SOCIAL DIMENSIONS OF INFORMATION AND COMMUNICATION TECHNOLOGY POLICY

T0138065

IFIP – The International Federation for Information Processing

IFIP was founded in 1960 under the auspices of UNESCO, following the First World Computer Congress held in Paris the previous year. An umbrella organization for societies working in information processing, IFIP's aim is two-fold: to support information processing within its member countries and to encourage technology transfer to developing nations. As its mission statement clearly states,

> *IFIP's mission is to be the leading, truly international, apolitical organization which encourages and assists in the development, exploitation and application of information technology for the benefit of all people.*

IFIP is a non-profitmaking organization, run almost solely by 2500 volunteers. It operates through a number of technical committees, which organize events and publications. IFIP's events range from an international congress to local seminars, but the most important are:

• The IFIP World Computer Congress, held every second year;
• Open conferences;
• Working conferences.

The flagship event is the IFIP World Computer Congress, at which both invited and contributed papers are presented. Contributed papers are rigorously refereed and the rejection rate is high.

As with the Congress, participation in the open conferences is open to all and papers may be invited or submitted. Again, submitted papers are stringently refereed.

The working conferences are structured differently. They are usually run by a working group and attendance is small and by invitation only. Their purpose is to create an atmosphere conducive to innovation and development. Refereeing is less rigorous and papers are subjected to extensive group discussion.

Publications arising from IFIP events vary. The papers presented at the IFIP World Computer Congress and at open conferences are published as conference proceedings, while the results of the working conferences are often published as collections of selected and edited papers.

Any national society whose primary activity is in information may apply to become a full member of IFIP, although full membership is restricted to one society per country. Full members are entitled to vote at the annual General Assembly, National societies preferring a less committed involvement may apply for associate or corresponding membership. Associate members enjoy the same benefits as full members, but without voting rights. Corresponding members are not represented in IFIP bodies. Affiliated membership is open to non-national societies, and individual and honorary membership schemes are also offered.

SOCIAL DIMENSIONS OF INFORMATION AND COMMUNICATION TECHNOLOGY POLICY

*Proceedings of the Eighth International Conference
on Human Choice and Computers (HCC8),
IFIP TC 9, Pretoria, South Africa,
September 25-26, 2008*

Edited by

Chrisanthi Avgerou
London School of Economics and Political Science
United Kingdom

Matthew L. Smith
International Development Research Centre
Canada
& London School of Economics and Political Science
United Kingdom

Peter van den Besselaar
University of Amsterdam &
Rathenau Institute
The Netherlands

 Springer

Social Dimensions of Information and Communication

Technology Policy

Edited by Chrisanthi Avgerou, Matthew L. Smith and
Peter van den Besselaar

p. cm. (IFIP International Federation for Information Processing, a Springer Series in Computer Science)

ISSN: 1571-5736 / 1861-2288 (Internet)

ISBN: 978-1-4419-4651-5   e-ISBN: 978-0-387-84822-8

Printed on acid-free paper

Contents

Part 4:   Panels

HUMAN CHOICE AND ICT POLICY: INTRODUCTION TO THE HCC8 CONFERENCE PROCEEDINGS

Chrisanthi Avgerou
London School of Economics and Political Science, UK

Matthew L. Smith
International Development Research Centre, Canada &
London School of Economics and Political Science, UK

Peter van den Besselaar
University of Amsterdam &
Rathenau Institute, The Netherlands

1.   Introduction

Since its launching in 1974, the Human Choice and Computers (HCC) series of conferences of the IFIP Technical Committee 9 (TC9)[1] has provided a forum for the study of the multiple facets of the dynamics of social change associated with information and communication technologies (ICTs). These conferences have captured the unfolding hopes and concerns about the interplay between the technologies we construct and our personal lives, organisations, and social institutions. Whether the message voiced by individual authors is optimistic and positive about the emerging socio-technical arrangements or worrying and critical, the "human choice" concept has always been pivotal in the discussions of the HCC conferences.

In HCC studies, as well as in kindred research streams such as Social Informatics [6, 17], Participatory Design [10, 23], and the Social Study of ICT [3], the shaping of ICT-mediated social arrangements is seen as resulting from the interaction among a broad range of categories of human actors. Early focus on engineers and managers of the innovating work place, each seen as endowed with the formal technical logic of their profession, has expanded to address the pervasiveness of ICT-mediated practices that comprise the so-called information society. Computer users juggling with multiple ICT artefacts at the work place, entrepreneurs taking risk with new-technology-incorporating products and processes, consumers, corporate executives creating competitive advantage with new business models, government regulators setting the norms of the innovation arena, NGO activists forging the values of ICT-mediated civil spaces, citizens

---

[1] The IFIP Technical Committee 9 (TC9) is dedicated to the study of the relationship of "Computers and Society" [http://is2.lse.ac.uk/tc9/]. See [22] for the proceedings of the first HCC conference.

Please use the following format when citing this chapter:

Avgerou, C., Smith, M.L. and van den Besselaar, P., 2008, in IFIP International Federation for Information Processing, Volume 282; *Social Dimensions of Information and Communication Technology Policy*; Chrisanthi Avgerou, Matthew L. Smith, Peter van den Besselaar; (Boston: Springer), pp. 1–13.

exercising their democratic rights in ICT-mediated government institutions, are only some of the roles through which the information society play of the early 21st century is enacted. HCC research deciphers the lines each of them performs, seeks to interpret their interests and, occasionally, exposes their unfulfilled role. It often witnesses conflicts, power dynamics, and the mismatch of bold rhetoric of revolutionary change with painstakingly slow action and reversals. Sometimes it dares to articulate recommendations, thus attempting to legislate either specific actor roles, or the direction of the enactment, though such attempts from scholars remain of dubious legitimacy and effectiveness within contemporary society [5].

Partly as a result of the broad scope of attention to multiple actors, the notions of choice and action have a broad meaning in HCC research. Choice is exercised not only in technical decision making settings, but in the streams of everyday practices of people's lives. The choices that construct ICT-mediated socio-economic institutions involve tacit knowledge; they are not confined to formal cognitive processes. Moreover, socio-technical choices are not merely cognitive, they are to a large extent ethical in character [4], and involve emotional human capacities [9]. Action too is not limited to professional conduct informed by analytical design models and planning techniques; it is improvisational, idiosyncratic, deeply political and culturally conditioned. It should be noted that these notions of action that are increasingly prevalent in HCC conferences are congruent with the concepts of the mutual constitution of human agency and social structure [15], of technology and society [7, 18], and of the social dynamics of technical change [13, 24] that became prevalent in social sciences in the last decade of the twentieth century.

This book, drawing its chapters from the 8th HCC on the *Social Dimensions of ICT Policy*, follows the same conceptual direction, but focuses in particular on human choice and action pertaining national and supra-national policy, thus shifting attention to efforts of collective actors shaping macro-level processes: governments, regulating authorities, citizens, social institutions, industries, universities, civil society organisations, etc. Policy involves purposeful action in a large variety of forms: the setting of a vision, the identification of problems to be overcome or opportunities not to be missed, the drafting of legislation, the mobilization and allocation of resources, the efforts to win public opinion and mobilise public support, the negotiations on intended ends and available means, the organisation of "projects", and the monitoring of results. This is neither a prioritised nor an exhaustive list, but it is indicative of the visible aspects of a collective process that seeks to steer individuals, institutions and technologies towards particular ends. There is, of course, a less visible side of action accompanying policy, such as citizens' often silent behavioural positioning in relation to a government initiative, incremental institutional adjustments, covert alignments of agencies with diverse interests which translate policy initiatives and their intended outcomes differently from their declared logic and aspirations.

The significance of government action in fostering ICT innovation and enabling society to cope with the destructive consequences of its pervasive diffusion is well documented in a number of publications [12, 14, 16, 19, 21]. National and regional governments and international development agencies such as the World Bank, have pursued policies for the advancements of ICT in various sectors, mainly aiming at harnessing the potential of ICT for achieving economic growth. Many governments sought to promote the development of ICT industries. Examples of such policies are the efforts of European countries to develop computer hardware manufacturing in the 1980s [12], and more recently the efforts of developing countries to become competitive producers of software [1, 11].

Government policy for the development of ICT industries is debatable. In particular, policies designed to protect local producers from foreign competition have proved risky, often developing complacency of local ICT firms regarding innovation by providing them a captive market, while depriving domestic users of state-of-the-art technologies at internationally competitive prices. On the other hand, fostering an ICT industry synergistically with domestic users bears mutual benefits for the learning and the development of capabilities that are considered necessary for the contemporary economy.[2] Thus, while particular protectionist policy interventions are controversial, there is a general consensus in the literature of industrial policy and economics of innovation that governments have a crucial role to play in creating the conditions for collaboration and competition among business firms producing and using ICT. Governments, for example, have a major role to play in securing the existence of a work force appropriately skilled for the knowledge economy, in regulating the providers - and in many cases providing themselves - telecommunications services, and in sponsoring R&D. Moreover, as ICT users themselves, governments are directly collaborating with ICT industry, for example for developing information systems infrastructures for national health care, and therefore they are interested in achieving synergistic gains.

Less controversial is the view that government should be addressing the emerging social issues that accompany ICT innovation. To begin with, there is a widely held expectation that governments will take initiatives to enable their citizens to participate in the information society. For example, governments are expected to use ICTs to strengthen democratic processes through e-government services that improve the transparency and responsiveness of state agencies. And as the Internet becomes a fundamental means for information and communication, governments are also expected to act to avoid social exclusion that occurs from lack of access to ICT and from lack of capabilities to participate in ICT-mediated social and economic activities. Moreover, there is general agreement that governments have a major legislative role to play in order to introduce institutions required for the information society. Personal data protection is one such area. Intellectual property rights (IPR) for information and software industries is another.

---

[2] The literature on economics of innovation elaborates on policies aiming at developing capabilities through geographically located partnership [2, 8, 20].

However there is less agreement about the extent to which governments are equipped to do these tasks and about the strategies to be followed. Additionally, government policies addressing the social dimensions of the information society are neither distinct from economic policy concerns, nor politically uncontroversial. Governments often stifle the democratic potential of the Internet with censorship; IPR legislation becomes a social convention that prevents technologically possible free access to information and software; and data protection clashes with concerns of national security. The policy dilemmas are greater in poor countries, many of which have neither public resources, nor developed markets to provide required telecommunications infrastructures for the information society. Moreover access to technology infrastructure is of limited developmental potential when literacy and job opportunities in the information sector are lacking. The HCC8 is dedicated to the study of such policy issues, and the chapters in this volume amply demonstrate the dilemmas and controversies of this area.

2.   Overview of the chapters

As in most conferences, individual contributions vary in terms of the extent to which they are theoretically and methodologically grounded and make convincing arguments. As editors of this volume of proceedings we were also aware that HCC conferences draw authors from a mix of academics', practitioners', and NGO activists' communities, each of them with their distinctive epistemic culture and rhetorical style. Each of the submitted papers was reviewed by two reviewers knowledgeable of its particular topic, as well as the conference programme chairs, and most of the accepted papers were revised substantially as a result of reviewers' comments and suggestions. In the resulting book some papers present well articulated, theoretically and empirically supported arguments in the contemporary academic tradition; others voice concerns or shed light on particular issues that need closer investigation and theoretical comprehension. Some chapters present research in progress, which although has not produced yet definitive conclusions, raises awareness of particular aspects of the emerging information society and stimulates consideration of appropriate policy action. In addition, we include in this book outlines of three panel discussions. We consider all these types of contribution valuable for the continuing effort to understand the nature and scope of human choice in the shaping of the information society.

We provide below an overview of the chapters we drew from the conference papers. The first chapter is the keynote presentation by Robin Mansell. Appropriately for a conference taking place in Africa, Robin Mansell focuses on the policy challenges confronting low income countries. She draws from her involvement in international networks and institutions that influence policy on media and communications – a policy area overlapping with ICT policy within the broader arena of efforts regarding the "Knowledge Society" – and proposes a research framework to support policy interventions that enable well being through sustainable development. Her framework suggests the need for research on human rights, communication and information, access and literacies, participatory communication, representation and critical assessment of strategic communication and information policies, and indicators of knowledge societies.

The rest of the book is structured in four Parts. Parts 1 to 3 contain chapters on the following broad thematic categories: the shaping of national and international ICT policies and their effects; harnessing the empowering capacity and ICT; and the shaping of the institutions of the information society. The fourth Part contains the panel descriptions.

Part 1: The shaping of national and international ICT policies and their effects

The chapters of this Part discuss specific cases or areas of national and international ICT policy, showing various facets of the policy making. They shed light on the way policies for the deployment of ICT and the mobilization of required resources and action are formed. The picture that emerges shows a variety of interactions across different levels of governance.

In *The argumentative structure of spatial data infrastructure initiatives in America and Africa,* Yola Georgiadou and Vincent Homburg point to the powerful influence of "myths", abstract tales that are neither true nor false, but rather are living or dead. These myths, in this case about spatial data infrastructures in Africa, are tales regarding the intention and purposes of new technologies that motivate and pervade policy. As the authors detail in their analysis, such myths can travel through time and space, from one context to another, mutating along the way as they are edited to account for contextual differences and to maintain legitimacy.

Ioanna Chine, in *ICT policy as a governable domain: the case of Greece and the European Commission,* illustrates how the development of a national ICT policy is sometimes subject to and interacts with controlling forces beyond the traditional state boundary. Drawing from Foucault's notion of governmentality, Chini argues that the Greek national government was subject to techniques of control from the supra-national European Commission that regulated and engendered self-regulation within the Greek government with respects to ICT policy. The end result, she argues, is a Greek ICT policy that is effectively shaped by these techniques to fit the strategic vision of ICT policy held in the Eurpoean Commission.

The relationship between Greek ICT policy and European policy is also examined in the next chapter, *National variations of the information society,* by Dimitris Boukas, who takes a different theoretical perspective from that of Chini, considering Greece as a case of semi-peripheral, middle-income countries. Boucas analysis of the Greek case draws from historical sociology to show the creation of differentiated national information society features that result from the interaction of the state and the national economy and society with global information society processes.

In *Technology, globalisation, and governance: research perspectives and prospects*, Diego Navarra and Tony Cornford discuss the use of ICT in government organisations as a phenomenon which transcends the nation state, manifesting a distinctive problematisation of the nature of citizenship, statehood and, citizen/state relations. This phenomenon, they argue, is central to the contemporary world and as yet has not received much attention in the literature. To compensate for this gap, they propose several research perspectives that might help to increase our understanding of the many different aspects of this phenomenon, including Actor-network Theory, New Public Management, and Transaction Cost theory.

In *Globalisation and national security issues for the state: implications for national ICT policies*, Jackie Phahlamohlaka examines policy concerns associated with security threats that emerge due to the increasingly interconnected nature of computer neworks, and the penetration of these networks into the social, political, and economic activities of a state. In this chapter, Phahlamohlaka provides a novel framework to begin to grasp the different types of national security threats that have evolved with globalisation. Following this, he explores the potential implications for ICT policy and makes an urgent call for more research in this rapidly changing and still underdeveloped area.

In *Next generation ICT policy in South Africa: towards a human development-based ICT Policy*, Walter Brown and Irwin Brown discuss ICT policy in terms of assumptions and values as to the ways and means that new technology can contribute to the development of a country. They point out that, like any policy, a state's ICT policy will have distributional impacts, intended or unintended, that benefit some and disadvantage others. As Brown and Brown document, despite significant advances in ICT diffusion in South Africa, the advantages of ICT have not been spread evenly among the citizens, for a variety of reasons. To rectify this situation for the next generation of ICT in South Africa, the authors propose that the various terminologies used to describe the various technologies should be collapsed into the term telecommunications. They argue that this would be a start towards the development of a simple and effective ICT policy that places human development at the core: a human development-based ICT policy.

Successful ICT diffusion and uptake depends, as other chapters in this volume argue, upon coherent policy that is not only well developed, but also well implemented. In his chapter, *Challenges of ICT policy for rural communities: a case study from South Africa*, Mpostol Jeremia Mashinini examines the rural community of Dr. S.J. Moroka in South Africa to uncover a myriad of challenges that need to be addressed to enable this community to derive human development benefits from new ICTs. Interestingly, the central challenge that Mashinini's study reveals is that, for a variety of reasons discussed in this chapter, a majority of the ICT policies designed to address these challenges were simply not being implemented.

Part 2: Harnessing the empowering capacity and ICT

The chapters of this Part examine efforts to exploit the potential of ICT to empower the population of a country to participate in the emerging information society and improve their well being. There are various areas of action to that end, including government initiatives to overcome the digital divide problem, the construction of information resources to support health care services, and education initiatives aimed to develop the technological and social capabilities for the information society.

Panayiota Tsatsou, in her chapter *Digital divides and the role of policy and regulation*, reviews current understanding of the digital divide problem and the role of policy and regulation for achieving digital inclusion. She presents data from interviews with policy makers, researchers, Internet service providers, and business agencies in Greece, which is a country with persistently low Internet adoption. Her analysis reveals problems related with culturally embedded decision making mechanisms. Thus Tsatsou concludes by identifying the need for socially accountable policies and regulations aiming to alter the traditional bureaucratic and techno-phobic culture, that her analysis suggests to be an obstacle to change, and to allow more scope for market forces.

In *Empowerment through ICT: a critical discourse analysis of the Egyptian ICT Policy*, Bernd Carsten Stahl shows that the rhetoric of ICT policy statements doesn't always match the reality on the ground. Using critical discourse analysis Stahl examines Egypt's ICT policy documents through the lens of critical theory to uncover the rhetoric and underlying intentions. In particular, he contrasts the ICT policy rhetoric and Egyptian social realities in the areas of empowerment and education. Stahl finds that the discourse of empowerment through ICT is not matched by equivalent government action and thus at best shows a lack of sincerity or at worst hides an oppressive intention that works to actively disempower citizens. Researchers and practitioners are advised to think critically when using such policy documents.

In *Egyptian women artisans: ICTs are not the entry to modern markets*, Leila Hassanin shows that ICT policy that establishes an enabling environment for ICT usage and human development benefits is a significant factor, but is certainly not the only one. Certain activities, such as selling crafts at a local market do not easily scale up to e-commerce, especially internationally, which requires a level of funding and a whole new set of technical, legal, and other expertise that are generally not available to the average SME. In this chapter, Hassanin's case study of Egyptian women craftmakers illustrates these challenges, and counters the fundamental assumption that ICT access will open up new markets for micro- and small businesses, enabling them to expand their sales and income.

Solomon Bishaw, in his chapter *Institutional strategies towards improving health information systems (HIS) in Sub-Saharan Africa*, discusses the challenges confronting the development of information infrastructures for health care. He identifies the difficulty of effective participation of relevant actors in the endeavours for the development of hospital information systems as a major obstacle, and draws from institutional theory to analyse the institutional processes and pressures that constrain, construct and empower participation.

In *A human environmentalist approach to diffusion in ICT policies*, Elaine Byrne and Lizette Weilbach remind policy makers that ICT policy needs also to be cognizant of the variety of contextual factors that make ICT diffusion and adoption a complex, and non-linear, process. Standard IT diffusion theory that gives credence to this approach apparently assumes uni-directional causality between the implementation of technology and its adoption. In contrast, Byrne and Weilbach present an extended and holistic model of IT diffusion based upon the human environmental model. Such a model, they argue, is more appropriate to capture the complex dialectical interactions of technology and context during diffusion.

In *ICT and socio-economic development: a university's engagement in a rural community in Yola, Nigeria,* Jainaba Kah and Muhammadou Kah explore theoretically and empirically the role of universities in the diffusion and use of ICT for socio-economic development. The authors cover a broad range of theoretical ground linking ICT, universities, and development including: economic theory on the role of universities in economic development, ICT and poverty alleviation, and a consideration of various factors that impede developmental outcomes from ICT interventions in Africa. To ground the discussion, the authors provide a detailed case description of the activities of one University in northern Nigeria aimed at promoting socio-economic development through, in particular, fostering increased techno-entrepreneurship and engaging with the community and industry.

In the last chapter of this Part, *Lessons from a dropped ICT curriculum design project: a retrospective view*, Roohollah Honarvar documents the development and disintegration of an attempt to develop a nationwide ICT curriculum for universities in Iran. Honarvar identifies a series of issues that emerged during the course of the project that eventually led to its termination despite a significant investment: the relatively rapid nature of change of ICT necessitating constant revision of the curriculum, the inability to provide the requisite flexibility due to centralised planning approach, lack of social orientation of ICT professionals, and the difficulties locating qualified lecturers to teach the curriculum. While these issues are specific to the Iranian context, they are also encountered by other countries looking to develop an ICT curriculum. Drawing from his experience, the author offers a series of potential solutions to these issues.

Part 3: The shaping of the institutions of the information society

The making of the information society requires new institutional mechanisms across a broad range of domains of human activity. The chapters in this Part discuss the formation of several such mechanisms: the governance of the Internet, legal regimes for accessing and using electronic entities such as software and academic publications, new forms of banking, social networking for various social causes, measures of the information society. They reveal deep controversies and contestations and, appropriately, some authors follow critical theoretical perspectives to analyse the areas of action they researched.

Jacques Berleur, in his chapter *15 years of ways of Internet governance: towards a new agenda for action*, deconstructs numerous official publications and declarations that have been contributing to the shaping of the governance regime of the fundamental technology infrastructure of the information society: the Internet. He is skeptical of the emphasis given to self-regulating market forces, raising concern that such a regime might not realize the "people centred" information society that is often presented as the desirable end of government policy. He points out the "multistakeholder" approach which is stressed within the much publicized World Summit for the Information Society forums, but which "is still to find its full meaning".

In *Governmental policies for ICT diffusion and leadership legitimacy in grassroots movements,* Magda Hercheui shows that ICT policy may result in unintended consequences that adversely impact the goals of the policy itself. Drawing on institutional theory, Hercheui's study documents one such unintended consequence of an ICT policy to fund ICT usage by informal environmental education groups in Brazil. While ICT usage by these informal communities was enhanced, the conditionalities placed upon the funding resulted in a significant centralizing shift in their decision-making structures. This shift worked to counteract their original intention of non-hierarchical structures based on democratic participatory ideals. Interestingly, these structural changes proved durable enough to last beyond the funding period. Consequently, Hercheui advises that we need to be especially aware of how ICT policies influence the governance structures of civil society organisations so that citizens can ensure that new ICT policy and democratic aspirations remain compatible.

In *Examining trust in mobile banking transactions: The case of M-PESA in Kenya*, Olga Morawczynski & Gianluca Miscione present their research in progress that examines the crucial role that interpersonal and institutional trust plays in a case of the use of a new mobile banking (m-banking) system in Kenya. Their preliminary findings suggest that while interpersonal trust in the agents representing the m-banking system is low, use still remains high due to institutional trust in the well-established mobile service provider.

Farid Shirazi, in *Social networks within filtered ICT networks: a case study of the growth of Internet usage within Iran,* describes how ICTs, such as blogs and mobile SMSs, are being used in Iran as a space for open social, cultural, political discourse in ways that otherwise were not possible. In response, however, the Iranian government has developed a sophisticated Internet censorship systems and have restricted ICT diffusion. This, Shirazi argues, has effectively restrained the growth and use of the Internet and inhibited civil freedoms, leaving Iran lagging considerably behind other countries in the region.

The working assumption of Kay Kimppa in *A no-IPR model as solution to reuse and understanding of information systems* is that, much like how intellectual property rights (IPR) protection makes the purchasing of drugs unaffordable to many lower-income countries, software intellectual property rights can inhibit the ability of organisations, especially small and micro-enterprises with little resources, to take advantage of highly useful software. Kimppa argues in this work-in-progress chapter, that the current software IPR regime inhibits the reuse of software as well as the understanding that users have of the system. To counter the current regime, Kimppa proposes a no-IPR model to replace the current IPR legislation.

In *Measuring information societies for development: a critical study of the Infostate framework*, Anouk Mukherjee critically examines the assumptions behind a framework that attempts to quantify and monitor the information society status of different countries with the goal of providing policymakers with the information needed to guide policy and investment decisions. Such frameworks and measurements are generally considered useful, as Robin Mansell suggests in her chapter: if states wish to determine ICT policy to bridge the digital divide and advance towards the information society, based upon empirical evidence, it is helpful to have measurement frameworks to gauge the current status of different states. However, such frameworks may oversimplify the process of the formation of knowledge societies and indeed mislead the policy making effort. Mukherjee takes the Infostate framework to task for its highly instrumental orientation and makes an argument for more multidisciplinary approaches to capturing the information society phenomena.

Mathias Klang, in *Open access barriers: an action research*, presents the first stage of research that explores the challenges of obtaining universal access to information. Klang points out that the current system of journal publication and subscription is increasingly inhibiting access to scientific knowledge, especially scholarly journals. To combat this, an open access movement is pushing for the creation of more systems of open access and open publishing to scholarly writings. Instituting a new system of open access, however, comes with its own set of difficulties. In particular, it produces a whole new set of challenges for universities and especially for university librarians. His action research in the Swedish context, uncovers problems relating to the research culture, administration of knowledge databases, and legal issues, among others.

Part 4: Panels

The HCC8 conference includes three panels on three important contemporary topics: Free and Open Source Software (FOSS), policies relevant for large scale projects for the development of information systems infrastructures, such as for national health systems, and the potential of ICTs to improve women's lives.

In their panel *Free and Open Source Software in low-income countries: emergent properties?*, Gianluca Miscione, Dorothy Gordon, and Kevin Johnston draw from experiences of the development and use of open source software in Africa and India. There tends to be a revolutionary hype about FOSS as a way of constructing and acquiring software that is vital for development by liberating software producers and users from the constrains of conventional business models. These panellists, while recognizing the developmental potential of FOSS, go beyond hype to discuss some of the requirements for effective FOSS practice, with particular emphasis on mechanisms of organisational learning.

In the panel *Evaluating 'Connecting for Health': policy implications of a UK mega-programme,* Jane Hendy, Ela Klecun, Kathy McGrath, Leslie Willcocks, and Terry Young draw lessons from a 10 year mega-project intended to implement an integrated ICT infrastructure in the UK National Health Service (NHS). As the panel description points out, "fully informatized" health care is a vision that all countries consider desirable, but no country has realized. The pannelist discuss various difficulties that have been slowing down, increasing costs and, in some cases, inhibiting the implementation of the UK NHS ICT programme.

In *Gender research in Africa into ICTs for empowerment,* Ineke Buskens, Gertrudes Macueve, Ibou Sane, and Ann Webb present and discuss the rationale, methodology and findings of GRACE, a three year research project studying the implications of the gender divide and the way it inhibits the potential benefits of ICTs for development in Africa. In addition to the overall presentation of GRACE as an international NGO initiative, the panel includes discussions of findings from some of its 14 sub-projects, including a study of women's use of telecentres and mobile phone networks in rural Mozambique and a study of the use of mobile telephony by women fishmongers and fish processors in Senegal.

3.   Conclusions

The chapters of this book demonstrate the multiplicity and complexity of interrelated issues that confront policy action intended to foster visions of the information or knowledge society. Many of these issues are studied in long-standing IFIP working groups, such as WG9.4 on ICT in developing countries, and receive attention in the biennial World IT Forum (WITFOR) of IFIP. Several other learned organisations and NGOs are also engaged in research and debate on aspects of policy that shape features of the information society.

The book demonstrates also current collective capacity of such research forums to articulate policy related issues and address them, at least analytically. Clearly, more research effort is needed, theoretically and empirically, to understand the unfolding socio-technical processes. More specifically, we need to achieve better understanding of the way through which existing social institutions, such as government mechanisms at national and international levels, NGOs and the market can contribute to the formation of socio-economic regimes that translate technology innovation to improvements of human life conditions, such as reducing poverty and delivering education that enhances human capabilities.

As we complete this book of proceedings three months ahead of the HCC8, we hope that this event will stimulate such further research, debate, and action.

References

[1]   Arora, A. & Gambardella, A. (Eds.) (2005). From underdogs to tigers: The rise and growth of the software industry in Brazil, China, India, Ireland, and Israel. Oxford: Oxford University Press.

[2]   Asheim, B.T. & Gertler, M.S. (2005). *The geography of innovation: Regional innovation systems.* In Fagerberg, J., Mowery D.C., and Nelson, D. (Eds.) *The Oxford handbook of innovation.* (pp. 291-317). Oxford: Oxford University Press.

[3]   Avgerou, C., Ciborra, C., & Land, F. (Eds.) (2004). *The social study of information and communication technology.* Oxford: Oxford University Press.

[4]   Avgerou, C. & McGrath, K. (2005). Rationalities and emotions in IS innovation, in Howcroft, D. & Trauth, E.M. (Eds). *Handbook of critical information systems tesearch: Theory and application.* (pp. 299-324). Cheltenham: Edward Elgar.

[5]   Bauman, Z. (1988). *Legislators and Interpreters.* Cambridge: Polity Press.

[6]   Berleur, J., Nurminen, M.I. and Impagliazzo, J. (Eds.) (2006). *Social informatics: An information society for all? In remembrance of Rob Kling.* New York: Springer.

[7]   Bijker, W.E. & Law, J. (Eds.) (1992). *Shaping technology/building society.* Cambridge, Massachusetts: MIT Press.

[8]   Cantwell, J. (2005). *Innovation and competitiveness.* (2005). In J. Fagerberg, D.C. Mowery, and D. Nelson (Eds.) *The Oxford handbook of innovation* (pp. 543-567). Oxford: Oxford University Press.

[9]   Ciborra, C. (2006) The mind or the heart? It depends on the (definition of) situation. *Journal of Information Technology.* 21(3), 129-139.

[10] Clement, A. & Van den Besselaar, P. (1993). A retrospective look at participatory design projects. *Communications of the ACM*, 36(4), 29-37.

[11] Commander, S. (Ed.) (2005) *The software industry in emerging markets.* Cheltenham: Edward Elgar.

[12] Coopey, R. (Ed.) (2004). *IT Policy: An international history.* Oxford: Oxford University Press.

[13] Edquist, C. (1997). Systems of innovation: Technologies, institutions, and organizations. London: Pinter.

[14] English, M. & Watson Brown, A. (1984). National policies in information technology: Challenge and responses. *Oxford surveys in information technology.* 1, 55-128.

[15] Giddens, A. (1984). The constitution of society. Outline of the theory of structuration. Cambridge: Polity Press.

[16] Kahin, B. & Wilson, E. (Eds.) (1997). *National information infrastructure initiatives: Vision and policy design.* Cambridge, Massachusetts: MIT Press.

[17] Kling, R., Rosenbaum, H., & Sawyer, S. (2005) Understanding and communicating social informatics: A framework for studying and teaching the human contexts of information and communication technologies. Medford, NJ: Information Today.

[18] Law, J. (Ed.) (1991). A sociology of monsters: Essays on power, technology and domination. London: Routledge.

[19] Lazonick, W. (2005). The innovative firm. In J. Fagerberg, D.C. Mowery, and R.R. Nelson (Eds.) *The Oxford handbook of innovation* (pp. 30-55). Oxford: Oxford University Press.

[20] Lundvall, B.-Å. (Ed.) (1992). National systems of innovation: Towards a theory of innovation and interactive Learning. London: Pinter.

[21] Mansell, R. & Steinmueller, W.E. (2002). *Mobilizing the information society: Strategies for growth and opportunity*. Oxford: Oxford University Press.

[22] Mumford, E. & Sackman, H. (Eds.) (1974). *Human choice and computers*. Amsterdam: North-Holland.

[23] Van den Besselaar, P. (1998) Technology & democracy, the limits to steering. *Proceedings of the participative design conference: Broadening participation*. Seatle: CPSR.

[24] Williams, R., Stewart, J., & Slack, R. (Eds.) (2005). *Social learning in technological innovation*. Cheltenham: Edward Elgar.

COMMUNICATION, INFORMATION, AND ICT POLICY:
TOWARDS ENABLING RESEARCH FRAMEWORKS

Keynote Presentation

Professor Robin Mansell
London School of Economics and Political Science, UK

1.   Introduction

In this presentation my aim is to set out a forward looking research agenda which I will argue can be further developed in a way that may contribute to a partial resolution of ongoing conundrums that confront those seeking to ensure that information and communication technologies (ICT) are put into service in ways that are enabling, rather than disabling. ICT-related policies and strategies are being developed by their stakeholders to support a range of important goals and aspirations associated with the wider policy agendas of low income countries. In such countries, there will inevitably be trade-offs among the competing claims of stakeholders for scarce resources of all kinds whether these are associated with investment in ICTs themselves or in the capabilities to design or use them in ways that are compatible with development aspirations, locally, nationally, or regionally.

Although ICT policies and strategies have become relatively well-accepted as components of broader policy making initiatives over the past decade – and despite the fact that ICTs are acknowledged as a target area in the Millennium Development Goals,[1] there is debate about how best to underpin these initiatives. Should they be informed by the outputs of research? If they should be, how should dialogues between researchers and practitioners be facilitated to ensure that all parties find such dialogues informative?

The first main section of this presentation draws on a "brainstorming" workshop which I chaired in December 2007 hosted by UNESCO. We brought leading researchers together to develop a research framework which would tackle issues and questions that we believe need to be given much greater attention if ICTs are to play a greater role in enabling a variety of development goals to be met. Our main questions were: *What new concepts are required to acknowledge*

---

[1] MDG 8: "In cooperation with the private sector, make available the benefits of new technologies—especially information and communications technologies", see: http://www.un.org/millenniumgoals/#.

Please use the following format when citing this chapter:

Mansell, R., 2008, in IFIP International Federation for Information Processing, Volume 282; *Social Dimensions of Information and Communication Technology Policy*; Chrisanthi Avgerou, Matthew L. Smith, Peter van den Besselaar; (Boston: Springer), pp. 15–28.

difference and the distinctiveness of today's knowledge societies? And, what evidence is there of effective learning on the part of different stakeholders?

ICTs are clearly implicated in the answer to the first question. I want to acknowledge at the outset that all societies are "knowledge societies". This point is often lost in the hyper reality that sometimes characterizes discussions about ICT policy. As Valerie Brown has argued, perhaps the most essential issue in debates concerning ICTs (as well as other innovative technologies and practices) is to recall the words of the anthropologist, Clifford Geertz. He suggested that it is crucial to give close attention to the commonsense questions and answers. Commonsense requires us to ensure that all citizens are "not just using their eyes and ears, but using them collectively, judiciously and reflectively to understand their own locality" [2, p. 51 citing 9]. In a similar vein, it is important to emphasize that any discussion of the role of ICT applications and of ICT policy in the service of development needs to understand concepts like the "knowledge society" as being very fluid ones. This is essential if we are to overcome the risk that our research becomes caught between "a hegemonic Eurocentrism, and a counter-hegemonic but reactionary epistemological nativism". In our discussions about what needs to be researched in the ICT field it is essential to keep this risk in mind, especially when we discuss theoretical standpoints and methodologies [6, p. 146].

The participants in the December workshop came from Bahrain, Benin, Canada, France, India, Mexico, Russia, Singapore, South Africa, Sweden, the United Kingdom, and the United States.[2] Most of the participants were academics but many had strong links to practitioner and policy making communities in their respective regions. They were all members of a world-wide academic association called the International Association for Media and Communication Research (IAMCR), a 2000-strong organisation founded in 1957 which has nongovernmental organisation status within the United Nations system and of which I was President until July 2008.[3] Although there is little direct overlap between members of this association and that of IFIP Technical Committee 9, I suggest that there are many opportunities for these disparate communities with an interest in the relationship between ICTs and society to learn from each other. IAMCR and TC9 members have overlapping interests in policy-relevant research and in influencing policy agendas and practices beyond the boundaries of academic institutions. In this presentation, I will suggest some of the research areas where I think we may have common cause.

The outcome of the workshop hosted by UNESCO was a new research framework which was partly intended to inform UNESCO's Medium-term Strategy 2008 – 2013. UNESCO's strategy has an overarching objective to build "inclusive knowledge societies through information and communication" [24].

---

[2] Also represented were several members of UNESCO staff. For a full account of the workshop, see: [23].
[3] See: www.iamcr.org.

This objective embraces efforts to enhance universal access to information and to foster pluralistic, free, and independent media and information structures.

Our aim in the workshop was to develop a forward-looking research framework that might provide guidance more generally in the commissioning of research that will provide critical assessments of developments in the communication and information field. Inequalities persist in knowledge societies at the local, national, and global levels and the research framework that we developed is intended to encourage work that will yield new insights for those involved in shaping ICT-related policy agendas and for those engaged in practical projects involving ICTs. We recognised that the strengths and weaknesses of research differs enormously in different places around the world and that any new research framework will need to be inclusive and to encourage the development of diverse theoretical and policy perspectives if it is to shape the future trajectory of work in this area. The next section sets out the central components of the research framework that emerged. The following section (s.3) highlights several areas within this framework which were deemed to be of very high priority.

2.   An Alternative Framework for Knowledge Societies Research

In 2005, UNESCO published a World Report entitled *Towards Knowledge Societies.* This document gave strong emphasis to the plurality of knowledge societies historically as well as in today's communication and information environments. The authors posed the question below and sought to differentiate between "knowledge societies" and "information societies" and to clearly indicate that there are no ready-made, off-the-shelf models that can be adopted to ensure that ICTs are developed and used in enabling, rather than disabling, ways.

"Does the aim of building knowledge societies make any sense when history and anthropology teach us that since ancient times, all societies have probably been each in its own way, knowledge societies? ...

The current spread of new technologies and the emergence of the internet as a public network seem to be carving out fresh opportunities to widen this public knowledge forum. Might we now have the means to achieve equal and universal access to knowledge, and genuine sharing? This should be the cornerstone of true knowledge societies, which are a source of human and sustainable development. .. The idea of the information society is based on technological breakthroughs. The concept of knowledge societies encompasses much broader social, ethical and political dimensions. There is a multitude of such dimensions which rules out the idea of any single, ready-made model, for such a model would not take sufficient account of cultural and linguistic diversity, vital if individuals are to feel at home in a changing world" (emphasis added) [21, p. 17].

In the light of this quotation, I want to argue that a high priority for any alternative research framework in this area is that it should mobilise research that challenges dominant paradigms that envisage a homogeneous knowledge society. Instead, a useful framework should be expected to critique the values embedded in ICT-related policies and practices, with the goal of redressing the tendency to privilege technology and to foster a narrow set of market-led values. A forward-looking research framework is required if we are to encourage a *rethinking of sustainable development in the context of knowledge societies.*

What might this mean? A rethinking or re-imagining of the kinds of knowledge societies which are more likely to foster enabling communication and information environments that contribute to greater efficacy, social justice, and well-being, is essential in the context of sustainable development goals. I am aware that there are some who would abandon the term "development" in order to move away from the progressive or neo-liberal value-laden perspectives embraced by Western traditions of research. This is an important debate that is ongoing within the wider community of researchers concerned with poverty eradication [8]. However, I suggest that the term "sustainable development" may be used to signal a departure from an uncritical stance with respect to the implications of strategies involving ICTs. In suggesting this, I also acknowledge that this terminology is itself controversial. However, I want to emphasise the need for dialogue aimed at encouraging translations between different meanings and interpretations of the goals of sustainable development and for ICTs. In the present context of developing a research framework that is sensitive to these issues, translation refers to the need for researchers to: "engage in, and try to connect to, knowledge formations and vocabularies that reside in other modernities and other temporalities that are either refused recognition, or are not adequately translated, in machines of knowledge production" [19, p. 3]. This suggests the need to encourage indigenous theory building and the development of models using a variety of languages.

There has been substantial critical analysis and discussion of the relationship between media and communication, and in the context of this conference, - ICTs - and development, since the work of Nora Quebral in the 1970s [20]. But, the mainstream research paradigm in this area is shifting towards a "social marketing" perspective which emphasises the ICT user as a customer/consumer.[4] In contrast, we urgently need to give priority to research which embraces a concern for the "power of peace and tolerance". Understanding the role of communication and information - and ICTs - in fostering mutual understanding, peace and reconciliation, arguably requires an effort to support the ambitions of others

---

[4] Social marketing was first developed by Kotler and Zaltman [13] to apply marketing to the solution of social and health problems. In recent literature it has also been used in the ICT and communication "for" development contexts.

through the acknowledgement of cultural diversity as well as of the need for knowledge sharing. Therefore, ICTs and mediated social systems of all kinds need to be examined using *alternative* research frameworks that can facilitate debates about the values that should be at the core of the initiatives by stakeholders to build inclusive knowledge societies. It should contribute to debates that are aimed at a discovery of the common and distinctive interests of all stakeholders. At very least there is an ongoing need to prise open development debates in a way that acknowledges the values that are at stake and the fact that people need to be empowered to make choices with respect to how their knowledge societies should be organised.[5]

In this regard, Amartya Sen's work offers a good starting point for an alternative framework for research on ICTs in the context of sustainable development. Sen's interest is in people's functionings, where "functioning" is understood as "an achievement of a person: what he or she manages to do or to be" [18, p. 7]. Functionings are related to capabilities and freedoms as, for example, in the freedom to access resources that contribute to well-being. Such freedoms are also closely associated with human rights and ethical conduct. Following Sen, a research framework should emphasise investigation of the multiple ways in which knowledge societies may be contributing to the well-being and achievements of human beings.[6]

Research is needed that can help to inform all stakeholders in knowledge societies about the ways in which varying combinations of information and communication relationships in local and global contexts can contribute to sustainable development. The uneven characteristics of knowledge societies and the relationship between their development and discrimination and poverty must be taken into account [see 22]. To start with there is a need to depart from perspectives that envisage a linear, technology-driven approach to the issue of ICT policy. There has been a proliferation of ICT platforms and there are increasing numbers of producers and co-producers of information. One benefit of these platforms is that there is renewed potential to use ICTs as a "tool for eradicating poverty because it makes people aware they have rights. As such, they cannot be marginalized or excluded. They have the right to be heard and to participate in the decisions that affect their lives" [12, p. 10].

Figure 1 highlights a cluster of research themes that I suggest need to become more prominent in future research relating to ICT policy and practice in line with an emphasis on human well-being rather than market-led values exclusively.

---

[5] For a comprehensive review of research traditions in the area of communication and media "for development", see [15].
[6] I acknowledge that there are many issues with respect to Sen's approach that need to be developed and/or critiqued, but I do not have the space here to do so. See for instance [5].

Figure 1: Research Framework
Rethinking sustainable development in the context of knowledge societies

Cultural Diversity	Governance	Media & Information Education

Human Rights, Communication and Information

Access and Literacies

Participatory Communication

Representation

Strategic Communication and Information Policies and Action Plans

Indicators of Knowledge Societies

A Repertoire of Research Methodologies and Methods

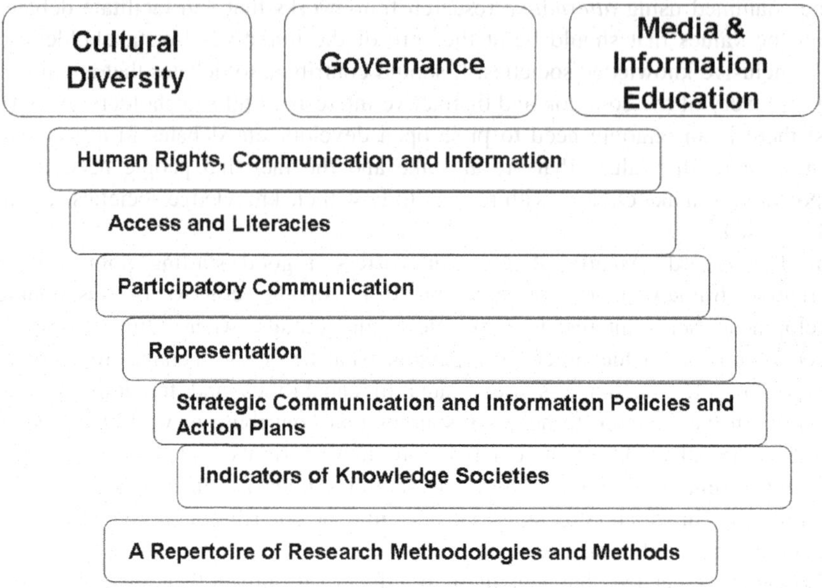

First, cultural diversity is inherent in the recognition of the plurality and variety of knowledge societies; second, governance, inclusive of all stakeholders, is an essential component of the processes and structures through which knowledge societies emerge; and third, media and information education are the means through which ICT applications can contribute to human well-being.

An alternative research framework should be informed by a consideration of, and sensitivity to, *communication, culture and context*. It needs to acknowledge that communicative environments of all kinds – ranging from interpersonal family relationships to large groups and organisations are mediated by older and newer ICTs in many different ways.[7] In a world in which there is a tendency towards atomised individuals and fragmentation, a major issue is to understand the potential for new communities and civil society actions to emerge within ICT-mediated environments.

Understanding the implications of diverse media, communication and information relationships requires attention to culturally specific contexts. This is as much the case with respect to governance processes and institutions as it is with respect to measures to enhance or protect cultural diversity. Actions to foster ICT use more generally that respect human rights through a wide variety of education measures are also needed. Research needs to embrace cross-cultural studies, to acknowledge the differences in the framings of issues and to assess how values

---

[7] Thanks to workshop participants for suggesting this phraseology.

inform specific norms of conduct in media, communication and information-related professions of all kinds.

Research is needed that develops theoretical and methodological approaches that focus on communication as a dynamic process involving power relationships and differences with respect to whether specific features of knowledge societies are empowering of individuals in terms of their well-being. Research should be transnational in its outlook and should focus on revealing the dynamics that give rise to the perpetuation of power differentials. These may be related to access to communication and information, inequality with respect to literacies, or to uneven capabilities for information and communication management.

Researchers need to avoid dichotomies between older and newer ICTs and between information "haves" and "have nots". Research must be conducted in a transversal way that contributes to integrated perspectives and which understands contemporary problems in multiple ways. It is important to compare the results of research undertaken from mainstream perspectives with those undertaken from the alternative perspectives I am advocating. The former often focus on the impact of the production or consumption of ICTs without giving sufficient attention to sustainable development issues. The alternative framework suggest here puts the emphasis on the well-being of social groups, for example, with respect to health, education and literacies, and human rights. It emphasises the ethical and moral considerations raised by developments in knowledge societies.

For many researchers, the academic reference points are often those drawn from the United States or other Western countries. Many of those in the scholarly community who focus on the issues of concern here remain unaware of alternative research frameworks and the literature that is already available.[8] Analysis of the relationship between ICTs, cultural diversity, and issues such as national sovereignty and independence, ownership and control, personal identity, and community participation, is essential, especially given ongoing tensions between the knowledge societies evolving within the global economy and those which are fostering indigenous expression. In this way we may move closer to understanding how ICT policy and practice can better contribute to sustainable development and peaceful human relations.[9]

Within this framework, there are several specific research domains that need to receive greater attention than they often seem to attract within the mainstream ICT research agenda.

3.   Specific research domains

As shown in Figure 1 above, issues of human rights, communication and information;   access   and   literacies;   participatory   communication;   and

---

[8] There are of course alternative research agendas being developed with the US, for example, see [16].

[9] See UNESCO's Universal Declaration on Cultural Diversity, adopted by the 31st session of the General Conference of UNESCO, Paris, 2 November 2001.

representation together with critical assessments of strategic communication and information policies (and action plans) and indicators of knowledge societies, need to be emphasised.

3.1   Human rights, communication, and information

Given the emphasis on human well-being and the implications of ICTs, particular attention needs to be given to examining how, and to what extent, information and communication-related rights are being respected in today's knowledge societies [see also 25]. The adoption of the United Nations Charter in 1945 and the Universal Declaration of Human Rights (UN UDHR) in 1948 obliged all States to establish, protect and enforce human rights at the global, regional, national and local levels. In particular, Article 19 of the UN UDHR declares that:

> *"Everyone has the right to freedom of expression and opinion; this right includes the freedom to hold opinions without interference and to seek, receive and impart information and ideas through any media and regardless of frontiers".*

There is debate about whether there is a need for the formal establishment of a "right to communicate", but it is clear that there is a strong relationship between recognition of the inherent dignity and equal and inalienable rights of all people and their right or entitlement to participate in communication and information environments. This relationship was acknowledged in the Millennium Declaration, 18 September 2000, which under "V. Human rights, democracy and good governance" resolves "to ensure the freedom of the media to perform their essential role and the right of the public to have access to information".

In this area, policy-making would arguably benefit from greater insight into the legal conditions for free speech and a free press in emerging and other democracies and how these can be sustained. We need to better understand the legal and other conditions that are enabling or constraining access to communication and information environments by different social groups and the way different ICT-supported environments contribute towards the promotion of human rights. In addition, we need to understand how issues of communication and information rights are understood from different standpoints in different countries and regions and, in particular, how information and communication (including media) production influences moral conduct and our understanding of others.

3.2   Access and literacies

In line with an emphasis on well-being, research on issues of access needs to be combined with research on capacity building with respect to the literacies required for functioning in knowledge societies. There are issues of the accessibility and affordability of communication and information environments of all kinds, but there are also issues of access to *relevant* content, not only by elites, but by all people.

Research in this area needs to move beyond simplistic and dualistic thinking. Investigations of the "digital divide" and counts of whether individuals have access to specific information and communication technologies are not helpful unless they are coupled with new insights into the dynamics of specific informational and communicative contexts. Access issues need to be rethought in terms of a wide range of communication and information capabilities or literacies, especially for young people. As Ulla Carlsson argues:

> *"Media and information literacy is needed for all citizens, but is of decisive importance to the younger generation - in both their role as citizens and their participation in society, and their learning, cultural expression and personal fulfilment. A fundamental element of efforts to realize a media and information literate society is media education"* [4].

Literacies need to be investigated with respect to different social groups and their specific needs taking age, gender, class, ethnicity, disabilities, and minorities into account. Access questions need to be extended to include literacies related, for example, to education, political participation, entrepreneurship, and the management of new kinds of networks of partnerships. We also need to give greater attention to differences in access and literacy levels among groups such as migrant labourers and the conditions that prevail for urban as compared to rural workers.

3.3   Participatory communication

Research in the field of participatory communication needs to encompass a variety of perspectives including developments in "citizen" or "networked" journalism [1]. From a governance perspective research is needed to understand the sustainability of emerging forms of participation by civil society members and the extent to which new communication and information environments can contribute to democratic participation, e.g., social networking using Facebook, MySpace, and a host of related Internet sites.

Changing patterns of media and information production and consumption need to be examined with attention to different social groups, such as young people and marginalised groups. ICTs are playing an important role in contexts where there is a need to mediate conflict. Research has shown that it is not appropriate to assume that there is an automatic relationship between the presence of a free and independent media or ICT sector and the strengthening of civil society and democracy in fragile states [see 11, 17]. We need to discover more about what policy frameworks are consistent with enhancing sustainability and how these *differ* in different countries or regions. Research in this area needs to be extended beyond the Western countries to investigate how communication and information environments are being mediated by older and newer ICTs from radio, to multimedia sites and through the growing use of mobile phones, with a focus on who is being included and excluded from these developments.

3.4   Representation

Today's societies are generating increasingly complex structures and systems for organising knowledge of all kinds. These embrace all forms of media and communication and information systems. They enable new forms of representation and entail many new conventions, norms, and standards. These are present in the mainstream and alternative media and communication systems. They are also embedded within the "codes" or conventions of the way information systems organise and enable access to information. Research is needed which focuses on the dynamics that lead to new learning systems and systems of knowledge production and consumption. We need to understand better what specific digital representations generate distrust and the processes through which authoritative voices come to the fore. Little is known about how new forms of digital representation of distant others, for example, have the potential to give rise to violence, conflict, suffering, and victimisation or about the implications of these representations for public opinion formation and for humanitarian action.

3.5   Strategic communication and information policies and action plans

The last three decades have seen the publication of many reports outlining recommendations for what have come to be known today as knowledge societies. In 1980 UNESCO published, *Many Voices, One World*, the report of its International Commission for the Study of Communication Problems also known as the MacBride Report.[10] In the 1990s, and continuing into the present, numerous countries have been encouraged to prepare strategies for reducing inequality in access to ICTs. This work has been supported by many governmental and intergovernmental agencies. At the global level, the Action Plan of the World Summit on the Information Society[11] and the initiative of GAID (Global Alliance for ICT and Development)[12] are two of the most visible interventions at present. Each of these has parallel local or national instantiations.

There is an ongoing need to assess the barriers to progress in these areas as well as the signs of positive developments. What are the major barriers at the macro and micro levels? How are they perpetuated and what power relationships continue to sustain them? In this area we need a much stronger coupling of political economy perspectives with those that focus mainly on social processes without regard to power relationships. Special emphasis needs to be given to participation, continuity, and discontinuity between the multiple stakeholders

---

[10] See [14] and [3].
[11] See http://www.itu.int/wsis/docs/geneva/official/poa.html.
[12] See http://www.un-gaid.org/en/about/ict4d.

including those entering partnerships, and enabling those at the local level to influence developments. We need to learn more about what the nature of participation and consultation has been, that is, how are people actually involved? How, for instance, has the development of ICT strategies and action plans influenced policy diagnoses in specific countries? What evaluation instruments have been, and are being, used? Where these are imported from other contexts, are they appropriate for various local contexts? The barriers and opportunities for bottom-up policy formation and implementation also need more systematic attention.

3.6   Repertoires of methodologies

All indicators - qualitative and quantitative - can be misleading if they are not interpreted in the light of contextual information. I suggest, nevertheless, that both have a role to play in providing informative maps of changes in knowledge societies. It is difficult, in the absence of empirical evidence, for stakeholders to consider the policy interventions that might be needed to enhance well-being if they have no information about the nature of communication and information-related inequalities and their expression in different places or at different times. Many of the global and universal efforts to develop quantitative indicators of knowledge societies are insufficiently fine-grained and they are often insensitive to differences within knowledge societies [7]. Ethnographic and related methods offer the potential to provide valuable information and insight because they can provide data about the myriad forms of communication and information mediation, community practices, meanings and representations, and perceptions of conflict or mutual understanding. In general, reflexive methods should be encouraged alongside the development of survey-based methods designed to produce quantitative indicators of knowledge societies.

Research is also needed to map deficits in qualitative and quantitative indicators. There are frequent differences of opinion about whether inter-country comparisons using various metrics are helpful. Some argue that such comparisons contribute to the notion that all societies should be progressing towards a homogeneous knowledge society, i.e., meeting similar indicator targets and benchmarks. Others argue that such indicators provide stakeholders within countries with a basis for choosing priorities for action. There are also differences of opinion about whether the highest priority should be given to developing indicators for transitional societies, taking into account what it is practical to achieve in these societies, or whether all countries should be included in such work. Notwithstanding these differences, I suggest that indicators need to be as people-centred as possible and that a wider range of indicators than we have at present is essential. The research community can contribute by developing indicators for national and cross-country comparison and offering critical assessments of how such indicators are interpreted and received.[13]

4.   Conclusion

The research framework that I have begun to flesh out here is concerned with transnational approaches to social change and transformation leading to human well-being in knowledge societies. It aspires to be holistic in the sense of inclusivity without privileging specific social science disciplines or methodologies. It is intended to be flexibly applied at the micro and macro levels of analysis and to encourage both context specific and comparative research. The goal is to promote understanding of knowledge societies as being distinct, but also, as being systemically interrelated.

As an alternative research framework to that which achieves visibility within the mainstream of ICT-related research, it is intended to encourage a strong commitment to critical assessments of standpoints that reflect only partially on the conditions and potentials for achieving well-being in knowledge societies as they are developing in specific places. The results of research conducted within this alternative framework are likely to yield counterintuitive insights which, in turn, may influence ICT policy decisions and actions in new ways and have a greater chance of contributing to sustainable development goals.

The second question I emphasised at the outset of this presentation was *"what evidence is there of effective learning on the part of different stakeholders?"* My overall assessment based on my own engagement with a considerable number of macro and micro level initiatives with respect to ICT policy and strategy, and with respect to bottom-up ICT implementations in low-income countries – in this case largely through the research of my PhD students – is that there is a continuing tendency to favour a search for universal models, to foster market-led values, and to privilege technologies over human aspirations and needs. However, more optimistically, there are signs of learning augmented increasingly by attention to the causes of inequality in society and to how those causes filter into specific ICT initiatives. Perhaps, awareness of power relationships is the first step on the part of stakeholders, including the research community, towards the shift in research priorities and towards the more context sensitive and enabling approach that I am advocating in this presentation. A further step, of course, is the active engagement of the research community with those whose everyday lives are preoccupied by the material conditions of people's lives and their specific engagement with ICTs.

References

[1]   Beckett, C. & Mansell, R. (2008). Crossing boundaries: New media and networked journalism, *Communication, Culture & Critique*, 1(1), 92-104.

---

[13] An initiative to redress the imbalance in coverage of statistics on ICT Access and Usage in Africa is discussed by [10].

[2]   Brown, V. A. (2006). Towards the next renaissance? Making collective decisions combining community, expert and organisational knowledge, *International Journal of Knowledge, Culture & Change Management*, 6(3), 43-55.

[3]   Carlsson, U. (2005). From NWICO to global governance of the information society, in O. Hemer and T. Tufte (Eds.) *Media and glocal change: Rethinking communication for development* (pp. 193-214), Buenos Aires: NORDICOM & CLACSO.

[4]   Carlsson, U. (2007). Some reflections on the background document, note prepared for the UNESCO Brainstorming Meeting, 20-21 December.

[5]   Clark, D. A. (2005). The capability approach: Its development, critiques and recent advances, GPRG-WPS-032, Global Poverty Research Group, at www.gprg.org

[6]   Dirlik, A. (2004). Spectres of the third world: Global modernity and the end of the three worlds, *Third World Quarterly*, 25(1), 131-148.

[7]   Dunn, H. & Johnson-Brown, S. (2008). Information literacies and digital empowerment in the global south, report prepared for *UNESCO and the IAMCR 50th Anniversary Conference*, July, Paris, at http://portal.unesco.org/ci/en/ev.php-URL_ID=26268&URL_DO=DO_TOPIC&URL_SECTION=201.html.

[8]   Institute for Development Studies (2007). Reinventing development research, *IDS Bulletin*, 38(2).

[9]   Geertz, C. (1983). *Local knowledge*, London: Fontana.

[10]   Gillwald, A. & Stork, C. (2007). Towards an African ICT e-index: Towards evidence based ICT policy in Africa, an initiative covering 17 countries, http://lirne.net/test/wp-content/uploads/2007/11/gillwald-and-stork-2007-b.pdf.

[11]   James, B. (ed) (2004). Media conflict prevention and reconstruction, UNESCO.

[12]   Khan, A. W. (2006). What UNECO is doing to Support Freedom of Expression, in UNESCO (ed) (2006). *Media Development and Poverty Eradication*, Paris: UNESCO.

[13]   Kotler, P. & Zaltman, G. (1971). Social marketing: An approach to planned social change, *Journal of Marketing*, 35, 3-12.

[14]   Mansell, R. & Nordenstreng, K. (2006). Great media and communication debates – WSIS and the MacBride Report, *Information Technologies and International Development*, 3(4), 15-36.

[15]   Manyozo, L. (2008). Communication for development: An historical overview, report prepared for *UNESCO and the IAMCR 50th Anniversary Conference*, July, Paris, at: http://portal.unesco.org/ci/en/ev.php-URL_ID=26268&URL_DO=DO_TOPIC&URL_SECTION=201.html.

[16]   McChesney, R.W. (2007). Communication revolution: Critical junctions and the future of media, New York: The New Press.

[17]   J. Putzel & van der Zwan, J. (2007). Why templates for media development do not work in crisis states: Defining and understanding media development strategies in post-war and crisis states, LSE Crisis States Research Centre (CSRC), London.

[18]   Sen, A. (1999). *Commodities and capabilities*, Oxford: Oxford University Press.

[19]   Shome, R. (2006). Interdisciplinary research and globalization, *The Communication Review*, 9, 1-36.

[20]   Quebral, N. (1975). Development communication, in J. Jamias (Ed.), *Readings in development communication* (pp. 1-11), Laguna: UPLB College of Agriculture.

[21]   UNESCO (2005). Towards knowledge societies, http://unesdoc.unesco.org/images/0014/001418/141843e.pdf.

[22]   UNESCO (ed) (2006). *Media development and poverty eradication*, Paris: UNESCO.

[23] UNESCO (2007). Communication and information: Towards a prospective research agenda, Report on a Workshop, UNESCOParis, 20-21 December 2007, available at: http://www.iamcr.org/

[24] UNESCO (2008). Medium-Term Strategy for 2008-2013, 34 C/4 at http://unesdoc.unesco.org/images/0014/001499/149999e.pdf; 35 C/5 (2010-2011) and 35 C/5 (20012-2013).

[25] Vega Montiel, A. (2007). A preliminary reading of the background document: Human rights, the fundamental framework, note prepared for the UNESCO Brainstorming Meeting, 11 December.

Part 1:

The shaping of national and international ICT policies and their effects

THE ARGUMENTATIVE STRUCTURE OF SPATIAL DATA INFRASTRUCTURE INITIATIVES IN AMERICA AND AFRICA

Yola Georgiadou
International Institute for Geo-Information Science and Earth Observation (ITC),
The Netherlands

Vincent Homburg
Erasmus Universiteit Rotterdam FSW, The Netherlands

Abstract   Policy, including technology policy, is made of language. Politicians, bureaucrats, and consultants use language to shape action and ways of thinking by fabricating rules that enable individuals to deal with unresolvable contradictions of everyday life. The evolution of geospatial ICT policy can be best understood through the language of spatial data infrastructure (SDI) initiatives and the analysis of their argumentative structure. We focus on how SDI has been rhetorically crafted over almost two decades and how the rhetoric ("myth") unfolds as SDI myths move from one context (North America) to the other (Africa). We conclude that despite apparent similarities, there are durable differences. In the American myth, there is a clamour for "metrics" which can demonstrate progress and knowledge generation through research. In the African context, a rhetorical move is made by aligning the SDI concept with overarching Information Society concepts as promoted by the African Information Society Initiative (AISI). We suggest further research directions to explore how ICT policy talk interacts with the context in which it takes shape as it travels in space and time.

Keywords: Spatial data infrastructure, rhetoric, ICTs in developing countries

1.   Introduction

Spatial data infrastructure (SDI) refers to the assembly of geospatial technologies and institutional arrangements and practices that allow for the disclosure and sharing of geospatial data among various levels of government, citizens, and corporations. Spatial data infrastructure (SDI) doctrines, such as "data should be collected at one level of government and shared between all levels", "it should be possible to combine seamlessly data from different sources

Please use the following format when citing this chapter:

Georgiadou, Y. and Homburg, V., 2008, in IFIP International Federation for Information Processing, Volume 282;
Social Dimensions of Information and Communication Technology Policy; Chrisanthi Avgerou, Matthew L. Smith,
Peter van den Besselaar; (Boston: Springer), pp. 31–44.

and share it between many users and applications" etc., underpin geospatial ICT policy, for example, in the European Union [13].

Geospatial ICT caught the imagination of American think tanks in the early years of the Clinton-Gore administration when complex and distributed information systems were re-conceptualized as information infrastructure (II). Similarly, geographical information systems, dealing with geospatial data, were also becoming more complex and distributed, and re-conceptualized as a spatial data infrastructure (SDI). A national II was expected to provide for the integration of hardware, software, and skills to make it easy and affordable to connect people with each other, with computers, and with a vast array of services and information resources [39], while the purpose of a national SDI was to advance the goals of a national II by avoiding wasteful duplication of governmental geospatial data and resources [40].

In the early days, SDI initiatives were phrased primarily in terms of economic considerations of sharing capital-intensive and basic geospatial data "among the widest possible group of potential users at affordable costs" [40, p. 2]. National II and SDI initiatives were frequently phrased in those days as information superhighways emphasizing predictability, procedures and efficiency of delivery, technical access guided by the needs of commerce and government, a key role for central government in directing a top-down construction of the information superhighway, and the assumption of harmonious collaboration between governmental agencies. Contemporary discourse now recognizes II and SDI also as strategic infrastructures for social progress, particularly in supranational settings.

In this chapter, we focus on SDI talk as a more or less persuasive doctrine [12] or myth [21]: a statement of intention towards some part of a target audience, where the intention is that the "myth" serves as (1) a common frame of reference that experts, administrators, and politicians use to enact social reality, (2) a link between argument and acceptance, and (3) a source of inspiration that guides a specific course of action. Bearing in mind the observation that technological and managerial "ideas" often travel [8] over space and time as they are rhetorically crafted, the research objective of this chapter is then to analyze and critically examine the myths that underlie SDI initiatives as they mutate while travelling from distant think tanks to various real world settings [8].

The remainder of the chapter is organized as follows. In section two, we define SDI talk as myth and outline the research strategy. In section three, we analyze and reflect upon the changing argumentative structure in the American and African SDI myths over space and time. Section four summarises preliminary conclusions and directions for future research.

2.   The language of SDI initiatives

SDI became stabilized as a concept in 1993 in a report commissioned by the United States National Research Council [28]. One of the contributing authors of this report, Prof. John McLaughlin, had coined the term in two influential key note speeches, delivered in 1991 first to a Canadian [20] and then to an Australian audience [19]. Ever since, the notion of a spatial data infrastructure (SDI) has been discussed intensively in think tanks populated by geospatial academics, as well as by practitioners, software vendors, and policy makers. Since its official American début in 1993, the concept has been expanded in the United States in a series of National Research Council reports [22-30], and picked up in other contexts such as India [9], the European Union [18], and in a series of global spatial data infrastructure conferences (GSDI). Concurrently, throughout the 1990s, various national governments (Australia, United States, Qatar, Portugal, the Netherlands, Indonesia, Korea, Japan, and the United Kingdom, to name a few examples) pioneered implementation of national SDIs.

In 2001, a position paper of the Economic Commission of Africa (ECA), titled *The Future Orientation of Geoinformation Activities in Africa,* and prepared under the guidance of Prof. John McLaughlin, signalled the official arrival of the SDI concept in Africa [3]. By that time, ECA's prestigious *African Information Society Initiative (AISI): An Action Framework to Build Africa's Information and Communication Infrastructure* was already in full swing of implementation but largely oblivious of geospatial ICT [38].

2.1   Myths as inspiring tales

Following Mosco [21], we define myths as hymns to progress, and as utopian visions or promises unfulfilled or even unfulfillable. Myths are composed by so-called *bricoleurs* [15]: experts, politicians, bureaucrats and consultants who, in language, attempt to fabricate rules that serve as a shared frame of reference that enables individuals and organisations to deal with contradictions that can never be fully resolved [15-17], eventually enabling the *bricoleur* to inflict changes in ways of thinking and doing.

Myths have a number of recurrent features: they often are ubiquitous, usually rest on soft data (selectively drawn examples) and soft logic (use of persuasive example), they "win" over competing ideas by persuasion in communicative processes rather than by hard factual evidence, and often are contradictory and unstable (susceptible to new styles, fashions, and fads). The act of persuasion commonly involves the correct choice of metaphor, which taps into or builds shared modes of thinking. An example of the use of metaphors in the global SDI discourse is the use of imagery of physical infrastructures in relation to geospatial databases [11].

The notion of myth has been fruitfully theorized about and applied in discursive approaches within policy sciences [10]. For instance Hood and Jackson [12] identified 99 "doctrines" of administrative argument, and Bekkers and Homburg [2] identified four major "myths" in national e-government programs of Australia, the United Kingdom, the Netherlands, Denmark, and the United States. Smullen [35] analyzed public management reform accounts to identify and explain similarities and differences of administrative reforms in the Netherlands, Sweden, and Australia.

It is important at this moment to emphasize two issues. First, by referring to myths, in no way do we look down upon strenuous processes of SDI development. In this study we merely focus on argumentative structures of SDI initiatives. Second, unlike theories, myths are not testable, and debunking them is of little value. What is of interest is what myths represent, and how myths may or may not contribute to established bases of meaning and experiences with, in this case, spatial data infrastructures. As such, myths are neither true nor false, but either living or dead [16].

2.2   Myths and context

Although a focus on the language of ideas, myths, and argumentation may be interpreted as a move away from the operational particulars of everyday practice, myths cannot be separated from the context in which language takes shape. Ideas, embodied in myths, can simply not be isolated from the institutional context in which myths are crafted, used, and interpreted. The link between myth and its institutional context is that myths lend themselves to imitation: either appealing myths are copied from one context to the other, or a myth is copied from a well-known, prestigious, global "template". In the context of public management reform, Sahlin-Andersson [34] has noted that ideas are edited as part of the imitative process; how myths are retold in specific countries, continents or institutional settings depends, in some unspecified way, on institutional context, for instance on which actors are privileged to speak, and the timing of the emergence of those privileged to speak. Sahlin-Andersson identifies two basic patterns related to imitation of ideas and practices throughout various institutional contexts. The first one is that imitative behaviour is natural when goals and technologies are ambiguous. The second one is that interests of international bodies are a source of widely held beliefs about what uses and technologies are appropriate [1, 34].

2.3   A research strategy for analysis and comparison

In the current research, we analyze SDIs as myths, with a special focus on how myths become domesticated across space and time. We focus on the time period between 1990 (when the notion of SDI was first explicitly used) and 2007, and attempt to reconstruct the transformatory journey of the SDI notion in the North American discourse, the way it was translated [24] in the sub-Saharan African discourse, and how it has subsequently travelled in the African discourse. The choice for Africa is based on the explicit reference to the translation from North America to the African Continent [24], but also on pragmatic grounds in the sense that one of the authors of this chapter actively participated in the African CODI conferences [3-7] in which the African SDI rhetoric actually took shape.

More specifically, policy documents, research reports, and conference transcripts were gathered and subsequently scanned for discrete, unique utterances, inferences, and phrases within particular orders of discourse. Then, bearing in mind we were primarily interested in the mobilizing and persuasive qualities of myths, we reduced a larger set of utterances to specific higher level concepts. These concepts [see also 2, 12] are:

- How SDIs are defined and what metaphors were being used to describe them;
- What SDIs are supposed to do (ambitions: what is aimed for and how the results should be accomplished);
- Justification for action; and
- Perceived barriers that should be overcome.

Additionally, the analysis was informed by means of additional interview data with one key informant. The method as described above is susceptible to at least two forms of criticism. First and foremost, like any semiformal method involving identification and clustering of linguistic acts, this approach is inevitably subjective. Second, some readers may think the approach is too informal and actually does not deconstruct meaning or reveal hidden macro-level power structures. Those readers are reminded that the objective of this exercise was not to relate linguistic acts with overarching power structures, but rather to illuminate and identify the mobilizing potential of SDI myths. As such, in the analysis, the reinterpretation of SDI over time, in various policy documents and resolutions, has taken precedence over the in-depth (and very time-consuming) analysis of specific written or oral texts.

3.   Findings: African and American SDI "bricolage"

3.1   The American myth 1990-2007

The American SDI myth takes shape in various documents of the National Research Council (NRC) [22-30]. By reading against the reports and documents from 1991 to 2007, it is hard to miss an overall mobilizing tone. Using metaphorical language, SDIs are described as physical infrastructure (1999-2007), information marketplaces (1991-1993), and (digital) commons (1999-2003), and are generally seen as opportunities that simply cannot be missed [26, p. 1, 2, 3, 6]. Once realized, SDIs are portrayed as mandatory for rationalized decision making, for instance for the promotion of public safety, fight against terrorist attacks, and dealing with contingencies. Barriers standing in the way of the inescapable technological sublime are uncertainty about policies and investments, and lack of incentives towards sharing of geospatial data (see Table 1 for a detailed analysis). SDI development is depicted as a rather technical game: existing geospatial databases are to be integrated into a network by following a nine step strategy [29,

p. 116], so that eventually "[a]ccessing spatial data should become as easy as turning on a light switch" [29, p.112].

By 2001, accounts of meagre SDI progress [25], later on also signalled in a Congressional Hearing of the Committee on Government Reform, increased the reflexivity in the American rhetoric. In reports published in 2001 and beyond, NRC's abandonment of the evangelical tone of its previous documents, and a pragmatic turn is apparent in at least three ways.

- There is a clamour for the development of specific hypotheses regarding SDI goals [25] and a quest for demonstrating possibilities rather than promoting them, preferably using metrics to monitor long-term success in the adoption and principles of SDIs;
- It is argued that responsibility for developing a significantly more modest version of a national SDI for America, the so-called National Map, should be placed on a single federal government agency, the United States Geological Survey (USGS), which is furnished with a research agenda that provides the scientific underpinning for USGS operations [27]; and
- Although the abstract level of formulating ambitions is never really abandoned, specific attention is paid to more modest ambitions, and an eye for modesty in implementation: "all of these needs and applications must be balanced against the reality that [...] it cannot be all things to all people and all applications [...] because this will generate unreasonable expectations and scepticism from data producers" [30, p. 127].

While the evangelical tone is forsaken in reports meant for an American audience, the 2002 NRC report *Down to Earth: Geographic Information for sustainable development in Africa* [24], despite addressing a heterogeneous African audience, resurrected the physical infrastructure rationale for investing in information infrastructure. *Down to Earth* was a component of the U.S. State Department's "geographic information for sustainable development" project for the world summit, focusing on sub-Saharan Africa. *Down to Earth* signalled that "...building infrastructure for geo[graphic] information use is becoming as important to African countries as the building of roads, telecommunication networks [...] The rationale for investing in information infrastructure is analogous to that for physical infrastructure" [19]. The report emphasizes that "[...] access to integrated geographic information allows civil society to hold government accountable; and government creates policies that determine public access to information and public participation in the decision process" [19]. It urges African countries and international development programs to consider using a standardized SDI, compatible with the emerging global spatial infrastructure, and conforming to the same standards, to achieve sustainable development.

Period	Metaphor	What is aimed for	Justification	Barriers
1999 - 2007	Physical infrastruct-ure or building construc-tion [29, p. 15]	Integrated databases with information about physical, social and economic geography that provides linkages between goverments, citizens, and private sector; "Streamlined" [22, p. 1] decision support for societal problems crossing functional and geographical boundaries [26]	The upcoming information society requires availability of geographic information [29, p. 1] Opportunity that simply cannot be missed [26, p. 1, 2, 3, 6] Sunk costs of existing, localized database; SDI "will be an enormous benefit to federal agencies, state and local governments, the private sector, and the public at large"	Unclear policy and social issues, for instance debate about access rights Uncertainty about impact of SDI investments on decision making Skills and competencies Lack of incentives to share data and engage in information partnerships
1991 – 1993	Information Market-place	Supply of information services critical to a national competitive position in a globalizing economic arena [29, p. 2]	SDI is necessary for the maintenance of competitive position	Traditional pricing strategies for spatial information products (token prices)
1999- 2003	Commons [23] or Quilt [30]	Distributed geospatial library from which users can extract data for own purposes, and contribute locally gathered resources to common repositories [23, p. 31] Civic and private sector involvement [25, p. 75]	Outcomes and benefits are hard to estimate / intangible yet an informed debate on societal issues, and rapid responses to contingencies may prove to be priceless [23, p. 89, 90] promote the safety and welfare of the people [30] Terrorist attacks and recent natural disasters have shown that current information can save lives, and protect public and private property Best available data are often are proprietary, or at the local, municipal, or county government level and are made available at significant cost or with restrictions (…) The greatest benefits will be an enrichment of entire national coverage.	Uncertainties related to information ethics, legal barriers (in particular intellectual property rights) Demarcation of public domain (versus commercial sphere) [23, p. 35] The greatest challenges will be coordination among hundreds of participants and developing incentives for state and local governments to share and standardize their data or metadata

Table 1: Summary of the American SDI Myth 1990-2007.

3.2   *The African myth 1999-2007*

On the African continent, the global sustainable development agenda converged in the first years of the new millennium with the pan-African information society initiative (AISI). The adoption of AISI by the African Union Heads of State Summit in July 1996, elevated AISI to an African "ICT constitution" of sorts, a regional framework to support the New Partnership for Africa's Development (NEPAD) and a mechanism for achieving the Millennium Development Goals (MDG). AISI called for the development of a national information and communication infrastructure (NICI) plan in every African country [36]. The AISI aims to realize by 2010 a sustainable information society in Africa where "information and decision-support systems are used to support decision-making in all the major sectors of the economy [...] access is available to international, regional and national 'information highways', providing 'off-ramps' in the villages [while] a vibrant business sector exhibits strong leadership capable of forging the build-up of the information society" [38].

The United Nations Economic Commission for Africa (ECA) was instrumental in the inception of AISI and the implementation of NICIs with support from other United Nation agencies and bilateral donors. In its effort to promote the economic and social development of the African Union, foster intra-regional integration, and promote international cooperation for Africa's development, ECA plays a critical role in helping build consensus around key African development challenges and in articulating common African perspectives and positions, which then form the basis for engagement with the international community. Its mandate and ability to convene senior policy makers, through ECA's annual *Conference of Ministers of Finance, Planning and Economic Development* and other development stakeholders, is pivotal in ensuring this role.

The AISI caused a reshuffling of ECA's own programmes including the launching of the Committee on Development Information (CODI), a subsidiary body of ECA, providing policy and technical guidance for the *"harnessing information for development"* programme. The programme's objective is to provide assistance to African governments in the fields of Spatial Data Infrastructure and National Information and Communication Infrastructure (NICI) development, under the umbrella of AISI. CODI has regularly convened voting delegates from African member states and international observers since 1999 in bi-annual conferences to discuss policy issues related to the implementation of AISI by the key players in the African communities of "geoinformation", "statistics", and "ICT".

The resolutions adopted in the five conferences of the CODI subcommittee on geoinformation to date, organized under the wings of the ECA, together with documents commissioned to consultants and endorsed or written by ECA can be read as Africa's hymn to SDI progress [3-7]. In the CODI proceedings, SDI is portrayed as embedding "raw materials", to be used for (1) sustainable development, (2) timely ("informed") decision making regarding food security, poverty alleviation, and environmental monitoring, and (3) the realization of overarching NEPAD objectives and Millennium Development Goals (see Table 2 for a more elaborate description).

Period	Metaphor	What is aimed for	Justification	Barriers
1999-2007	Raw material [3, 4]	Backbone for sustainable development as well as decision making regarding food security, poverty alleviation, environmental monitoring and control and natural resources management [3] Delivery of spatial information to widest possible group of potential users	Critical need for timely information for decision making [3, p. 4] Realization of NEPAD objectives, Millennium Development Goals and WSSD	Lack of resources at all educational levels Low awareness of value of spatial information by policy makers Lack of implementation methodology
1999-2005	Information Marketplace		Investment value and national benefits of spatial data [3, p. 4] Economic potential [37, p. 1] Service delivery industries that depend on location and spatial knowledge will benefit from reduced transaction costs and will be stimulated, leading to more economic activity [37]	Low awareness of the value of information (especially spatial information) by government policy makers and senior management. Lack of implementation methodology
2003-2007	Evolving phenomenon	Alignment of SDI initiatives with overarching AISI initiatives (NICI)	National, strategic and financial need for sound decision making Fundamental geospatial datasets are required for informed decision making	No implementation methodology

Table 2: Summary of the African SDI Myth 1990-2007.

If one reads the African tale as a myth to progress, the tale initially thrives on hymns to rationalized decision making in national single nation settings, but soon snowballs into rhetoric that addresses more complex objectives like poverty alleviation, food security, and natural resources management. Throughout the period covered in the analysis the cast of obstacles remains stable; in various

CODI documents, as well as in auxiliary studies, there are continuous references to lack of resources, lack of awareness, and lack of support (in the sense of methodologies) to guide action. Use of imagery is restricted to occasional references to backbones for decision making regarding a host of abstract goals and to information markets.

The relative paucity of "content" in the African Tale is counterbalanced by its relative richness in "procedures". To counteract the high degree of heterogeneity (different forms of knowledge, different forms of governance, etc) in the African tale consensus could be reached only when a common platform has been agreed upon, in the shape of shared procedures of evidence [32]. The quest for "procedures" has been part of the solution suggested in the *Down to Earth* report ("developing countries should consider using a standardized SDI" [24]) and is the single most persisting feature of the African Tale. With no single source of information or instruction on how to proceed to set up a national spatial data infrastructure the quest for procedures resulted in three iterations:

- The compilation of a SDI Implementation guide for Africa [5] was attempted under the auspices of ECA as "guidelines on concrete steps to implement SDIs in Africa, targeted to all those that have a key role to play in promoting, adopting, developing or implementing spatial information infrastructure in their home countries" [4] and reinforced by appeals of representatives from member States, academia, professional bodies, and other sectors [30];
- During the actual compilation of the guide the practical difficulty of developing a "how to" step-by-step guide for something that defies computation was resolved by organizing the material of the SDI Implementation guide for Africa as "chess" moves and options [30];
- With progress still elusive in 2005, the third iteration portrayed African SDI as an AISI implementation tool, thus aligning SDI implementation procedures with the broader and successful NICI implementation procedures in Africa.

In November 2007, ECA published a report titled *E-strategies: National Information and Communication Infrastructure (NICI): Best Practices and lessons learned* [27]. In this report, African national SDI initiatives are reframed as "geo-enabling the NICIs" [27] in an argumentative turn reminiscent of SDI piggy-backing on II more than ten years earlier in North America. The report concludes that the "development, deployment and use of ICTs within the economy can contribute to and accelerate the socio-economic development process provided some critical success factors and conditions are addressed at all levels" [27]. Forty-five critical success factors and conditions are listed in [27], including good governance and rule of law, functioning democracy and democratic institutions, prevailing peace, national unity and national security, sub-regional stability and peace, and stable economic policy environment. The tautology suggested by these prerequisites — ICTs contribute to development, under the condition of development — is difficult to miss.

4.   Conclusions and future work

In this chapter, we showed how the concept of SDI was developed, transformed, and translated in the North American context in which it was conceived, how it travelled to an African context, and how it was translated in that particular context over time. We used basic rhetorical analysis and the concept of myths to show how bricoleurs of the NRC (in North America) and CODI (in Africa) enact reality. Reflecting on Sahlin-Andersson's notions of imitation of ideas [34], a number of observations (and subsequent research directions) can be noted.

First, the CODI bricoleurs seem to have copied some of the metaphors of the more generalized North American SDI tale. The perceived obstacles remain constant, throughout the process and in the comparison between the North American tale and the African tale, with a number of usual suspects being (1) lack of resources, (2) lack of awareness, and (3) lack of incentives for governments and private sector corporations to enter into information partnerships.

Second, the "corrective turns" in the SDI rhetoric (responding to faltering progress) display how in the North American and in the African tales, myths are edited in specific ways to account for differences in institutional context, presumably in order to seek legitimacy for the idea of SDI. In the United States, emerging practices include the use of metrics, a focus on a single agency with a unique role, and knowledge generation through research. In Africa, the absence of a pan-African legislative SDI framework and research, paradoxically considered as luxury given the urgency of the challenges in Africa, lends a characteristic twist to the emerging "corrective" practices, while some uniformity with the rest is still evident. SDI metrics emerge again as a prominent practice, but this time subservient to a broader agenda — in the guise of NICI compliant implementation steps — and at a high political risk. Overall, what can be witnessed is that the SDI myth in North America is aligned with theory development and theory use in the clamour for best practices and demonstrated uses of SDI, whereas in Africa, SDI is interwoven with the political agenda of AISI and the NICI community.

All in all, the way the SDI – conceived as a myth – has been developed and translated in time and space shows that – in a yet unspecified way – it interacts with the context in which the myth takes shape. NICI and SDI discourses unfolded in Africa in a context marked by the overwhelming support to NEPAD, which signalled the ideological convergence of the ECA and the African Union with the neoliberal agenda of international financing institutions after decades of disagreement and acrimony between the "international community" and African leaders [31]. In order to identify core elements of the process of translation, future work has to focus on a number of issues.

First, an obvious candidate for further exploration is the organisation field of foreign aid to Africa —a world-wide network populated by formal, "giving" and "taking", national and multinational organisations pursuing and financing development— in which translation takes place [33]. At least two intermediate spaces of the organisation field can be distinguished, a regional and a national one.

In the regional intermediate space, ECA and the Conference of Ministers of Finance, Planning and Economic Development articulate common African perspectives and positions, which form the basis for engagement (and further translation of these positions) with international financing institutions and bilateral donors. In the national intermediate space of a single country, ministries and other government and non-government organisations —arguably reconfigured to communicate with structures similar to those of the donors by a process of "contact infection" [14]— engage in a technical game. In this technical game, a seemingly impossible feat is attempted: the transfer of a "thing" —e.g. a water management system, a professional practice, a legal framework or an idea— from one context to the next in such a way that the "thing" remains identical while it is transformed to accomplish the desired impact in the destination context [33]. Second, further research should be directed to the micro processes of translation: of how myths, not in an abstract way, but in processes of bilateral and multilateral communication at conferences, in think tanks, etc., are edited, and are or are not vulnerable to varying degrees of professionalization of bodies, variety in cognitive, and technical skills, etc.

Myths serve as a link between argument and acceptance in intermediate spaces of the foreign aid organisation field and in micro processes of translation. In its composition, the myth may refer to resources such as legitimacy, power, skills, and money. These resources, however, are not simply available "out there", but are dispersed over the variety of organisations operating in the foreign aid field. Myths then are not only composed in a way that inspires action, but also in a way that enables translation and communication between developing countries and donors.

References

[1]   Barzelay, M. & Gallego, R. (2006). From "new institutionalism" to "institutional processualism": Advancing knowledge about public management policy change.. *Governance*, 19(4), 531-557.
[2]   Bekkers, V.J.J.M. & Homburg, V.M.F. (2007). The myths of e-government: Looking beyond the assumptions of a new and better government. *The Information Society*, 23(5), 373-382.
[3]   CODI I (1999). Report of the first meeting of the committee on development information (CODI I): Harnessing information for development, Subcommittee on geoinformation 28 June - 2 July 1999. Addis Abeba: Economic Commission for Africa.
[4]   CODI II (2001). Report of the second meeting of the committee on development information (CODI II): Development information and decision making,

Subcommittee on geoinformation, 4 - 7 September 2001. Addis Abeba: Economic Commission for Africa.

[5] CODI III (2003). Report of the third meeting of the committee on development information (CODI II): Information and Governance, Subcommittee on Geoinformation, 10 - 13 May 2003. Addis Abeba: Economic Commission for Africa.

[6] CODI IV (2005). Report of the fourth meeting of the committee on development information (CODI IV): Information as an economic resource, Subcommittee on Geoinformation, 23 - 28 April 2005. Addis Abeba: Economic Commission for Africa.

[7] CODI V (2007). Report of the fifth meeting of the committee on development information (CODI V): Employment and the knowledge economy, Subcommittee on geoinformation, 29 April – 4 May 2007. Addis Abeba: Economic Commission for Africa.

[8] Czarniawska, B. & Sevón, G. (2005). *Global ideas: How ideas, objects and practices travel in the global economy*. Copenhagen: Copenhagen Business School Press.

[9] Department of Science and Technology (2001). *National spatial data infrastructure (NSDI) (Strategy and action plan)*. Bangalore: Task Force on NSDI, Department of Science and Technology.

[10] Fisher, F. & Forrester, J. (eds.) (1993). *The argumentative turn in policy analysis and planning*. London: Routledge.

[11] Georgiadou, Y., Puri, S.K., & Sahay, S. (2006). The rainbow metaphor: spatial data infrastructure organization and implementation in India. *International studies of management and organization*, 35(4), 48-71.

[12] Hood, C. & Jackson, M. (1991). *Administrative argument*. Aldershot: Dartmouth.

[13] INSPIRE Directive (Joint Research Centre, E.C.E.I., Italy), (2007). Directive 2007/2/EC of the European Parliament and of the Council of 14 March 2007 establishing an infrastructure for spatial information in the European Community (INSPIRE). Published in the official Journal on the 25th April 2007.

[14] Kühl, S. (2005) Organisationen in der Weltgesellschaft: Zur Rolle der Entwicklungshilfe bei der Diffusion von Organisationen. Working paper 2, www.hsu-hh.de/download-1.4.1.php?brick_id=UGo1B67ZfyPIcU7N.

[15] Lévi-Strauss, C. (1987). *Anthropology and myth: Lectures 1951-1982*. New York: Blackwell Publishers.

[16] MacIntyre, A. (1970). *Sociological theory and philosophical analysis*. London: MacMillan Publishers.

[17] March, J.G. & Olsen, J.P. (1989). *Rediscovering institutions*. New York: The Free Press.

[18] Masser, I. (2004) The future of spatial data infrastructures, in ISPRS Workshop on Service and Application of Spatial Data Infrastructure. Hangzhou, China.

[19] McLaughlin, J.D. (1991).Spatial data infrastructures: the next LIM challenge. *Proceedings of the 1991 Conference on Land Information Management,*, (pp. 8-20), University of New South Wales, Australia: New South Wales, Australia.

[20] McLaughlin, J.D. (1991).Towards a national spatial data infrastructure. In *Proceedings of the Canadian conference on GIS*, (Ed.), (pp. 1-5), Canadian Institute of Geomatics: Ottawa, Canada.

[21] Mosco, V. (2004). *The digital sublime: Myth, power and cyberspace*. Cambridge: The MIT Press.

[22] National Research Council (1995). *A data foundation for the national spatial data infrastructure*. Washington DC: National Academy Press.

[23] National Research Council (1999). *Distributed geolibraries: Spatial information resources*. Washington DC: National Academic Press.

[24] National Research Council (2002). *Down to earth: Geographic information for sustainable development in Africa.* Washington DC: National Academy Press.

[25] National Research Council (2001). *National spatial data infrastructure partnership programs: Rethinking the focus.* Washington DC: National Academy Press.

[26] National Research Council (1994). *Promoting the national spatial data infrastructure through partnerships.* Washington DC: National Academy Press.

[27] National Research Council (2007). A research agenda for Geographic Information Science at the United States Geological Survey. Washington, DC: National Academies Press.

[28] National Research Council (1990). *Spatial data needs: The future of the national mapping program.* Washington DC: National Academy Press.

[29] National Research Council (1993). *Toward a coordinated spatial data Infrastructure for the nation.* Washington DC: National Academy Press.

[30] National Research Council (2003). Weaving a national map: Review of the U.S. Geological Survey concept of The National Map. Washington DC: National Academies Press.

[31] Owusu, F. (2003). Pragmatism and the gradual shift from dependency to neoliberalism: The World Bank, African leaders and development policy in Africa. *World Development*, 31(10), 1655-1672.

[32] Rottenburg, R. (2006).Code-switching, or why a metacode is good to have. In B. Czarniawska and G. Sevón, (Eds), *How ideas, objects and practices travel in the global economy* (pp. 259-274), Copenhagen: Copenhagen Business Press.

[33] Rottenburg, R. (2002). *Weithergeholte Fakten: Eine Parabel der Entwicklungshilfe.* Stuttgart: Lucius & Lucius.

[34] Sahlin-Andersson, K. (2002). National, international and transnational constructions of New Public Management. In T. Christensen and P. Laegreid, Eds), *New Public Management: The transformation of ideas and practice)*, Ashgate: Aldershot.

[35] Smullen, A. (2007). Translating agency reform (rhetoric and culture in comparative perspective). Rotterdam: Erasmus University.

[36] United Nations Economic Commission for Africa (2007). African Information Society Initiative (AISI). An action framework to build Africa's Information and Communication Infrastructure. Addis Abeba: United Nations Economic Commission for Africa.

[37] United Nations Economic Commission for Africa (2001). The future orientation of geoinformation activities in Africa: A position paper, ECA/DISD/GEOINFO/DOC/01, Endorsed by the second meeting of the committee on development Information, development information services division (DISD). Addis Abeba: United Nations Economic Commission for Africa,.

[38] United Nations Economic Commission for Africa (2003). SDI implementation guide for Africa. Endorsed by the third meeting of the committee on development information. Addis Abeba: United Nations Economic Commission for Africa.

[39] US President (1993). Executive order 12864. United States Advisory Council on the national information infrastructure. Federal Register, 58, 179.

[40] US President (1994). Executive Order 12906 on national spatial data infrastructure. Federal Register, 59, 71.

ICT POLICY AS A GOVERNABLE DOMAIN: THE CASE OF GREECE AND THE EUROPEAN COMMISSION

Ioanna Chini
London School of Economics and Political Science, UK

Abstract   This chapter explores ICT policy as a domain that emerges out of the interplay of national and supra-national efforts. Against this backdrop, the chapter investigates the case study of Greek ICT policy, under the important influences of the European Commission. Foucault's concept of governmentality is constructively used as a theoretical lens to inform the analysis of the empirical data. I argue that ICT policy in Greece has been constituted as a governable domain. An array of techniques which embody the rationale of the Commission's outlook of ICT policy are regulating the conduct of Greek administrators, who, in turn, willingly self-regulate their behaviour in order to keep the relationship going. In effect, the empirical investigation and theoretical analysis of the research presented in this chapter challenge the way ICT policy is traditionally viewed as the product of rational deliberation of a country.

Keywords: ICT policy, Greece, European Commission, governmentality

1.   Introduction

The pervasiveness of information and communication technology (ICT) in society, and the perception that it can form the basis of a national competitive advantage has led to a flurry of national policies geared towards strengthening the society's capacity to adopt and skilfully adapt ICTs. Proactive institutional intervention from governments, be it as part of a neoliberal *laissez-faire* approach or as part of social welfare discourse, has been a legitimate step to take [26, 27].

The appreciation of ICT as providing a distinct competitive advantage has prompted the involvement of regional and international authorities in joining in the ICT policy field, as the issue was deemed to be too important to allow uncoordinated action or inaction to stifle the economic potential. Therefore, regional authorities, such as the European Union, supranational organisations, such as the OECD, and international organisations, such as ITU and the World Bank, have all stepped forward to create their own ICT visions, backed by policies and programmes of action. The chapter investigates what happens at the intersection of these international demands with national ICT policies.

Please use the following format when citing this chapter:

Chini, I., 2008, in IFIP International Federation for Information Processing, Volume 282; *Social Dimensions of Information and Communication Technology Policy*; Chrisanthi Avgerou, Matthew L. Smith, Peter van den Besselaar; (Boston: Springer), pp. 45–62.

National ICT policies have been the focus of academic research for a number of years. Two distinct traditions can be discerned with researchers approaching the topic on the one hand from a localised perspectives, zooming in on a single policy or programme of action, and on the other hand from a bird's eye view, attempting to account for the overall outcomes of year-long interventions. A tendency to understand ICT policy as unambiguous and technical has led to an underestimation of its political nature and implications [3, 22]. A third stream of research, which overcomes this shortcoming, taking a critical approach striving to understand the ideologies embodied in ICT policies, is under-represented, but gaining ground.

The chapter is empirically based on a case study of ICT policy in Greece in relation to the European Union and demonstrates how Greek governments have conceptualised and made ICT policy, while being influenced by the political decisions and programmes of action of the European Commission[1]. The prevalence of contexts worldwide where supra-national organisations play a role in national political decisions begs further investigation, of which this research is an example.

The study explores how the international momentum to create ICT policy is being acted upon in the case of a state which has experienced late modernity [36], has limited technological tradition, and has historically been a late adopter of technological revolutions [47]. The research reveals the vital role the European Commission has played in making available and enforcing the strategic direction, the implementation framework, and the funding. The significant loss of autonomy in this area by Greek state officials was never resisted; the active intervention of the Commission has been welcomed, even as its obtrusiveness has increased through time.

Governmentality is used as the analytical lens through which the analysis of the case is done. The concept was initially developed by Foucault [13, 14], and later by Rose [40] and Dean [6, 7]. The analysis of government is concerned with the techniques that have been used in order to shape conduct so as to achieve certain ends. Tracing the lines of thought, discourses, and programmes of action constitutes its method of enquiry. The concept of governmentality can be more simply understood as a way of exploring how willing subjects are created, that is, subjects whose behaviour is regulated through a series of techniques. The concept is essentially different from simple enforcement or dependency. Agency is required, not negated.

This chapter argues that in the case of Greece the European Commission has rendered the area of ICT policy a governable domain by framing the issues around ICT policy, and utilizing a series of procedures which effectively govern and shape the conduct of Greek policy makers. The state officials in Greece actively engage with the techniques of government and willingly assert their status of subject by acting in ways that please the Commission.

---

[1] From now on the European Commission will be referred to as simply the Commission.

The chapter goes on to review the literature in ICT policy, thus helping to position this piece of work within the existing body of knowledge. The concept of governmentality is discussed and a few elements are extracted to help operationalise it for the purpose of the chapter. In the analysis, key elements of the case study are presented through the lens of governmentality and conclusions are drawn as to the extent to which the concept has helped improve our nuanced understanding of the case.

2.   ICT policy

ICT policy constitutes a fluid and fragmented area of study, as it has predominantly been of the "adjectival" type [5], focusing on substantive policy issues. Different themes have emerged as important through time: from the development of national competitive advantage through micro-electronics production [10, 11], to telecommunications liberalization [9, 29, 34], national information infrastructures [21, 35], and software outsourcing [4, 12]. The information or knowledge society has been the focus of recent research [2, 30, 31, 46].

The majority of the research takes a localised approach, placing particular policy initiatives at its focus. They provide in-depth, contextual knowledge of the factors that brought a policy to life or of its implementation outcomes [18, 25, 39]. Treating specific policies as independent objects of research, these analyses fail to trace historical interdependencies, and fall short of accounting for the influence of globalised conditions. A further methodological criticism pertains to the difficulty of discerning the impact of a specific policy from all the relevant factors at play [37].

On the other hand, a variety of studies examine the macro effects of ICT policy for developmental goals. Occasionally drawing on an economic rationality, these studies aim at formulating prediction models or at expressing causal relationships [22, 43-45, 48]. In this stream of thought, Iosifidis and Leandros [20] investigate the results of the interventionist policies of the Greek state over the private sector and the civil society in order to foster the creation the information society

Research of this sort allows for a more comprehensive view of the impacts of ICT policy. However, the relatively short time frames examined can lead to overestimation or underestimation of different types of impact, and may not allow for trickle-down effects or spin-offs to be observed [37].

A third significant group in the literature consists of studies that have an ideological approach to ICT policy. The basic premise is that decisions and policies about ICT are rarely the outcome of rational deliberation, but serve instead other ideological purposes. Ideologies become an integral part of policymaking not only because they provide a useful lens through which a new and uncertain situation can be interpreted, but also because they come bundled with acceptable and legitimate courses of action [15, 38]. Studies in this stream usually take as their object of study a policy document or declaration. Their intention is to uncover the hidden ideological assumptions that are embedded in the policy discourse and which shape the form and goals of policy itself.

Such research has examined ICT policies of national governments [8, 17, 24, 42]. The European Union's rhetoric on the information society has been ideologically critiqued as upholding the economic aspects at the detriment of social and cultural considerations [16, 19].

This tradition has produced a number of intriguing studies. A shortfall of this type of research is that studying policy declarations does not equate with studying ICT policy. Ideologies do not exist in a vacuum, nor do they diffuse without active human intervention. Instead, they form part of a material arrangement which sustains them and allows them to have real-world effects. Thus, it makes much sense to open the focus from the ideological study of policy documents to the material arrangements that bring them to life [15, 23].

The existing research on ICT policy has not looked into the phenomenon of ICT policy being led by external, usually supranational, organisations which communicate the visions about the information society and control significant sources of funding. Exploring such a situation can bring forward different interpretations of the reasons why ICT policy is pursued, the conditions under which this is done, and the effects is has on the socio-economic fabric of society. This is where this research contributes.

3.   Governmentality

The concept of governmentality appears in Foucault's later lectures and writings as a way to move forward with the question of knowledge and power and to explore the domain of government as the "conduct of conduct" [13, p.220]. The idea of governmentality tries to bring to light the collective, taken for granted, thought involved in practices of government, which is rarely challenged [14]. The prevalent question "who is governing" becomes "how the governing of ourselves and others happen".

This question can be answered by pursuing an analytics of government [7, 40]. The goal is to understand the underlying rationale hidden in the complex nexus of institutional relationships and programmes of action. Instead discussing of ideology, the analytics of government is concerned with thought as it is embedded in material arrangements and technical means of shaping conduct. Foucault uses the term regimes of practice to denote the complex assemblage of institutions, programmes of action, techniques and technologies through which truth is produced.

Foucault is thus exploring a process of subjectification: the way in which agents are constituted as subjects and are brought to willingly conduct themselves accordingly. The strength of the concept lies in its emphasis on how conduct is shaped in the different locales and how individuals create themselves as subjects and locally produce truth through the regimes of practice at play. In this way, governmentality does not negate agency; to the contrary, it requires agency so as to allow for the individual to act and either reinforce or challenge the regime of practice.

Providing a more flexible interpretation of government and power, as well as a way to investigate the material and technical arrangements in which mentalities of government are embedded, the concept of governmentality appears to be a fruitful lens for looking into a regulated domain such as the domain of ICT policy in Greece. It is possible to move away from the question of "who governs" and proceed to discuss how governing is taking place and how all parties involved regulate their conduct according to the desired ends, the *telos* of the government.

Methodologically, the analysis of government is concerned with "how" questions. The emphasis is on deciphering how conduct in specific domains is regulated by studying the technical means in which such regulation is inscribed in order to be effective.

Dean [6, 7] argues that when pursuing an analysis of government the regimes of practice can be analysed along four closely intertwined, but relatively autonomous, dimensions. Firstly, forms of visibility render certain aspects of government visible, while others remain obscure and unchallenged. The visual dimension of government, expressed through charts, diagrams, images and tables, helps define what or who is to be governed, assigns roles, and constitutes identities. Secondly, regimes of practice can be analysed in terms of the technical aspects of government, i.e., the procedures, instruments, techniques, vocabularies, and technologies by which government is accomplished. This corresponds to the *techne* of government and is congruent with the emphasis on how thought operates by being embedded in real-world arrangements. The third dimension looks into the question of thought and is aiming to establish the kinds of knowledge claims that are being upheld as valid. In effect, this is a quest to understand the rationality of government. Finally, the fourth element concerns the formation of identities for those that govern and those that are being governed. What capacities and attributes are they invested with and how are they to comport themselves?

This chapter will focus on the second of these elements, the technical means of government. It will discuss the different means used to constitute the field of ICT policy as a governable domain, and will attempt to demonstrate the types of technical and material means on which government has been inscribed. In this quest, the boundaries between techniques, identities, forms of visibility, and the *telos* of government will inevitably be blurred; however, for reasons of size restrictions, these will not be the focus of this chapter.

4.   Methodology

4.1   Data collection

Data for the study was drawn from two domains. Firstly, twelve semi-structured interviews were conducted with policy makers in the European Commission. These included people from various departments, such as the Fund for Regional Development, the Social Fund, the Directorate-General for Enterprise and Industry, and the Directorate-General for the Information Society. A common denominator for all the interviewees was that they were, either at the time of the interview or in the past, involved in making ICT policy inside the Commission. They were also all involved in negotiations with the Greek side in order to monitor or help in the implementation of the policies.

Secondly, forty semi-structured interviews were conducted in Greece with stakeholders involved in different areas of ICT policy, including past and present state officials working on ICT policy from the formulation to its implementation, past and present civil servants, consultants and IT implementers, involved in co-financed IS projects, public procurement managers in IT companies, and trade union representatives and public procurement managers in IT companies.

Because the domain of ICT policy was particularly fragmented, different groups of informants were aware of only some of its facets. As such, the themes to be discussed in the interviews were determined after carefully considering the experiences and position of each informant within the field. The overarching themes that transcended the field study pertained to understanding how individuals made enough sense of the technological innovations around them to create a developmental vision, how they reached decisions about the types of actions to be pursued, how they managed the relationship with the European Union, and how they understood the outcomes of their efforts. The informants were encouraged to explain their concerns and aspirations, their day-to-day realities, and their opinions. The researcher compiled a storyline of events on which the majority of accounts converged and thereafter treated the opinions as part of the informants' identities and assessed them accordingly.

Alongside the interviews, written material was gathered and analysed. The websites of the Commission and the Greek information society office were scrutinised, as they contained vast amounts of information on their activities, highlighting their concerns at different points in time. Apart from the widely available information, the researcher was lucky enough to be offered some access to the informants' private archives, thus gaining access to material often forgotten. The field study resulted in the collection of three hundred pages of personal notes and more than a thousand pages of printed material.

4.2   Data analysis

The study is a case study dealing with a contemporary phenomenon [49]. The phenomenon appears, however, to be particularly defined by path-dependent processes, and so a historical perspective was deemed necessary to allow us to understand the structural elements of the case. The work of Mason, McKenney *et al.* [32] guided the collection and analysis of the data. Analysing the data consisted of determining patterns, trying out causal chain scenarios, and establishing empathy with the protagonists of the story [32]. The researcher's impressions were compiled in an analytical narrative [33], which highlighted important and recurrent themes, as well as temporal and causal linkages. The analytical narrative recounted the policies designed and implemented on ICT for almost two decades, 1985-2006, tracking in parallel the history of Greek and European ICT policy. For the purposes of the chapter, only data from the later stage, 1999-2006, is considered.

5.   Case study

5.1   Case background

Greece joined the European Community in 1981, but has neither managed to reach levels of economic growth and development similar to those of other EU members nor to achieve full integration. Located in the geographical periphery of the EU, Greece also has remained peripheral socio-economically [47]. Greece has, however, been particularly influenced by the EU, by both its "hard" policy measures, such as regulations, and its "soft" approaches, such as targets and benchmarks, developmental plans and financial incentives [41, 50]. Greece is a net beneficiary of Community funding [28]; financial assistance has been received since 1987 in various areas, among which ICT.

A Community Support Framework (CSF) is an EU instrument which groups all the funding to be made available to a member-state in a given time frame, so that the goals of cohesion and integration can be pursued. Operationally, CSFs are broken down in smaller sub-programmes which are sector- or theme-specific (e.g., shipping or human capital creation). The negotiation of a CSF determines the domains where funding is to be channelled, the types of interventions to be pursued, the overall rationale of the intended intervention, the criteria of evaluation, as well as the budgets. In the timeframe of six years the funds need to be funnelled into specific projects, while the projects need to be finished two years after the end of the CSF. For each CSF, a management and monitoring mechanism is set up in the member-state in order to evaluate the progress of the CSF on an annual basis.

Greece has been making policy decisions on ICT for the past two decades. ICT policy and ICT investment has revolved around the funds made available from the European Commission. Horizontal, ICT-specific programmes of action were negotiated with the Commission as sub-programmes under the CFSs, and implemented nationally. These IT-specific operational programmes, initiated in 1987, proved to be the driving force behind any orchestrated governmental effort regarding ICT.

To briefly summarise what has happened before 1999, the first CSF was initiated in 1987, the second in 1993, and the third in 2000. In each one, there was provision and funding to carry out developmental IT interventions, although the criteria for what was considered developmental shifted with time. In CSF1, large data centres were created for key areas of the public administration. In CSF2, the creation of physical and informational infrastructures was funded. In CSF3, the priorities were the liberalisation of the telecommunications, and the use of the Internet, particularly in e-government services. The Commission was jointly involved in the monitoring and operational management of the programmes up until the end of the CSF2, effectively co-determining their course. It relinquished its operational monitoring role in favour of a more executive one from the CSF3 onwards.

5.2   Narrative

Around the turn of the century, the theme of the information society gained increasing visibility. In 1999, a group of eight advisors, public servants and academics, led by the prime minister's Advisor for the Information Society, created the White Bible for Greece's entry into the information society. This non-binding policy paper documented its authors' vision for the role of ICT in the country's progress.

Concurrently, the country's administration was negotiating with the Commission the formulation of CSF3, which would be co-financed to a large extent by the Commission. Successfully negotiating and signing the CSF3, and maximizing the amount of funding were key political targets for the government. With the global rise to prominence of the issue of the information society, a sub-programme focusing on institutional intervention for the adoption of ICT was also being negotiated by the PM's Advisor to the Information Society. The White Bible was the wild card used in the negotiations to demonstrate the country's proactive and strategic planning for the information society.

CSF3 was signed in the spring of 2000, and the sub-programme for the information society, called OPIS (Operational Programme Information Society), was one of the first sub-programmes to be agreed upon and signed. It included the provision of a 3 billion fund to be funnelled into projects of information systems and IT-enabled change by the end of 2006. The projects had to be selected on the basis of specific criteria, and were to be incorporated in one of four categories: education and culture, public services to citizens, assistance to businesses, and telecommunications.

The majority or the available funds was committed towards providing online services to citizens, i.e., in projects of e-government. All authorities were urged to put forward proposals for projects which were visibly outwards-facing, linking the administration to the citizens. Projects of back-office computerization were not deemed congruent with the spirit and the criteria of the programme. Citizen orientation was the key criterion to be fulfilled.

A complex organisational structure was implemented to carry out the programme, involving a funds managing authority, a project management and implementation authority, and an observatory. The funds managing authority was responsible for the selection, monitoring, and evaluation of the projects. The implementation authority was responsible for assisting with project management when the organisations were not deemed to have the capacity to run their projects.

Finally, the observatory would gather data to influence policy and to report to the Commission to enable benchmarking.

During the course of the 6-year period of the programme a number of further attempts were made to create new ICT strategies. In 2003, a new strategy was drafted, introducing a set of different priorities from the White Bible. A final version was never created as the national elections of 2004 brought a different party in power. OPIS came to an overhaul, as the leadership changed completely. In 2005, the new leadership which had been in office for less than a year initiated the creation of, yet again, a new strategy called the Digital Strategy.

As the Digital Strategy was being created, the EU called on member-states to articulate how they planned to pursue the targets of the Lisbon Strategy, which was agreed in 2000 with the strategic vision to make Europe a competitive knowledge-based society. Member-states had to express their plans in a National Strategic Reference Framework (NSRF), which would be negotiated with the Commission. The NSRF would form the basis of further negotiation for funding for the subsequent period 2007-20013. As had happened six years before, the newly written Digital Strategy formed an integral part of the Greek NSRF and secured a new co-financed programme for ICT.

6.   Analysis

The storyline has indicated the existence of a co-constructive relationship between Greece and the Commission in creating the Greek ICT policy. I argue that the domain of ICT policy has been constituted as a governable field, where the Commission heavily influences the conduct, the decisions, and the policies of Greek policy makers. In the next section, different facets of this relationship are explored, in order to demonstrate not only its existence, as it manifests itself through technical means, but also the extent of its pervasive outcomes.

6.1   Procedures in regimes of practice

A number of procedures which came as part and parcel of OPIS constituted powerful elements in the regime of practice and through their operation effectively shaped the conduct of Greek policy makers and implementers.

6.1.1   Complying with the aims

As suggested above, the Commission had clear development targets, which it was trying to achieve through member-states. Although it could not straightforwardly dictate the directions to be followed, as in areas of telecommunications policy, it managed to effectively do just that through the negotiation process of the CSFs. Although all CSFs had a clear mandate, which matched the strategic priorities of the EU and the vaguely expressed developmental goals of Greece, CSFs 1 and 2 had lax enough procedures to allow individual decisions to be made nationally, even when they contradicted the official mandate.

CSF3was, however, a much more tightly coupled programme, and when it came to ICT, OPIS embodied the then preoccupation of the Commission with e-government. E-government had gained much credibility in the Commission for a number of reasons. Firstly, e-government could prove to be an effective means of European intervention within the national public administrations, for which the Commission could find little support in the treaties. It was envisaged that e-government could be the catalyst of public sector reform, which would, through the creation of interoperable systems, allow the tighter coupling of public administration across Europe. Also, e-government was a technological solution to the crisis of transparency and accountability that had struck the Commission [1]. For all these reasons, the Commission placed e-government high in its informal list of priorities. It insisted, though, that any funding under OPIS be channelled to projects of services to citizens. OPIS was negotiated and agreed with this outlook, and it thus became the instrument in which the specific ideas of the Commission about what was considered legitimate technological intervention to achieve a particular type of development were inscribed.

6.1.2   Procedures of acceptance

Another set of procedures and devices that defined the regime of practice was the array of procedures of acceptance of projects that were deemed suitable for funding. This role was entrusted to the staff of the funds managing authority who were accountable to the Commission and the Greek state if funds were committed to projects which were later found unsuitable or incongruent with the criteria.

Three distinct devices can be identified. Firstly, the acceptance criteria which had been set and agreed with the Commission framed the types of eligible projects. Projects needed to have an obvious orientation towards the "citizen-made-customer" if they were taking place in the context of the public administration (which was more often than not the case). If projects were in the telecommunications sector they needed to strengthen competition and not favour the incumbent.

The obvious result of the above and other acceptance criteria on the ground was that they defined the way in which projects were described and represented when submitted for approval. As a result, innumerable projects titled "Project for the creation of Web portal for the provision of electronic services to the inhabitants of [...]" were submitted and approved. Consulting companies also swiftly changed their product line to offer products that would allow their clients to obtain approval. The acceptance criteria shaped the conduct of a wide array of stakeholders, who were willing to change their expectations and desires to fit with what was being put forward as legitimate, and in so doing irreversibly defined the direction of information systems diffusion.

Two further devices are also interesting: the development goals and the maturity tables. The former was meant to measure the potential of a project to spur socio-economic development, for example by counting the number of employment opportunities to be created. The latter was meant to assess the capability of the organisation to undertake the project, by having experience in similar projects or by having experts in the project management team. If they were not deemed to be "mature" enough to manage the project themselves, the project could only be approved if the project management was outsourced to professionals.

Both of these devices were particularly resisted and distorted in practice, in essence making them just another formality void of content. The development goals reflected the preoccupation of the Commission with the creation of employment for skilled work, as it was expressed in the Lisbon Strategy in 2000. In practice, the number given often reflected the number of temp cleaning staff that would be laid off and re-employed in the specified time frame. To get over the maturity tables, expert academics would often be included in the project management team for a nominal fee, and would later leave the team.

6.1.3   Procedures of financial administration

Perhaps the most important form of regulation of the conduct which had the greatest impact on the character of the results was the procedures of financial administration. These related to monitoring of the progress of IS projects and reporting both internally and to the Commission. These procedures had been put in place by the Commission to prevent the mismanagement of funds, something that had happened in previous CFSs. These procedures of financial management fundamentally shaped the conduct of all involved and meant that the economic rationality prevailed over other competing rationalities.

An invention that demonstrates the above point was the separation of an IS project in two parts: the "financial object" and the "technical object". The financial object included the budget and the expenses of a project. The technical object was comprised of the actual information system of the IS-mediated intervention. The financial object overshadowed the technical object in formal and informal discussions, in the controls and assessments, and in the monitoring of individual projects and of the whole OPIS programme. From the speeches of public figures to the informal chats in the corridors of the OPIS building, discussions revolved around the amount of money spent, or committed to be spent. The level of expenses of a project was used as a proxy for judging its progress. The information system which was used as the main monitoring tool for the progress of the programme, named Ergosys, could record financial information, but could not keep track of information regarding actual deliverables or products. The staff often improvised their own database applications to allow them to track the progress of the information system itself.

One of the most destructive effects of the supremacy of the financial object over the technical object was that it created two incompatible goals for all those involved in the process. They could either try to deliver according to the financial object, i.e., do the bare minimum that would allow them to claim back the expensed from the Commission, or they could try to uphold the importance of the technical object, i.e., the need to implement information systems that make a difference. The second goal was sidestepped in favour of the first, and so spending money in accordance with the Commission's regulations became more important than making a difference with IT. The developmental goal was lost.

The preoccupation with the financial administration was liked to a high-level discourse on absorption rates, i.e., how much of the available funds were funnelled to projects at any time, an amount that was being reported by the Commission at regular intervals. The discourse on absorption of funds was made material in a multiplicity of rules, procedures, instruments, and technologies. The motoring reports were filled in for all projects monthly, quarterly, and annually by the projects' beneficiaries and IT contractors, detailing all expenses for all projects. The reports were uploaded in Ergosys and became the object of scrutiny by the Greek management of OPIS and the Commission. Administrators in both sides (Greece and the Commission) lamented having become "accountants". The evaluation targets of all stakeholders involved in the implementation were expressed not in terms of number of projects finished but of volume of funds absorbed. The chart showing the expenses in juxtaposition to the available budget was published every month on the website, and was occasionally the issue of public outcry, when the Greek media discovered that "Greece is losing money", not that Greece is failing to make useful interventions with IT.

Overall, financial administration was the major way of regulation of conduct in the Greek efforts to do ICT policy. The vocabulary of funds absorption was set by the Commission and embraced, with some complaining but with no serious objections, by the Greek administration. Even though they could have resisted the imposition of the economic rationality, in the same way that they resisted the maturity tables, they willingly took up the discourse and reified it, by, for example, reproducing it through the media or in the political scene. These processes of financial administration also formed the identities of the people involved: they were administrators that tried to make the numbers work, instead of trying to make the interventions work. They were "accountants".

6.2   The "IT strategy" as an example of self-regulation

Having seen a number of examples where conduct was regulated by providing clear directions, it is important to show an example where conduct was self-regulated based on what the agents felt they were expected to do. For this, I demonstrate how the instrument of the "IT strategy" was used by Greek policy makers.

The narrative of the case study points to the creation of three Greek IT strategies in the course of six years. Two of them were created just before the negotiation of CSFs, in 1999 and 2005. One of them was created in 2003 half-way through the programme. These temporal coincidences and the interview responses of the creators of these strategies highlight the reasons why their creation was felt imperative. The White Bible in 1999 was meant to show to the Commission that

Greece was a trustworthy partner with a well considered plan about what to do with IT. The IT strategy was thought to make right the very poor results of the IT programmes in CSF2. Without proof of commitment the Greek policy makers thought that the Commission would not agree to an ICT programme in CSF3.

The reasons that were hinted at for the creation of a new IT strategy in 2003 were similar. Programme OPIS had got off to a slow start with very low absorption rates which sparked fierce criticism from the Commission in the annual Monitoring Committees. A new strategy was meant to reassure the Commission that, despite the problems in implementation, there was still determination to do ICT policy.

In 2005, nearing the completion of programme OPIS and the negotiation of CSF4, yet another strategy was created. The new leadership reluctantly expressed their certainty that had it not been for their strategy the Commission would not have approved another ICT programme under the CSF4.

This constitutes a striking example of self-regulation of conduct. The Greek administrators and policy makers acted in ways that they believed were congruent with what the Commission expected from them. They willingly governed and shaped their conduct according to what they thought were the appropriate ways to keep the Commission satisfied. The self-governing of conduct could signify that the regime of practice was potent enough to make them behave in certain ways, even in aspects of their conduct where they did not experience the direct influence of techniques of government.

7.   Discussion

ICT policy in Greece has, in effect, been a product of the relationship between Greek authorities and the European Commission. The way this relationship unfolded and manifested itself, as well as its results, have largely remained obscure. This chapter argued that viewing the phenomenon through the analytical lens of governmentality would bring to light interesting facets which would allow us to develop a more nuanced understanding.

In analysing the case study evidence was provided to support the contention that ICT policy has been defined as a governable domain. By looking into the technical means in which governing is embedded and which make governing material and durable, a wide range of procedures which constituted a regime of practice were discussed. It was showed how the acceptance criteria defined the legitimate IT interventions to be pursued, while making a whole array of stakeholders regulate their conduct so as to fit with the specified requirements. On the other hand, some devices were demonstrably covertly resisted and subverted in their everyday enactment, thus pointing to the fact that not all attempts to regulate conduct are successful all the time.

The analysis has shown that procedures of financial administration, along with an array of technological artifacts and associated discourses, were particularly successful in not only shaping conduct, but also creating identities and framing the issue. An array of procedures about the financial management of the information society was developed to closely regulate the conduct of the disobedient Greek administration who had in the past distorted the efforts and intentions of the Commission. Although financial mismanagement was still occurring, the regime of practice was extremely successful in making the information society a question of budgets and expenses instead of IT interventions. The discourse on funds absorption, although initiated by the Commission, was avidly taken up by all involved and was reproduced in the media and the politics, effectively showing the only legitimate way to discuss technological progress.

On the other hand, taking the creation of IT strategy as an example, the Greek administration was shown to self-regulate its conduct by acting in the ways they felt responded best to the Commission's expectations. The IT strategy was not a response to a rational need. The rationality behind its creation was not formal rationality. Instrumentality was part of the response and there are questions to be asked as to the extent to which the self-regulation of conduct was merely a superficial external manifestation of a desirable behaviour, or whether it had indeed formed an identity which participants shared and acted accordingly. Such questions are not, however, pertinent to understanding how ICT policy got constructed and acted upon in the specific context and under the influence of particular institutional relations.

Finally, rounding up the discussion, I would like to suggest that the concept of governmentality and its related concept of regimes of practice provide a particularly fruitful analytical lens in dealing with situations of multilevel relations. Because they assume power in all relations, power becomes an enabler instead of a sterile fight over resources. Thus, they can inform much more subtle and nuanced analytical accounts. An important challenge that has to be addressed, however, is the difficulty in operationalising concepts which Foucault has defined loosely and used imaginatively.

8.   Conclusion

In this chapter I have attempted to examine the example of ICT policy in the case of Greece under the influence of the Commission with the help of Foucault's ideas on governmentality [13, 14]. The aim has been to better understand the phenomenon of creation of ICT policy as it emerges out of the interplay of two levels of government. The motivation for this research has been the multiplicity of cases where ICT policy is not solely the product of national deliberation, but the emergent product of a process where the European Commission (or similar international bodies) is promoting a strategic vision and also makes available the funding for its implementation.

The existing literature remains silent about the phenomenon of institutional intervention from regional and supranational organisations in the national interpretations and policies on ICT. Although some research, mainly from the critical tradition, have challenged the neutrality of the European Union's ICT policies [15, 16, 19, 38], similar critiques have not been applied to national ICT policies. On the contrary, these are viewed largely uncritically, although such research has produced a wealth of information about individual approaches to national ICT policy [22, 43-45, 48].

I have argued for an alternative approach in understanding ICT policy as a governable space, where the rationale of the Commission's vision of the information society is embodied in material practices which regulate the behaviour of Greek administrators. Simultaneously, administrators in the national level also self-regulate their conduct in ways that are thought to be compatible with what they feel is expected of them, also making use of technical means of government. The contribution of the chapter is twofold. On the one hand, it uses a novel theoretical approach in examining ICT policy to come up with a more subtle discussion of the situation. The lens of governmentality has enriched the analysis of the phenomenon, allowing for nuanced observations of the social agents and their institutional environments to be drawn. It thus provides an interesting alternative to theories of power and coercion, particularly as the relational, diffused character of power allows attention to be placed on the material (and technological) arrangements that structure social contexts. On the other hand, the chapter contributes through its empirical investigation in the reframing of an area of study. The findings shed light into an aspect of ICT policy that has received very little attention, namely the interplay of two different levels of governance of ICT policy.

Further research needs to investigate the other three dimensions of the regimes of practice, i.e., the rationalities of government, the forms of visibility and the formation of identities. Although some links were drawn here, a more thorough exploration could yield interesting insights. Also, further research could be directed towards investigating whether the results of the study are supported in other contexts which look similar to this one, for example in contexts of the development agencies and international donors in relation to developing countries.

Acknowledgements

Funding for this research was provided by the Propondis Foundation, in Greece. I am deeply grateful for their continuing support, without which the research would not have taken place.

References

[1]   Alabau, A. (2005). The European Union and its eGovernment development policy: Following the Lisbon strategy objectives. Madrid: Ed. Fundacion Vodafone.

[2]   Berleur, J., Galand, J.-M. (2005). ICT policies of the European Union: From an information society to eEurope. Trends and visions, in J. Berleur and C. Avgerou (Eds.) *Perspectives and policies on ICT in society: An IFIP TC9 (Computers and Society) handbook*, New York: Springer.

[3]   Bijker, W.E. (2001). Understanding technological culture through a contructivist view of science, technology, and society, in S. Cutcliffe and C. Mitcham (Eds.) *Visions of STS: Counterpoints in science, technology and society studies* (pp. 19-34), Albany: State University of New York Press.

[4]   Carmel, E. (2003). The globalization of software outsourcing to dozens of nations: A preliminary analysis of the emergence of the 3rd and 4th tier software exporting nations, in S. Krishna and S. Madon (Eds.), *The digital challenge*, Ashgate: Aldershot.

[5]   Colebatch, H.K. (2002). Policy. 2nd ed., Maidenhead: Open University Press.

[6]   Dean, M. (1996). Putting the technological into government. History of the human sciences, 9(3), 47-68.

[7]   Dean, M. (1999). *Governmentality*. London: Sage Publications.

[8]   Diso, L.I. (2005). Information technology policy formulation in Nigeria: Answers without questions. *The International Information & Library Review*, 37(4), 295-302.

[9]   Dutton, W. (1992). The ecology of games shaping telecommunications policy. *Communications Theory*, 2(4), 303-328.

[10]   English, M. & Brown, A.W. (1984). National policies in information technology: Challenge and responses. *Oxford Surveys in Information Technology*, 13(1), 125-142.

[11]   Evans, P.B. (1992). Indian informatics in the 1980s: The changing character of state involvement. *World development*, 20(1), 1-18.

[12]   Forbes, N. & Wield, D. (2002). The Indian software industry: Miracle in the making or a high-technology "sweet-shop"?, in N. Forbes and D. Wield (Eds.) *From followers to leaders*, London: Routledge.

[13]   Foucault, M., (1982). The subject and power, in H. Dreyfus and P. Rabinow (Eds.) *Michel Foucault: Beyond structuralism and hermeneutics*, Brighton: Harvester.

[14]   Foucault, M. (2007). Security, territory, population. Lectures at the College de France 1977-1978. Basingstoke: Macmillan.

[15]   Galperin, H. (2004). Beyond interests, ideas and technology: An institutional approach to communication and information policy. *Information society*, 20(3), 159-168.

[16]   Garnham, N. (1997). Europe and the global information society: The history of a troubled relationship. *Telematics and informatics*, 14(4): p. 323-327.

[17]   Garnham, N. (2000). 'Information society' as theory and ideology: A critical perspective on technology, education and employment in the information age. *Information, communication & society*, 3(2), 130-152.

[18]   Gil-Garcia, J.R. (2004). Information technology policies and standards: A comparative review of the states. *Journal of Government Information*, 30(5/6), 548–560.

[19]   Goodwin, I. & Spittle, S. (2002). The European Union and the information society: Discourse, power and policy. *New media & society*, 4(2), 225-249.

[20]   Iosifidis, P. & Leandros, N. (2003). Information society strategies in the European context: The case of Greece. *Southeast European and Black Sea studies*, 3(2).

[21]   Kahin, B. & Wilson, E. (Eds.) (1997). *National information infrastructure initiatives: Vision and policy design*. MIT Press: Cambridge & Massachusetts.

[22]   King, J.L., et al. (1994). Institutional factors in information technology innovation. *Information systems research*, 5(2), 139-169.

[23]   Kumar, K. (2005). *From post-industrial to post-modern society*. Oxford: Blackwell Publishing.

[24]   Kuppusamy, M. & Santhapparaj, S. (2005). Investment in information and communication technologies (ICT) and its payoff in Malaysia. *Perspectives on global development and technology*, 4(2), 147-167.

[25] La Rovere, R.L. (1998). Diffusion of information technologies and changes in the telecommunications sector: The case of Brazilian small- and medium-sized enterprises. *Information technology & people*, 11(3), 194-206.

[26] Land, F. (1983). Inaugural lecture. Information technology: The Alvey report and government strategy, London: London School of Economics and Political Science.

[27] Land, F. (1990). Viewpoint: The government role in relation to information technology. *International Journal of Information Management*, 10, 5-13.

[28] Majone, J.M. (2003). The politics of southern Europe: Integration into the European Union. Westport: Praeger Publishers.

[29] Mansell, R. (1993). The new telecommunications: a political economy of network evolution. London: Sage.

[30] Mansell, R. & Streinmueller, E. (2000). *Mobilizing the information society strategies for growth and opportunity*. New York: Oxford University Press.

[31] Mansell, R. & Wehn, U. (1998). Knowledge societies: Information technology for sustainable development. Oxford: Oxford University Press.

[32] ason, R., McKenney, J., & Copeland, D. (1997). An historical method for MIS research: Steps and assumptions. *MIS Quarterly*, 21(3): p. 307-320.

[33] ayntz, R. (2004). Mechanisms in the analysis of social macro-phenomena. *Philosophy of the social sciences*, 34(2), p. 237-259.

[34] Mosco, V. (1988). International Telecommunication What Price Policy? Toward a Theory of the State and Telecommunications Policy. Journal of Communication, 38(1), 107-124.

[35] Mosco, V. (1998). Myth-ing links: Power and community on the information highway. *Information Society*, 14(1): p. 57-62.

[36] Mouzelis, N. (1995). Modernity, late development and civil society, in J.A. Hall (Ed.) *Civil society*, (pp. 224-249), Cambridge: Polity Press.

[37] Mueller, M. & Lentz, B. (2004). Revitalizing communication and information policy research. *The Information Society*, 20(3): p. 155-157.

[38] North, D.C. (1990). Institutions, institutional change and economic performance. New York: Cambridge University Press.

[39] Qureshi, S. (2005). E-government and IT policy: Choices for government outreach and policy making. *Information technology for development*, 11(2), 101-103.

[40] Rose, N. (1999). Powers of freedom. Cambridge: Cambridge University Press.

[41] Schlesinger, P. (1999). Changing spaces of political communication: The case of the European Union. *Political communication*, 16: p. 263-279.

[42] Selwyn, N. (2002). E-stablishing and inclusive society? Technology, social exclusion and UK government policy making. *Journal of Social Policy*, 31(1), 1-20.

[43] Shih, E., Kraemer, K.L. & Dedrick, J. (2007). Research note: Determinants of country-level investment in information technology. *Management science*, 53(3), 521-528.

[44] Shih, E., Kraemer, K.L., & J. Dedrick, (2008). IT diffusion in developing countries. *Communications of the ACM*, 51(2): p. 43-48.

[45] Silva, L. & Figueroa, E. (2002). Institutional intervention and the expansion of ICTs in Latin America: The case of Chile. *Information, Technology and People*, 15(1), 8-25.

[46] Steinmueller, W.E. (2002). Knowledge-based economies and information and communication technologies. *International Social Science Journal*, 54(171), 141-153.

[47] Thomadakis, S.B. (1995). The Greek economy and European integration: Prospects and threats of underdevelopment, in D. Constas and T.C. Stravrou (Eds.) *Greece prepares for the twenty-first century*, Washington: Woodrow Wilson Center Press.

62   Social Dimensions of ICT Policy

[48] Tigre, P.B. J, B.A. (2001). Brazil meets the global challenge: IT policy in a postliberalization environment. *The Information Society*, 17(2), 91-103.
[49] Walsham, G. (1995). Interpretive case studies in IS research: Nature and method. *European Journal of Information Systems*, 4(2) 74-81.
[50] Wincott, D. (2003). Beyond social regulation? New instruments and/or a new agenda for social policy at Lisbon? *Public administration*, 81(3), 533-553.

NATIONAL VARIATIONS OF THE INFORMATION SOCIETY: EVIDENCE FROM THE GREEK CASE

Dimitris Boucas
London School of Economics and Political Science, UK

Abstract   Identifying an empirical gap in the examination and analysis of the information society (IS) in semi-peripheral and middle income countries, the paper seeks to address the evolving characteristics and forms of the "Greek case" of the IS, stressing the dialectic between European policy and the national socio-cultural, political and economic idiosyncrasies, the weaknesses encountered, and the role of the state in articulating the global and the national through rhetoric and policy. Drawing on historical sociology, I propose that the historically developed relationship between the state, and the national economy and society will interact with global IS processes, creating differentiated national IS outcomes. The emphasis of the study is on the period 1998-2006, which includes the first comprehensive IS strategy in Greece and provides the opportunity to assess preliminary results of the policies adopted.

Keywords: Information society, IT policy, state, implementation politics

1.   Introduction

The concept of the "information society" (IS) denotes a new techno-socio-economic paradigm around information and communication technologies (ICTs), involving a set of significant economic and social transformations and bearing implications for governance and potential for development and quality of life [6, 33, 57].[1]

This chapter examines how trust can emerge and be sustained in the context of mobile transactions, through an ethnographic study of M-PESA, a mobile banking system deployed in Kibera—one of Africa's largest slums.

---

[1] As the term "information society" has been deployed to capture different kinds and scales of social (economic, political etc.) transformation, a definition will be inadequate. Our working definition of IS: a form of economic and societal organisation at various levels, which emerges when the diffusion of ICTs interacts with pre-existing social, economic, cultural, political arrangements, which involves new patterns of living and working, and where, in addition, information and knowledge are considered central assets for competitive advantage, profit, growth, and employment.

Please use the following format when citing this chapter:

Boucas, D., 2008, in IFIP International Federation for Information Processing, Volume 282; *Social Dimensions of Information and Communication Technology Policy*; Chrisanthi Avgerou, Matthew L. Smith, Peter van den Besselaar; (Boston: Springer), pp. 63–79.

A central question in relevant debates has been whether the IS formation constitutes a radical break with previous societal arrangements. In this respect, some speak of the IS as a new type of society in a deterministic way [2, 3], while others prefer to identify continuities with industrial capitalist societies and place ICTs in context, trying to identify the profound transformations deriving from the articulation between new technologies and pre-existing economic, social, political, and cultural processes [1, 33, 47]. The former approaches imply some kind of homogenisation lens and anticipate a uniform IS, while the latter allude to variation and context-specific differentiations of the ICT paradigm. Contrary to previous research, recent agendas have placed emphasis on the interplay between society and technology in the IS outcomes. National variations are gradually becoming accepted and attributed to different national political and socio-cultural circumstances, as well as different institutional structures and traditions, which are seen to influence not only the outcome of IS policy, but also practice. Moreover, they are expected to reflect often conflicting ambitions and aspirations of different arrays of involved actors and users.

Indeed, "national cases" of the IS are beginning to become objects of study both in the European context [8, 22, 46] and beyond [7]. What seems to be missing, however, is an examination and analysis of the IS in semi-peripheral and middle-income countries. In this paper I examine the evolution of the IS policy in the Greek context, in conjunction with the evolution of similar policies at the EU level. In doing so, I limit my analysis to IS policies in Greece during the 1990s and up until 2006, a period which includes the introduction of the first comprehensive IS strategy as well as its reception and preliminary effects.

My argument is that the unfolding of any national IS is a contested process feeding on previous, historically rooted, social, economic, cultural, and political arrangements. Specifically, I propose that the historically formed state/society relation at the national level is expected to inflect global IS processes in quite idiosyncratic ways, leading to differentiated national IS trajectories and outcomes. My research question is: What are the IS policies implemented in Greece in the period under examination and how have they interacted with pre-existing national characteristics (as encompassed broadly in the state/society relation)?

The structure of the paper includes a brief background presentation of IS policies at the EU level and in Greece. Subsequently, it provides a concise picture of the current situation of Greek IS based on certain ICT diffusion indicators. These provide a preliminary picture of "lagging behind". In order to explain why this is the case, the paper uses a state/society approach based on tools from historical sociology. A brief presentation of the state/society approach is followed by an account of the historical evolution of the state/economy/civil society relation in Greece. The characteristics of this relation are then used to identify continuities and explain constraints of the IS in Greece at present, as they emerge from a set of in-depth interviews with key IS actors. Conclusions are drawn, including implications for future studies of national case of IS.

2.   IS policy at the EU level

An IS vision has been, since the 1990s, communicated at the EU level, with the intention of promoting diffusion of ICTs at various geographical scales, including national, sub-national, regional, supra-national, EU-wide, and even beyond. The 1993 European Commission White Paper on growth, competitiveness, and employment was the first influential policy document communicating this vision, revealing the importance attached by policy makers to the opportunities and challenges for European competitiveness, growth and employment, particularly in skilled jobs and new services [13].

Subsequently, the well-known Bangemann Report was produced for the March 1994 meeting of the European Commission in Corfu. The report set out the following priorities: a) promoting the use of information technologies; b) providing basic services at a European level; c) creating an appropriate regulatory environment; d) developing training in new technologies; and e) improving technological and industrial performance [14]. These proposals were followed by the action plan "Europe towards the information society", designed by the Commission in July 1994 [15].

The EU Lisbon summit in March 2000 declared the goal of making Europe the most competitive knowledge-based economy[2] while maintaining social cohesion and cultural diversity [10]. Moreover, a new open method of inter-state coordination was adopted for the translation of European goals into national policies, through European guidelines, best practices, references indicators, but also room for national diversity through targets and measures fitting each nation's case [44]. The new method was applied to IS policies in the "eEurope 2002: An Information Society for All" initiative, launched in December 1999. This outlined ten priority areas for joint action by the Commission, the member states, the industry and the citizens [16]. The subsequent "eEurope 2005" action plan set out to stimulate Internet services, applications and content, to improve the underlying infrastructure (promotion of broadband, awareness of security matters) and to promote ICT skills and ICT-based opportunities. Recently, the i2010 EU plan aims at promoting a borderless information space and internal market for electronic communication, ensuring inclusion, accessibility, and quality of life.

The EU IS policy, particularly the eEurope initiatives, has had an impact on the formulation of strategic national programmes. Recently there have been certain degrees of convergence with regard to the tone and content of the IS policies adopted. Nonetheless, as IS policy-making in the national context still rests with the authority and power of the member states, similar frameworks might lead to different translations, according to the different state/society traditions in different member states of the EU [41]. As a result, many possible forms of the European

---

[2] A knowledge-based economy has been defined as one where knowledge is being created, diffused, and deployed in accelerated ways through ICTs; where increasingly sophisticated products codify and manage knowledge; and where there is a perception of knowledge as a strategic asset for individuals, firms, and nations [45].

IS are expected, depending on technological developments, interaction with users, as well as national policies and the general societal culture. The role of the state is particularly important in articulating international policy imperatives with national specificities.

3.   IS policy in Greece

The first policy document regarding the IS in Greece was the 1995 White Paper "The Greek Strategy for an Information Society: A Tool for Employment, Development and Quality of Life", which served as a means of setting the IS agenda in the Greek context. It echoed the discourse of opportunity associated with the new technology and was mainly concerned with the inadequate national infrastructure, which limited electronic transactions and access to new products and services both for firms and for households. Most of its actions have been funded by the 2nd Community Support Framework (CSF): the development of a national infrastructure linking universities, technological institutes and public research institutes, the promotion of an e-commerce environment for business, or actions to raise public awareness of e-commerce [9, 25].

While all operational programmes of the 2nd CSF included funding for the IS, the operational programme Kleisthenis (1994-2000) was the key IS initiative. Its central aim was the modernisation of public administration through an integrated approach to IT, including development of infrastructures, applications and training in the design and implementation of each separate project. In parallel, the digitisation of the public telecomms operator (OTE) network, the development of certain fibre optic rings, and the creation of the national network for research and technology (EDET) were important telecommunications initiatives. During this period a small number of IT firms of significant size developed, the IT sector was consolidated and entered the Athens stock market in the end of the 1990s.

Like in all other EU countries, the first major step towards the implementation of the IS was the liberalisation of telecommunications sector, which until the late 1980s was based on a state monopoly in telephony and telecommunication services. In the wake of the early EU IS documents, a series of laws carried forward the liberalisation of telecommunications, starting from value-added services and mobile telephony services (Law 1892/90 and 2075/92) and culminating with Law 2860/2000; after 31 December 2000 all restrictions including those on the provision of voice telephony and the network infrastructure were removed and full competition was officially established, under the supervision of an independent regulatory authority, the National Telecommunications and Post Commission (EETT) [38].

In 1999, a more strategic and comprehensive second White Paper titled "Greece in the Information Society: Strategy and Actions" was prepared by ten policy experts based on international experience and feedback from the Ministries regarding the actions and steps that had been taken vis-à-vis the IS. Its rhetoric emphasised the potential of ICTs for competitiveness and better public services, present in the early EU documents, together with the requirement of building human skills to take advantage of these opportunities. The imperative of universal access and the prevention of new types of social exclusion, reminiscent of similar concerns in EU documents, were also highlighted [26].

Following from the White Paper, through the eEurope initiative of 1999 and the Feira Summit of June 2000, the Greek government proposed a systematic "Operational Programme for the Information Society" (OPIS), linking it to funds within the structure of the 3rd CSF. This was an innovative horizontal programme, involving a number of government departments, and aiming to implement the essential features of the 1999 White Paper.

The OPIS objectives over the period 2000-2006, with the corresponding shares of national and EU funding, were: a) to address issues of infrastructure and training in education and promote Greek cultural heritage (17%); b) to provide better services to the citizen and improve the quality of life through the deployment of ICTs in public administration, health and welfare, transport and the environment (37%); c) to promote the economy through actions to increase competitiveness and employment and to help SMEs enter the digital era (24%); d) to enhance telecoms liberalisation, development of broadband and local networks and facilitate access for remote areas and disadvantaged groups (19%). The OPIS also included a technical support for the above actions (3%) [9, 39].

According to Law 2860/2000 several bodies were set up to manage and implement the OPIS: a) The Management Authority, operating under the Special Secretariat for the Information Society was established within the Ministry of National Economy, which deals with the design of action lines for the OPIS, the follow-up and control of their implementation, as well as supervision of financial, legal, and logistical aspects; b) The Monitoring Committee comprising representatives of ministries, public organisations, economic and social partners and having a supervisory and advisory role; c) The IS S.A., a public not-for-profit organisation which is charged with the administration of public calls for tender for projects seeking funding under the OPIS, while also providing assistance and advice to government and other public and private institutions in the implementation of the OPIS; d) The IS Observatory, aiming at transferring expertise and best practice relevant with IS issues, as well as providing training tools and supervising benchmarking studies [5].

4.   Current picture of the IS in Greece

In 2000, when the OPIS had just begun, Greece was significantly behind the EU-15 average in ICT infrastructure and use, with the exception of fixed and mobile telephones. Table 1 shows an increase in PC and Internet usage for individuals and PC and Internet possession for households between 2001 and 2003, but this increase cannot be characterised as a take-off; on the contrary, falling rates were observed between 2003 and 2004 [12].

Indicator	2001	2003	2004
% population over 15 using PC	20.8	27.1	25.9
% population over 15 using Internet	10.6	19.9	19.7
% population over 15 with email address	6.5	12.4	12.5
% population over 15 using Internet to interact with public authorities	3.5 (2002)	6.1	7.2
% households having PC	23.3	30.5	29.9
% households having Internet access	12.4 (2002)	15.2	17.1
%households with broadband connection	-	1	1
% population having mobile phone	49.5	64.7	69.4

Table 1: Evolution of basic IS indicators in Greece.

At the enterprise level, in 2003 92% of firms with 11-250 employees possessed PCs (94% in the EU), 82% were connected to the Internet (83% in the EU), while 48% had also a website (52% in the EU). These tendencies were reinforced through the "eBusiness" action of the OPIS, resulting in an 87% Internet connection in 2004 (90% for the EU-15). Very small enterprises (up to 10 employees) lagged significantly behind the EU average in 2003. The "Go-Online" programme for small enterprises, which subsidises initial purchases of ICT and also provides training, is expected to have an important contribution in this context (according to a recent survey, 60% of small entrepreneurs were of the opinion that the programme could sufficiently address their needs) [11, 40].

Although the support of investment towards broadband infrastructures has been one of the fundamental priorities of the OPIS, in 2004 only1% of households and only 21% of enterprises were connected with broadband, percentages that were by far the lowest in the EU-15 and among the lowest even in the EU-25 [18, 40].

In the public sector, diffusion and deployment of ICTs has been limited in almost all areas, which also explains the low use of Internet-mediated interaction with public authorities (7.2% of the population over 15 in 2004). Exceptions have been certain parts of the TAXIS Net project (addressing fiscal procedures), as well as the area of education and training, with the development of the advanced Greek Research and Education Network (GRNET) [17].

In 2006, Greece presented among the lowest percentages in EU-25 (including the new EU accession countries) in the following categories: Internet usage at least once a week by individuals (23% compared to 47% for EU-25), Internet access by households (23% compared to 52% for EU-25), and PC usage among the population (33% in 2005). Internet access among enterprises was about 94% (93% for EU-25), but broadband access was 58% (74% for EU-25), while broadband Internet access by households was 4%, the lowest percentage in the EU-27 [19].

5.   The Greek IS in historical perspective

Notwithstanding certain "success stories" Greece is still significantly behind not only in terms of ICT diffusion, but also with respect to the overall economic, social, cultural, and institutional aspects of the IS project. The few attempts to assess the Greek IS situation have stressed that policy formation has been accompanied by inadequate or unsuccessful policy implementation [5]. I would rather treat implementation impediments as symptomatic of broader characteristics of the national context in question that have been developed over time. These (social, economic, political, cultural) dimensions have been consolidated into structural elements and have informed social practices. The fact that Greece has historically shown receptiveness to the idea of modernisation at a first level, but has found difficulties in the actual absorption and deepening of new ways of living and working [56], further legitimates a historical approach.

5.1   State/society: Embedded autonomy and state capacity

Being interested in capitalist diversity and national variations, I adopt a state/society historical theoretical approach. The value of a state/society approach is related to alerting the researcher to the historical unfolding of a national economy/society relation (and inescapably the role and evolution of the specific national state in this unfolding). As such, it prepares the ground for an adequate comprehension of the outcomes of what has been operating as the IS project at the international level by considering pre-existing historically formed (at the national level) economic arrangements, social relations, cultural characteristics, institutional traditions, together with the role of the particular state in socio-economic development. By doing so, however, it does not rule out the (global) structural context in which such national variations are placed, but highlights the anticipation that the impact of IS global processes will depend on the nature of the society and the state (seen through the state/society relation) under examination.

Comparative political economy and political sociology have been preoccupied with state/society debates at least since the 1970s, when demands to "bring the state back in" were responding to "society-centred" approaches which were seen as attributing to the state a secondary position in terms of analytical importance [43, 48]. The ensuing state-centric theories were stressing the notion of "state autonomy", which initially communicated the idea of independent state bureaucratic and policy-making activity, was subsequently coupled with the idea of embeddedness of state mechanisms into the wider society, resulting in the notion of "embedded autonomy", which denotes that states "are embedded in a concrete set of social ties which binds the state to society and provides institutionalised channels for the continual negotiation and renegotiation of goals and policies" [20, p. 12]. Based on comparative research, Evans [20] argues that the ways in which states are coupled with their societies vary significantly and this relates to the role of the state in the economy, which can be either developmental or detrimental to economic development (or a mixture of both).

The concept of embedded autonomy sought to overcome the division between state autonomy and embeddedness into the social structural context. Evans claims that the more state bureaucracies approach Weber's ideal type (i.e., based on meritocratic recruitment, secure careers and rewards, and independence from external interferences) the more they can contribute to economic development [21]. However, autonomy from external interference (from business, church, military, etc.) is not enough and it is only through embeddedness into society (close societal links) that such policies can have successful outcomes [27].

The degree to which the state enjoys embedded autonomy also affects the capacity of the state, which involves resource endowment, quality of leadership and political institutions, as well as tradition of governance, national culture and previous political decisions [49, p. 2]. It presupposes capable public bureaucracies, together with competent leadership and the ability of the state to organise social contracts and promote goals in democratic ways. This in turn calls for the participation of societal forces and the promotion of an active civil society and eventually a healthy and organic relationship between state and society [29].

The analytical notions of embedded autonomy and capacity of the state are taken to express the embeddedness of state mechanisms in wider societal arrangements and their institutional capabilities (ample or limited) to promote social projects. These two (not mutually exclusive) concepts are expected to capture the IS development process at the national level as a social process.

In the following section, I adopt a historical perspective claiming that the specific state/economy/civil society relation, as has been historically shaped in Greece, can serve as explanatory device of current developments in the Greek IS.

5.2   State, economic development, and civil society in Greece

The dominant reading of Greek history places Greece in the capitalist semi-periphery, as well as the late-late development paradigm (i.e., economies where industrialisation only happened after 1929), which is associated with an increased role of the state or state-controlled institutions [36].

The gradual integration of the Greek economy into the world market and the process of urbanisation in the late 19th century gave an important role to the state for building infrastructure, regulating prices and exports, etc. The articulation of agriculture with industry took place in ineffective ways and resulted in a quite limited domestic market. Increasing urbanisation led to rising unemployment for large segments of population drawn in urban centres and created pressures for those segments of urban population to be absorbed in public bureaucracies [51].

As a result, the public sector size augmented and public administration became fragmented and inefficient, while state support and regulation became gradually linked with clientelism which was used as a vehicle for absorbing social tensions. On the other hand, since state structures were already in place before industrialisation took off in the 1930s, a tendency emerged for the private sector to operate under the protective mechanisms of the state (e.g., seeking increased subsidies, enjoying protection through high tariffs or other kinds of favourable treatment), rather than building its own independent capabilities [32]. Further, these practices were applied in asymmetrical ways between industries or within an industry, with certain economic groups enjoying privileged access to public resources. The above processes gave the state anti-developmental structural features, which had an impact on the industrialisation and development prospects [37, 54]; in contrast with Western Europe in the 1950s and 1960s, light industry and consumer goods dominated in Greece.

Further, the late industrialisation of Greece, as well as the role of the state in economic development, have also affected the character of civil society.[3] Firstly, insufficient industrialization prevented the development of traditional industrial unionism, with much lower rates of unionisation than Western Europe. The union movement in Greece has been characterised by considerable fragmentation, which has made collective action difficult, while it has facilitated the development of links between individual unions and the government and other political entities. In contrast to the corporatist arrangements in Western Europe, Greece has demonstrated asymmetric corporatist arrangements, with state-dependent trade unions and at the same time weakness of the state vis-à-vis business interests, something which has limited effective collective decision-making and the negotiation of social pacts [31]. Other parts of civil society have either been more or less dependent on the state (e.g., social movements like the feminist movement, the Church etc.), or have been powerful but reactive to any reform that would affect their privileges (e.g., the professional associations of lawyers, doctors, or engineers). Clientelism has also had a significant impact on civil society, potentially drawing citizens towards individual political participation and thus impeding the formation of horizontal associations to promote common goals and interests [37, 50].

After the dictatorship (1967-1974) and into the post-1974 era, the Greek governments focused on economic development and accession to the EU. After 1981, when the newly elected PASOK socialist government sought to accommodate its voters by creating new posts, clientelism took a new form as it moved from personalised relationships to a practice operating through parties. Populism and short-term practices led to an exacerbation of economic indices and of the condition of public enterprises. On the other hand, trade unions became more dependent on the state due to their politically-appointed leaderships, while PASOK also exerted great influence on professional associations and civil society associations.

In socio-cultural terms, the prevalence of clientelism, together with weak trade unions and social movements, as well as the polarisation engendered by the Civil

---

[3] Following Sotiropoulos, we take civil society to be "a wide-ranging set of social interaction and collective action taking place in the public space available between the individual household, on the one hand, and the state apparatus, on the other" [52, p. 10].

War (1944-49), the reliance on the family and disassociation from broader social collectivities, have contributed to social heterogeneity and have prevented the development of a universalistic and collective culture [42].

5.3   Analysing the current picture of the Greek IS

The dominant characteristics of Greek state, politics, economy, and society emerging from the historical evolution have been seen as features to some extent common in the South European context. Since the 1970s, south European countries have been witnessing processes of democratisation, Europeanisation, and modernisation and have approximated Western and Northern Europe in terms of partisan politics and economic change. Nonetheless, the Southern European state and its patterns of public policy outputs have continued to exhibit legacies that impede substantial change (in certain sectors more than in others) [24].

During the 1990s the ambitious socio-economic "modernisation" project of Prime Minister Simitis (1996-2004) set out to secure the position of Greece at the core of EU both in economic (including incorporation in the core of the Eurozone) and in political terms [23]. The comprehensive IS strategy, as demonstrated through the 1999 White Paper and the OPIS, has to be seen in this context.

In what follows I try to present a more detailed picture of the problems encountered in the implementation of the IS strategy based on data obtained through a set of elite interviews carried out between 2005 and 2006 with key state actors involved in the OPIS, as well as with representatives from the IT sector. These interviews were unstructured and in-depth based on a topic guide of general questions. They were also complemented by my personal observations of the IS evolution over the period 1998-2006, including important meetings, conferences, and debates in which we have participated. The presentation attempts to link the evidence with the particular components of the state/society relationship shaped historically as outlined in section 5.2.

5.3.1   Policy processes

The public policy process in Greece has been often seen as hierarchical, with complex relations between ministers and personal advisors operating across ministries, weak support from civil service, and the absence of think tanks and policy communities that would provide technocratic legitimation [30]; as a result, political initiatives suffer from antagonisms and competing interests within government agencies. Moreover, such antagonisms are exacerbated through highly conflictual relations between the political parties, based on opposing social identities and patronage systems [23].

Regarding the OPIS, there has been from the beginning a significant problem of antagonism between ministries as to the allocation of responsibilities. As a senior member of the team designing the OPIS remembers: "the whole programme run the risk of being abandoned, as the three ministers involved...all wanted to break the OPIS and receive separate chunks of pertinent CSF funds directly for their ministries... Ultimately the deadlock was resolved at the level of the Prime Minister with two ministries taking the responsibility, namely the ministry of National Economy and the ministry of Interiors. This duality, which was necessary for the programme to be approved, has taken its toll in terms of delays, coordination difficulties, and antagonisms and enmities with regard to who 'carries the flag' of the information society in Greece". Rivalries were constant throughout and the absence of a continuous IS vision at the prime ministerial level perpetuated them.

5.3.2   Bureaucracy, public procurement, and the IT sector

The historical evolution presented in 5.2 has ascribed to bureaucracy certain characteristics that often describe the "Southern European model of bureaucracy" and that have been persistent in Greece in the beginning of the 21st century. Firstly, political clientelism at the top level, meaning the political party-mediated appointments at the top levels of bureaucracy, as well as promotions and transfers to high civil service. Secondly, political clientelism at the low levels, i.e., selective recruitment at entry-levels jobs in public administration. Thirdly, lack of an institutionalised administrative elite with considerable political and social stature and a corresponding lack of Weberian bureaucratic culture based on rational/legal expertise. Fourthly, the uneven character of the public sector, with unbalanced distribution of personnel and resources [53]. These characteristics have participated crucially in the evolutionary course of IS in Greece.

On the one hand, there has been observed an overall incapacity of the state to carry out, monitor, and implement certain IT projects. As a central figure of the Management Authority remarked, "The most obvious reason for this has been the lack of project management personnel both capable and aware of the contours of the Greek reality that could navigate through a labyrinth of problems and procedures". On the other hand, as a senior member of a large IT firm put it: "Implementation has also been impeded by the complexity of the legal, administrative, and institutional framework for IT projects". This seems to have characterised public procurement mechanisms as a whole, reflecting the fragmentation of public administration that has been formed historically. Indeed, members of the Special Secretariat have reported that the perpetuation of obsolete structures (e.g. different departments for telephony, IT and Internet, and different departments dealing with procurement for those technologies) has blocked or delayed significantly projects, particularly those of an innovative nature. It is important to stress that the first projects did not start until about 2 years after the launch of the OPIS.

In addition, incorporation of a project in the daily administrative routines have been particularly difficult as lack of understanding and motivation on the part of employees. All in all, the public sector is inadequate as provider of digital products and advanced applications, as well as consumer of digital products and services. Its rationalisation and digitisation is seen as pivotal in ICT-related social transformation [4].

The historical characteristics of Greek capitalism and its relationship with the state have been reflected in the current state/IT sector relations in Greece. The incomplete industrialisation and the resulting small market has been reflected in an IT sector of limited scope, with very few SMEs and large enterprises and a vast majority of small and micro firms. This has differentiated Greece from other national cases where large ICT firms have acted as leading edge technological innovators (e.g., Nokia in Finland). Further, the relationships of dependence of firms on the state observed in the industrial era have been reproduced in phenomena whereby the IT firms, although private, have relied extensively on state promises for funding that either have not been materialised, or, have not been accompanied by appropriate monitoring of industrial performance [55]. As an advisor to the former Special Secretary remarked, "the private sector in Greece is mainly retail, with very low value-added, waiting mainly for the public sector to implement projects. This tendency is dominant in the IT sector…the market does not create its own dynamic, but waits from the state to generate projects". This has been confirmed by other state actors, as well as IT representatives in a relevant meeting in February 2006 to which the author was granted access.

Moreover, clientelism and micro-corruption have been frequently involved in IS project allocation and have been accompanied by a defiance of rules and codes of conduct during implementation. Lack of IT expertise has often resulted in public administration succumbing to pressures from the IT sector to purchase products and adopt solutions in accordance with what specific IT firms have to offer. The relevant committees involved have either obstructed allocation of projects or have made bribery commonplace, while the IT firms in Greece have been used to the logic of bribing every committee for allocating or evaluating a project.

More specifically, there has been observed the phenomenon of a small number of hegemonic firms able to appropriate the majority of projects, with obvious implications for fair competition. As a former Management Authority member reports: "The practice of such firms was either to bribe the pertinent committees in order to get the project, or to establish such connections and relationships with ministry employees and cadres, which gave them early access to information as to what the specifications of the project were and as a result comparative advantage in the preparation of their proposals for the project in question. In many cases, these dominant firms were in the position to create the specifications themselves". These phenomena led another interviewee to remark: "Characteristics of the industrial era are replicated in exactly the same way today. We have state dependent enterprises and the logic of appropriation of resources, funds etc by the small segment of 'the selected'".

Overall, the absence of formal procedures guiding IT actions have perpetuated unhealthy relations of dependence and distrust between the state and the IT firms, which in turn have prevented the development of patterns and relations of mutual accountability, trust, and smooth cooperation between the private and the public sector. The state/IT sector relation has reflected the overall state/economy relations, which have been historically characterised by over-regulation and strict legal frameworks on the one hand, while suffering on the other from an unhealthy relationship of mutual dependence which involves corruption and patronage in the allocation of favours and contracts [28].

5.3.3   Civil society

On the other hand, the historically unbalanced state/civil society relation and the general lack of collective spirit is reflected in the limited part of civil society in the evolution of the IS project in Greece. Social networks and local communities that could help advance the IS (as has happened in Finland, for instance) by increasing awareness, have either been absent or characterised by inertia. Indeed, the wider social forces and civil society groups do not seem to have comprehended the dimensions of IS developments or have simply shown a logic of appropriation. As a senior EDET member argued: "The OPIS articulated policies that were out of touch with the Greek context and were not acceptable by the Greek society. Conflicts of interests and local communities did not help the promotion of ICTs, either because actors were acting out of their own interest and only regarding their own interest or because local communities were not in a position to understand".

In parallel, there have been examples of civil society acting through a culture of short-termism and quick profit-making. In addition, the issue of inadequate investment culture has frequently come up in our interviews. For instance, it has been suggested that IT sector representatives have repeatedly reacted against the prospect of spending funds on education programmes (something that would indirectly boost demand) and have instead demanded channelling them towards direct purchases of IT equipment. Generalising, it can be argued that the culture of short-termism has been a drawback in the realisation on a social level of multiplier economic and social effects resulting from the promotion of the IS.

5.3.4   IS, state capacity, and embedded autonomy in Greece

During the period 1998-2006, the Greek state has demonstrated limited capacity regarding the promotion of the IS; the design of a comprehensive OPIS has been confronted by implementation problems. Specifically, there has been inadequate leadership in understanding and communicating the IS vision at the societal level and in organising it as a central socio-economic project in the political agenda; a lack of appropriate political institutions and of a political culture that would serve such a broad and all-encompassing project; the presence of an anti-Weberian state bureaucracy, devoid of the rational-legal expertise and the administrative culture needed to contribute to socio-economic development; a lack of participation of broader social forces towards the IS development goals.

To put it in slightly different terms, in the context of IS, the Greek state/society coupling has demonstrated limited "embedded autonomy". On the one hand implementation of policy has been enmeshed in various personal and institutional interests, clientelistic relations, and micro-corruption (inadequate autonomy of the state from society). On the other hand the IS project has been designed top-down without social dialogue and with subsequent limited mobilisation of civil society, while the links between state and entrepreneurs at the local level have been weak (inadequate embeddedness of state into society).

6.   Conclusions

Despite following closely the EU rhetoric and policy, the unfolding of the Greek IS has come up against significant delays and impediments. At the state level, obsolete institutional arrangements, inadequate coordination and implementation mechanisms, and the lack of Weberian bureaucratic culture, have delayed project implementation. At the industry level, the IT sector in Greece has been characterised by a vast majority of small and very small enterprises, has not been competitive enough, and has been implicated in complex relationships with other productive entities and the public sector. At the societal level, lack of awareness, ignorance, and technophobia vis-à-vis the new technologies have been observed, due to inadequate education/training, inadequate communication of the national vision, and the absence of driving forces like those of civil society. Apart from the sphere of private consumption (e.g. through mobile telephony) the IS project has not been meaningful to large segments of the Greek population.

I have analysed this picture by resorting to the history of the Greek social formation and by adopting a state/society approach. I have argued that incomplete industrialisation, a complex relationship between the state, the economy and politics, a fragmented, over-bureaucratic and inefficient public administration, inactive civil society, collective spirit and social heterogeneity, as well as the operation of clientelism, have all contributed to the contemporary picture of the Greek IS. Moreover, "state capacity" and "embedded autonomy" can be useful concepts in understanding the current standing of the Greek IS and the associated implementation problems.

The goal of this paper has been twofold: firstly, to provide a critical account of the IS in a specific national context and its particularities; secondly, to draw on this case in order to lead to theoretical propositions as to the impact of the particular state/society configuration and the role of the state on IS in a national context. The methodological implication of this research is that historical studies of societies can be informative of contemporary IS developments. The Greek case shows that national variations should be taken seriously in discussions of the IS, as the adoption and implementation of IS policies is a contested process that comes up against historical societal legacies. These legacies are expected to contribute to the trajectory and eventual physiognomy of any national IS (as further research in the Greek and other cases in future might demonstrate).

References

[1]   Avgerou, C. (2002). *Information systems and global diversity*. Oxford: Oxford University Press.
[2]   Baudrillard, J. (1988). *Selected writings*. Cambridge, Polity.
[3]   Bell, D. (1976). The coming of post-industrial society: A venture in social forecasting. Harmondsworth, Penguin.
[4]   Caloghirou, Y. (2003). Implementing information society development strategy in Greece. *Seminar on Information Society as Tool for Regional Development*, Salerno.
[5]   Caloghirou and Constantelou (2006). Addressing the complexity challenge: Some reflections on the non-linear route of putting policy into practice. *European Communications Policy Research Conference (EuroCPR)*, Seville.
[6]   Castells, M. (1996). *The rise of the network society*. Oxford: Blackwell.
[7]   Castells, M. Ed. (2004). *The network society: A cross-cultural perspective*. Cheltenham, UK: Edward Elgar.
[8]   Castells, M. & P. Himanen (2002). *The information society and the welfare state: The Finnish model*. Oxford: Oxford University Press.
[9]   Constantelou, N. (2001). In search of a vision: Information society policies in peripheral and middle-income countries. Athens: National Technical University.
[10] Council of the European Union (2000). *Conclusions of the Lisbon European Council*. SN 100/00. 23-4 March 2000.
[11] EDET (2004). 2003 Market study for e-commerce. Resource document. E-Business Forum. www.ebusinessforum.gr (in Greek). Accessed October 2005.
[12] EDET (2005). 2004 National survey for new technologies and the information society. E-Business Forum. www.ebusinessforum.gr (in Greek). Accessed October 2005.
[13] European Commission (1993). *Growth, competitiveness, employment: The challenges and ways forward into the 21st Century. A white paper*. Luxemburg: Office for Official Publications of the European Communities.
[14] European Commission (1994a). Europe and the global information society: Recommendations to the European Council. Brussels: European Council.
[15] European Commission (1994b). *Europe's way to the information society: An Action Plan*. COM(94) 347. Brussels: European Commission.
[16] European Commission (2000). eEurope 2002: An information society for all: Action Plan prepared for Feira European Council. Brussels: European Commission.
[17] Eurostat (2003). *Statistics on the information society in Europe*. Luxembourg: Office for Official Publications of the European Communities.
[18] Eurostat (2005). *Internet usage by individuals and enterprises*. Luxembourg: Office for Official Publications of the European Communities.
[19] Eurostat (2007). *Statistics on the information society in Europe*. Luxembourg: Office for Official Publications of the European Communities.
[20] Evans, P. (1995). *Embedded autonomy: States and industrial transformation*. Princeton, NJ: Princeton University Press.
[21] Evans, P. & J. E. Rauch (1999). Bureaucracy and growth: A cross-national analysis of the effects of "Weberian" state structures on economic growth. *American Sociological Review*, 64(5), 748-765.
[22] Falch, M. & A. Henten (2000). Digital Denmark: From information society to network society. *Telecommunications Policy*, 24(5), 377-394.
[23] Featherstone, K. (2005). Introduction: 'Modernisation' and the structural constraints of Greek politics. *West European Politics*, 28(2), 223-241.

[24] Gunther, R., Diamandouros, N.P., & Sotiropoulos, D. (Eds) (2006). *Democracy and the state in the new southern Europe*. New York: Oxford University Press.

[25] Hellenic Republic (1995). Greek strategy for the Information Society: A tool for employment, development and quality of life. Athens: Hellenic Republic.

[26] Hellenic Republic (1999). *Greece in the information society: Strategy and actions*. Athens: Hellenic Republic.

[27] Hobson, J. M. (1998). The historical sociology of the state and the state of historical sociology in International Relations. *Review of International Political Economy*, 5(2), 284-320.

[28] Kazakos, P. (2001). *Between state and market*. Athens: Patakis (in Greek).

[29] Kotzias, N. (2004). *The active democratic state*. Athens: Kastaniotis (in Greek).

[30] Ladi, S. (2005). The role of experts in the reform process in Greece. *West European Politics*, 28(2), 279-296.

[31] Lavdas, K. (2005). Interest groups in disjointed corporatism: social dialogue in Greece and European 'competitive corporatism'. *West European Politics*, 28(2), 297-316.

[32] Lyberaki, A. & E. Tsakalotos (2002). Reforming the economy without society. *New Political Economy*, 7(1), 93-114.

[33] Mansell, R. E. & Steinmueller, E. (2000). *Mobilizing the information society: Strategies for growth and opportunity*. New York, N.Y: Oxford University Press.

[34] May, C. (Ed.) (2003). *Key thinkers for the information society*. London: Routledge.

[35] Miles, I. (1996). The information society: Competing perspectives on the social and economic implications of ICTs. In W.Dutton (Ed.), *Information and communication technologies: Visions and realities*. New York: Oxford University Press.

[36] Mouzelis, N. (1986). *Politics in the semi-periphery*. London: Macmillan.

[37] Mouzelis, N. (1995). Modernity, late development and civil society. In J.Hall (Ed.), *Civil Society: Theory, history, comparison*. Cambridge: Polity.

[38] OECD (2001). *Regulatory reform in Greece*. Paris: OECD.

[39] OPIS (2000). Operational programme for the information society. Ministry of National Economy. www.infosociety.gr (in Greek). Accessed May 2005.

[40] OPIS (2004). Operational programme for the information society Performance Review 2003. www.infosociety.gr (in Greek). Accessed September 2005.

[41] Perrons, D. (2004). Globalisation and social change: People and places in a divided world. London: Routledge.

[42] Petmesidou, M. (1996). Social protection in Greece: A brief glimpse of a welfare state. *Social Policy and Administration*, 30(4), 324-347.

[43] Phillips, N. (2005). Special section: The state debate in political economy. *New Political Economy*, 10(3), 335-342.

[44] Rodrigues, M. J. (2002). Introduction: For a European strategy at the turn of the century. In M. J. Rodrigues (Ed.), *The new knowledge economy in Europe* (pp.1-27). Cheltenham: Edward Elgar.

[45] Rodrigues, M.J. (2003). *European policies for a knowledge economy*. Cheltenham: Edward Elgar.

[46] Sancho, D. (2002). European national platforms for the development of the information society. In J. Jordana (Ed.), *Governing telecommunications and the information society in Europe*. Cheltenham: Edward Elgar.

[47] Sassen, S. (2002). Towards a sociology of information technology. *Current Sociology*, 50(3), 365-388.

[48] Skocpol, T. (1985). Bringing the state back in: Strategies of analysis in current research. In P. Evans, D. Rueschemeyer and T. Skocpol (Eds), *Bringing the state back in* (pp. 3-37). Cambridge: Cambridge University Press.

[49] Smith, D., Solinger, D, & Topik, S. (Eds.) (1999). *States and sovereignty in the global economy*. New York: Routledge.
[50] Sotiropoulos, D. (1996). Civil society and the Greek state in the Third Hellenic Republic. In C. Lyrintzis, E. Nikolakopoulos and D. Sotiropoulos (Eds), *Society and politics*. Athens: Themelio. (in Greek).
[51] Sotiropoulos, D. (2003). Aspects of Babylonia: Interpretations of the post-war development of welfare state in Greece. In D. Venieris and C. Papatheodorou (Eds), *Social policy in Greece: Challenges and perspectives*. Athens: Ellinika Grammata (in Greek).
[52] Sotiropoulos, D. (2004). Formal weakness and informal strength: civil society in contemporary Greece. Discussion Paper 16. London: LSE Hellenic Observatory.
[53] Sotiropoulos, D. (2006). Old problems and new challenges: The enduring and changing functions of the southern European state bureaucracies. In R. Gunther, P. N. Diamandouros and D. Sotiropoulos (Eds), *Democracy and the state in the new southern Europe* (pp 197-234). New York: Oxford University Press.
[54] Tsoukalas, C. (1977). *State, society, work*. Athens: Themelio (in Greek).
[55] Voulgaris, Y. (2003). Greece and the information society: Particularities and strategic choices. *Contemporary Issues* (in Greek).
[56] Voulgaris, Y. & Sotiropoulos, D. (2002). Information society, sociology and technology. Operational Programme for Information Society. www.ebusinessforum.gr/teams/teamsall/view/index.php?ctn=60&language=en (in Greek). Accessed 15 December 2004.
[57] Webster, F. (2006). *Theories of the information society*. London: Routledge.

TECHNOLOGY, GLOBALISATION, AND GOVERNANCE:
RESEARCH PERSPECTIVES AND PROSPECTS

Tony Cornford
London School of Economics and Political Science, London, UK

Diego D. Navarra
International Institute for Geo-Information Science and Earth Observation (ITC),
The Netherlands

Abstract   The purpose of this chapter is to introduce global ICT programmes, defined as new and universal modes of organising mediated by technology and enacted through a novel mix of policy instruments, international institutions, business interests, and techno/managerial concepts. Largely unexplored in various fields, including information systems as well as many other social sciences studying innovation and digital technologies, such programmes are interesting, not least because of their projected ability to promote innovation and achieve new mechanisms of governance. The chapter argues that a new theoretical understanding for the study of such programmes is needed in order to explore them as a means of technology transfer and to better understand systems of innovation in the developing world.

Keywords: Globalisation, governance, networks, e-government.

1.   Introduction

Joseph E. Stiglitz in his book "Globalisation and Its Discontents" [46] points out that the greatest disparity between developed and less developed nations is not anymore only or principally a matter of natural resources, or even of human capital (increasingly mobile as it is), but is the growing divide in access to organisational capacity and the extent to which this impedes the coordination and exploitation of informational resources. This organisational capacity is often directly associated with the ability to embody ICT within networked structures that link government to economic and social development in new ways. As Castells suggests, late capitalist societies exhibit such network-based social and economic structures, both within government and administration and beyond in the economy and wider civil society [9, 10, 13]. These structures are increasingly identified as *the* significant instrument for the expansion of liberal capitalism through innovation and new forms of decentred concentration, alias new modes of

Please use the following format when citing this chapter:

Cornford, T. and Navarra, D.D., 2008, in IFIP International Federation for Information Processing, Volume 282;
Social Dimensions of Information and Communication Technology Policy; Chrisanthi Avgerou, Matthew L. Smith,
Peter van den Besselaar; (Boston: Springer), pp. 81–94.

organising based on digital networks and assembling complex meshes of activities and territories that cross conventional borders [45].

As a consequence, across the world it is possible to identify a movement, or a strong set of claims, for the introduction of programmes to shift from "government" as a primary responsibility of the unitary state, to "governance" by and through networks of institutions and individuals (and technological entities too, as discussed below), acting in partnership, held together by relations of trust, and transcending many old and established boundaries [6]. The webs of power and knowledge that these initiatives enact are often presented as being fundamental to the dynamics of technological, organisational, and social innovation in both developed and the developing socio-economic contexts. Mobilising technological capacity, the diffusion of networking and communication infrastructure and the stabilisation of the Internet as the new platform for global communications (telephony, data and images, broadcasting), is often understood as central in this process of change. Indeed, ICT is often identified as a primary actor in enabling national and regional economies to develop new social and organisational capacity and exploit new knowledge assets. This, it is proposed, can then lead to a better ability to participate in the wider global economy and serve as a primary means to achieve social and economic development [50].

However, this is not an easy or obvious path to follow, and meets many challenges in both developed and developing regions of the world. The sense of breakdown or crisis of the welfare state seen in many developed countries might be seen as one consequence of the fundamental shift that is implied by such developments in the contract between capital, labour, and the state, while the developing world faces formidable challenges in responding to this new reality. Typical challenges for developing countries include the creation of institutions in support of the new global and electronic markets as well as providing an enabling policy environment that can support social inclusion and offer institutional transparency while building regimes for foreign investment and participation in global trade [19, 47].

This can be conceptualised in terms of what Rose and Miller term a new and distinctive "programme of government" [43], understood as a specific contemporary problematisation of the question of the nature of the State and the drivers of its power and legitimacy. What we see emerging is a programme of government that draws heavily on information and communication technology, and which transcends the nation state, offering a distinctive problematisation of the nature of citizenship, statehood, and citizen/state relations - what we term here as *global ICT programmes*. These represent a programme of government that expresses a fundamental commitment to the proposition that ICT and informational resources can significantly increase organisational coordination and effectiveness in the business of government (Stiglitz's "organisational capacity") and on a scale that takes us beyond the nation state. Such programmes seek to support transactions taking place among diverse social and economic actors, organisations, and institutions which operate in a global space. Examples of such global ICT programmes can be found in the widespread commitment to e-government as a technology of transformation, in the establishment of global electronic markets for primary resources, in health information systems and bio-surveillance, or in the establishment of global projects to address climate change through carbon trading, organic agriculture, and land and water management.

The primary characteristics of global ICT programmes include:

- the establishment of new networked and distributed modes of organising mediated by technology and operating in the area of government, policy making, regulation and infrastructure development – often on a scale that goes beyond any one country;
- the application of a "toolbox" of policy instruments and guidelines to build and operate such systems, often identified with the general goal of promoting better (or good) governance, harnessing the market and the power of education and information;
- the presence of a common set of institutional and technical actors that operate across contexts and domains, building synergies as they mobilize and develop their technical and managerial knowledge resources.

These programmes themselves are fundamentally global. This is not a question of their application area going beyond the state (though it often will), but of the character of the mobilization that enacts and sustains them. In this mobilization we see three important drivers that bring a global dimension: first, the technologies applied are universal and generic (e.g., the Internet, data management, web sites); second, the values and goals they inscribe are universal (e.g., liberal capitalism, good governance, management and planning methodologies)[1]; third, the networks of agencies which carry them out are universal including bilateral and more often multilateral development and financial institutions such as the OECD, World Bank, and UN bodies, but also business schools, international management consultancies, technology companies, and the institutions of the scientific elites.

Of course, in emphasizing the global and universal character of these programmes – the scale of the materials out of which they are conceived and constructed – we do not want to imply that they operate across the world always in the same way. Indeed, quite the opposite. It is in the character of global ICT programmes that they mutate in local environments; operating as what Sassens calls formats of electronic space, which are inflected by the values, cultures, power systems, and institutional orders in which they are embedded, being appropriated and re-made in various ways in various settings [44]. In the end the "globality" of these programmes is not found in any flat uniformity, but in their interconnected diversity.

We should also be clear that there is nothing inherently good about global ICT programmes. They seem to serve a certain ideology of liberal modernity, with

---

[1] In the context of the present paper, liberal capitalism and good governance are not intended to be equivalent, compatible or complementary, but as essential values of reference for the definition of the goals and priorities implicitly or explicitly linked to Global ICT Programmes.

perhaps a strong Anglo-Saxon bias in their technical/rational and managerial character. They can and should be challenged; among other reasons we could suggest for their cultural myopia and insensitivity, their naive utilitarianism, their allegiance to certain power elites, or their fragility in the face of context and diversity. However, this chapter is not such a critique, rather we seek to understand and outline relevant research perspectives and prospects for global ICT programmes.

Global ICT programmes are usually explicitly linked to transformative agendas; they aim to make a big difference and change things. Examples would include e-government projects to "re-invent" government, regional health information systems, or programmes established within the frameworks of international development activity and focused on the notion of "good governance" [15]. Good governance in particular is often identified as an obligatory passage point for access to wider development and aid programmes and thus to participation in the global economy. The term "governance" as used here signifies something specific in terms of the changes that are expected within such programmes. Governance in general refers to a changed condition of recorded rule, a new process of governing, or a new method by which society is governed [42], with society understood as more than encompassed by the state. Thus, the OECD gives governance a global dimension as "the way society collectively solves its problems and meets its needs [...]. In a framework of good governance, government services across administrative levels co-ordinate their activities in *order to enhance the global effectiveness of policies and minimize conflicting action*" (our emphasis) [37].

Implicit in such programmes is a fundamental change in the relationship between state and citizens; potentially increasing the importance of citizens' and other mediating body's participation and feedback, and their role in policy formulation, implementation, and enforcement. E-government programmes, for example, are often noted for the way in which they describe and project a distinct conceptualisation of the citizen – as customer or consumer – but also as participant.

Programmes of e-governance then project a distinctive conceptualisation of how ICT is implicated in the blurring and re-shaping of the boundaries of the state, the establishment of new local and global institutional regimes, and in offering new modalities of governance. The legitimization and implementation of global ICT programmes is achieved through international and transnational initiatives and produces a variety of new organisations, control structures, formal and informal rules and codes of practice, all of which start to delineate a new (and not always very coherent) global governance architecture. And yet we see no single or coherent theoretical perspective that can be applied to study such phenomena and the structures of governance that emerge out of the diversity, complexity, but strongly totalising character of these programmes.

Such views lead us to ask some new but fundamental questions: how are we to understand such programmes and what is their contribution to the processes and dynamics of globalisation? How can we explain their character, using what theoretical perspectives? And, how should we link such programmes to contemporary notions of governance and social and economic innovation? To start to address these questions we argue for the need to develop new theoretical frameworks and new conceptual categories. In the next section we review the literature on technology, globalisation, and governance. The third section explores three well known epistemological approaches in the discipline of Information Systems and assesses their potential for research in this area. The fourth section returns to the questions above juxtaposing them to the research perspectives identified in section three. Conclusions follow.

2.   Technology, globalisation and governance: Global ICT programmes and development

Technological progress in the field of information handling, data storage and retrieval systems, networking, and communication is typically identified as the prime driver of social and economic change in the last three decades. Manuel Castells for instance, suggests that globalisation can best be understood by looking at the processes of interconnection that create a global information society [9-11, 13]. He stresses that ICT has facilitated the emergence of a "network society" based on the a-spatial nature of flows of finance, information, and knowledge. Other authors parallel the phenomenon of globalisation to a programme of modernity based on the advancement and expansion of global capitalism, market principles, and economic efficiency [5, 22-25, 27, 41]. As Avgerou & Madon point out, these ambitions are premised on the adoption of organisational processes from business practice, for example Total Quality Management, process re-engineering and business planning, and are sponsored by international organisations and technology suppliers to facilitate the introduction and diffusion of new forms of organisation and governance as, for instance, in e-government programmes [23, 15, 35].

Both in seeking to promote and to regulate the forces released by the process of globalisation, new mechanisms of regional and global governance have been put in place, which stand in an ambiguous relationship with existing mechanisms of national accountability [28]. Exclusive attention to the national level of aggregation becomes less useful in the light of the changes occurring in the organisation of economic activities, which increasingly tends to diminish the capacity of nation states to act freely even within their boundaries. Castells has argued that the world is being transformed from a "space of places" into a "space of flows" [11, 12], making the nature of the dialectical relations between these spaces and the consequences of these relations key issues for understanding the changing contours of state governance, but also for national and regional development.

Karl Polanyi's in his magisterial work *The Great Transformation* [40] suggests that the greatest difficulty in establishing a new economic order is contained in the social structures which will enact it. In the present time of institutional reconstruction, these ideas are still valid in defining the important distinction between "embedded" and "disembedded" economic orders. In the difficulty of achieving domestic stability without triggering conflict at the international level, it is possible to appreciate the differences between local and disembedded forms of governance and the emergence of an architecture (leading in Polanyi's time to the Bretton Woods international agreement and institutions) for the management of economic transactions by means of bilateral but primarily multi-lateral institutions and collaborations, projecting the activities of the nation state into the international realm. This is what led to Polanyi's prediction of the end of "capitalist internationalism". But, although according to Peter Evans [17] his findings have been disproved by the evident international organisation of production in the past 60 years, it is nonetheless possible to appreciate the way in which the introduction of ICT into governance structures contributes to a new great transformation in the balance between market and state authority as it has been defined since the end of World War II.

Ciborra provides a conceptualisation of the aspirations of global ICT programs in such terms, emphasising the strong role of technology as an actor: "characterised by the extension of the links (networks) to individuals and organisations they support. Software guarantees the standardisation of the linkages, for seamless transfer of data and access to powerful databases, which can also track usage and profile users" [4]. Ciborra conceptualises these novel structures as "grid technologies" – technologies that serve to achieve both a decomposition and a re-composition of existing highly institutionalised activities initially found in a collection of heterogeneous and fragmented systems [45]. These grids then come to support a system of decentred concentration, alias the relocation, sharing, and coordinated use of diverse resources (including organisational capacities) almost irrespective of their geographical, cultural, or organisational context. Such a move serves to decompose and distribute through the grid (networks) things that were previously monolithic or local – what Foster calls "host centric services" [21].

To bring together ICT, management ideas, and the networks of organisations and institutions engaging in developmental efforts, and to expose the emerging governance arrangements they imply is not easy. Such global ICT programmes present a difficult, diffuse, and challenging object of analysis and, as we show below, this is an area that does not surrender immediately to the theories in good currency in the discipline of Information Systems. For example, the ways in which the transfer of technology and organisational forms are combined in global ICT programmes will be associated with such diverse areas as agreements related to trade and the introduction of market supporting regulations in the area of telecommunication, labour mobility, intellectual property, and information services, as well as participation in global financial and transport networks, education and training programmes, research and development capacity, and overall strategies for social and economic development.

A number of influential reports have been written by multilateral donor and international standard setting organisations on the underlying rationale, effects, and potential of ICT, e-government, and information society initiatives to promote development and reform; in effect promoting a global ICT programme. For example, according to the First Annual Report of the Information and Communication Technologies Task Force of the United Nations: "while domestic policies are needed to harness ICT for development effectively, *international policies* forged in multilateral institutions will increasingly define the range of policy options available to developing countries" [7] [emphasis added]. Similarly, according to Okot-Uma [38] "E-Governance seeks to realize *processes* and *structures* for harnessing the potentialities of information and communication technologies [...] for the purpose of enhancing *Good Governance*" (emphasis in the original).

Most countries, those with ambitions for development, see an imperative in the rapid diffusion and consolidation of ICT, a process that depends on a number of factors including establishing basic infrastructure, but also investment in research and development by the public and private sectors, sustaining centres of academic excellence, building local industrial and organisational capacity, and then intertwining each element to create dynamic and self-sustaining "systems of innovation" [36]. However, the transition to a developing and dynamic economy and a "good governance" society demands epochal passages and implies efforts beyond any narrow trickle-down rhetoric. It seems to demand a re-shaping of government – its re-invention - in a form that aligns with the new demands emerging from local stakeholders who increasingly see themselves and their interests in terms of a participation in a global society. In short, such a route to development is not only difficult to achieve, but costly and risky [5, 24, 40].

3.   Research perspectives

Since the 1970s a variety of emerging theoretical approaches, such as population ecology, neo-institutional theory, resource dependence theory, and transaction costs economics, have been proposed as ways to view organisations as "open systems" with structures and internal processes that are determined primarily by environmental factors [39]. However, "because technology had always been regarded as an internal attribute of the organisation, they have proved difficult to combine an interest with technology and innovation [and] the open systems perspectives that have come to dominate macro-organisational research" [39], and especially so for the research and study of network forms of organisations.

Here we assess three potential approaches that may allow us to penetrate further and to explore global ICT programmes as complex and encompassing socio-technical arrangements. We have chosen to assess here the contrasting approaches of Actor Network Theory (ANT) drawn from Science and Technology Studies (STS), Transaction Cost Analysis (TCA), and New Public Management

(NPM). Each provides a potentially important perspective for expanding our understanding of the phenomenon. ANT allows us to study the role of formal and informal actors, human, social, and material, and their struggles for the maintenance and expansion of power and legitimacy. New Public Management, on the other hand, takes an unequivocal perspective of modernisation and reform, drawing on business and managerial models, and views technology as essentially a package or instrument that can enable certain technical/rational programmes of action. Transaction Costs Analysis in contrast takes the transaction as its unit of analysis, and helps to reveal ICTs as agents of optimisation, serving efficiency in organisational structures and institutional arrangements.

To be sure we cannot suggest that these choices represent the only potential theoretical means to explore global ICT programmes, or that they are ontologically compatible. What we do, however, suggest is that in the contrast between them we may be able better to illuminate aspects of global ICT programmes

ANT is one important strand of work that has attempted to transcend the problems identified by Podolny et al. [8, 31]. ANT builds on techniques of sociology, anthropology, and history to allow us to examine technology as an actor located within networks of hybrid interests. The initial development of ANT was concerned with the sociology of science and was pioneered at the Ecole des Mines in Paris [8]. Later work has included a focus on information and communication technology [32]. ANT rejects any distinction between technology and society proposing that both should be studied the same way using same language and metaphors. According to ANT, a technological innovation is developed and adopted through the building of a heterogeneous network of alliances of human and non-human actors, or actants.

ANT does not distinguish between human and non-human in assigning agency, nor does it specify a conventional unit of analysis; the network can be small or large, in the latter case micro-actor networks are "blackboxed" within the larger. Applying ANT's epistemology it is possible to move through these units of analysis as necessary. ANT does not establish a clear framework for the study of networks governance arrangements, fundamentally a distributed view. Thus, ANT has been criticised for stopping at the identification and description of actors and the networks they adhere to, and as being more persuasive as a means to study events at the local level, but not able to encompass the role played by history and context as innovation unfolds, nor to understand what mattered for the various actors at a specific moment in time [29].

An interesting example of the use of ANT for the study of global ICT networks across developing countries can be found in Braa et al. [4]. The authors draw on actor-network theory to analyse the processes of local translations and alignment with surrounding political institutions and actors in the context of technology transfer to build health information systems. They adopt ANT to extend Castell's network analysis [9] to bridge the global and local dimensions of technology transfer in a dialectic of opposition through counter (local) networks to the dominant (global) ones for the development of information infrastructure standards for health information systems in South Africa, India, Cuba and Mozambique. Their findings stress the highly political nature of the development of such infrastructures, which are also influenced by the institutional and economic settings of these countries, suggesting that institutionalisation, understood as local appropriation, can reinforce the sustainability of the aspirations of such networks, in this case to achieve national health information systems that can serve development goals.

The second theoretical perspective that may help in the study of global ICT programmes is Transaction Cost Analysis (TCA) which focuses on the translation of technological artefacts and interests into complex institutional settings and the consequences. This theory has been widely used in information systems research to examine governance arrangements and pricing mechanisms, for example for IT contracts and outsourcing, as well as in the study of e-commerce and e-business [2, 16, 34, 48]. TCA analysis of IT contracts allows for the study of the hierarchical elements of a contract in terms of command structures and authority systems, ruled-based incentive systems, standard operating procedures, non-market based pricing systems, and informational dispute resolution mechanisms.

Lee [33] for example argues that IT Service level, transfer of IT assets and staff, pricing and payment terms, warranty and liability, dispute resolution mechanisms and termination, intellectual property rights, and information security and confidentiality, are the most important dimensions in an IT sourcing contract. While this approach has been for the most part applied to business systems the characterizations given above by Lee suggest that there is potential to apply a similar conceptual scheme to global ICT programmes; seeing them as essentially a new transactional framework that will have institutional consequences.

Our final potential theoretical point of departure is New Public Management (NPM). Within the context of the public administration and e-government - itself deeply implicated with the re-definition of the boundaries of the nation state [9] – analysis is often associated with a large body of literature under the name of New Public Management (NPM) [14, 15, 18, 20, 30]. This literature places emphasis on the creation of more effective governance and organisational arrangements to increase the state's ability to offer services (if not itself provide them), using novel institutional arrangements, increasing the use of market-oriented mechanisms, and introducing the concept of "partnership" between the public and the private sector, not only as a way to share risks and expenses of experimentation, but also to create and exploit an information infrastructure that is better able to provide efficient service delivery as well as innovation in policy.

Theoretical perspective / Key issues	Actor Network Theory (ANT)	New Public Management (NPM)	Transaction Costs Analysis (TCA)
Territory & Context	Situated social actors, groups with overlapping and shifting interests, participants in different social worlds	Organisations as formal units, formal organisational arrangements, hierarchy of authority	Small groups and individuals, task groups and their interaction, organisational resources and rewards
Form of Authority, Regulation & Governance	Actor/environment Translation and Inscription	Package as milieu, Instrumental/ managerial	Allocate resources to reduce transaction costs
Citizenship	Membership and negotiated social meaning	Citizen as Customer	Contractual & Transactional
Ideology	Fulfilment through evocation of meaning	Modernisation, management and reform	Market, Firm
Research Interests	Maintenance and/or expansion of power	Organisational performance and order	Organisational forms, governance, structure

Table 1 Actor Network Theory, New Public Management and Transaction Costs Analysis of global ICT programmes.

Both New Public Management and Transaction Costs approaches advocate that technology works best through the formation of appropriate incentive structures, and via its assumed capacity to increase users' choice through contestability (for instance within electronic markets, through informational and interactive resources for citizens/customers, or by competitive outsourcing).

It is interesting then that research on processes of ICT development within these theoretical traditions has generally been concerned with the study of how technologies are used to facilitate activities or processes taking place within quite narrowly defined organisational and market boundaries. However, and in contrast to the global programmes considered here, the TCA literature, and to a degree NPM too, is based on the assumption that some constraining contract (and the assumed means to enforce it) can act as the key governance mechanism to ensure a successful partnership for the exploitation of ICT applications, and thereby ignores the situation where such relationships for global ICT programmes are typically embedded: namely not primarily between customers and providers of services, but also between diverse political and social institutions and settings.

This is part of the reason why an integral component of moving to a macro-level of analysis is found in efforts to align formal and informal structures and the transactions taking place so as to achieve (if not design) better or more appropriate governance arrangements [49]. This means looking also at the environmental externalities that become relevant as structures are transformed from techno/managerial fantasies into accepted and legitimate routines across the multiple realities that constitute the contexts of use [1].

Table 1 summarises these three theoretical perspectives and contrasts their potential contribution for the study of Global ICT Programmes with respect to their view of territory and context, forms of authority (including regulation and governance), ideology, and their interpretation of what constitutes "citizenship".

4.   Conclusions and prospects

In this chapter we have attempted to establish global ICT programmes as an object of study and explored some potential theoretical perspectives that might be used in studying them. The choices of theoretical approach we have made have drawn upon relevant strands of recent work in the field of information systems. We find each of the theories considered to have some potential, but each to be limited or partial. Each can help us explore some of the characteristics of these programmes, as networks of artefacts and institutions comprising policy making as well as operational and transactional systems, in alliance with certain dominant technical and managerial concepts. From ANT we may appreciate their hybrid nature and dynamic emergence as interests coalesce and align; from NPM we understand their appeal to managerial rationality and the market; while from TCA we draw the ideas of transactional efficiency matched to organisational forms. In each case we can see that they serve to capture some of the characteristics, but none presents itself as the obvious choice. In brief, theorizing global ICT programmes is work to be done. In this more attention will need to be paid to the organisational and governance challenges they pose, and especially the risks and challenges faced in developing an effective and coherent international governance architecture which can meet the challenges of the 21st Century. However, we do not see, as yet, in the literature strong strands of relevant research that explores the distinct character of global ICT programmes.

This may be because Global ICT programmes offer for analysis a rather different set of issues with respect to technology than is usually studied in the discipline of information systems. In this new order neither technological infrastructures, institutional arrangements, nor cultural specifics can be taken as stable or given, but must be seen as in a process of change and transformation. It is in this way fundamental for global ICT programmes to seek flexibility, both in the ways they change and mutate when implemented in (and across) local environments as well as to facilitate transitions from, to, and among developing and developed countries via the translation of ideas and interests. For example, the transport success story of the Brazilian city of Curitiba, or the micro-credit model of the Grameen bank from Bangladesh. This underscores the need for research that can frame these programmes in a way that can reflect the diversity of cultural and political contexts they inhabit, as well as the need to encompass in research itself the diversity of organisational ecologies [3].

We thus emphasise the status of global ICT programmes as transnational movements or mobilizations and as representing a new form of governance. They also project a distinctive conceptualization of how ICT is implicated in shaping (constraining and liberating) peoples' lives through the blurring and re-shaping of the boundaries of the state, the establishment of new local and global institutional regimes, the offering of new arenas (markets) for interaction. In this we see them as representing a key transition in global governance, associated with technological change and the potential of ICT and related knowledge activities to offer new modalities of governance, itself central to processes of globalisation [26]. They represent, we argue, a fundamental challenge to the notions of geographical location, boundary regulation, and the jurisdiction of the nation state. They also project a new world where co-operative outcomes, fluid collectivities, and trust based relationships become essential requirements if states and their citizens/customers are to be able to develop and exploit organisational capacities.

Unfortunately, this dynamic is not being paralleled by a similar evolution in the relationship between the political and technological domains (internally and more importantly transnationally), and thus the governance models that we see emerge from global ICT programmes are often incoherent and unbalanced, and not appropriate to current challenges. For example, according to the First Annual Report of the Information and Communication Technologies Task Force of the United Nations: "while domestic policies are needed to harness ICT for development effectively, *international policies* forged in multilateral institutions will increasingly define the range of policy options available to developing countries" [7] [emphasis added]. Meanwhile a plethora of international bodies and various other social and economic institutions struggle to delineate their responsibilities, while national governments are *de facto* more responsive than creative in addressing these challenges.

References

[1]   Andreu, R. & C. Ciborra (1998). Organisational learning and core capabilities development: the role of IT, in R. Galliers and W. Baets (Eds.), *Information Technology and Organisational Transformation*, Wiley: Chichester.

[2]   Ang, S. (1994) Toward conceptual clarity of outsourcing. *Business Process Re-Engineering*, 54, 113-26.

[3]   Avgerou, C. (2002). IT as an institutional actor in developing countries. in IFIP WG 9.4. 2002. Bangalore.

[4]   Avgerou, C., Ciborra, C., & Land, F.F. (2004) *The social study of ICT: Innovation, actors and contexts*. Oxford: OUP.

[5]   Beck, U. & Ritter, M. (1992). *Risk society: Towards a new modernity*. London: Sage Publications.

[6]   Bevir, M. & Rhodes, W.R. (2004). Interpreting British governance. *British Journal of Politics and International Relations*. 6, 129-164.

[7]   Birkmeyer, J.D. & Dimnick, J.B. (2004). The leapfrog group's patient safety practices, 2003: The potential benefits of universal adoption.

[8]   Callon, M. (1986). Some elements of a sociology of translation: Domestication of the scallops and the fishermen of St Brieuc Bay, in J. Law, (Ed), *Power, action and belief* (196-233), London: Routledge & Kegan Paul.

[9]   Castells, M. (1986) *The rise of the network society*. Massachussetts: Blackwell Publishers.

[10]   Castells, M. (1997) *The power of identity*. 1997, Cambridge, Mass: Blackwell.

[11]   Castells, M. (2000) *The rise of the network society*. 2nd ed. Information age ; v.1. Oxford: Blackwell. xxix, 594 p.

[12]   Castells, M. (2000). *Informational capitalism and social exclusion*. UNRISD.

[13]   Castells, M. (2001). *The internet galaxy*. Oxford: Oxford University Press.

[14]   Christensen, T.P.L. (Ed.) (2002). *New public management: The transformation of ideas and practice*. Ashgate: Aldershot.

[15]   Ciborra, C. & Navarra, D.D (2005). Good governance, development theory and aid policy: Risks and challenges of e-government in Jordan. *Journal of Information Technology for International Development*, 11(2).

[16]   deLooff, L. (1995). Information systems outsourcing decision making: A framework, organizational theories and case studies. *Journal of Information Technology*, 10(4), 281-297.

[17]   Evans, P.B. (2005). Counter-hegemonic globalisation: Transnational social movements in the contemporary global political economy. *Handbook of Political Sociology*, 655-670.

[18]   Ferlie, E., MacLaughling, K., & Osborne, P. (Ed.) (2001). *New Public Management: current trends and future prospects*. London: Routledge:

[19]   Force, D. (2001). Creating a development dynamic. Digital Opportunity Task Force: New York.

[20]   Fortin, Y.H.V.H. (2000). *Contracting in the new public management: From economics to law and citizenship*. Amsterdam: IOS Press.

[21]   Foster, I. et al. (2004). The physiology of the grid: An open grid services architecture for distributes system integration.

[22]   Giddens, A. (1984). *The constitution of society: Outline of the theory of structuration*. Cambridge: Polity Press.

[23]   Giddens, A. (1985). *The nation-state and violence. A contemporary critique of historical materialism*. Vol.2. London: Polity.

[24]   Giddens, A. (1990). *The consequences of modernity*. 1990, Cambridge: Polity in association with Blackwell.

[25]   Giddens, A. (1991). *Modernity and self identity: self and society in the late modern age*. Cambridge: Polity Press in association with Basil Blackwell.

[26]   Giddens, A. (2006). *Europe in the Global Age*, London: Polity.

[27]   Hall, S., et al. (1992). *Modernity and its futures. Understanding modern societies : an introduction*, Oxford: Polity Press in association with the Open University.

[28]   Held, D. & McGrew, A. (2002). *Governing globalization: power, authority and global governance*. Cambridge: Polity Press.

[29]   Howcroft, D., Mitev, N., & Wilson, M. (2004). What we may learn from the social shaping of technology approach, in *Social Theory and Philosophy for Information Systems*, J. Mingers and L. Willcocks, (Eds), Wiley: Chichester.

[30]   Larbi, G.A. (1999). The new public management approach and crisis states. United Nations Research Institute for Social Development: Geneva.

[31] Latour, B. (1987). *Science in action: How to follow scientists and engineers through society*. Milton Keynes: Open University Press.

[32] Latour, B. (1999). *Pandora's hope: Essays in the reality of science studies*. Cambridge, Mass: Harvard.

[33] Lee, M. (1996). IT outsourcing contracts: Practical issues for management. *Industrial Management and Data Systems*, 1996. 96(1), 15.

[34] Malone, T. & Yates, J. (1987). Electronic markets and electronic hierarchies *Communications of the ACM*, 30(6), 484-497.

[35] Navarra, D.D. & Cornford, T. (2005) ICT, innovation and public management: Governance, models & alternatives for e-Government Infrastructures. *European Conference of Information Systems*.

[36]. Nelson, R.R. (1993). *National innovation systems: a comparative analysis*. New York: Oxford University Press.

[37] OECD (2001). *Local partnerships for better governance*. 2001, Organisation for Economic Cooperation and Development.

[38] Okot-Uma, R. (2001). Electronic governance: Reinventing good governance. World Bank: Washington.

[39] Podolny, J.M., Stuart, T, & Hannan, M.T. (1996). Networks, knowledge, and niches: Competition in the worldwide semiconductor industry, 1984-1991. *American Journal of Sociology*, 102(3), 659-89.

[40] Polanyi, K. (2001) *The great transformation: the political and economic origins of our time*. 2nd Beacon Paperback ed., Boston, MA: Beacon Press.

[41] Poster, M. (1984) *Foucault, Marxism and history: mode of production versus mode of information*, Cambridge: Polity.

[42] Rhodes, R. (2000). Governance and public administration, in J. Pierre (Ed.), *Debating governance: Authority, steering and democracy* (pp. 54-90), Oxford: OUP: Oxford..

[43] Rose, N. & Miller, P. (1992). Political power beyond the state: Problematics of government. *British Journal of Sociology*. 43(2).

[44] Sassen, S. (2002), Towards a sociology of information technology. *Current Sociology*, 50(3), 365-388.

[45] Sassen, S. (2006). *Territory, authority, rights: From medieval to global assemblages*. Woodstock: Princeton University Press.

[46] Stiglitz, J.E. (2002). *Globalization and its discontents*. London: Allen Lane.

[47] UNDP (2003) Information and communication technologies for development in Human Development Reports. New York: United Nations Development Programme.

[48] Willcocks, L., G. Fitzgerald, et. al. (1996) To outsource IT or not?: Recent research on economics and evaluation practice. *European Journal of Information Systems*, 5(3), 143-160.

[49] Williamson, O.E. (2000). The new institutional economics: Taking stock, looking ahead. *Journal of Economic Literature*, 2000. 38(3), 595-613.

[50] WSIS (2004). Financing ICT for development: A review of trends and analysis of gaps and promising practices. ITU: Geneva.

GLOBALISATION AND NATIONAL SECURITY ISSUES FOR THE STATE: IMPLICATIONS FOR NATIONAL ICT POLICIES

Jackie Phahlamohlaka[1]
CSIR, South Africa

Abstract   The national security issues most impacted upon by globalisation are generally found to fall into three categories: the nature of security threats in a globalised world, the effects of the phenomenon of globalisation on the pursuit of national security, and the erosion of the exclusivity of the state as a provider of national security. In this chapter I examine the security risks associated with ICT, and in particular the Internet which is not constrained by territorial boundaries traditionally defining states and their sovereignty. Also, I point out the need for developing and implementing agile security related ICT policies to remain on the national security research agenda of all states.

Keywords: Globalisation, national security, information and communications technologies, national ICT policies, security threats

1.   Introduction

There is a general agreement in the literature that systematic studies analysing the link between globalisation and national security are necessary, but lacking. Cha [4] for instance points out that in spite of the plethora of literature on security and globalisation, there is relatively little work written by security specialists that interconnects the two. Because both globalisation and national security are multidimensional constructs whose bringing into operation is mainly enabled by Information and Communication Technologies (ICT), the lack of a systematic study of their interconnections presents a challenge for security related national ICT policies. So challenging are these constructs that most states are taking their time in publicly pronouncing their national security policies, let alone their ICT related national security policies. In an earlier study upon which this chapter draws, completed as part of the Executive National Security Programme (ENSP) by the author [10] in June 2007, a research approach was proposed that could be used by other interested researchers in further systematic studies linking globalisation and national security.

---

[1] Permission to use the results of the analysis from the Commadant Research Paper (CRP) of ENSP 15/07 was granted by the South African National Defence College.

Please use the following format when citing this chapter:

Phahlamohlaka, J., 2008, in IFIP International Federation for Information Processing, Volume 282; *Social Dimensions of Information and Communication Technology Policy*; Chrisanthi Avgerou, Matthew L. Smith, Peter van den Besselaar; (Boston: Springer), pp. 95–107.

Realising that most of the analyses attempting to draw a link between globalisation and national security were not based on or did not use any well researched theoretical perspective, we developed a framework in the ENSP study that combined the Ripsman and Paul [11] analysis framework and the process-based research framework proposed by Roode [5], to guide our analysis. A brief description of the framework is presented in section 3. Following this framework and the approach just mentioned, the author found that the national security issues most impacted upon by globalisation, generally fall into three categories: *(1) the nature of security threats in a globalised world*, (2) *the effects of the phenomenon of globalisation on the pursuit of national security,* and (3) *the erosion of the exclusivity of the state as a provider of national security*.

The proposed research approach is important because most of the literature attempting to link globalisation and national security was found to be very shallow and unhelpful from a research point of view. In line with this observation, Siponen [13] conducted a literature review on Information Systems (IS) security research between 1990 and 2004 and found that IS security research is chronically underdeveloped in terms of theory.

In this chapter, the results of the ENSP paper analysis are used to argue and demonstrate that globalisation renders the development and the implementation of ICT policies that are compliant to traditional national security requirements difficult across all states. The argument and the demonstration are structured in line with the identified national security issues most impacted by globalisation presented in the preceding paragraph.

The rest of the chapter is organised as follows. In the next section, the key concepts used in the chapter, namely globalisation, national security and the state are explored. This is followed by a discussion of the key national security issues for the state most impacted upon by globalisation after which a detailed argument on what the author considers the implications of these issues to be for security related national ICT policies is presented. The chapter ends with a concluding discussion.

2.   The key concepts explored

Taken separately, the literature on globalisation and national security is not scarce. As well, their definitions, perspectives and descriptions are vast and varied. As pointed out in the introduction, however, it is systematic studies analysing the link between globalisation and national security that are necessary, but lacking. The brief exploration of these concepts as presented below represent only a tiny fraction of what has been written in scholarly journals, books and conference proceedings, let alone the volumes of text available on the Internet.

2.1   Globalisation

Globalisation is described and defined in many different ways. Frost [7] quotes several sources, each differently describing globalisation. Amongst others, he quotes Friedman's description of globalisation as a "dynamic, ongoing process involving the inexorable integration of markets, non-states, and technologies to a degree never witnessed before." Frost also quotes the National Security Strategy issued by the White House in December 1999 which defined globalisation as "the process of accelerating economic, technological, cultural and political integration." The literature is loaded with many other descriptions and definitions, although most are very shallow.

Frost then arrived at his own description of globalisation as "a process leading to greater interdependence and mutual awareness (reflexivity) among economic, political and social units in the world, and among actors in general. It is an ideology with multiple meanings and lineages, sometimes appearing to be loosely associated with neo-liberalism and with technocratic solutions to economic development and reform, but also linked to cross-border advocacy networks and organisations defending human rights, the environment, women's rights or world peace" [8].

Guillen [8] writes in conclusion that definitions and timing aside, one of the persistent problems afflicting the study of globalisation is that it is far from a uniform and inexorable trend. Rather, globalisation is a fragmented, incomplete, discontinuous, contingent, and in many ways contradictory and puzzling process. Its study attracted and continues to attract great interest, with an explosion in the number of articles and books on globalisation published in the economic, sociological, and political literatures. He then identifies and discusses what he calls the five key debates: 1. Is it really happening? 2. Does it produce convergence? 3. Does it undermine the authority of nation-states? 4. Is globality different from modernity? 5. Is a global culture in the making? He goes into details in addressing each of these questions and an interested reader can consult the cited reference.

From the exploration of this concept as presented, and in relation to national security, this author concludes that globalisation is about the creation, protection, and sustenance of national interests in the process of global interaction.

2.2   National security

National Security as a concept is associated with the history of the United States of America following the Second World War, with the US Congress passing the first National Security Constitution in 1947. It traditionally had to do with the protection of the state against external aggression through economic, military, political, and diplomatic means. Recently however, it has been broadened to include human security – a people-centred approach to security, linking development to security and broadening both the identification of possible threats and the actors responsible for producing and resolving insecurity.

The literature indicates that there are as many definitions of National Security as there are students. One definition that caught the author's eye is the one given by David Jablonsky [9], who defines national security as that part of government policy whose objective is to create national and international political conditions that are favourable to the protection or the extension of vital national values against existing or potential adversaries.

According to Jablonsky, national security is defined in terms of the respective elements of the power base of a state, and is allotted differing priorities within different states, depending on the declared vital and national interests of such a state. All definitions of national security include the *concept of national power*, without which it is argued, there can be no security. The elements of national power fall into either of the two categories of determinants of power. The *natural determinants* and the *social determinants*. The *natural determinants* (geography, resources, and population) are concerned with the number of people in a nation and with their physical environment. *Social determinants* (economic, political, military, psychological, and informational) on the other hand concern the ways in which the people of a nation organize themselves and the manner in which they alter their environment [9]. From the literature, one can define national security as: *The provision of security to the state and of human security to its citizens as well as the protection of national and human interests together with state borders through the projection of national power.*

To understand national security, one must understand the elements of national power and how they interrelate. It is convenient to organize the study of national power by distinguishing between natural and social determinants of power. For instance, resources are a natural factor, but the degree to which they are used is determined socially. Population factors, in particular, cut across the dividing line between both categories. The number of people of working age in the population affects the degree of industrialization of a nation, but the process of industrialization, in turn, can greatly alter the composition of the population.

Jablonsky points out that where people live will influence what they possess, that the number of people will influence how much they possess, what their historical experience has been will affect how they look at life, how they look at life will influence how they organize and govern themselves, and all these elements weighed in relation to the problem of national security will influence the nature, size, and effectiveness of the armed forces.

It is further argued that as a consequence, not only must each separate element be analyzed, but the effects of those elements on one another must be considered, indicating that these complexities are compounded because national power is both dynamic and relative. There is a formula to develop a rough estimate of "perceived" national power - focused primarily on a state's capacity to wage war:

$Pp = (C + E + M) \times (S + W)$ in which:

Pp = Perceived power

C = Critical mass: population and territory

E = Economic capability

M = Military capability

S = Strategic purpose

W = Will to pursue national strategy

One of the lessons from this formula is that the more tangible elements (C, E, M) that can be quantified objectively also involve varying degrees of subjective qualifications. The formula demonstrates that national power is a product-not a sum of its components. It thus serves as a reminder of the importance of relational and contextual aspects. In demonstrating the usefulness of this formula, reference is made to how the United States discovered in Vietnam that no matter how large the sum of the more tangible economic and military capabilities in relation to an adversary, their utility is determined by the intangibles of strategic purpose (S) and national will (W).

2.3   The state

The State as a concept used in this chapter refers to the modern state, historically linked to the Peace of Westphalia that in 1648 ended the thirty years' religious war in Europe. Several historians tell us that it was during the Peace of Westphalia that stipulations were made to the effect that the citizens of nations needed to be subjected to the laws of their own governments [14]. States or governments can be classified according to how much autonomy they allow their subsystems such as churches, unions, colleges, and other organs of civil society freedom to run their own affairs

Totalitarian states permit little or no subsystem autonomy. They have an official and dogmatic ideologies to which all social institutions must adhere. Democratic states give a high degree of independence to subsystems. There are some limits for the conduct of any private association, but in general, a democratic state will allow as much autonomy as is consistent with the general well-being of the society [14]. Labour unions for example can strike without fear of state reprisal, except when the nation's security is affected. No subsystem has absolute freedom, but most are allowed to run their own affairs unless they threaten the public interest.

States differ not only in the degree of initiative they allow all subsystems but also in the way political power is distributed among its different levels. Nations can be classified as unitary states or federal states, depending on the way they distribute government authority. For example Great Britain, France, Italy, Israel, and most other nations are unitary states. A single national government exercises supreme power and can override the decisions of local governments. Such actions are unlikely in federal states such as the United States, Germany, Australia, and

Canada where power is divided between the national government and provincial governments.

This brings us to the end of the exploration of the key concepts used in this chapter. We now return to the national security issues most impacted upon by globalisation in order to lay a foundation for our argument regarding the implications and the associated challenges related to the development and implementation of national ICT policies.

3.   The national security issues most impacted upon by globalisation

Ripsman and Paul [11] performed an impressive literature review on globalisation and national security out of which they distilled three batches/sets of propositions regarding military doctrines and defence policies, for a total of nine propositions. A summary of the batches and their corresponding propositions is presented below. The first batch concerned the *nature of security threats in a globalised world,* the second concerned *the effects of the phenomenon of globalisation on the pursuit of national security*, and the last related to *the erosion of the exclusivity of the state as a provider of national security.*

Their framework of analysis entails investigating the validity of these propositions by examining the military doctrines and defence policies of four categories of states which they describe as the Major Powers and Global Social Forces, the States in Cooperative Regional Subsystems, the States in Competitive Regional Subsystems, and the Weak and Failed States as well as by studying empirical data on national military establishments since the late 1980s.

The three batches with the nine propositions about these categories of states are briefly described next.

BATCH A. The nature of security threats in a globalised world:
Proposition 1: A shift in the nature of wars from Clausewitzian interstate wars to "wars of a third kind." Civil ethnic wars and wars between small states have taken the place Clausewitzian interstate wars.
Proposition 2: States, particularly the United States, face the challenge of "post-industrial warfare." This concept refers to a new kind of threat: global assault by unprofessional, ideological combatants, operating in deprived areas, targeting civilians and businesses.
Proposition 3: National security increasingly includes the non-defence areas of trade, ecology, and health as threats are increasingly economic, environmental, and disease-related.

BATCH B. The effects of the phenomenon of globalisation on the pursuit of national security:
Proposition 4: National conscription and the size of the military apparatus are declining.

Proposition 5: Defence spending is declining.

Proposition 6: National military doctrines are abandoning offence in favour of defence or deterrence.

Proposition 7: Military establishments are shifting from being war fighters to police forces.

BATCH C. Erosion of the exclusivity of the state as a provider of national security:

Proposition 8: States are privatizing security by including non-state actors in defence activities.

Proposition 9: States are increasingly pursuing security through regional institutions.

By combining the Ripsman and Paul's analysis framework, with all the above propositions and the process-based research framework developed by Roode [4] in the ENSP study, the author was able to generate a set of questions enabling a deeper probing into these national security issues most impacted upon by globalisation. Roode's process-based approach is based on the taxonomic framework of Burrell and Morgan [3].

The purpose of the taxonomic framework of Burrell & Morgan is to create a set of perspectives on the problem space, in which one consciously traverses the problem space (with its underlying ontological and epistemological assumptions) in order to develop a richer understanding of the nature of the concept under investigation. But unlike Burrell and Morgans' framework, Roode's approach allows the researcher to deliberately pose different questions to explore different aspects of the problem or situation at hand. According to Roode, the researcher is not required to accept the assumptions associated with one question, but merely enquires about different facets of the research problem to obtain as much information about it as possible. One may choose to focus only on one type of question, for instance the "How does" type question(s) in a particular study. The framework for the approach is shown in Figure 1.

(**What is?**) With this question the fundamental nature or essence of the research problem is first explored. The question aims at exposing the structure of the problem or the meaning of the underlying concepts or ideas. The purpose is to enquire radically and critically about the problem domain and its accompanying paradigm(s) in order to be able to describe the problem precisely and unambiguously. The fundamental assumption here is that such universally accepted descriptions for the concepts, ideas, and problems do exist.

(**Why is?**) The purpose of this question is to explain the real-life behaviour or characteristics of the phenomenon or problem. In doing so, the focus is on determining relationships between aspects of and/or variables within the problem domain. There is a fundamental assumption underlying this question, namely that these relationships, when uncovered, can be used to generalise about the problem domain and causal consequences.

(**How does?**) In answering this question the phenomenon or problem is directly observed and described as it manifests itself in reality.

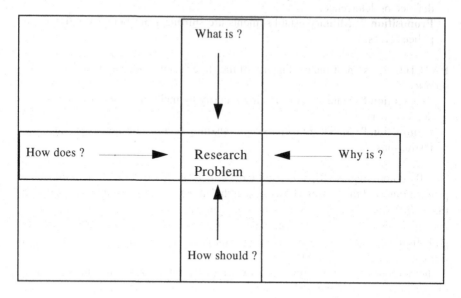

Figure 1: Research questions space (Roode, 1993, p. 11)

(**How should?**) This question focuses on the conclusions, implications or normative aspects of the research results. It is an evaluation of the results or new insights obtained during the research. In some cases it might lead to prescriptive conclusions regarding the problem domain - in other cases it might enhance the understanding of the problem domain or redefine it.

The two research questions that the ENSP study sought to address were:

> *What are the national security issues of the state most impacted upon by globalisation?*

> *What institutional means could be put in place in order to effectively deal with this impact to enhance the security of the state?*

For the design of the study, these research questions were mapped onto the Ripsman and Paul's research approach, not according to separate categories of states as described by Ripsman and Paul, but several sub-questions were raised instead, in accordance with the process-based research framework for each batch of propositions. In other words, synchronizing the Ripsman and Paul's framework for analysis and the process-based research framework gave us two major benefits. First, it gave us a framework for raising the research questions and aligning them with a sound theoretical process as well as a basis, in the form of propositional batches, on which further questions, using the process-based research framework, could be raised for a deeper analysis. For instance, the sub-questions corresponding to each of the propositional batches raised in the next section were found to be appropriate.

It is in discussing the said further probing questions in the next section that implications for security related national ICT policies we examine in this chapter will become apparent.

4.   Implications of these issues for security related national ICT Policies

BATCH A. The nature of security threats in a globalised world:

What is the current nature of security threats in a globalised world?

Cyber warfare poses a large threat to highly computerised societies. For instance, within the context of globalisation, which state can claim a good capability to understand the full scale of its vulnerability within its information infrastructure and all its networks? Could a national ICT policy be developed that could be founded on the principle of protecting and exploiting the use of cyberspace? The latest information warfare literature reports increasing methods for conducting distributed attacks and identity theft on the internet, called botnets [1]. Botnet attacks include email spamming, distributed denial of service, port scanning, remote exploitation of vulnerabilities, and self propagation to expand the botnet's size. Combined with the asymmetrical nature of information warfare and the possible inapplicability of national and international laws, it is difficult for a state to declare ICT application dominance in the projection of its national power. Unlike traditional weapon technologies, access to ICT no longer requires substantial financial resources or state support. Terrorists, drug cartels, organised crime, spies, and hackers can, with relative ease, access and offensively use ICT to support their causes and thus easily pose as threats to national security of any state.

National borders are becoming irrelevant in the global and information environment and globalisation and ICT remove the differentiation between international and domestic threats. The rapidly changing nature of the threats enabled by globalised ICT infrastructure makes vulnerabilities difficult to understand and to identify.

There is no front-line to ICT enabled information warfare. Potential battlefields are anywhere networked systems allow access.

How then do states develop sufficiently agile ICT policies to deal with this current nature of security threats in a globalised world?

BATCH B. The effects of the phenomenon of globalisation on the pursuit of national security:

How does globalisation positively contribute to national security of the state?

Globalisation facilitates interaction among groups that define themselves in terms of values, for instance human rights groups and women advocacy groups, across national boundaries. It changes and accelerates the pace with which people interact, communicate, and do business.

Computer networks and the Internet, for instance, democratise access to information and knowledge. Computer networks enable states to differently exercise their national power, especially through their effective use of information and communications technologies. States across the globe are able to rapidly move goods, information, and services.

The global economy increasingly relies on complex, interconnected network control systems for communications, energy distribution management, air, land and sea traffic management, and financial transactions. National assets can no longer be protected by traditional military and/or mechanical security means only. Because these global effects have no boundaries, they must be addressed both locally and internationally.

How does globalisation negatively contribute to national security of the state?

In a globalised world, all states face competition amongst themselves and other forms of non-state organisation. Technological globalisation makes it possible, through television and access to the Internet, for the disadvantaged and impoverished people around the globe to see how things are in other parts of the world in relation to their own, resulting in pressure being put on their own states for the improvement of their livelihood. States have limited avenues to influence the agenda of multinational businesses and agencies as well as less capacity to control information flow, goods, and services across its borders. International organised crime uses the computer network infrastructure to undermine state efforts in curbing their illegal activities. Highly networked and computerised nations are more vulnerable to cyber warfare. There are winners and losers in the global world as its effects are uneven. The question then becomes who must lose and to what extent? Or as Dexter [6] puts it, the nuances of who wins and loses what, when, and how are equally important.

Schwab paints a very gloomy but real picture on this question from a developing country's point of view:

> *"The nations of the developing world are essentially non-participant observers, watching helplessly as their commodity prises rise or fall, bond rates tumble or soar, interest on borrowed capital fluctuates, while currencies flood or evacuate the market place. Their domestic*

businesses can be made or broken in a split second, even as prices received for their agricultural or mineral products and the very amounts they can sell abroad are calculated in London, Paris, New York, Chicago, or Milan" [12].

For instance, the only sources of national security economically in the small country of Granada, the bananas, have to be opened for trade liberalization. If the sellers in Granada cannot determine the selling price of the only commodity that they have due to liberalised markets, what would this mean for the continued existence of that state?

BATCH C. Erosion of the exclusivity of the state as a provider of national security:

What are the visible signs that the exclusivity of the state as a provider of national security is being eroded?

Frost's [7] argument is compelling on this question. He argues that the combination of technology, international institutions, local governments, and non-state actors is diluting the states' monopoly on governance and creating new forms of power. He says that although states remain sovereign, their leaders are choosing to shift some of their power to international institutions because of the need for new rules to govern global transactions and to respond to new global threats. In effect, states are choosing to share their power with multinational business, international organisations, and sub-state social groups.

States are directly and indirectly compelled to comply with the international economic system due to economic globalisation. It is difficult to distinguish in cyberspace among the actions of terrorist, criminals, and nation states and thus difficult for states and their institutions to protect themselves against cyber attacks. Consequently, developing ICT policies to effectively deal with these on a state by state basis is a challenging task.

5.   Concluding discussion

Following a structured approach and the results of an earlier study that the author undertook, we have demonstrated in this chapter that globalisation renders the development and the implementation of ICT policies that are compliant to traditional national security requirements difficult across all states.

There are several implications for security related national ICT policies following the current nature of security threats pointed above. Key amongst them are Internet governance and e-government policies.

Most developed, as well as some of the developing states, have e-government systems in which satellite and other forms of wireless communication systems are used. While enhancing communication and effectiveness, they also increase the vulnerability of these states to information warfare. These kinds of threats require that policies that are based on anticipapted scenarios be considered during the development of communication systems to guarantee sufficient protection. As Baskerville [2] points out, agile information security development that anticipates threats and rapidly deploys necessary safeguards in the context of shifting systems landscapes amid pervasive systems threats needs to be developed. Advanced firewalls and virtual private networking can be used to fragment the organisational information system into security compartments and to extend a secure network architecture across unsecured public networks such as the Internet. I fully agree with Baskerville that while these are useful tools, research into techniques for applying these tools in dynamic environments is lacking. Approaches and methodologies in support of emergent security, necessitated by rapidly changing nature of threats enabled by ICT and the Internet, are urgently needed.

The underlying concern with both globalisation and national security is that of the safeguarding of interests, both human and national interests. Because ultimately national security is about the security of the individual citizen, the protection of the individual's interests by the state is as important as the protection of the interest of the state. In a globalised world, the capability with which states successfully navigate these webs of interests will determine the extent to which they are advantaged or disadvantaged by globalisation.

With the Internet not being constrained by territorial boundaries traditionally defining states and their sovereignty, the goal of developing agile security related ICT policies and their implementation must remain on the national security research agenda of all states. Even if it were possible to develop the various ICT policies to address the specific vulnerability areas mentioned earlier on in this section, integrating them into national security assurance would remain a challenge, but an important research area for all states.

References

[1]   Ahn, G., Paxton, N, & Pearson K. (2008). Understanding IRC bot behaviors in network-centric attack detection and prevention framework, *Proceedings of the 3ʳᵈ International Conference on Information Warfare and Security*. University of Nebraska, Omaha, USA, 24-25 April 2008.

[2]   Baskerville, R. (2004). Agile security for information warfare: A call for research. *Proceedings of the European Conference in Information Systems*.

[3]   Burrel,G. and G. Morgan,G. (1979). *Sociological pradigms and organizational analysis*, London: Heinemann.

[4]   Cha, V.D. (2000). Globalisation and the study of international security. *Journal of Peace Research*, 37(3), 391-403.

[5]   Dewald Roode, D. (1993). Implications for teaching of a process-based research framework for Information Systems. In Smith, L. (Ed.). *Proceedings of the International Academy for Information Management Conference*, Orlando, Florida.

[6]   Dexter, P. (2006). Globalisation: solidarity forever, Financial Mail, 07 May 2004, available on http://www.fm.co.za/cgi-bin/pp-print.pl. Accesses 26 June 2006.

[7]   Frost, E.L. (2002). Globalisation and national security: A strategic agenda, in R.L Kruger, and E.L. Frost, (Eds.) *The global century, globalisation and national security*, Hawaii: University Press of the Pacific.

[8]   Guillén, M.F. (2000). Is globalisation civilizing, destructive or feeble? A critique of five key debates in the social-science literature. *Annual Review of Sociology*, 27 (June 2000 Version).

[9]   Jablonsky, D. (2001). National power. In Cerami, J.R., Holcomb, J.F, Jr. (eds). *U.S. Army war college guide to strategy*.

[10] Phahlamohlaka, L.J. (2007). Globalisation and national security issues for the state. CRP, South African National Defence College, South Africa, June 2007.

[11] Ripsman, N.M and Paul, T.V. (2005). Globalisation and the national security state: A framework for analysis. *International Studies Review* 7, 199–227.

[12] Schwab, P. (2001). Globalisation and Africa, in Africa: A continent self-destructs. New York: Palgrave.

[13] Siponen, M. (2005). A critical assessment of IS security research between 1990-2004. *Proceedings of the European Conference in Information Systems*.

[14] Trager, F.N. & Simonie, F.L. (1989). An introduction to the study of national security, in Frank, N. Trager and Philip, S. Kronenberg (eds.), *National Security and American Society, Theory, Process, and Policy*, Manhattan: University press of Kansas.

NEXT GENERATION ICT POLICY IN SOUTH AFRICA:
TOWARDS A HUMAN DEVELOPMENT-BASED ICT POLICY

Walter Brown
Monash University South Africa, South Africa

Irwin Brown
University of Cape Town, South Africa

Abstract   This chapter discusses the critical link between human development and information and communications technology (ICT) policy in South Africa. Through a review of relevant literature, the status of human development and ICT growth in South Africa was investigated. The findings showed that South Africa is lagging behind many similar developing countries in terms of both ICT growth and human development. The South African ICT policy environment was analysed and found to lack a strong emphasis on human development. A human development-based ICT policy is advocated, and recommendations for achieving this are made.

Keywords: Human development, ICT policy, Next Generation Networks

1.   Introduction

According to the United Nations Development Programme's (UNDP) Human Development Reports, South Africa's Human Development Index (HDI) ranking (a measure of the population's life expectancy, education, literacy, and gross domestic product (GDP) per capita) declined 35 places between 1990 and 2005, while nearly all other developing countries showed significant gains [36]. Numerous papers have been written on how ICTs can contribute towards human development [7]. In South Africa, this clearly has not happened, despite its ICT infrastructure being one of the most sophisticated in Africa [2]. ICT diffusion and utilization in South Africa is limited to a small segment of the population whose HDIs are equivalent to many high income economies [2]. A large proportion of the population remains disadvantaged, with very low ICT service levels, and HDI levels equivalent to many low income economies [2]. As a result South Africa's average HDI of 121 places the country below countries with similar population levels, but significantly smaller economies such as Colombia (HDI rank 70), Thailand (74), Vietnam (109), and Egypt (111) [36].

Please use the following format when citing this chapter:

Brown, W. and Brown, I., 2008, in IFIP International Federation for Information Processing, Volume 282; *Social Dimensions of Information and Communication Technology Policy*; Chrisanthi Avgerou, Matthew L. Smith, Peter van den Besselaar; (Boston: Springer), pp. 109–123.

The focus of general ICT policy tends to be on the technology and ownership structures. This chapter suggests an urgent need for a rethink towards a more human development-based ICT policy in order to extend modern ICT services for the benefit of all South Africans. In the next section a review of the state of South Africa's human development and ICT growth is presented, followed by a discussion and critique of the current South African ICT policy focus. Implications of the findings are then considered. In conclusion, recommendations for moving towards a more human development-based ICT policy focus are made.

2.   Human development in South Africa

Human development has been defined as "the process of enlarging people's choices. Their three essential choices are to lead a long and healthy life, to acquire knowledge and to have access to the resources needed for a decent standard of living" [23]. The UNDP has developed a means of assessing human development in a nation through the use of the HDI [36]. The state of human development in South Africa is well documented in reports compiled and published by the UNDP [36]. These reports and others show that South Africa is a complex country, deeply divided into a developed "first economy", and an under-developed "second economy" [29]. Those few within the "first economy" reside and work in highly developed first world enclaves with access to sophisticated ICT infrastructure. The majority operate in the "second economy", residing in deprived urban enclaves, or in rural areas afflicted by extreme and chronic poverty [30].

As mentioned, South Africa is, as a result, ranked 121st on the HDI index, placing it in the lower half of the medium human development classification [36]. The lowest ranked country is Niger at 177 [36]. In this section, key South African issues relating to the HDI are discussed, followed by a review of South Africa's ICT growth in comparison to other countries.

2.1   Economic and social inequalities

The standard of living of a country is assessed by GDP per capita [36]. South Africa performs well on this indicator in comparison to other African countries. However, the GDP per capita masks the level of inequality between socio-economic groups within a country since it presents an overall average score. To assess the level of economic inequality in a country the Gini coefficient is used [36]. South Africa's inequality is reflected in a high Gini coefficient of 57.8. The richest 10% of its citizens consume 33.1 times more than the poorest 10%. Only one country, Botswana, has a higher GDP per capita and lower HDI rank than South Africa [36]. The implication is that both Botswana and South Africa are inefficient users of national wealth for human development.

South Africa's history of race-based segregation has led to social inequalities along racial lines. These exacerbate the economic inequalities reflected by the Gini coefficient. Classification along racial lines has been retained by the post-apartheid South Africa as a means for monitoring progress in efforts aimed at reversing racially based inequalities [9, 31]. Despite constituting 79% of the population, 76% of the lowest wage earners are Black South Africans [31]. 75% of the highest wage earners are White South Africans who represent just 10% of the population [31]. Reversing this social divide has proven to be extremely complex. Used appropriately, and with enabling policies, ICTs can and should be used to help reduce these inequalities.

2.2   Life expectancy

Life expectancy at birth reflects the ability of a population to lead a long and healthy life [36]. It is as such heavily influenced by poverty and health pandemics such as HIV/AIDS. South Africa has declining levels of life expectancy [36]. Poverty and the HIV/AIDS crisis are the primary causes. South Africa's average life expectancy is 31 years below Japan's 82.3 years [36]. As with standard of living indicators, life expectancy amongst the economically advantaged is high, but the decline is evident amongst the disadvantaged majority. It follows that ICT policy focused on the use of ICTs to assist in poverty eradication and health work should be a key priority in South Africa.

2.3   Access to mother tongue education

Education, and its less tangible but more profound concepts of knowledge and wisdom, is a critical component of human development [36]. Post-apartheid South Africa has succeeded well in expanding school enrolment to all South Africans, but quality remains problematic as reflected by the country's poor performance in the International Reading Literacy Survey of 2006 [14]. This chapter highlights just one possible contributing factor to poor educational performance - access to mother tongue education at an early age. With just 13% of young African children able to access early childhood education in their home language, compared to 62% in the next lowest region, East Asia and Pacific [35], Africa's children are clearly at a significant disadvantage. They are obliged to learn how to learn in a foreign language from a very early age. South Africa, with eleven official languages [2] and several more regional dialects, faces a daunting task in delivering high quality cost-effective education to all its citizens. ICTs present an invaluable opportunity to ameliorate this national challenge. To be effective, ICTs need supportive policies and regulatory systems that focus on education as an important component of human development.

2.4   ICT growth in South Africa

The analysis of human development has shown that South Africa faces immense challenges related to inequalities in standard of living, life expectancy, and education. ICTs can play an enabling role in addressing these challenges. In this section, South Africa's ICT growth over the past few decades is compared against other countries with similar characteristics. The costs associated with enabling technologies such as broadband interconnectivity are highlighted.

In the 1970's, South Africa shared similarities in population, economic levels and ICT development with Colombia, South Korea and Spain (see Figure 1). During the past thirty years South Korea's GDP per capita grew forty-fold, and Spain's thirteen-fold while South Africa's GDP per capita only quadrupled, barely keeping up with inflation [20]. To support economic growth during the same period, South Korea's fixed line access grew by a factor of 31.8 compared to South Africa's 2.7. In the early 1980's, South Korea introduced a national development policy of "One Family One Telephone", and delivered on it [27]. By 2005/2006, South Korea had joined the ranks of high income countries, and led the world in the Digital Opportunity Index (DOI), a new composite measure of ICT development that takes into account ICT access, use and affordability [19]. In contrast, Colombia and South Africa were ranked 80 and 86 respectively on the DOI [19]. This contrast reveals the close interrelationship between ICT development and economic development, with each reinforcing the other.

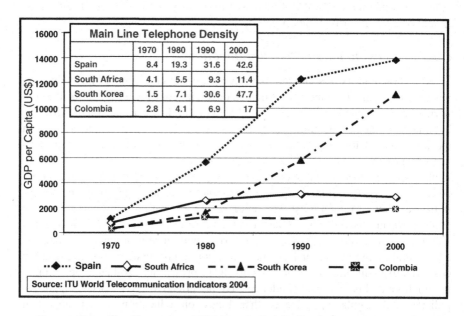

Figure 1: Thirty-Year Economic and ICT Growth: Five Similar Countries Compared [20].

The benign economic growth in South Africa over the period is mirrored by the limited growth in telephone density. During the apartheid era (pre-1994) the telecommunications infrastructure was developed to support the White-dominated "first economy". Little effort was expended on developing infrastructure for the majority of the population. In the immediate post-apartheid period after 1994, efforts were made at increasing telephone density amongst the disadvantaged, but this effort could not be sustained. Many "second economy" consumers that were provided with telephone services were unable to afford it, and lines were disconnected [8]. Mobile phone services introduced in 1994 [34] became effective substitutes for fixed line access, but their affordability remains a matter of great concern [8, 30].

Commercial Internet services were launched in South Africa in 1994 [2]. There was rapid growth from 1994 to 2000, but this was short-lived. The Internet was only affordable and accessible to those operating in the developed "first economy". Growth therefore stagnated as levels of saturation were reached in the "first economy" [2]. To date the number of Internet users per capita remains below 10%, due to the high cost and inaccessibility of Internet services to the majority of the population [2].

Affordability of ICTs is essential for human development [19]. Table 1 below compares typical South African broadband prices to Japan [15, 17]. Broadband tariffs are falling as illustrated in Table 1, but these decreases are not deep or fast enough to realise the full benefits of the full range of ICTs services as enablers of human development. In fact, the Table demonstrates the paradoxical situation that the most developed countries (e.g., Japan) often have the cheapest ICT services. In developing countries such as South Africa with much greater needs for the human development support services that ICTs offer, prices are much higher. Mobile services have partially bridged the information divide, but their knowledge delivery capacity cannot be compared with high speed fixed broadband infrastructure. Furthermore, sophisticated, leading edge data and multimedia mobile services are pervasive in the "first economy", whilst in the "second economy", simple voice and possibly SMS services are the norm [2].

Bandwidth	South Africa			Japan		
	Bandwidth limit	Price per Month (US$)		Bandwidth Limit	Price per month (US$)	
Price Change	-	Feb. 2006	Apr. 2008	-	2003	2004
192kb/s	3GB	87.54	49.14	Nil	0.25	0.11
512kb/s	10GB	207	171.71	Nil	0.70	0.31
1Mb/s	10GB	238	193.71	Nil	1.38	0.61
Data Source & Notes	http://www.interprise.co.za Access dates as per price data			Prices based on 47Mb/s http://www.itu.int/ubiquitous UNS Japan Case Study		

Table 1: Broadband Price Comparisons between South Africa and Japan [15, 17].

The analysis has revealed that ICT growth and development in South Africa has generally been unequal. Telecommunications services, with the exception of basic mobile telephony, are largely available to those that can afford it in the developed "first economy", with ICTs in general having little impact on human development in the "second economy". Efforts have been made to reach underserved communities through, for example, multipurpose community centres with mixed results [2]. In the next section, a review of ICT definitions and meanings are presented before ICT policy in South Africa is examined.

3.   Review of ICT definitions and meanings

The rapid growth of ICTs, and the commercial interests associated with them, led to fragmentation in the ICT industry and a proliferation of technical terms and acronyms. This proliferation of terms has tended to confuse and misdirect ICT policy makers and ICT users alike. Fragmentation has spawned a new divide between the "Bellheads" who built, own and defend the traditional telecommunications public switched telephone network (PSTN) infrastructures, and the "Netheads" who build, operate, and defend the Internet [32]. Policy makers have been misled by these superficial divisions, protecting "Bellheads" from competition and allowing competition by many "Netheads" while restricting their range of services to protect the "Bellheads" [6]. In this section, well-known ICT definitions are re-examined with the specific objective of supporting this chapter's proposal for a fundamental review of national ICT policies in South Africa, by returning to the original meanings of terms, and focusing attention on the human development potential of ICTs.

Before embarking on a review of selected components of ICTs, it is useful to review the prevailing definitions of the ICT acronym itself. The following definitions provide a good starting point:

Wikipedia [37]: "an umbrella term that includes all technologies for the communication of information".

Richard Heeks [13]:"'electronic means of capturing, processing, storing, and communicating information' ICTs are based on digital information held as 1s and 0s, and comprise computer hardware, software and networks".

The United Nations Development Programme (UNDP) [35]: "information-handling tools — a varied set of goods, applications and services that are used to produce, store, process, distribute and exchange information. They include the 'old' tools such as of radio, television and telephone, as well as the 'new' ICTs of computers, satellite and wireless technology and the internet".

Even within this limited range of definitions, significant differences in actual or perceived meanings are apparent. The Wikipedia [37] definition stresses the communications aspect of ICTs, Heeks [13] emphasises the digital IT aspects, and the UNDP [35] prefers a broader meaning encompassing both communications and information processing. The UNDP definition has a potentially misleading bias: the classification of selected methods of providing ICTs as "old" or "new" tools. Returning all definitions of ICT components to their original meanings will help policymakers and consumers of ICT services to focus on the services themselves, and not the manner in which they are delivered, or the technologies they use.

The definition of technology as used in the ICT acronym also needs to be reviewed and simplified for policy-making purposes. Wikipedia [37] defines technology as "a broad concept that deals with a species' usage and knowledge of tools and crafts, and how it affects a species' ability to control and adapt to its environment". Using such a definition for technology, the very ancient "African talking drum" could be described as an ICT. It was used to transmit information which affected the user community's ability to control and adapt to their environment [24]. Reverting to this simple meaning of the term "technology" should assist policy makers in refocusing attention on the benefits to be derived from the use of technology, and not on the technology itself.

The base line definitions in the following reviews were taken from the standard Oxford Dictionary.

3.1   Telecommunications

Telecommunications: *Derived from the Greek words "Tele" meaning "far, at a distance", and "Communications", the act of imparting or transmitting information*. The definition is agnostic to the technology used to move information from one place to another, and to the content and form of the information. The term applies equally to voice, numerical data or graphic images. Reverting to the term telecommunications to describe any form of electronic communications would simplify policy formulation and regulation of the industry, and would improve user understanding and therefore assimilation and use. It would also be consistent with the desire for convergence of the ICT industry, and with the emerging concept and definition of Next Generation Networks (NGNs) [16, 18].

3.2   Telegraphy

Telegraphy: *Tele – Gk. far, at/from a distance: Graphē – Gk. writing*. The first digital electronic telecommunication, the *"Telegraph"* required a graphic input/output interface to enable satisfactory communications. Personal computers mobile telephones, broadband wireless and fibre optical cables have replaced the original Morse code telegraphic system and its wired infrastructure, but the principles remain unchanged. The Internet-based email "telegraph" has become a critical component of the knowledge society. The complexity of its current policy and regulatory control provisions has prevented this first ICT from benefiting the majority of South Africa's citizens.

3.3   Telephony

Telephony: *Tele – Gk. Far, at/from a distance: Phōnē – Gk. voice*. The success of telephony was immense soon after its invention. It led to a cacophony of illogical ICT policies such as the United Kingdom's Telecommunications Policy of 1888 [21], which protected the British Post Office's monopoly for 75 years by legislating that a telephone was a "telegraph", and that a telephone call was a "telegram". The ICT industry has introduced a variety of acronyms and jargon to describe small variations in the manner in which telephony is delivered. We now have "old" telephony or Public Switched Telephone Networks (PSTN) [35]. Voice over Internet Protocol (VoIP), Value Added Networks (VANs) which are little more than private telephone networks, global Skype telephone services, and a wide variety of telephone systems differentiated only by the fact that they use radio (wireless) as the main transport platform. This cacophony of terms and jargon continues to increase as new ICT technologies present slightly differentiated applications and delivery opportunities. The commercial interests of the ICT industry are such that great pressure is exerted on policymakers and regulators to differentiate similar services for short term commercial gain. This chapter proposes that the best defence against such pressure is to rationalise and simplify all ICT definitions. By defining and classifying just one product, telecommunications, and obliging the ICT industry to compete on how best to deliver the richest and most cost-effective telecommunications to consumers, effective use and growth of information services would be promoted.

3.4   Radio

Radio: *The process of* "wirelessly" *delivering telecommunications through the air* (include Television here). The early use of the radio frequency spectrum to enable telecommunications was initially unencumbered by autocratic government policy and regulatory controls. Its value was nevertheless such that greed, stock fraud, and patent infringements encouraged close scrutiny by governments and their law enforcement agencies [5]. The control of the radio-frequency spectrum became highly politicised. These controls resulted in numerous classifications of telecommunications products delivered over radio transmission paths (e.g., radio, television, walkie-talkie, cell phone; wireless). South Africa's failure to provide high quality affordable broadband connections to the country's majority "second economy" citizens can be partly attributed to the complex system of classification and controls governing the use of the radio-frequency spectrum. Reducing the number of unique ICT classifications that govern spectrum allocation can help focus policy and regulatory systems on the human development potential of this resource.

3.5   Data

Data: (a) known facts or things used as a basis for inference or reckoning (b) quantities or characters operated on by a computer etc. The introduction of computers to process and transport data spawned a new data communications industry. The main feature that differentiated it from other forms of communications technology was the coding method used. Data in analogue form was modulated into a digital format and demodulated by the receiving terminal to reproduce the data in its original analogue form. In the evolving NGNs [18], all forms of data will be transported in digital formats. In reality, they already are, but just routed or switched differently. This renders the term data communications obsolete, as it can be included under the broad rubric of telecommunications.

3.6   Information

Information: *(a) Something told, knowledge; (b) items of knowledge; (c) news.* Information is the core product of the ICT industry. For the purposes of policymaking and regulation there are only two information components of the ICT acronym: the unregulated information processing elements (IT) that enable information storage and processing, and the heavily regulated communications elements that transport processed or unprocessed information from one unregulated processing terminal to another. There seems little reason why the unregulated IT elements that encompass information processing functions should play any role in ICT policymaking or regulation, and yet they do. South Africa's current national ICT policy, the Electronic Communications Act of 2005 [10], has gone a long way to separating the IT sector from the communications sector, but still includes as its primary objective to "*promote and facilitate the convergence of telecommunications, broadcasting, information technologies and other services contemplated in this Act*" [10]. Simplifying this policy by focusing only on the transmission and receipt of information, i.e., telecommunications would be of great value. Such simplification would ease the regulatory process and promote the use of ICTs for human development. As technological advances enable more cost-effective delivery of any type of information in any mode, the retention of complexity in policies and regulatory controls is counterproductive. Telecommunications, the act of imparting or transmitting information over distance, would seem to be an adequate rationalization for control purposes.

3.7   Computers

Computers (and "Computer networks" aka the Internet): (a) *Calculating machines (b) Electronic machines used to process information.* The Internet, often defined as a network of computers, may use complex arithmetic processes to enable telecommunications, but its main input/output product is information transported from one place to another. The Internet is clearly a telecommunications network that uses computers as key components. It is most certainly not a computer network that uses telecommunications networks to compute. This potential to confuse and fragment the ICT industry was recognised early in the life of the Internet [12]. As early as 1963, the architects of the Internet anticipated the deep divisions and fragmentations that the overlapping computer and telecommunications industries could cause, and specifically described the nascent Internet as follows: "*The ARPA theme is that the promise offered by the computer as a communication medium between people, dwarfs into relative insignificance the historical beginnings of the computer as an arithmetic engine.*"

And *"It is not proper to think of networks as connecting computers. Rather, they connect people using computers to mediate. The great success of the Internet is not technical, but in **human** impact"* [12].

This profound statement was to a large extent ignored, as the industry fragmented. The emerging NGN [16, 18] offers an opportunity to converge all thinking, reverting to the single term telecommunications to describe all modes of transporting information, and fostering the selection of the most effective quality assured technologies available.

3.8   Summary of the discussion on ICT definitions

If all forms of moving information from one place to another could be allowed to revert to the original all-embracing term for the process - telecommunications, the policy and regulatory processes would be eased significantly. Technological advances enable full convergence of all fragmented forms of telecommunications. It is therefore possible for ICT policy focus to shift to the use of ICTs for human development. The guiding principles for policy reform could be reduced to:

Simplicity: The cumbersome licensing laws and control mechanisms add significantly to entry costs, impede effective competition, raise user prices, and effectively slow down national growth and local participation.

Focus on Information: National ICT policies should focus on the principal product of ICTs - the information needed for human, social and economic development, rather than technological complexity, commercial interests, or ownership issues.

Affordability and quality: New policies should encourage innovation at all levels. They should maximize the opportunities presented by new technologies to reduce infrastructure costs and access prices.

Ubiquity: National ICT policies should be continuously reviewed to ensure that access to all forms of telecommunication services will become available to all segments of the community. NGNs provide an invaluable opportunity to ensure ubiquity, effectiveness and ease of use of information products [16, 18].

Competition: National ICT policies should promote competition by lowering barriers to entry, and by monitoring the industry to ensure that dominant market power is not abused. Competition policy should focus equally on encouraging new competitive entrants, and on the competitive structures of the industry as a whole.

4.   ICT policies in South Africa

It is not the purpose of this chapter to present a rigorous analysis or review of South Africa's national ICT policy. Several studies have undertaken such analyses, and most have concluded that South Africa's current national policy, represented by the Electronic Communications Act of 2005 (ECA) [10], is reasonably well constructed and intentioned [4]. It is effective implementation that remains elusive, however [4]. It has been observed that *"South Africa continues to descend down international scales of competitiveness and e-readiness in the telecommunications sector*" [4]. This section discusses the major issues that impede effective implementation of the current policy.

4.1   Little focus on the utility of ICTs

The imperatives for rapid development of ICTs in South Africa are well known and desired by South Africa's political and social leaders. The Electronic Communications Act began as the Convergence Bill, in line with recommendations of a sector analysis report published by the Yankee Group in 2003 [38]. The Yankee Group report emphasised the convergence of broadcasting and telecommunications, which became the dominant theme of the ECA. A high-level examination of the ECA indicates three dominant themes: licensing, broadcasting, and the structure and funding mechanism of the Universal Service and Access Agency of South Africa. The major focus of the act is control and enforcement, with little focus on the content or utility of ICTs.

4.2   Licensing delays

Implementation of the ICT licensing changes resulting from the ECA has been extremely costly, time consuming, and frustrating for existing and new ICT businesses. ICASA, the state ICT regulator, has limited capacity to convert all existing ICT licenses to the new competitive arrangements in the short term demanded, and has consequently delayed the licensing of new entrants. This has delayed the growth of the critical South African ICT industry, especially its expansion to effectively service the needs of South Africa's majority "second economy" citizens.

4.3   Slow implementation of policy

Evidence of the slow implementation of policy reform is the process of local loop unbundling (LLU). Releasing the relatively large number of fully depreciated copper cable for competitive use by SMEs, especially in the under-serviced low income urban areas would go a long way towards introducing broadband services in these areas. The Department of Communications has studied this possibility extensively, and set a target of 2011 for completion of LLU [11]. Even the South African President's expression of exasperation over this delay has had little effect on the lengthy LLU liberalization process [26]. Meanwhile, South Africa's broadband prices remain high in comparison to the developed world [15, 17], and out of reach to the communities that need them most for development.

4.4   Ownership of ICT businesses

An important feature of national ICT policy is the concept of ownership of ICT business entities. Although this aspect is not covered specifically in the ECA, a separate legal provision stipulates the levels of Black South African ownership and management control of ICT business entities [3]. The Department of Trade and Industry (DTI) has been tasked with warehousing all Black Economic Empowerment (BEE) Charters [3]. The BEE charters are clearly aimed at reversing the historical exclusion of Black South Africans from economic activity. The fine balance of redressing historical injustices while developing a modern high technology ICT driven knowledge society can, and has in some instances resulted in conflicts and contradictions. Lengthy delays in the introduction of effective competition in the ICT sector have slowed economic development [8]. The controversy surrounding recent proposals to amend the ECA to license Infraco, the proposed state-owned national and international broadband provider [25], and efforts to prevent private sector international fibre optic cables from landing in South Africa, created controversy and embarrassment for the government [1, 22, 33].

5.   Discussion and implications

Despite a well-formulated and well-intentioned ICT policy environment in South Africa, several problems persist. The analysis above has identified the lack of focus on the utility of ICTs, licensing delays, slow implementation of policy, and a fixation on ownership of ICT businesses as problematic. These issues may be the reason why ICTs seem to be having little effect on human development in South Africa's "second economy". A human-development-based ICT policy would make the key elements and components of human development explicit in the policy framework. Licensing delays and slow implementation of policy are at odds with the urgency required to address the socio-economic deprivation in poor communities. A focus on ownership structures, while necessary to address racial inequalities, also diverts attention away from speedy delivery of services to the poor. In addition, government has tended to adopt a techno-centric approach to implementation of services in under-served areas with generally disappointing results [28]. By ignoring critical human development components and community participative issues in ICT for Development (ICT4D), many initiatives have failed [8, 28]. Simplifying South Africa's ICT policy and regulatory systems through simplification and rationalization of the underlying definitions of the ICT industry, focussing on the human development utility of ICTs, and promoting unfettered competition in a horizontally structured NGN industry would be an elegant starting point for this development.

6.   Conclusion and recommendations

South Africa is faced with immense socio-economic problems emanating from the many divides created by apartheid. ICTs present a means of addressing some of these problems. Simpler human development-focused ICT policies and regulatory systems are a prerequisite for the introduction of affordable ubiquitous modern ICT products and services to all South Africans.

This chapter has very briefly summarised the human development challenges faced by the South African nation as a whole. A sample of key statistics reveals that South Africa's ICT growth is lagging behind equivalent emerging economies. If South Africa is to join the global knowledge society, the country will need highly effective ICTs that are accessible, affordable, and used by the majority of South Africans. Creating such an ICT environment demands simple yet effective human development-based ICT policies and regulatory systems that can be implemented quickly and transparently. Such simplicity will encourage ICT service providers and consumers to participate more in the process of development. A human development focus will ensure ICTs have a positive impact on standard of living, life expectancy and improved education especially in the marginalized "second economy".

The following recommendations are offered as additional activities that can lead to early policy and regulatory changes to support improved human development through improved use of ICTs.

Recognition: Begin high level dialogue using all available forums to create or reinforce awareness of the link between ICTs and human development. South African government organs, ICT industry representatives, and civil society should be included in these discussions.

Research: Initiate research programmes aimed specifically at ICT policy reforms. Action research projects, for example, will allow for monitoring of the intervention process and enable the identification of any policy or regulatory barriers that impede successful achievement of the research objectives. These will provide potent arguments for the required reforms.

Advocacy: Opportunities to create awareness and influence key role players in the human development process should be utilized.

Development: The introduction of a national NGN Forum should be encouraged, focused on developing consensus on the nature and form of the concept. The desired NGN Forum could be a new stand alone initiative, or a special focus group within existing forums, societies or associations. The forum or focus groups should preferably comprise multi-disciplinary groups to analyse and initiate action programs along the lines of the many highly influential NGN forums that exist in virtually all regions of the world except Africa.

Systematic implementation of the above proposals should result in a change in South Africa's ICT environment, and consequently South Africa's overall development and entry into the global knowledge society.

References

[1]   Barron, C. (2007). SA undersea broadband cables are in a tangle, Business Times, 16th Sep, http://mybroadband.co.za/news/Telecoms/1328.html, Accessed 30 November 2007.

[2]   Brown, I., Collins, T., Maleka, B., Morrison, D., Muganda, N., & Speight, H. (2007). Global diffusion of the Internet XI: Internet diffusion and its determinants in South Africa: The first decade of democracy (1994-2004) and beyond. *Communications of the Association for Information Systems*, 19, 142-182.

[3]   DTI: Department of Trade and Industry (2004). ICT empowerment charter working group, http://www.thedti.gov.za/bee/beecharters.htm, Accessed 24 April 2008.

[4]   Esselaar, S., Gillwald A., & Stork C. (2006). South African telecommunications sector performance review 2006. LINK Centre Public Policy Research Paper No 8, Witwatersrand University, South Africa.

[5]   Fayant, F. (1907). Fools and their money, *Success Magazine*, 9-11, 49-52 Available at: http://earlyradiohistory.us/1907fool.htm, Accessed 30 November 2007.

[6]   Frieden, R. (2002). Revenge of the Bellheads: How the Netheads lost control of the Internet, *Telecommunications Policy*, 26 (7-8), 425 – 444.

[7]   Gilholly, D (2005). Innovation and investment: Information and communication technologies and the Millennium Development Goals. United Nations Information and Communications Technologies Task Force.

[8]   Gillwald, A. & S. Esselaar (2004). South African ICT sector performance review. LINK Centre Public Policy Research Paper No 7, Witwatersrand University, South Africa.

[9]   Government of the Republic of South Africa (1998). Employment Equity Act No. 55, Government Gazette, 19 October, 1998.

[10]   Government of the Republic of South Africa (2006). Act No. 36 of 2005: Electronic Communications Act 2005. The Government Gazette Volume 490 number 28743 dated 18th April 2006.

[11]   Government of the Republic of South Africa (2008). Notice to invite public participation in the Local Loop Unbundling process, http://www.info.gov.za/speeches/2008/08022908451001.htm, Accessed 01 May, 2008.

[12]   Hauben, M. (n.d.) History of ARPANET, http://www.dei.isep.ipp.pt/~acc/docs/arpa.html, Accessed 30 November 2007.

[13]   Heeks, R. (1999). Information and communications technologies, poverty and development. Institute for Development Policy and Management, University of Manchester.

[14]   IAEA: International Association of Educational Achievement (2007). PIRLS 2006 international report, Boston: TIMSS & PIRLS International Study Centre, Lynch School of Education, Boston College.

[15]   Interprise (2008). ADSL Pricing.

[16]   ITU: International Telecommunication Union (2004). ITU-T recommendation Y.2001 (12/2004) - General overview of NGN.

[17]   ITU: International Telecommunications Union (2005). Ubiquitous network societies: The case of Japan. ITU, http://www.itu.int/ubiquitous. Accessed 01 May 2008.

[18]   ITU: International Telecommunication Union (2007). Trends in telecommunications reform: The road to Next Generation Networks (NGN). ITU.

[19]   ITU: International Telecommunication Union (2007). World information society report 2007: Beyond WSIS. ITU and United Nations Conference on Trade and Development (UNCTAD).

[20]   ITU: International Telecommunications Union (2008). World telecommunications/ICT indicators database, http://www.itu.int/ITU-D/ict/publications/world/world.html, Accessed 01 May 2008.

[21] Levy, B. & Spiller, P. (2002). The institutional foundations of regulatory commitment: A comparative analysis of telecommunications regulation, *Journal of Law, Economics, and Organization*, 10(2), 201-246.

[22] Mochiko, T. (2007). State demands slice of Seacom pie, Business Report, 23rd Aug, http://mybroadband.co.za/news/Telecoms/1068.html, Accessed 30 November 2007.

[23] OECD (2003). OECD glossary of statistical terms. http://stats.oecd.org/glossary/detail.asp?ID=1265, Accessed 01 May 2008.

[24] Ong, W. (1977). African talking drums and oral noetics, *New Literary History*, 8(3), 411-429.

[25] Polity.org.za (2007). Broadband Infraco Bill, http://www.polity.org.za/, Accessed 30 November 2007.

[26] Presidency: Republic of South Africa (2007). President Mbeki meets the ICT Advisory Council, http://www.thepresidency.gov.za/show.asp?type=pr&include=president/pr/2007/pr08 24821.htm, Accessed 30 November 2007.

[27] Reynolds, T., Kelly, T. and Jin-Kyu, J. (2005). Ubiquitous network societies: The case of the Republic of Korea. ITU, Available at http://www.itu.int/ubiquitous. Accessed 30 November 2007.

[28] Roode, D., Speight, H., Pollock, M., & Weber, R. (2004). It's not the digital divide – it's the socio-techno divide! *Proceedings of the 13th European Conference on Information Systems*, Turku, Finland, June 14-16, 2004.

[29] SARPN: South African Regional Poverty Network (2004). Readings on the second economy, http://www.sarpn.org.za/documents/d0000830/index.php, Accessed 19 December 2005.

[30] Skuse, S., & Cousins, T. (2007). Managing distance: Rural poverty and the promise of communication in post-Apartheid South Africa. *Journal of Asian and African Studies*, 42(2), 185-207.

[31] Stats SA: Department of Statistics, South Africa (2003). Census 2001, http://www.statssa.gov.za/SpecialProjects/Census2001/Census2001.htm Accessed 22 July 2003.

[32] Steinberg, S. (1996). Netheads vs. Bellheads, Wired, 4.10, http://www.wired.com/wired/archive/4.10/atm.html, Accessed 30 November, 2007.

[33] Stones, L. (2007). Undersea cable plan tangled in acrimony, Business Day, 5th Sep, http://www.businessday.co.za/articles/article.aspx?ID=BD4A556150, Accessed 30 November 2007.

[34] Telkom (2006). Highlights of the telecommunications history of South Africa. Telkom, http://www.telkom.co.za/, Accessed 06 December 2006.

[35] UNDP: United Nations Development Programme (2004). Regional human development report: Promoting ICT for human development in Asia 2004: Realising the Millennium Development Goals. UNDP.

[36] UNDP: United Nations Development Programme (2004 to 2006). Human development reports 2004, 2005, 2006. UNDP, http://hdr.undp.org/en/reports/. Accessed 30 November 2007.

[37] Wikipedia (2008). Wikipedia, http://www.wikipedia.org/, Accessed 01 May 2008.

[38] Yankee Group (2003). South African communications, 2002-2008: Market review and analyses. The Yankee Group, 31 St. James Ave., Boston MA 02116.

CHALLENGES OF ICT POLICY FOR RURAL COMMUNITIES:
A CASE STUDY FROM SOUTH AFRICA

Mpostol Jeremia Mashinini
Sithabile Technology Group, South Africa

Abstract: It is alleged that rural people in South Africa are being excluded from the rest of the world in terms of communication and exchange of information due to lack of appropriate ICT policies. This research used grounded theory method to study the local authority of Dr S.J. Moroka in order to understand the limitations of the South African ICT policy for poor rural communities. It found lack of leadership for integrating multiple policy initiatives and evidence of a culture of non-compliance with policies. These are major challenges that need to be addressed. This chapter makes several practical suggestions for the integration of isolated, disadvantaged, and poverty-stricken rural communities into the rest of the world, enabling them to benefit from ICT-related services on a sustainable basis.

Keywords: Traditional leadership, grounded theory method, ICT Policies, rural communities, South Africa

1. Introduction

Some intellectuals and policy makers question whether poor people living in rural areas in developing countries such as South Africa need to be provided with advanced communication technologies and even warn about the potential harmful effects of attempting to transform poor rural communities into cyber communities [4]. They point out that the provision of clean water, roads, improved primary health care, and schools for teaching people to read and write as a means of improving their quality of life are far more important than providing people in rural communities with computer access to data networks. Nevertheless, the South African Government has been making efforts to provide communication services to rural communities and enable them to be included in an increasingly more electronically connected world.

Hence, this paper seeks to answer the question how can the current ICT policies of the South African Government aiming at the formation of cyber communities in rural areas improve quality of life in these areas? At present South African rural communities are being excluded from the rest of the world in terms of communication, exchange of information, and usage of ICT-related services.

Please use the following format when citing this chapter:

Mashinini, M.J., 2008, in IFIP International Federation for Information Processing, Volume 282; *Social Dimensions of Information and Communication Technology Policy*; Chrisanthi Avgerou, Matthew L. Smith, Peter van den Besselaar; (Boston: Springer), pp. 125–137.

This chapter seeks to explore existing challenges and provide suggestions for action that may enable the integration of isolated, disadvantaged, and poverty-stricken rural communities into an increasingly relying on ICT world. The structure of the chapter is as follows. Firstly, the background to the environment where the research was conducted is provided. Secondly, the research methodology used to collect and analyse data is described and justified. Thirdly, there are discussions on key findings such as the current challenges, causes of the challenges, and how these challenges can be corrected. Finally, conclusions drawn from this research are summarised.

It has become obvious that in the face of major challenges such as the total lack of even the most basic infrastructures in a community, namely roads, clinics and schools, that any ICT policy needs to be designed to play a role in addressing or helping to eliminate these critical problems.

1.1   Background of Dr. S.J. Moroka (research area)

Dr. S.J. Moroka was identified as a rural area ideally suited to the aims and objectives of this research because of the lack of basic services, lack of suitable infrastructure, and social challenges, among others. It is a rural area that has some exposure to ICT usage and related services on a small scale. It is a local authority situated within Mpumalanga province. The population is estimated between 1 million to 2 million people and it covers an area of about 267,626 hectares. It is governed by a local authority under the leadership of a Mayor (Molefe) and King Mayisha III (Ndebele King). Prior to the 1994 elections, Dr. S.J. Moroka was governed by traditional authorities while administrative activities were carried out by the King and the local Chiefs. During the apartheid regime, few infrastructural development projects were initiated within this area as it was subject to a separate development policy.

This historical situation created a number of challenges that continue to face Dr. S.J. Moroka. These challenges can be summarised as follows: poor infrastructure, unattractive investment opportunities owing to traveling distances, a scattered population, and a shortage of skilled labour. The road network into Dr. S.J. Moroka has suffered from the lack of infrastructural development. Access to even the most basic of services, such as primary health care and education, is difficult due to the lack of transport. Lack of buying power and the extremely slow and low level of economic activity preclude the establishment of a vibrant, service-orientated financial services sector on which to base development. Dr. S.J. Moroka lacks sufficiency in clinics, medical doctors, and other health related services.

This situation forces patients seeking medical help to travel to the nearest clinic and from there they are referred to a distant regional hospital that is servicing communities far beyond its capacity. Cultural and ethnic differences continue to make communication and co-operation difficult in the delivery and administration of key services and projects. A poor economic environment has contributed to the high level of abject of poverty within the Dr. S.J. Moroka community. There is a heavy reliance among people on state pensions and children's grants.

According to the Government Report [6], a number of problems exist with regard to the use of ICT in rural areas and attempts to deliver good quality services to all rural people using ICT. Admission of failure to achieve this initiative resulted in the South African Cabinet, led by the President Thabo Mbeki, organising visits to various areas to evaluate whether or not community needs are being met. Prompted by concerns expressed by several rural communities [6], a commission was established within the President's Office headed up by Prof. W. Nkuhla to investigate the problems. The following problems were identified (in no specific order): low level of community literacy, lack of ICT awareness, ICT programs currently implemented do not produce adequate results, inadequate ICT infrastructure, a process of policy formulation that is not suitable for the community needs. Many rural communities share common problems associated with education, health, land, and job opportunities.

1.2   Landscape of current ICT policies in South Africa

According to the South African Minister of Communication [8], "the history of ICT policies in SA did not address the needs of all people. Apartheid skewed the manner in which telecommunication infrastructure was established in South Africa". As a result the telecommunication network embodied the characteristics of racial duality. For example, in black formal townships the telephone infrastructure existed, but it was inadequately provided and maintained, while in neighbouring white urban areas the telecommunication infrastructure was well established and supported. In black rural areas, there was a total absence of telecommunication networks [5].

Furthermore, under the previous political dispensation, there was no prospect of rural communities being brought into the mainstream of the conventional telecommunications network as income levels were extremely low and economic activity was often at a standstill. Issues of affordability and privatisation have been priorities for the government to ensure proper empowerment [1].

Convergence within ICT, where current technology allows multiple operations to take place in parallel (such as the ability of a single cable to carry both voice and data) further enhances the potential role to be played by ICT in service delivery to rural communities. In recognising the power of convergence, whereby a single multi-purpose community centre in a rural area can be positioned to serve citizens, the government has recognised the importance of how essential it is to provide accessibility to infrastructure to all people. This has led the government to strive to meet the demand to achieve universal service as urgently as possible. The delivery of universal service is largely dependent on human resource capacity within the industry. Therefore, the National Department of Communications was established to ensure that ICT policies are developed and well implemented. Furthermore, the department was set up to ensure that proper communication and dissemination of information from the national government through the Provincial and to the local authorities was carried out. It initiated an internship programme whereby more than 1,000 students are being trained in each ICT sector. The department's mandate includes the provisioning of a "one-stop-service" government information centre for all ICT policies in South Africa to be coordinated centrally [2].

2.   Research methodology

In this research we used the grounded theory method to address the research question. Grounded theory allows the following benefits. Firstly, it allows a close interaction with the rural community and the researcher. Secondly, the analysis of the different categories by means of identifying properties and dimensions is described together with their relationships and connections. This ensures a better understanding of how to co-ordinate the different relationships. Thirdly, the grounded theory method provides for different types of conditions that address the research question. Fourthly, this method might be more reflective of reality especially the current challenges regarding the status of ICT policies and their leadership that this research seeks to address. Fifthly, the researcher using a grounded theory approach tends to be collaborative and discursive in nature, being in continuous interaction with ideas and in the generation of ideas through constructive criticism and discourse. Sixth, this method has no preconceived ideas; it is shaped and detected by the data from the respondents. Lastly, it is not rigid but flexible as the situation changes. Hence this method set up a framework on how to ensure effective data collection and analysis.

Data was collected through interviews in a number of organisations. The organisations that were selected are those that form part of the rural community and they perform specific roles and provide certain core services. The key organisations that were selected are indicated as follows.

- Organisations that were actively involved in educating and training community members on ICT, community services, and general skills training. These organisations were Siyabuswa Education Improvement Development Empowerment Trust (SEIDET), KwaNdebele Computer Education Centre (KCEC), Kusile Self Help Association for the Disabled (KSHAD), Super Web Trust (SWT), and Nogijima CC.
- Organisations that are involved in church-related services such as preaching the gospel of God, initiating projects through churches, for example, feeding schemes for those who do not have food, donations of clothing and blankets, training people on self-help projects such as gardening, sewing and so on. Such organisations include the Apostolic church, the Methodist and Faith Mission churches.
- Organisations that are involved in political activities such as deciding on key strategic policies and projects will be implemented within the area. Civil organisations form part of the labour movement within political

groupings that play a role in protecting workers' rights in different working environments. These organisations are the African National Congress (ANC), the Pan African Congress (PAC), the Democratic Alliance (DA), and other smaller local parties such as Sindawonye MaNdebele.

- Traditional structures being all organisations under the leadership of the Kings and Chiefs, governed by traditional authority. They are mainly grouped according to the language spoken, cultural activities practiced, and location. The structures are further responsible for all the traditional and cultural affairs of the community. The leaders were Ngwenyama Mayisha II (the main leader), Chief P Mahlangu, Chief S Mgwezani, and others.

- Economic structures that are mainly involved in business related activities. The main focus being agriculture services where people practice small-scale farming in their own backyards. Small businesses are also assisted in how to grow their businesses to become big corporates through such economic structures. Some of the organisations that are actively involved include the National African Federated Chamber of Commerce (NAFCOC), Small Medium African Farmers Union (SMAFU), and *stokvels* (an informal way of investing money on a small scale).

- Groups of professionals with different expertise such as nursing, lawyers, medical doctors, police officers, and administrators were part of the selected people. Non-professional individuals, namely, those people who do not have any experience and are called unskilled labour, were also interviewed. The selection of the different organisations and people was considered to be exploratory. Therefore, the research was limited to those organisations and individuals that operated within Dr. S.J. Moroka in terms of services. These comprise the selected groups from which data was collected.

Hence, interviews were conducted according to the different roles of the respondents and ordinary people (users) included in this research. Letters were also sent to all the leaders of the communities explaining the research to be conducted. The letters sent were followed by formal gatherings with all the different leaders, namely, traditional, political, civil society, and the like. The rural community consists of people with diverse cultures and different languages. For example, most of the questions were asked in Ndebele. The researcher had the ability to read and write the same language. As a result, different languages were used when asking questions in order to make sure that all the respondents understood the questions asked.

The analysis followed the open coding technique of grounded theory to uncover, name, and develop concepts. In this way, we opened the text and exposed the thoughts, ideas, and meanings contained therein. Without the first analytical step, the rest of the analysis and communications that follow could not occur. Open coding allowed the data to be broken down into discrete parts, closely examined and compared for similarities and differences. Events, happenings, objects, and actions that were found to be conceptually similar in nature or related in meaning were grouped under more abstract "categories".

3.   Discussion of key findings

The key findings are grouped together in accordance with the main concepts, properties, and dimensions detected in the data. However, the core idea emerging from the grounded theory method is that the leadership required to integrate the different elements is not effective as this stage. For example, the challenges arising from policies not being implemented include a lack of capacity and processes, and the inappropriate recognition of leadership roles. Appropriate leadership is needed to provide the necessary training, ensure implementation, plan strategies, align policies, and consult with all relevant stakeholders. The key findings of our research are described in some detail below.

3.1   Current status on challenges in rural areas

The major challenges identified by the respondents were grouped into the following categories. Firstly, the low level of education in rural areas results in a lack of skills to perform key operational activities that could benefit the community. Hence, most of the people living in rural areas are unskilled, while those with skills move to urban areas to seek better work. Furthermore, the high demand for farm labouring means that children under the age of ten often work on farms, and thus receive no education at all. Secondly, the lack of general infrastructure and poor road quality are major challenges. Roads are not designed for heavy vehicle transport. The import and export of goods is thus severely restricted. The existing gravel roads cross streams and are full of potholes, often making it impossible for road users. The electrical infrastructure, installed and supported by ESKOM, is unreliable and unstable; in windy or wet conditions, the power goes off. Furthermore, the present supply does not meet consumer demand, which has resulted in power cuts.

Thirdly, lack of ICT infrastructure within South Africa. In terms of backbone and bandwidth, this infrastructure is provided exclusively by Telkom. However, Telkom has a deployment strategy that concentrates on urban areas as opposed to rural areas. Lack of financial support to maintain the existing infrastructure has become another major obstacle. Thus, the lack of ICT infrastructure negatively impacts on the entire infrastructure and poses a grave threat to the implementation of ICT services in rural areas. Fourthly, lack of environmental scanning to ensure that projects satisfy user requirements and add value to citizens, an appropriate needs analysis is required. It has happened in the past that authorities have established projects which were not needed by the community members and thus there was no return on the money spent.

Fifth, lack of policy implementation. Policies serve as the underlying structure to plan and ensure proper guidance of the different ICT-related services. In the current situation not all stakeholders are involved in the development of such policies. Therefore, both the policies themselves and their implementation are inadequate. Most of the projects thus fail in terms of clear deliverables, milestones, associated risks, and so on. Sixth, economic challenges, rural areas are characterised by challenges, principally the lack of financial resources. Funding is limited, if not non-existent, especially for ICT projects. The major challenge for people applying for grants is that they are required to provide guarantees, balance sheets, and previous credit records. Lastly, social challenges. Social challenges directly impact on the daily life of individuals and the community as a whole. The major problem is the high rate of unemployment. Among the consequences of unemployment are poverty, depression, alcoholism, drug addiction, and crime. In situations of poverty diseases arise and spread that further impact on the well-being of the community. Although not all poverty-stricken people turn to crime, certain people who have no food to feed their children sometimes resort to theft.

3.2   Current status on leadership in rural areas

According to our analysis of the data from the respondents, there are different leadership divisions, such as community leaders, church leaders, traditional leaders, political leaders, etc. Traditional leadership is seen by the community as the principal leadership role, the one which makes things happen. Traditional leaders are currently recognised as the true leaders of the people. In many instances, they are born leaders, not elected by the community, but rather groomed to be good leaders. Being natural leaders, traditional leaders have many followers. One of the reasons why they are so highly respected is that they act in accordance with the will and needs of their people. Traditional leadership is therefore directly linked to the community. This could explain why a project introduced by the local council without endorsement of traditional community leaders might not be adopted. Even though the project may be viable, it first requires the approval of the traditional leadership.

3.3   Current status on policy development life cycle

The main driving force that served as the central nervous system of the policies we studied has been the policy development life cycle [2]. The first phase of the life cycle model is the policy development process. This process outlines all the processes that need to be followed when developing any of the policies. The current state is that policy development has reached saturation stage, where there are too many policies being developed almost daily.

The challenges of developing such policies include the capacity to develop policies, the ability to consult with all the relevant stakeholders, and the communication process currently used. At this stage, the policies being developed do not address the needs of the people. They are often seen as irrelevant to the society.

The second phase is policy implementation. This process is non-existent, particularly in the rural areas. Policies currently are not being implemented due to lack of capacity and the fact that they are irrelevant to the needs of the people.

The third phase is policy monitoring. If policies are implemented, they need to be monitored and measured against defined goals. Monitoring will help to ensure and confirm that they meet their goals. Monitoring will also help to identify gaps during implementation so that adjustments can be made in order to address problems and therefore close gaps. However, our research could not study this stage of the policy process. As policy implementation is non-existent, no monitoring is taking place.

The last phase of the policy process is policy evaluation. Evaluation should be designed to measure and understand the impacts on policy of both internal and external elements such as changes in the political landscape, economic issues, social challenges, internal regulations, and so on. Owing to the fact that policies are not being effectively developed, implemented or monitored, no evaluation is taking place either.

3.4   Reasons why policies are not implemented

There are various reasons why policies could not be implemented. This section discusses some of them. The assumption often made about rural people is that they are not educated. Thus they are ignored when it comes to decision making. It is assumed that they cannot add value to the development of policies, even though in the end such policies will affect them. To complicate the challenge, the government, when communicating information via the media, mainly uses Internet services with separate Web sites for the each department. That is where many of the government tenders, vacant positions, departmental services, and so on are announced. Consequently, members of the community are not always aware of what is happening in their own environment. In many instances they just see things develop without being informed or even asked for their input. For example, if the local authority wants to install electricity, they will start digging holes and planting poles without informing the community beforehand. In such instances the community may even resist a project which is beneficial to all. At times a local council would call all people who are living in the same area into a meeting called an Imbizo. The major challenge at such meetings is to prevent the ruling political party from addressing only those issues that directly affect it. The input from opposition parties is not often taken into account. Therefore the Imbizo does not play a meaningful role in the community and is not an appropriate vehicle for distributing information to the community

The South African government is still in the early stages of ICT policy development. There is a shortage of skills in various areas, namely ICT-related services, medical doctors, professional engineers, nurses, and other professions. The major challenge is the lack of skills in policy development, implementation, monitoring, and evaluation. As a result of the skills shortage in the country, policy implementation cannot take place. In addition, people have limited knowledge and skills within the policy development framework. Even the government approach does not assist in addressing this challenge. The government has different spheres, namely national, provincial, and local. Each of these spheres have different roles. For example, the local sphere will provide basic community needs and ensure that policies are adopted and used correctly. The provincial sphere will be responsible for implementing and monitoring policies. The national sphere will be mainly responsible for developing, evaluating, and monitoring policies. A problem occurs when officials are not involved throughout the whole process; for example, on a national level when policies are developed that do not include officials from provincial and local government. The government has practically adopted a centralised approach to policy development. In other words, the national government is the sole entity responsible for initiating various policies. The reason why these policies do not work is that most of the policy developers live far away from the people for whom they are developing these very policies. This is a top-down approach, top being the national department in question and down being the local authority and the community.

The Parliament portfolio committees had about thirty-four policies to be finalised during the 2006/7 financial year. In the end, the different committees only managed to finalise ten policies in terms of development. Implementation has not yet started in some and by the time it does there might be a need to amend some of those policies. The main challenge is the lack of an implementation strategy that will guide the process of policy development and ensure its success. Before any policy is finalised, it must be published in the Government Gazette. Only a few people have access to this document and it is not generally available in rural areas. The key challenge is the ability to read and understand how the Gazette works. In certain areas the Gazette is sold, but the local community cannot afford to buy it.

Furthermore, the industry regulators are often the ones that make the situation inoperable. ICASA is one of the regulators that promote competition within the communication industry in network services, VOIP, security, and so on. The giants of the telecommunication industry such as Telkom are there to provide communication services, even to marginalised areas. The motive for issuing communication licenses by the regulator was to introduce effective competition within allocated areas. Even though small companies have been granted permission to operate in a certain areas, the big giants will still compete with them in those areas. In some other instances, there are many regulations such as the Information Technology Act, Chapter 5E Special, that clearly specify the operations of ICT. Such policies were designed by the Department of Public Service and Administration mainly to ensure uniformity within State departments, interoperability, and ability to interface systems and so on. This policy framework - called the SITA house of values - ensures that each State department uses SITA methodology for the procurement and acquisition of other services. However, the framework does not satisfy the needs of all the departments. All the departments are still forced to use SITA's services regardless of the value received. The framework was designed five years ago, so much has changed in the meantime. Hence, the framework is irrelevant and not flexible.

3.5   How can the current situation be improved?

This research resulted in the following suggestions on how to overcome the above challenges. The assumption often made about rural people is that they are not educated. Indeed, currently about 85% of the people in rural areas are uneducated and have low-level skills. Therefore, appropriate training programmes need to be designed to address the gaps that have been identified. Furthermore, people need to be educated with respect to human rights and need to be taught how to initiate as well as embark on projects that could help them financially. The education process needs to link up with external challenges. As technology advances, there is a need to match the education process to the current skills set to enable direct and proper usage of technology. Funds need to be invested in the establishment of training centres that will serve as centres of knowledge and as sources of information.

Rural communities, like urban ones, receive vital core services from government departments. To ensure premium quality with respect to service delivery, capacity building and maintenance of sustainable skills are imperatives. There is a shortage of skills in different sectors: ICT, engineering, and science, to name a few. Government needs to train people in the skills that are lacking as part of enhancement of service delivery by the government. Skills transfer initiatives are to be encouraged and promoted; those who have been trained need to ensure that the appropriate skills are taught to fellow staff members.

Rural areas have their own unique challenges. Environmental scanning could help gain insight into the underlying and related dynamics. Amongst others, aspects that need investigation and interrogation when remedial projects are launched incorporate: local challenges, the political situation, economic situation, social, and technology issues. The aspirations of the rural communities, their strengths and weaknesses need to be leveraged to ensure rural community buy-in and successful execution of projects.

Project management principles have to be adopted to ensure the success of any large scale operation. Execution of projects based on best practice often give the assurance that a project will be delivered on time, within budget, and the end product is a fit for purpose, hence ensuring customer satisfaction. The policy development life cycle should not constitute an exception. Policy development initiatives need to adopt project management principles to ensure timely delivery and within given financial and other related constraints. Management of policy development, implementation, monitoring, and evaluation within the context of a project office will give an insightful understanding on related issues and risks and the situation could easily be presented in a dashboard format to enhance interpretation and expedite related decision-making processes.

To establish a solid ICT infrastructure in rural areas as a prerequisite to the provisioning of ICT-related services requires adequate funding. government needs to create an environment whereby big business will be attracted and encouraged to invest as well as operate in rural areas. Incentives have to be introduced to turn around the current situation where companies are not willing to provide support and maintenance of services in rural areas as the profit margins are either very marginal or non-existent. Government funding could also help local structures such as Non Governmental Organisations (NGOs), Community Based Organisations (CBOs), and civic organisations to identify and promote local talent within the rural areas. There is a dire need for multinational companies like Microsoft, Hewlett Packard, and International Business Machines (IBM), who are directly involved in ICT, to invest in rural communities by providing ICT-related solutions that will benefit the communities. Also, government in its yearly budget allocation needs to make provision for funding in respect of development of ICT in rural areas.

To foster the participation of big business as well as forge the appropriate relationship between big business and government, it might be relevant to establish an ICT forum. The forum could be used to serve as a platform where all key stakeholders responsible for the provisioning of ICT-related solutions could share information, knowledge, and strategies as well. Also, the forum would enable all role players to keep abreast of technological advancements and emerging technologies and initiate development of relevant policies for implementation.

A policy framework is necessary to give a route map to guide the process of policy development life cycle to ensure effective service delivery. Flexibility needs to be built into the framework to accommodate the dynamism of rural environments that are subject to external forces which might be political, economic, and social or labour related in nature. Furthermore, consideration needs to be given to the high rate of unemployment in the country which might imply denial of access to the technology by the intended users as affordability could pose a serious problem.

The policies need to be aligned to the basic needs of the people. Current policies are developed with either minimum or no consultation with affected people; consequently, developed policies do not take into account all the requirements of the people. Testing of policies will ensure that policies are evaluated against the needs of the people. Review of policies needs to be done on a continuous basis to assess their validity and relevance as well as introduce pertinent amendments for implementation.

Implementation of applicable policies and related amendments has to be guided by an implementation strategy. The strategy will outline the strategic objectives to be met and the approach to be adopted in accomplishing the desired end state. The accompanying implementation plan will detail project work packages to be executed, related resource plans, timeframes, and related budgets.

Emphasis has to be placed on the participation of the affected people to ensure the success of any ICT-related project that has to be implemented. Projects implemented in rural areas are no exception. The people targeted by projects within a rural setting have to be identified from the outset as key beneficiaries as it essential to understand their background, their major challenges, their expectations and know in advance whether a project will address their requirements and be able to manage the expectations of those affected and communicate accordingly.

Successful projects are underpinned by an effective communications strategy. The strategy identifies the content to be communicated, the recipients of various types of communications, the frequency of each communication type as well as the communication channels.

4.   Summary and conclusion

This chapter focused on the difficulties confronting policy makers attempting to integrate isolated, disadvantaged, and poverty-stricken rural communities into the rest of the world through the provision of ICT-related services on a sustainable basis. It presented findings from a case study of the current ICT policy efforts of the South African Government for the formation of cyber communities in rural areas intended to improve quality of life in these areas.

Our research showed that the policy development process followed in South Africa has reached saturation point, with many policies being developed but never implemented. Hence the main finding of our research is that the implementation of policies is virtually non-existent and consequently there is little policy monitoring and no evaluation.

We found lack of leadership for integrating multiple policy initiatives. Leadership is required to glue all the different elements together and ensure that the environment is scanned in order to understand existing challenges and plan for effective implementation action. Moreover, we found strong evidence of a culture of non-compliance with policies, which is a major challenge that needs to be addressed.

References

[1]   Barendse, A. (2003). Innovative regulatory and policy initiatives at increasing ICT connectivity in South Africa. Netherlands: Elsevier Science Ltd.
[2]   Casaburru I, V. (2003). The Input of the Minister of Communications for the parliamentary media briefing, 20 February 2003. Cape Town: Parliament.
[3]   Glaser, B. & Strauss, A. (1967). The discovery of grounded theory: Strategies for qualitative research. New York: Aldine.
[4]   Moodley S. (2001) The challenge of e-business for the South African Ltd. Durban: Polity Press.
[5]   Morris, M.L. & Stavron, S.E. (1993). Telecommunication needs and provision to underdeveloped black areas in South Africa, telecommunication policy. Republic of South Africa: Butterworth-Heinmann.

[6]   South African Government (2001). E-government policy. Pretoria: Department of Public Service and Administration,

[7]   South African Government (2003). Statistic of South African annual report 2003, Pretoria: Government Printers.

[8]   South African Government (2002). Annual report. Cape Town: Government Printers.

[9]   Strauss, A. & Corbin, B. (1998). The basics of qualitative research: Techniques and procedures for developing grounded theory. London: Sage.

Part 2:

Harnessing the empowering capacity and ICT

DIGITAL DIVIDES AND THE ROLE OF POLICY AND REGULATION: A QUALITATIVE STUDY

Panayiota Tsatsou
London School of Economics and Political Science, UK

Abstract   This chapter aims to answer the research question: what is the role of internet policy and regulation in digital divides in Greece? I argue that Internet policy and regulation account significantly for the persistence of digital divides in Greece. The chapter draws on literature that views the role of policy and regulation in digital inclusion as problematic and proposes a more dialectical view of the interactions between politics and technology, so that the democratic and participatory potential of the Information Society can be approached more critically. The chapter explores the research question empirically through in-depth individual interviews with elite actors in the Greek Information Society. Elite actors who are involved in various areas of policy and regulation in the Greek Information Society are in the position to account for the role of internet policy and regulation in aspects of digital exclusion from more than one perspective. Thus, the chapter argues about the significant role of decision-making in the Greek case of digital divides, providing the grounding upon which research outside Greece could rely on to look at other cases of digital divides and at the role of policy and regulation accordingly.

Keywords: Digital divides, Greece, policy, regulation, interviews

1.   Introduction

This chapter reports on ongoing research into digital divides in Greece. The part of the research reported here examines factors of influence for digital divides in Greece which operate at the level of decision-making. The central question addressed is: what is the role of Internet policy and regulation in digital divides in Greece?. It is argued that Internet policy and regulation frameworks account significantly for the persistence of digital divides in Greece.

Although other forces such as social psychology, economics, technology design, and innovation parameters could be considered in researching digital divides, this chapter looks at decision-making on policy and regulation in order to explore specific aspects of digital divides in Greece. The emphasis is grounded in

Please use the following format when citing this chapter:

Tsatsou, P., 2008, in IFIP International Federation for Information Processing, Volume 282; *Social Dimensions of Information and Communication Technology Policy*; Chrisanthi Avgerou, Matthew L. Smith, Peter van den Besselaar; (Boston: Springer), pp. 141–160.

the interest that decision-making discourses and practices present for understanding and explaining the case of Greek divides, as briefly illustrated later in the chapter.

In what follows, the conceptual and research foundations of the work are established and the key discourses in the field reviewed. This allows more specific issues relating to digital divides and the role of decision-making to follow, introducing the reader to the conceptual framework and research scope of this chapter with regard to the case of Greek divides. The chapter then reports briefly on major methodological issues, as well as on the findings obtained from in-depth individual interviews of elite actors in the Greek Information Society. It is worth noting that, due to space limits, this chapter provides an overview only of the interview findings, with the discussion being by no means exhaustive. Nevertheless, it aims to provide the ground where further research on some of the issues at stake will be conducted. It concludes with an overview of the argument supported throughout and with information about the next phases of the research.

2.   Digital divides: new divides, new discourses and emerging research challenges

2.1   Digital divides: an overview

The digital divide is arguably an "umbrella concept" that traditionally "describe unequal access to technologies or digital exclusion at an international as well at a local level" [5]. Other scholars [25] define digital divides in rather broad terms as "the uneven spread of the new media". On the other hand, the OECD has offered a more elaborate understanding of digital divides, underlining the fact that behind digital divides there is a range of "interlocking divides":

"The importance of ICT to both economic and social development explains the priority of bridging what has come to be known as the 'digital divide'. This is, in fact, a whole series of interlocking 'divides' – the gaps that separate segments of society as well as whole nations into those who are able to take advantage of the new ICT opportunities and those who are not" [32].

On the basis of the above OECD definition, digital divides can be understood as a complex phenomenon that relates not only to access to and use of new information and communication technologies (ICTs) and of the products provided through them, but also to the social, economic, and political contexts where technology is used and developed. This definition attempts to contextualize the phenomenon of digital divides, illustrating not only its complexity but also its various explanations. Nevertheless, no absolute and complete definition of the phenomenon exists, since "the problems of the digital divide have been and probably will continue to be moving targets" suggesting that "the term's definition should be similarly mobile" [16].

Beyond purely definitional terms, digital divides have been a shifting area of research [8] and there is controversy about both the extent of their existence and their features: "[t]he 'digital divide' is one of the most discussed social phenomena of our era. It is also one of the most unclear and confusing. What after all is the digital divide" [47]? Others [2, 6] wonder whether the term digital divide has a real meaning, when "digital" refers to a range of technological artefacts, goods, contexts, services, applications, etc.

The initial literature on digital divides stresses technological advances or inequalities as resulting in racial employment balances [1], whereas others have discussed digital divides with respect to ICTs in general [41, 12]. On the other hand, the term "divide" per se implies a strict dichotomy represented by the "'all or nothing' scenario" [16] and the "social stratification" [47] approach. Scholars have recently and increasingly criticised this dichotomy arguing that it lacks "sufficient sociological sophistication" [48].

Due to the complexity of digital divides and the importance they hold for this chapter, the discussion that follows attempts to deliver a more insightful discussion of digital divides in conceptual, research, and pragmatic terms.

2.2   Digital technologies & divides: beyond access and use?

In March 2007 less than 17% of the world population were Internet users [21], suggesting the persistence of digital divides globally. Does this figure constitute the only aspect or element of digital divides?

Primarily conceived as unequal access to indispensable resources, digital divides have drawn researchers' attention to dichotomous socio-economic and demographic differences as the main source of divisions. However, empirical surveys, commentaries on empirical findings, and other scholarly works (30, 31, 29, 20, 45, 49, 44, 23] have provided contrasting findings with regard to existing inequalities and the role of demographics.

In an attempt to overcome the simplistic "bipolar societal split" between haves and have-nots – or users and non-users - Warschauer [46] demonstrates the meaningful role of physical, digital, human, and social resources in posing barriers that hinder equal access to and use of new information technologies. As far as Internet technologies in particular are concerned, although "social divisions in internet access continue to exist" [50], skills, abilities, breadth of online activities, means of overcoming potential barriers to functional use, as well as the "techno-culture" [41] are also among the increasingly important parameters of divides that we should look at. Others argue about the relative and graduated differences between users and non-users, deriving from structural inequalities in skills for and usage of ICTs [17, 38]. These arguments are closely linked in turn to the issues of "cohort" and "awareness" that Katz and Rice [22] sharply identify as other divides. Moreover, the term "competency", implying technological and educational skills in the use of ICTs, has been looked at the literature, while Silverstone and Haddon [42] have shown that these skills are strongly dependent upon individuals' goals of use and their disposable time/temporal capital among other factors at work.

Drawing on the necessary parameter of contextualization, we see that digital divides are not just inequities in technological facilities deriving simply from socio-economic inequalities. They also relate to informational gaps that stem from contextual settings which intensify existing socio-economic inequalities, thus creating significant psychological parameters that matter [7]. In an ethnographic study of 20 single-parent and 20 elderly households, Haddon [18] argues that not only the evident financial constraints but also everyday routine, limited sociability, and the pressing limitations of daycare restrict single-parents' understanding of media utility. Likewise, the same study finds that the elderly are marked by unwillingness to familiarize themselves with ICTs, and that, due to their limited past experiences of ICT use, they do not see ICTs as good value for money.

By critically reviewing the above facets of digital divides, this chapter explores Internet adoption as one of the critical aspects of digital divides in Greece. It explores Internet adoption in Greece by conducting an empirical examination of the political and regulatory context of Internet adoption in the country. Internet adoption plays a leading role in the development of digital divides overall, while at the same time allowing other forms of digital inclusion and participation to be looked at. In terms of contextualization, this chapter contends that the Internet is an inseparable part of social life, while Internet adoption is tightly linked to political and regulatory parameters in the field, as discussed below in Section 2.3.

2.3   Digital divides and interaction with policy and regulation: a forward-looking proposal

How do digital divides relate to policy and regulation?

The role of politics in digital divides is well illustrated by the debate between defenders and opponents of the welfare state model. This debate constitutes part of the recent discussion about the deconstruction of the legacy of the welfare state under the imperatives of liberty and independence [3]. In contrast to neo-liberal views that support de-regulation, there continues to be literature that argues that the state has a significant role to play in technological innovation since it significantly influences the availability of resources, the establishment of legal frameworks, and the development of investments [27]. On the other hand, the necessity of control by the state has become problematic, since popular discourses perceive the democratic potential of the Information Society as clearly serving market goals, competitiveness, and trade [26]. This debate acquires new interest as social rights and services go hand-in-hand with communication-related issues such as "media access, public service broadcasting, universal telephone service, trade and investment of global telecommunications, media education, and cultural identity" [28]. In this regard, communications influence the parameter of societal inclusion, with the latter posing further challenges to policy setting and regulation making [19].

Departing from the above theory-based discourses, the following OECD indicators illustrate how digital divides are commonly measured: access lines and channels, mobile and Internet subscribers, broadband subscribers, availability of Digital Subscriber Lines (DSL), households with access to the Internet and to a home computer, Internet penetration by size class; Internet selling and purchasing by industry, telecommunication services revenue, telecommunication infrastructure investment, R&D expenditure, trade in ICT goods, contributions of ICT investment to GDP growth, top 50 telecommunications firms and IT firms[1]. Also, in the annual OECD IT Outlook series [37, 36, 34] countries with completely different socio-economic, political, and cultural characteristics are compared mostly in terms of technological and market development.

From the above list, it is evident that the Internet is considered the key technology in the Information Society and that emphasis is placed on market indicators of development. What seems to be missing from the above list are indicators that relate to the ways in which socio-cultural and decision-making mechanisms respond to the rapidly changing technological environment. The lack of "institutional and cultural analyses" [4] seems to deprive research of the potential to provide a fuller picture of the mechanisms that determine the course of new digital technologies and of the Internet in particular in multiple contexts. In addition, the currently missing societal perspective would allows us to look, in Preston's [40] words, at significant implications "for public policies and strategy...which may serve to challenge or enhance the kinds of thinking and considerations that currently inform policy decision-making or practices". These implications relate to the mission of policy and regulation to coordinate the mediation process with a view to shrinking divides between the communicator, the medium, the receiver and the circulation of content.

On the one hand, policy is at the centre of the discussion about the deconstruction of the welfare state legacy under the imperative of liberty and independence [3]. In the media and communications literature, policy has mostly been looked at from a political economy perspective (Melody, Mansell, Garnham, Smith and others), although recently Garnham's work introduced some cultural considerations to the field. This chapter argues that the focus needs to be not so much on the power relations behind institutional- and political economy-centred mechanisms of the policy-making processes, but rather on the ways in which such mechanisms reflect and correspond to society's needs on the basis of what "products" a policy delivers. This is attempted to some degree by Mansell [25] in the discussion of digital entitlements and empowerment of people, where she argues that social needs and cultural differences do not inform media policy to the extent they should, as policy is surrounded by a rhetoric that addresses the digital economy vision resulting in persistent digital gaps between citizens.

Regulation, on the other hand, is a rather technical and complicated area of activity that has little to do with welfare or with neo-liberal policy ideologies and social policies. Empirical studies in media and communications critically discuss

---

[1] A full list of the 15 ICT indicators used in OECD standards to measure the Information Society can be found at www.oecd.org/sti/ICTindicators.

regulation mostly with respect to how it jeopardizes ordinary people's interests and it favours the market. The debate between "citizens" and "consumers" in relation to market competition, public interest, and the state illustrates the controversy between civil society and the market, as well as the rather unclear role of media and communications regulation [24]. The question "citizen and/or consumer" goes beyond rhetoric and attempts to capture whether ordinary people are identified with the market and the consumer's interests or distinguished on the basis of regulatory provisions for inclusion, participation, and citizenship.

On the basis of the above critiques of the role of policy and regulation in digital inclusion, this chapter aims to explore the role of policy and regulation in Greek divides. However, no specific aspects of policy and regulation are to be explored, as this chapter looks at policy and regulation in a rather open way and on the basis of a constantly evolving and complex framework that carries different weight for different actors in the Information Society. The following section introduces the interest that the case of Greek digital divides presents, and the role of policy and regulation.

3.   Case-study of Greece

Why are Greek digital divides an interesting case to study?

Greek digital divides are understood in this chapter as the persistently low Internet adoption in Greece. For the purposes of the chapter, I aim to briefly discuss political, regulatory, and technology penetration characteristics of Greek divides, so that the importance of this case and the ways in which it fits the conceptual and research framework of the chapter are illustrated.

In political and regulatory terms, the Greek government started to liberalise and privatise the broadcasting and telecommunications market in the early 1990s. So far, the Greek governmental and legislative authorities are not willing to let market forces act freely. Indicative of this is the fact that in January 2006 the European Commission (EC) sent a formal request to Greece asking for information regarding its compliance with the Court of Justice (CoJ) ruling of 14 April 2005 with respect to the country's failure to implement the liberalisation of electronic communications by the established deadline. In addition, the report published by the OECD on regulatory reform in Greece demonstrates the culture-related difficulties that the authorities of the country face in shaping the Information Society: "although most Greeks will benefit from regulatory reform, the resistance of many protected groups to needed change is hard to overcome" [33]. The OECD pays particular attention to existing administrative barriers [33] and to the tight state control of the economy and of the supposedly independent regulatory process as factors that obstruct regulatory reform and the creation of a competitive telecommunications market in Greece [35]. The OECD therefore highlights the need for "structural change" [35] which supports the criticisms in the literature that the introduction of ICTs has been driven by the private sector while the public sector is lagging behind [43].

In terms of technology penetration indicators, Greece has long been slow in the diffusion of network technologies and services. On the basis of the Information Society indicators set by the eEurope and i2010 initiatives, the latest national survey reports uneven diffusion of various types of digital technologies in Greece [14]:

1. In 2006, DVD penetration was 71% and electronic games console penetration was 26%;
2. An increase was recorded in the possession of desktop computers, from 39% in 2005 to 42% in 2006, as well as in portable computers (laptops) from 11% in 2005 to 16% in 2006;
3. Palmtop computers are still at the same very low level, only 2%, as in 2005;
4. Household access to the Internet increased from 24.2% in 2005 to 27.4% in 2006;
5. Terrestrial digital television shows a low penetration, at 8% in the regions of Attiki, Thessalia and Salonica (where the required infrastructure exists);
6. Awareness of terrestrial digital television is at low levels, with only 2 out of 10 people being aware of it; and
7. One half of the Internet users who are mobile phone users possess a mobile which can connect to the Internet.

Beyond the above general figures, the 2005 national survey of new technologies usage [15] illustrates the increasing penetration of ICTs in Greece for the years 2001-2003 and the stagnation of new technology adoption for the years 2004-2005. Indicatively, in 2005 the five-layered indicator of new technology use increased by only 0.3% (13.6%), whereas the percentage of the population not using new technologies decreased by 2.7% [15]. Moreover, Internet use in the general population increased in 2005 (24.6%) only by 0.1% compared to 2004 (24.5%) while still being lower than in 2003 (25.2%). Computer use decreased from 34.2% in 2003 to 32.2% in 2004 and increased from 32.2% in 2004 to 34.3% in 2005 [15].

Even when looking at Greece in a broader European context, one can see that fundamental Internet indicators, such as Internet adoption and use, remain at surprisingly low levels. More specifically, in the Eurobarometer survey of 2005 [11] Greece is at the very bottom of the EU25 Internet use list, with only 24% of the population using the Internet. Spain and Italy are far closer to the EU-25 average (49%), with Portugal having the next lowest percentage (27%) after Greece[2].

How does policy and regulation account for the above delays in Internet technologies adoption in Greece? From a regulatory perspective, telecommunications regulation in Greece has been marked by a long history of delays and inconsistencies. According to the 10th EC report on the implementation of the EU Electronic Communications Regulatory Package [10],

---

[2] Internet usage in the EU25 ranges from 85% in Netherlands to 24% in Greece [11].

five countries, among which Greece, had not implemented the framework one year after the deadline. As a result, the Commission launched infringement proceedings for non-notification, and proceedings were pending before the European Court of Justice against Belgium, Greece, and Luxemburg [10]. This is an instance that gives support to the idea that, regardless of the globalization trend in regulation, national state strategies and dynamics should not be underestimated [39].

Hence, the chapter looks at the case of Greek divides from an Internet adoption perspective and takes into consideration the fact that "societal change takes more time. It requires organisational changes, a shift in mindsets, modernization of regulation, different consumer behaviour, and political decision" [9]. Aiming to explore the role of decision-making mechanisms in the case of Greek digital divides, Section 4 reports on the methodology applied and the findings obtained from in-depth interviews with twelve elite actors in the Greek Information Society.

4.   In-depth interviews with elite actors in Greece: methodology and key findings

This section presents the methodology applied and some of the findings obtained from in-depth individual interviews of twelve elite actors in the Greek Information Society. These interviews aimed to trace the major factors that affect the development of the Internet in Greece, particularly in connection with the processes through which policy and regulation are established. Section 4.1 provides some methodological insights on issues of sampling and interview perspective. Section 4.2 presents the main interview findings, pointing to the implications for further research.

4.1   Sampling: Expertise and interview perspectives

Twelve interviewees were selected by ordering a list of key policy, regulatory, activist, and research bodies in the Greek Information Society. Members of those bodies who play a role in ICT dissemination activities were contacted and some of them were selected and interviewed. Table 1 presents the interviewees' expertise, as well as the three different interview perspectives adopted during interviewing.

INTERVIEW SAMPLE EXPERTISE	INTERVIEW PERSPECTIVE		
Policy & Regulation	**Scope interviews**	**Bottom up**	**Theory driven**
Special Secretary of the Operational Program 'Information Society' (OPIS) in Greece	□		
President of the National Committee for Electronic Commerce & General Secretary of Commerce	□		
Director of Telecommunications, Hellenic Republic National Telecommunications and Post Commission	□		
Officer of the EC DG Information Society	□		
Research	Scope interviews	Bottom up	Theory-driven
The Head of Research and Development in the SafeNetHome Project (Safer Internet Action Plan) in Greece			□
Associate Professor and Head of Broadband Wireless & Sensor Networks at the Athens Information Technology Institute (AIT)			□
Associate Dean, AIT			□
Internet Bodies	Scope interviews	Bottom up	Theory-driven
President of the 'Association of Greek internet Users' (EEXI)		□	
Legal Consultant of EEXI		□	
President of SAFENET (the Hellenic self-regulation body) and SAFELINE (the Hellenic Hotline)			□
Auditor, Hellenic Data Protection Authority (DPA)			□
Market	Scope interviews	Bottom up	Theory-driven
Officer of the Federation of 'Hellenic Information Technology & Communications Enterprises' and Product Manager of FORTHnet		□	

Table 1: Interview sample and interview perspective.

The interviews were of three types: scope, bottom-up, and theory-driven. For scope interviews, which emphasize the scope and focus of the research, four interviewees from the broader policy and regulation domain in the Greek Information Society were selected. All four interviewees were in a position to report on the Information Society in Greece, while representing some of the official decision-making authorities of the country. For bottom-up interviews, which emphasize issues that derive from the web of social actors, three interviewees were selected. All three were actors associated with Greek society in general and with the community of Greek Internet users in particular, reporting thus on digital divides in Greece from the perspective of their grassroots connections. For interviews led by theory, which emphasize issues deriving from the literature, five interviewees were selected. All five were actors in research areas related to the benefits, risks, and implications of Internet adoption and to the ways in which Greek society perceives such benefits, risks and implications.

The above categories of interviewees cover the field of experts in the Greek Information Society, whilst their classification into three interview categories allows the study to examine all issues of interest from more than one perspective. For instance, the interviewees in the category of "scope" interviews represent the official political and regulatory authorities in the field, whereas the interviewees in the "bottom-up" category raise their voices with respect to societal aspects of digital divides. Lastly, the interviewees categorised as "theory-driven" are actors with an insight stemming mainly from contemporary research on digital divides.

4.2   Critical overview of findings

This section presents the interview findings and highlights their implications for future research. In general, complex interconnections between societal and decision-making forces in the Greek context came to the fore in the interviews and significant remarks for the evolution of the Greek Information Society were made regarding the ideology-power complex. I present the findings in relation to the following themes of interest: the Information Society and the Internet in Greece, the public and the Greek Information Society, Internet policy and regulation in Greece, other social forces at work, and points of reference.

4.2.1   Information Society and the Internet in Greece

The first theme looks at the Greek Information Society and its main characteristics. The interviews confirmed the empirically demonstrated low level of Internet adoption in Greece, argued about "Greek distinctiveness", and pointed in particular to the liability of the country's political authorities:

> "...we are talking about the diffusion of broadband services in Greece, the Internet, and what we actually see when TV cameras go to Ministers' offices is the picture of Jesus Christ because it is this that 'sells', whereas we have not seen any picture of a laptop on Ministers' desks to show that the Minister uses new technologies himself" (Associate Dean, AIT).

The interviewees added to the knowledge base of the study insight into the critical role that specific features of the Greek public administration have played. They interviewees mainly referred to regulatory delays and lack of modernisation and dominance of bureaucracy in the Greek public administration, with the latter being marked by inefficiencies, failures, and highly techno-phobic culture and practices. The inefficiency and lack of modernisation in the public administration in Greece is argued by the Special Secretary of the Operational Program Information Society (OPIS), who manages the political initiatives taken in the

Information Society, having an insider's view of the Internet decision-making in Greece:

> "...the lack of previous experience in promoting new technologies contributes to the persistent difficulty with respect to the harmonious cooperation of the public authorities in charge and to the drawing of a common policy line on the Information Society... Besides, the time-consuming bureaucratic processes in the country as well as the lack of modernisation of public administration are important barriers to the timely and efficient implementation of the Information Society program."

The interviewees resorted mostly to bibliographic and research sources when making their arguments about socially unaccountable, bureaucratic, inefficient, and non-technocratic decision-making in the country. Actors involved in ICT research, such as the Head of Broadband Wireless & Sensor Networks and the Associate Dean at the AIT, brought up examples where the bureaucratic operation of the public administration in Greece accounts for the policy and regulation failures in the Greek Information Society:

> "These [regulatory delays] are very indicative of the dominant bureaucratic mechanisms in our country, although we are not being affected by it as we are used to be.... bureaucracy in Greece is much greater than in other countries and thus... one of the reasons is the lack of penetration of electronic means and services in the public sector ...in order for a draft of legislation to be signed, ten signatures must be collected. It could be electronic signatures so that it takes just one day. However, now, just the signing of draft legislation takes two months in Greece" (Associate Dean).

> "...why are we talking about broadband...since politicians themselves do not perceive the benefit of e-services, how can we contribute to their diffusion" (Head of Broadband Wireless & Sensor Networks)?

It is also worth reflecting on the authorities' own evaluation of how they are structured and operate. Here, we can find references to the lack of collaboration between authorities, to absence of formal and systematic campaigns for public awareness-raising, and to the limited and socially dissociated scope of activities and services provided by the authorities. Indicative are the words of the Auditor of the Hellenic Data Protection Authority (DPA), who indirectly points to the directions where the authorities in charge should improve and work more in:

> (Auditor of the Hellenic DPA): "...the truth is that we are very few auditors working here. This is a problem that will hopefully be solved shortly. A second problem is that, at least technically and beyond the law, we do not have the necessary means to carry out extensive audits, to explore the operational systems in depth and to use advanced technical tools.

Interviewer: However, do you participate in joint actions with other policy and regulatory bodies in the country?

(Auditor of the Hellenic DPA): I would not say that we participate and collaborate in such a way. We collaborate with other bodies only in some cases. Eeem...but there is no particular and regular cooperation line that we follow. For example, we were asked to legislate in order to implement the EU Privacy Directive and there was no collaboration developed from our side with any other authority.

Interviewer: ...and what about the interest in increasing people's awareness about how to protect their personal data on the Internet?

(Auditor of the Hellenic DPA): *You know.... if we are talking about information provided to people... eeem... I would not say that. There is no particular awareness campaign carried out by us, something that we know we should promote further. Eeem...as people are interested in that as well. For example, last year...in our annual report these issues were mentioned, and when the DPA President announced our report the public was pretty interested in it..."*

On the other hand, market-players in the field emphasize the phenomena of the lack of modernisation and the traditionalism in the Greek public administration sector. Of particular interest is the argument made by the Officer of Federation of Hellenic Information Technology & Communications Enterprises (SEPE) about people's unwillingness to use new technologies such as the Internet in the public administration sector:

"...unlike what happens in other European countries where policies are vertical, straightforward, clear, and mandatory for the stimulation of Internet use in every field of social life...in Greece there is no such functionality of policy and regulation making on the Internet...this is due to the 'old-fashioned' identity of the Greek public sector which has not become modernised enough, as well as because of the reluctance of governors to promote the Internet as a tool for the necessary modernisation of public administration."

Thus, even the interviewees who are not directly linked to the decision-making mechanisms mentioned particularities concerning attitudes, traits, and cultures in the Greek public sector in order to explain the drawbacks of the country's Information Society. In essence, the interviewees highlighted a research area that has been hugely overlooked in the relevant research conducted in Greece, whilst they approached cultural traits and attitudes to new technologies as matters that go beyond the boundaries of ordinary people's everyday living.

4.2.2   The public & Internet policy and regulation in Greece

Beyond general trends and characteristics of the Greek Information Society, the interviewees made proposals regarding the establishment of appropriate societal and political conditions that will diffuse new technologies in Greek society. More specifically, they claimed that decision-making in Greece needs to be more socially accountable. The Special Secretary of OPIS described the deeply rooted weaknesses of the decision-making process in Greece in the following way:

> "Practically speaking, we design all our future activities in accordance with existing social concerns and needs... This, however, cannot happen through marketing or any such kind of promotion of our efforts. Instead, we decided to act more drastically and practically in order to come closer to the citizen through making decisions and designing policies that would have a practical impact on citizens' everyday lives... we want a more socially-accountable policy on the Information Society that will identify the different needs and demands of different groups of people in society".[3]

This brings to the fore the importance of awareness raising and incorporation of the Internet in citizens' everyday life, as well as the contribution that policy and regulation can make accordingly. The Director of Telecommunications at the National Regulatory Authority argues in this respect:

> "I think that what would be very stimulating for the Internet in Greece - this is besides something that I believe at the personal level as well - is e-government, so that citizens get familiarised with online services and realize the benefit of those services. I am afraid that the public sector is still very behind. We are talking about infrastructures and wires, but citizens need to come across new, useful, and important for their everyday lives online public administration services."

These arguments importantly support the notion of "sociology of policy and regulation", while the role of the appropriate IT education is further underlined. Those working in education and awareness-raising research initiatives pointed to the remedial role that education and training in the safe and beneficial use of the Internet can play. Interviewees such as the Head of Research and Development at the SafeNetHome Project, underlined the negative impact that the current lack of thorough IT training and education in Greek schools has on Internet adoption and safe use of the Internet in the country:

---

[3] In this conceptual framework, the Special Secretary of OPIS evaluated regulation. He argued that societal forces have not been taken into account by the authorities of the country and mostly by the previous government:
"Special Secretary: The main mistake is that local particularities have not been taken into account.
Interviewer: Have you, therefore, identified a lack of social considerations in the designing of policy and regulation on the information society?
Special Secretary: There used to be such a lack".

> *"...we do invest a lot in education... it is just unacceptable that there is no computer or Internet training in primary schools in Greece. At the age of 12 and 13 it is already too late to teach a child... what we propose is training about computer and Internet use from the age of 6, when the child goes to primary school for the first time... parents have to be more informed about the Internet too..."*

However, the question about the interface between politics and society and how their interaction can be explained on the basis of interdependency and complexity has been largely left unanswered by the interviewees. By mostly representing elite bodies of action in the Information Society, the interviewees viewed the solution to digital divides as coming from the political and regulatory fields of action, while they expressed the view that the public in Greece lacks citizenship being thus unprepared to drive change. The Officer of the EC DG Information Society and one of the official EU regulatory voices in the Information Society maintains that the society of ordinary people in Greece is hugely inactive, arguing that this as a distinct Greek phenomenon that leads the Greek society to playing no role in decision-making:

> *"In other countries and mainly in the Anglo-Saxon and Scandinavian counties there are civil societies which are organised in such a way that active civil teams come to existence, take measures and communicate with the public authorities, protect citizens' rights and consumers' rights, etc, etc... In Greece the characteristic of atomism is socially dominant and therefore collective social action is far less existent."*

When the interviewees were asked about the possible immediate contribution of society to decision-making, most supported a top-down approach. Even elite actors who aim to increase public awareness of the Internet failed to see the contribution that ordinary people can make through participating in the overall decision-making process. It comes as a surprise that those who argued in favour of more socially-accountable processes do not find any space for citizens to actively participate in decision-making, challenging somehow the idea of participatory democracy. Indicative are the words of the Head of Research and Development in the SafeNetHome Project, who aims to increase awareness of the Internet in the Greek society through promoting the Safer Internet Programme:

> *"Interviewer: Do you think, however, that Greek civil society may have a role to play in regulation and policy making on the Internet?*
>
> *Head of Research and Development in the SafeNetHome Project: ...no... I am afraid... how can society participate? ...society is not interested... I don't think that at the moment there is a potential for social action. It is something like a chain... people need to get more interested and stimulated about the Internet first..."*

Only the Director of Telecommunications at the National Regulatory Authority placed some emphasis on the catalytic role of public consultations in decision-making. This elite actor pointed to the persistent gap between the public and decision-making and provided an alternative to the top-down solution that most of the interviewees proposed:

> *"Public consultations is a practice that was given particular attention in the last four-five years in order for the unlimited registration of the opinions and proposals of all involved parties to be achieved. Therefore, participants can be enterprises and telecommunications services providers, consumer bodies, as well as everyday people and individual consumers. In general, there is no limitation on who is eligible to participate."*

These arguments acquire even more importance since the public was considered by the interviewees to be the ground where politics is based and political culture is shaped. This contradiction indicates that the professional status and profile of the interviewees and the resulted power-ideology complex significantly determine the thread between cause and solution with respect to digital divides in Greece and as this is perceived by the elite actors in the country. Whereas they considered societal forces important, they mostly see change as stemming from policy and regulation and less from the dynamics lying in the web of social activity and mobilisation.

4.2.3   Other social forces at work

The above contradiction becomes even more obvious in the fourth theme where the interviewees pointed to the additional role that market development and continuous education can play in the development of the Internet in Greece, while criticizing the role that media propaganda has played in the dismissal of new technologies by the majority of people in Greece. Media propaganda and negative advertising of the internet on TV were regarded by market-players in particular as key factors that enhance negative social attitudes to the Internet, leading thus the interviewees to strongly pessimistic theses as far as the role of citizens in closing digital divides in concerned:

> *"...we constantly see the media presenting the Internet in a negative way. For example, child pornography and some occasional incidents of suicide on the Internet are presented by the media much more extensively than the benefits of the Internet. We believe that this contributes significantly to social fear, obscurantism, and ignorance about the Internet"* (Officer of SEPE).

Additionally, pragmatic factors that influence Internet adoption in Greece, such as a lack of sufficient infrastructure and of satisfactory online services, high cost of internet services and networks, as well as lack of social action and institutional organisation were all brought up as additional parameters to explain digital divides. This constitutes an important addition to the knowledge base of the study, as these pragmatic factors have not been examined in-detail in the context of the study. Indicatively, the President of the Association of Greek Internet Users

(EEXI) brings to the fore the high cost of access to high speed Internet as problematic for the broader diffusion of Internet technologies in Greece:

> "The problem is that the existing infrastructure hinders the Information Society in our country. The Internet is very expensive...can you find an ADSL connection at a cost of less than 50 Euros per month? Where do we live, in Monaco? The enterprises cannot afford such an amount and ADSL is a technology which, whereas Europe is abandoning, Greece is only now discovering...what research in Greece has shown is not only lack of use but also low quality of use, especially in young age groups..."

4.2.4   Points of reference

Finally, the fifth and last theme approached in the interviews takes a rather reflexive approach, shedding light on the role of professionalism and "conflicts of interest" in the interview discourses. For instance, the difficulty that many of the interviewees faced in using a socially accountable language can explain the politically driven recommendations they made and the underestimation of the public's role in bringing about change in the Information Society. In particular, the interviewees who participate in policy- and regulation-making used a politically grounded language in their efforts to explain the current situation and the possible future of the Greek Information Society.

Hence, the liability of the political and regulatory authorities of the country contrasts the elite actors' arguments about the marginal role that civil society can play in decision-making and regardless of their arguments in favour of more socially-accountable policies and regulations in the field. On the other hand, culture seems to be lying both in politics and society, bringing up issues of bureaucracy, non-modernisation, and techno-phobia as critically important for the course of digital divides in the country and establishing a rather complex picture of mindsets and practices in decision-making procedures. These findings also highlight the need for further research in order this complexity to be disentangled.

5.   Concluding remarks

Overall, this chapter aims to illustrate that we cannot view technological innovations as an autonomous field of life and work. It argues that decision-making in Greece has a role to play in the digital divides in that country.

This chapter goes beyond problematic accounts of Internet access and use, as it explores Internet adoption and digital inclusion by looking at decision-making in the field. Also, although other digital technologies could be looked at and various other perspectives could be taken into consideration (physical resources, infrastructure, digital resources, applications and content, human resources, education, etc), this chapter looks only at decision-making, namely policy and regulation, as both influencing and being subject to today's rapidly changing digital environment.

After reviewing the debates and discourses on digital divides, this chapter briefly presents some of the challenges and implications for policy and regulation making. It then proposes an in-depth examination of the role of decision-making, while attempting, in Section 3, to make sense of this proposal with regard to the case of Greek divides. In Section 4, this chapter reports on the methodology applied and the research findings obtained from interviewing twelve elite actors in Greece.

The discussion of the interview discourses confirms the validity of the underlying links between digital divides and policy and regulation making. The central argument articulated in the interviews is that current decision-making mechanisms in Greek Information Society is characterised by a bureaucratic, traditional, and techno-phobic culture, deterring the development of the Information Society in the country and reflecting, to some extent, cultural traits that dominate the Greek environment overall. Thus, the interviewees argue in favour of socially-accountable policies and regulations in the country, so that the authorities come closer to society and pave the way for broader Internet adoption. However, the elite actors failed to answer questions about how politics can change societal culture and how decision-making mechanisms will represent societal needs and desires properly if not with the active participation of civil society in decision-making. Nevertheless, they highlighted certain aspects of the complex network of ideology and power relations, and they indicated key practices and discourses in the Greek Information Society. In addition, other parameters such as delayed market development, media propaganda, and lack of IT education in Greece complete the complex picture of digital divides in the country. Lastly, discrepancies in the texts concerning the need for more socially-accountable policies and regulations, on the one hand, and the widely neglected role of the public in the closing of digital divides, on the other hand, raise the rhetoric applied by the interviewees.

Although the analysis focused on a rather small number of interview discourses, this chapter provides an insight into the possible interconnections between political, social, and technological factors in the shaping of digital divides, indicating the validity of the conceptual and research framework of the study. The chapter also paves the way for more focused, empirically rich, and exhaustive research in the future, as this research is still ongoing. The next stages of the research consist of a large-scale survey of ordinary people (both Internet users and non-users) in Greece who will provide a bottom-up account of the role of policy and regulation in Internet adoption in Greece and in connection with ordinary people's culture and attitudes towards the Internet. Finally, follow-up focus group interviews, with a sub-sample of surveyed individuals, will conclude the empirical research, aiming both to provide some qualitative depth to the survey findings and to integrate with the data collected in the in-depth interviews with elite actors.

References

[1]   Angwin, J., & Castaneda, L. (1998). The digital divide: High-tech boom a bust for blacks, Latinos. San Francisco Chronicle, 4 May.

[2]   Brady, M. (2000). The digital divide myth. E-commerce Times, www.ecomercetimes.com/story/3953.html.

[3]   Calabrese, A. (1997). Creative destruction? From the welfare state to the global information society. Javnost/The Public, 4(4), 7-24.

[4]   Calabrese, A. (1999). Afterword. In A. Calabrese & J.-C. Burgelman (Eds.), Communication, citizenship, and social policy: Rethinking the limits of the welfare state (pp. 311-314). Lahnham; Boulder; New York; Oxford: Rowman & Littlefield Publishers, Inc.

[5]   Cammaerts, B. & Audenhove Van L. (2003). Dominant digital divide discourses. In B. Cammaerts, L. Van Audenhove, G. Nulens & C. Pauwels (Eds.), Beyond the digital divide: Reducing exclusion, fostering inclusion. Brussels: Brussels University Press.

[6]   Chaney, H. (2000, March 12, 2000). The US "digital divide" is not even a virtual reality. Bridge News.

[7]   Chen, W., Boase, J., & Wellman B. (2002). The global villagers: comparing internet users and uses around the world. In B. Wellman & C. Haythornthwaite (Eds.), The Internet in Everyday Life. Oxford: Blackwell.

[8]   Compaine, B. M. (Ed.). (2001). The digital divide: facing a Crisis or Creating a Myth? Cambridge; MA; London: MIT Press

[9]   EC. (2002). eEurope benchmarking report: eEurope 2002. Brussels. COM (2002) 62 final.

[10] EC (2004). Communication from the Commission to the Council, the European Parliament, the European Economic and Social Committee and the Committee of the Regions. European Electronic Communications Regulation and Markets 2004. COM (2004) 759 final. Brussels, 2.12.2004.

[11] EC (2006). Safer internet. Eurobarometer 203/Wave 250 survey (December 2005 - January 2006). Publications: May 2006.

[12] Frissen, V. (2003). The myth of the digital divide. In B. Cammaerts, L. V. Audenhove, G. Nulens & C. Pauwels (Eds.), Beyond the digital divide: reducing exclusion, fostering inclusion (pp. 17-33). Brussels: VUB Brussels University Press.

[13] Gaskell, G. (2000). Chapter 3: Individual and group interviewing. In M. W. Bauer & G. Gaskell (Eds.), Qualitative researching: with text, image and sound. A practical handbook. London: Sage.

[14] Greek Information Society Observatory. (2007). Study for measuring the indicators of the eEurope and i2010 initiatives for the years 2006 and 2007. Athens: Greek Information Society Observatory.

[15] GRNet. (2005). National survey on new technologies and the information society. (in Greek). Athens

[16] Gunkel, D. J. (2003). Second thoughts: Toward a critique of the digital divide. New Media and Society, 5(4), 499-522.

[17] Hacker, K., & Van Dijk, J. (2003). The digital divide as a complex and dynamic Phenomenon. The Information Society, 19(4), 315-326.

[18] Haddon, L. (2000). Social exclusion and information and communication technologies. Lessons from studies of single parents and the young elderly. New Media & Society, 2(4), 387-406.

[19] Henten, A. (1999). Will information societies be welfare societies? In A. Calabrese & J.-C. Burgelman (Eds.), Communication, Citizenship, and Social Policy: Rethinking

the Limits of the Welfare State (pp. 77-90). Lahnham; Boulder; New York; Oxford: Rowman & Littlefield Publishers, Inc.

[20] Hoffman, D., Novak, T., & Scholsser, A. (2001). The evolution of the digital divide: Examining the relationship of race to internet access and usage over time. In B. Compaine (Ed.), *The Digital Divide: Facing a Crisis or Creating a Myth?* (pp. 47-98). Cambridge: MIT Press.

[21] Internet World Stats. Usage and population statistics. Retrieved from http: www.internetworldstats.com/stats.htm, [Accessed 10/19/07].

[22] Katz, J., & Rice, R. (2002). *Social consequences of the Internet: Access, Involvement and Interaction.* Cambridge, Mass.: MIT Press.

[23] Kirkup, G. (2001). Getting our hands on it: Gendered inequality in access to information and communications technologies. In S. Lax (Ed.), *Access Denied in the Information* Age. New York: Palgrave.

[24] Livingstone, S., Lunt, P., & Miller, L. (2007). Citizens, consumers and the citizen-consumer: articulating the citizen interest in media and communications regulation. *Discourse & Communication*, 1(1), 63-89.

[25] Mansell, R. (2002). From digital divides to digital entitlements in knowledge Societies. *Current Sociology*, 50(3), 407-426.

[26] Mattelart, A. (2003). *The information society: an introduction.* London: Sage.

[27] May, C. (2002). *The information society: a sceptical view.* Cambridge: Polity Press

[28] Mosco, V. (1999). Citizenship and the technopoles. In A. Calabrese & J.-C. Burgelman (Eds.), *Communication, citizenship, and social policy: rethinking the limits of the welfare state* (pp. 33-45). Lahnham; Boulder; New York; Oxford: Rowman & Littlefield Publishers, Inc.

[29] NTIA. (2000). Falling through the net: toward digital inclusion. US Commerce Department.

[30] NTIA (2001a). Falling through the met: a survey of the "Have-Nots" in rural and urban America. In B. Compaine (Ed.), *The Digital Divide. Facing a Crisis or Creating a Myth?* (pp. 7-15). Massachusetts: MIT Press.

[31] NTIA (2001b). Falling through the net: Defining the digital divide. In B. Compaine (Ed.), *The Digital Divide. Facing a Crisis or Creating a Myth?* (pp. 17-46). Massachusetts: MIT Press.

[32] OECD (2000). Learning to bridge the digital divide. Paris: Organisation for Economic Co-operation and Development.

[33] OECD (2001) Greece set to reap maximum benefits from regulatory reform. Paris: OECD.

[34] OECD (2002a). Information technology outlook 2002. Paris: OECD.

[35] OECD (2002b) Regulatory reform in the telecommunications industry in Greece. Paris: OECD.

[36] OECD (2004). Information technology outlook 2004. Paris: OECD.

[37] OECD (2006). Information technology outlook 2006. Paris: OECD.

[38] Perri 6 with Jupp, B. (2001). *Divided by information? The "Digital Divide" and the implications of the new meritocracy.* London: Demos.

[39] Preston, P. (2001). *Reshaping communications: Technology, information and social change.* London; Thousand Oaks; CA: Sage.

[40] Preston, P. (2005). ICTs in everyday life: Public policy implications for Europe's way to the information society. In R. Silverstone (Ed.), *Media, technology and everyday life in Europe: from information to communication* (pp. 195-211). Aldershot: Ashgate.

[41] Selwyn, N. (2004). Reconsidering political and popular understandings of the digital divide. *New Media & Society*, 6(3), 341-362.

[42] Silverstone, R., & Haddon, L. (1996). Television, cable and AB households. A report for Telewest plc: University of Sussex:, Graduate Research Centre in Culture and Communication.

[43] Voulgaris, Y. and D. Sotiropoulos (2002). *Information society, sociology and technology*. Athens: Operational Programme for the Information Society. (in Greek).

[44] Walsh, O. E., Gazala, M. E., & Ham C. (2001). The truth about the digital divide. In B. Compaine (Ed.), *The digital divide. Facing a crisis or creating a myth?*. Massachusetts: MIT Press.

[45] Walton, A. (1999). Technology vs African-Americans. *Atlantic Monthly* 283(1), 14-18.

[46] Warschauer, M. (2003a). *Technology and social inclusion: rethinking the digital divide*. Cambridge, Massachusetts: MIT Press.

[47] Warschauer, M. (in press). A literacy approach to the digital divide. In M. A. Pereyra (Ed.), *Las mulialfabetizaciones en el espacio digital*. Malaga: Ediciones Aljibe.

[48] Webster, F. (1995). *Theories of the information society*. London: Routledge.

[49] Wilhelm, A. (2001). From crystal palaces to silicon valleys: Market imperfection and the enduring digital divide. In S. Lax (Ed.), *Access denied in the information age*. New York: Pargrave.

[50] Wyatt, S., Thomas, G., & Terranova, T. (2002). They came, they surfed and then went back to the beach: Conceptualizating use and non-use of the internet. In S. Woolgar (Ed.), *Virtual society? Technology, cyberbole,* Reality (pp. 23-40). Oxford: Oxford University Press.

EMPOWERMENT THROUGH ICT:
A CRITICAL DISCOURSE ANALYSIS OF THE EGYPTIAN ICT POLICY

Bernd Carsten Stahl
De Montfort University, UK

Abstract   ICT is often promoted as a solution to a range of social ills. This is particularly true for the use of ICT in developing countries. ICT deployment can address numerous issues but its overall aim is the empowerment and emancipation of individuals with the aim of improving society. This chapter takes a critical approach to such discourses and asks which claims to emancipation are raised and how they are underpinned. Using a Habermasian framework, the chapter undertakes a critical discourse analysis of the Egyptian ICT policy. This important document, which has inspired much African ICT policy, is analysed to identify the validity claims it raises. These claims, many of which are explicitly aimed at emancipation and empowerment, are then contrasted with social realities as well as the overall structure of the policy document. This comparison shows that empowerment is not only not achieved, but arguably not a primary aim of the policy in the first place. Instead, claims to empowerment are used to legitimise particular aims which conflict with empowerment. The chapter concludes with a critical reflection of the chosen approach and findings.

Keywords: Information society, policy, ICT, social movements, institutions

1.   Introduction

Governments and international agencies spend huge amounts of money on projects aimed at promoting the use of information and communication technology (ICT) in so-called developing countries [61, 63]. The immediate aim of such investment is typically economic growth [50, 79]. It is usually recognized, however, that economic growth is no end in itself. Economic growth is meant to produce employment, create welfare, and improve the lot of all members of society. Its purpose is to allow people to live a fulfilled life according to their own design. Briefly, the final aim of the promotion of ICT in developing countries is the empowerment of the members of society.

This chapter will shed doubt on the empowering effect of ICT. It will do so by undertaking a critical discourse analysis of the Egyptian Information Society Policy. This policy document is of pivotal importance having been presented by

Please use the following format when citing this chapter:

Stahl, B.C., 2008, in IFIP International Federation for Information Processing, Volume 282; *Social Dimensions of Information and Communication Technology Policy*; Chrisanthi Avgerou, Matthew L. Smith, Peter van den Besselaar; (Boston: Springer), pp. 161–177.

Egypt at the World Summit on the Information Society and having inspired numerous comparable policies across the African continent. The discourse analysis will be based on some of Jürgen Habermas' ideas. I will use this approach to focus on two important areas of possible empowerment: political participation and education. The result of the analysis is that ICT has disempowering effects which are known to the agents involved and arguably intended from the outset. The chapter ends with a reflection on the findings and the methods employed.

2.   Critical research in IS

Critical research is often seen as the third possible research approach, as an alternative to positivist and interpretive research [22, 68]. I believe that this categorization of three research "paradigms" is misleading because it wrongly suggests that the paradigms are mutually exclusive and that they constitute all possible choices. Instead, I suggest a definition of critical research according to critical intention and critical topics and the resulting choice of theory [74, 75], all of which will be discussed below. The extensive debate on critical research has found its way into the field of Information Systems, where a number of special journal issues and books evidence that it is becoming increasingly recognized [45].

2.1   Critical intention

The term "critical research" usually stands for research that is grounded on the assumption that society can and should be improved. At the basis of this assumption one can find Marx's view of history as a series of class struggles [57] and a corresponding conflictual view of society [43].[1]

Critical research is built on the tenet that realities are socially constructed but that they often become reified and objectified. Critical researchers do not simply accept the status quo as the best possible world; they want to know what is "wrong with the world rather than what is right" [83, p. 112]. They aim to open up discursive closure, to facilitate new descriptions and to initiate new discourses [1]. Critical research wants to challenge accepted realities and promote resistance. It cannot be comfortable; it disturbs the quiet and challenges established authorities.

2.2   Critical topics: Empowerment and emancipation

The critical intention is mirrored by the choice of research topics, theories, and methodologies. Critical research concentrates on those topics that promise a chance of redeeming the critical intention. The typical topics of critical research

---

[1] One could call this view of critical research with its emphasis on the Marxist roots the "continental European" perspective of critical research. As Harvey [40] points out, there is a different tradition of critical theory in the Anglo-American world. I will concentrate on the European tradition, which should not be misunderstood as implying that all critical research is of a Marxist nature.

are thus power, empowerment, and emancipation [16, 44]. Power is usually perceived as a pervasive influence on human action, rather than straightforward projection of political or military potency [62]. Critical researchers are interested in how power is created and legitimized. The aim of studying power is to identify those who are dominated and to help them represent their claims better, to empower themselves [56, 18, 26].

Another concept related to power and empowerment and central to critical research in IS is emancipation [2,3, 42, 66, 81, 20, 82, 59]. The idea of emancipation is to "help eliminate the causes of unwarranted alienation and domination and thereby enhance the opportunities for realizing human potential" [48, p. 69]. Emancipatory concerns are frequently linked to concepts that appear to hinder emancipation such as alienation [68] authenticity [69], identity [35] or a limited rationality [54, 17, 71, 82, 23]. Critical researchers in IS have investigated matters of power and empowerment in systems failure [88], the digital divide [52] or gender issues in IS [51].

In this chapter I will use the terms "empowerment" and "emancipation" synonymously. The main concern is to see whether ICT is used for purposes of empowerment. Answering this question raises considerable theoretical problems. The above definition of empowerment as the avoidance of domination, alienation, subjugation, etc. has some intuitive appeal. However, it is difficult to translate into practice. Who is to define what constitutes an empowering practice? Can we as academics prescribe people to be empowered? And what are we to do if their views differ from ours? The solution to this intricate problem may be to look at the research subjects' claims to empowerment. Rather than making material suggestions, we follow the procedural idea that people need to define their own understanding of empowerment (see [76]). My analysis of empowerment through ICT is thus based on the view of Egyptian politicians, administrators and users.

The concept of emancipation is of particular importance with regards to development, as development seems to promise the overcoming of oppression and alienation. It is relatively easy to see how a relationship between emancipation and democracy could be construed where the participative aspects of democracy are constitutive of emancipatory developments. The contemporary debate about empowerment and participation in the development literature is considerable [13, 14, 72, 87] and this chapter does not do it justice. This is justifiable because the chapter does not inquire into substantive emancipation but only aims to identify the role that emancipation plays in ICT policy and whether assumptions and rhetorical devices bear critical scrutiny.

3.   Critical theory: Habermas's discourse

There are a large number of theories employed by critical scholars. In the continental European tradition there tends to be an explicit link of critical theories to Marxism. The most prominent examples of this are the theories developed by the so-called Frankfurt School of critical research, which is linked to names of its members such as Horkheimer, Adorno, Marcuse, and others. Their theoretical approaches were further developed by the second and third generation of critical scholars including Habermas, Apel and Honneth. It is relatively uncontentious to state, however, that other theoretical developments can also lay claim to being critical in the sense of the word suggested here. These include theories such as postmodernism, postcolonialism, or poststructuralism. Prominent critical theorists whose work has been used in IS include Foucault or Bourdieu [12, 53].

I do not wish to engage in a debate on the merits of the respective theoretical approaches. I believe that all of them have the potential to contribute to the critical intention of promoting emancipation. Some explicit observations on Habermas's theory will be necessary to render the chosen methodology understandable.

Rationality is a central concept for Habermas. It represents a disposition to give reasons for one's actions. This can best be understood in the framework of his Theory of Communicative Action (TCA) [38,39]. The anthropological basis of this theory is that we are intrinsically social beings who require social interaction to survive and thrive. Communication is aimed at facilitating cooperation. Communicative action stands for those pieces of communication where the speakers mutually respect each other as autonomous moral beings. Whenever we communicate, each utterance carries several validity claims: those of truth (*Wahrheit*), legitimacy (*Richtigkeit*), and authenticity (*Wahrhaftigkeit*). A further condition of successful communication, which in English-language literature is often counted as a fourth validity claim, is that of clarity or comprehensibility.

It is part of the nature of communication that we do not always agree on the validity claims of all utterances. If this is the case, then discourses take place. Discourses are acts of communication that aim at clarifying contentious validity claims. Discourses are characterized by the attempt to emulate the so-called "ideal speech situation", where the only criterion that will decide their outcome is the quality of the argument [37]. The ideal speech situation is never realised in discourses but it is a necessary condition of the possibility of discourses.

The Habermasian framework has been widely read and applied in IS [49]. Communicative action requires speakers to accept the fundamental equality of others and is thus intrinsically ethical. In IS research these ideas have been applied in two major directions: a critique of research methods and approaches and the attempt to create more "socially informed" methods and theories [55, p. 164]. The latter aspect, the attempt to use Habermasian discourse theory to inform practice, is closely aligned with the critical intention to change current practices and to emancipate users of IS. This ethical ideal is linked to the ideal speech situation, which is taken as an normative ideal used to model reality [9, 81].

Examples of Habermasian research in IS range from fundamental explorations of the impact of ICT on communication [31] to applied considerations of how IS development processes can be improved [29, 81]. The areas of application of these thoughts range from e-government / e-democracy [41] to e-teaching / e-learning [73] and the definition of the field of the field of information systems [42].

The attempt to base research on Habermas's theories can also produce problems. There is the egalitarian assumptions that all stakeholders should be equal and the resulting bias toward participatory approaches, which often runs counter to capitalist hierarchies [46]. There are the intricacies of language and the problem of meaning, which a Habermasian researcher must take seriously [19]. Furthermore, there are also fundamental and conceptual problems with the application of Habermas's theories in organisational practice. Chief among them is the dichotomy of ideal and real discourses and the resulting question of the theoretical status of real discourses.

4.   Critical methodology – A Habermas inspired discourse analysis

There is no generally recognized critical methodology [60]. Part of the reason for this is the nature of critical research, which, by definition, cannot consist of the "application" of a theory to a given situation. I will briefly outline the methodological approach chosen for this research.

In order to identify contradictions between rhetoric and reality in the Egyptian ICT policy, I decided to undertake a critical discourse analysis (CDA) (cf. [32, 33, 34, 21]) using a Habermasian framework. Examples of CDA in the literature (cf. [35, 80]) demonstrate a central problem of the method, namely that it requires extensive discussions of the text. Since I intended to analyze a whole policy framework, this would not have been feasible in a research chapter.

I therefore decided to follow a novel way of doing critical discourse analysis, pioneered by Cukier et al. [24, 25]. This method is based on Habermas's validity claims [55]. It aims to identify these claims, using quantitative and qualitative measures, and thereby explicate the hidden assumptions of texts and discourses. Validity claims are discovered and coded by using a guiding question for each of the four claims: truth, legitimacy, sincerity, and clarity. To help identify claims, I followed the guiding questions put forward by Cukier et al. [22, 23]. Drawing on these questions, texts were coded and validity claims in each text were determined. During the coding several individual claims were noted as frequent and worthy of their own category or sub-category. The main advantage of this approach to critical discourse analysis over traditional methods is that it allows the analysis of a larger body of texts.

The method was applied to the Egyptian Information Society policy. The policy documents can be accessed from the Ministry of Communication and Information Technology's (MCIT) homepage (http://www.mcit.gov.eg/index.asp) under the link "E-Bridges".

MCIT was chosen because it is the government department responsible for ICT. It is also the trendsetter among the Egyptian ministries and the organisation primarily responsible for policy and implementation of ICT in Egypt. The ICT policy is of high importance in Egypt and is supported by President Mubarak. MCIT was set up in 1999 to realize the National Project for Technology

Development [27]. External business observers view MCIT as a reliable partner and a forerunner of reform in the Egyptian administration [5]. A clear sign of the internal importance of MCIT and its aim of furthering ICT use in Egypt is the fact that its first minister, Dr. Ahmed Nazif, was promoted to the position of Prime Minister in August 2004.

It was decided to use the online version of the policy rather than the full text, on the assumption that it would have been possible to update it and thus reflect current changes. The online version consists of 43 web pages with a length varying from ½ to 10 pages when printed out. It gives an overview of the intended use of ICT in Egypt and its contribution to the information society in general. The seven most important policy areas, including e-business and e-government, are outlined in five web pages each, which discuss the intention, principles, implementation, current state, and planned action for each. I identified a total number of 1247 validity claims. In the following data analysis, I describe the findings stemming from these documents. References in curly brackets { } refer to the different texts. The exact references can be found in [74], Appendix B.

5.   ICT and empowerment in the Egyptian ICT policy

In this section I present and discuss the findings of the CDA. I will start by identifying claims to empowerment through the use of ICT in two areas: democratic participation and education. Subsequent to the presentation of the claims, I will discuss the results of the discourse analysis and, where appropriate complement this by alternative descriptions of social reality.

5.1   Democracy and participation

In one of the central speeches promoting the ICT effort in Egypt, the Egyptian President Hosni Mubarak [64] said that the purpose of information technology is to facilitate a "better living to all the Egyptians". A similar reference to "enhancing the quality of life for each and every Egyptian" was repeated by the President [65]. Empowerment of the Information Society is the explicit aim of Information Society Development Office, an organisation charged by MCIT with promoting the information society (ISDO, 2005). All of this suggests that empowerment is indeed a central aim of the use of ICT.

This empowering idea is repeated throughout the policy document. The information society, which is the centre of attention of the ICT policy, is said to be a society where "citizens are empowered [...]" {2}. Different aspects of the policy empower different stakeholders such as the Egyptian IT community {17}. The empowerment includes participation and explicitly mentions that ICT will allow "genuine participation of citizens, including traditionally marginalized segments of the population" {2}. Two groups discussed specifically are women where ICT training is meant to "close the gender gap" {17} and "enhance the role of women in managing commercial activities" {27} as well as disabled people {13}, specifically the visually impaired {47}.

This development of participation will lead to "greater opportunities for all" {3}. Part of the process will be increased transparency, for example in the banking industry {27}, as well as national and international solidarity {54}. A particular emphasis is given to freedom, especially the market freedom to do business and be successful, thereby overcoming the problem of poverty. Participation is to be supported by e-government which will "bring the benefits of the emerging global information society to the largest possible segment of the population" {19} and allow for "community participation" {20}. Best of all, the potential of ICT is not something we will have to wait for much longer. "A fully functioning, effective Egyptian Information Society is now just around the corner" {53}.

5.2   Limits of participation

The emancipatory rhetoric of ICT and the information society is contrasted starkly by social realities. Political participation as an expression of empowerment is highly limited. Egypt officially claims to be a democratic system but the implementation of a "presidential republic" where the main power holder is nominated by the People's Assembly and then confirmed by referendum leaves little space for political freedom. Compared to other countries Egypt's political system may be relatively liberal and allow for limited opposition activities [67]. Egypt also seems set for a further course of political liberalization with the recent creation of a National Council for Human Rights, the appointment of the first female judge, the cancellation of state security courts [6]. Also, Egypt has traditionally allowed greater openness and accountability in political decisions than neighboring countries [28]. On 26 Feb 2005 President Mubarak announced a multi candidate election for the position of President in 2005. The election was widely regarded as fraudulent, leading to the imprisonment of Mubarak's main rival. Also, Egypt is still ruled under Emergency Law.

While the external political environment does not appear to be conducive to personal empowerment, a closer look at the policy itself shows that the empowering claims are not taken seriously and not followed through. The general gist of the policy document is one of top-down development of ICT applications most of which are geared for specific stakeholder groups. Of 256 claims which identify a stakeholder, 156 refer to the government itself. The large majority of the remaining stakeholder claims (71) refer to businesses. Citizens are only identified as stakeholders 20 times. And where they are recognised as stakeholders they are invariably seen as passive recipients of government services. In the 16 of the 17 cases where an omission of relevant stakeholders was identified, these missing stakeholders were the citizens. No input from citizens to the development of the information society is sought.

A strong example of this exclusion of citizens from empowering participation is the "e-government" section of the policy {19}-{23}. The focus of e-government is the efficient provision of services to citizens, and, more importantly, to investors. Citizen input or even e-democratic participative models are not considered. Where decisions have to be made which stakeholders will be served first, business invariably wins the day over citizens {23}. The analysis of the text allows the conclusion that e-government does not involve any influence on political decisions. Also, e-government is very much seen in terms of e-commerce with one of the case studies and success stories of e-government {22} describing an online billing system. The problems of equating citizens and consumers [77] are generally ignored.

5.3   Empowerment through education

It has become conventional wisdom that, in order to participate in society and lead a fulfilled life, one needs a certain amount of education. The Egyptian ICT policy reflects this standpoint and uses ICT as a lever for improving the provision of education to its citizens. The e-learning initiative aims to provide equal opportunities for learning "regardless of age, gender, class, or geographical location" {15}. ICT is meant to improve all levels of education. On the most basic level it will "strengthen attempts to eradicate illiteracy" {17} and "encourage people to overcome illiteracy" {18}. At the same time the provision of ICT facilities in schools and universities will improve the quality of learning. It will provide much-needed capacity of higher education and increase the "competitiveness of [Egypt's] graduates" {13}. Teaching technology will also allow continuing education and life-long learning. A specific emphasis is placed on teaching ICT skills as these are seen as important for the job market and for international competitiveness {11}.

The policy concedes that there are problems, most notably those of access, usage, skills {4}, but also the general level of literacy and overcrowding of the educational system. However, the very use of ICT is seen as the solution to these and the correct usage of technology in education will take care of them. In order to persuade students to learn ICT skills, the government has set up a Basic Skills Training Program which is available free of charge to every young Egyptian and is even linked to a stipend {17}. Additionally, the government has initiated several programs which are aimed at spreading ICT around the country in a manner that will guarantee access to technology for everyone interested {11}. International cooperation, for example with UK universities, will help overcome the shortage problem of higher education {17}.

5.4   Limits of educational empowerment

The Egyptian education system faces serious problems. The level of illiteracy in the Egyptian population is close to 30%. Literacy is a concept that is hard to define, but literacy as a condition of participation in an information society is a multi-facetted competence that requires intensive educational effort [58]. It seems to be an unrealistic assumption that the mere provision of technology will solve the problem of illiteracy. It furthermore stands to reason that the introduction of ICT will produce more need for traditional education rather than alleviate pressure.

The Egyptian educational system is not well equipped to deal with the challenges of the information society. It performs poorly when compared to other developing countries, partly because of its bureaucratic structure and its outdated pedagogical model [86]. On top of this there is the demographic development with the number of secondary school graduates doubling from 375,000 to 650,000 from 2003 to 2005 alone and a further expected in crease to 800,000 in 2007 and 1,200,000 by 2017 {13}. Even a perfect system would find it extremely hard to deal with this sort of challenge.

The solution outlined in the government policy, namely to leverage technology to solve the problem, will most probably not solve it. It is insensitive to contextual, political, and pedagogic issues. It concentrates on technical matters, most notably on the provision of equipment and technical access, which, at best, will be preconditions for a successful use of ICT. In the document on e-readiness entitled "The Way Forward" {12}, the government concentrates on technicalities of access provision that are so advanced that they would have little relevance even in the most developed societies. The concentration on technology allows sidestepping the more difficult social issues behind the education problem (Warschauer, 2003). Solutions are suggested, such as the use of schools as publicly accessible Internet cafes {15}, {17} which go counter to the established use of ICT. Finally, the literature on e-teaching and e-learning which suggests that the introduction of technology into education may introduce new problems (Stahl, 2004) is ignored.

ICT education, which is praised as a solution is in practice organised so that it is impossible for students to fail. Due to the lack of equipment, ICT education is often done theoretically without access to technology. And even where technology is available, it is often not made accessible to students because it is perceived as being too valuable [86]. The policy itself demonstrates that the government is not following through on its emancipatory promises. If education is to lead to empowerment, then one would expect that teachers and students as main stakeholders would have a say in its provision. However, rather than seeing students as active participants of education, they are passive recipients. Where stakeholders of education are explicitly named, we find the names of major corporations {17}. Education is not seen as an end in itself or as a means of empowerment but rather as a way to produce "human capital" and make Egypt attractive to foreign investment. Literacy or education are named relatively frequently as benefits of ICT (37 times) but this number pales in comparison to economic benefits, which are cited 110 times.

In general, the use of ICT is promoted as a way of solving the very serious problem Egypt is facing with regard to educating its rapidly growing population. However, the discourse concentrates on technical matters, thus leaving unexplored the more important underlying questions such as the purpose of education (cf.

Sahay, 2004), the pedagogical fit of technology, and the greater social issues including illiteracy.

5.5   *Summary of findings*

The above description of the research findings supports the conclusion that the use of ICT in Egypt on the national level of the Information Society Policy is actively disempowering. There is a strong empowering rhetoric. This empowering rhetoric is an important aspect of the promotion of ICT because it lends legitimacy to the endeavour. This empowering promise of ICT is not kept. The Habermasian framework allowed me to identify contradictions between the rhetoric and the underlying intention. The critical discourse analysis demonstrated that the rhetorical validity claims are contradicted within the policy itself. The general gist of the policy document is one of one-sided economic liberalism that is fundamentally unconcerned with the individual empowerment.

6.   Reflections

Critical research aims to be reflective. In order to live up to this standard, it needs to reflect on itself. Weaknesses, biases, alternatives and assumptions must be subject to critical reflection. This goes beyond the usual discussion of limitations and must question the heart of the research.

6.1   *Theory and methodology*

There are a number of questions one could raise about the use of concepts, theory and methodology in this piece of research. A visible omission of the chapter is the lack of a definition of "development". The term is contentious and divisive [30] and a discussion would add little to the chapter. Egypt is a developing country by most standards and the use of ICT is linked to efforts of development, however defined.

Another problematic aspect might be the use of theory. Does the chapter do justice to Habermas? A possible answer is that the question is of limited relevance for critical research. For critical research it is more important to follow the "emancipatory spirit than to the authoritative letter of any particular Critical Theorist" [3, p. 3]. Critical research is not a matter of applying a theory correctly but of using theoretical guidance to promote the critical intention [10, 83].

An important part of the critical reflection aims at clarifying the assumptions and biases the research is based on. The most important bias is that the argument was developed in the western tradition of thought whose applicability to Egypt is not obvious. This raises the difficult problem of the transferability of thoughts between cultures [84, 78, 77]. Without being able to argue this point conclusively here, I believe that the aim of emancipating and empowering people is universal and can be applied to non-western environments as well as to western ones. I concede that empowerment may take a different form in the Arab world than in the west. In order to accommodate this, I emphasized a concept of empowerment as employed by the Egyptian government itself.

6.2   Exclusion of other stories

By developing the present narrative I had to choose which aspects to discuss and which to neglect. This story therefore hides a multitude of other possible stories which may also be worth exploring. There are a few obvious candidates for alternative critical narratives of ICT use in Egypt. One of them is the international political order with its important influence on Egyptian politics. Western democracies seem to agree that peace and quite in the Middle East (again, a western description) is a political aim of high importance and they therefore stabilize the Egyptian government as best as they can. One can easily draw a line from Egyptian politics to the struggle of Israel and the Palestinians but also to other political developments in the Middle East. This, in turn is linked with questions of the desirability of certain types of government over others. There is an important connection to religious matters and the west's attempt to limit the political power of Islam. This, in turn is linked to the worldwide fear of terrorism, which influences western policies.

Another issue is that I have attempted to present the narrative in as linear and unequivocal a fashion as possible in order to make it more accessible to the reader. While I hope that I was successful in so doing, I realize that I may have neglected some important aspects. One of these is the concept of resistance. In the attempt to show that ICT is used for disempowerment I did not pay attention to the idea of resistance. Any Foucauldian scholar will know that for Foucault there is no power without resistance [36]. Space constraints precluded us from exploring these aspects. Critical research is never finished and always needs to be contextualized. I therefore believe that the omission of resistance and other observations counter to our narrative is justified by the fact that this chapter is only one contribution to a larger discourse.

Another omission is that of positive effects of ICT. This chapter has taken a negative stance and attempted to show that emancipatory rhetoric may hide oppressive agendas. This does not imply that all use of ICT in developing countries will always have to be oppressive or alienating. There are many good examples in the literature where ICT had emancipatory effects, either by design or by chance. Similar stories could be told about ICT in Egypt. The relationship between such cases of emancipation and the greater ICT policy is an issue worthy of further exploration.

7.   Conclusion

In this chapter I have undertaken a critical discourse analysis of the Egyptian ICT policy with the aim of identifying claims to empowerment. These were then contrasted with other claims in the document as well as the social realities within which empowerment should take place. The outcome of the analysis is that empowerment is much cited in the policy, but that it is not followed through. There may be several explanations for this. One that I have argued for is that empowerment is used as a rhetorical device meant to create legitimacy for the policy despite a lack of real policy interest in empowerment. There are further explanations, which may interact and support the first one. Egypt finds itself faced by severe challenges, which render empowerment difficult to achieve in any circumstances.

This chapter should not be misunderstood as a contribution to conspiracy theories in general. I do not believe that there are large numbers of evil bureaucrats in the Egyptian government that conspire to keep the average Egyptian from reaching their potential (even though I cannot rule out that there are some of these, either). What I have tried to show is that there is a lack of sincerity when dealing with potentially empowering use of technology and that the policy document betrays this lack when analyzed in detail.

The chapter should not be misunderstood as implying that nothing good can come from the use of ICT in Egypt either. Whether intended or not, the use of technology tends to have results which are conducive to individual or collective emancipation. Even a strongly oppressive regime cannot avoid successful acts of resistance.

The purpose of the chapter is thus not to paint too bleak a picture but to point out that even a relatively high level analysis such as the one presented here can point to problems of aspirational texts such as the Egyptian policy. Researchers as well as practitioners are thus well advised to be careful when using such policy documents and to question the underlying beliefs, assumptions, and intentions. Critical research aims to promote emancipation. By questioning whether emancipatory claims are viable and consistent, I hope to have contributed to a continued discussion of the use of ICT in Egypt. I am sure that ICT can contribute to empowerment and emancipation in Egypt and elsewhere. But to be successful, such emancipatory aims must be taken more seriously than the Egyptian policy makers have arguably done. If this is accepted as a starting point, then the next and considerably more complex question will be how such emancipatory intentions can be implemented and what this will mean for developing as well as developed countries.

References

[1]   Alvesson, M. & Deetz, S. (2003). *Doing critical management research*, London: SAGE.
[2]   Alvesson, M. & Willmott, H (Eds.) (2003). *Studying management critically*, London: SAGE.
[3]   Alvesson, M. & Willmott, H (Eds.) (1992). *Critical management studies*, London: SAGE.
[4]   Alvesson, M. & Willmott, H. (1992). On the idea of emancipation in management and organization studies. *Academy of Management Review*, 17(3), 432 – 464.

[5]   anonymous. (2004). Two for TE? It's been an exciting year for the telecommunications industry. *Annual Business Economic and Political Review: Egypt.* available: www.oxfordbusinessgroup.com [accessed 01.11.2004], 125–128.

[6]   anonymous. (2004). Wind of change - Egypt says it wants to reform, but how much? *Annual Business Economic and Political Review: Egypt.* available: www.oxfordbusinessgroup.com [accessed 01.11.2004], 23 – 24.

[7]   anonymous (2004) Silicon Wadi - Egypt is making a bid to be the Arab world's IT hub, *Annual Business Economic and Political Review: Egypt*: available: www.oxfordbusinessgroup.com [accessed 01.11.2004], 129 – 130.

[8]   anonymous (2004). Different Interpretations - Egypt and the United States share similar goals, but don't always see eye to eye, *Annual Business Economic and Political Review: Egypt.* Available: www.oxfordbusinessgroup.com [accessed 01.11.2004], 17 - 18

[9]   Apel, K. -O. (1988). *Diskurs und Verantwortung: das Problem des Übergangs zur postkonventionellen Moral*, Frankfurt: Suhrkamp.

[10] Avgerou, C. (2005). Doing critical research in information systems: some further thoughts. *Information Systems Journal,* (15),103 - 109

[11] Avgerou, C. (2003). The Link Between ICT and Economic Growth in the Discourse of Development, in M. Korpeal, R. Montealegre, & A. Poulymenakou (Eds.), *Organizational Information Systems in the Context of Globalization* (pp. 373-386) Dordrecht: Kluwer.

[12] Avgerou, C., McGrath, K. (2007). Power, rationality, and the art of living through socio-technical change. *MIS Quarterly*, 31(2). 295–315.

[13] Bebbington, A., Guggenhein, E., Olson, E., Woolcock, M. (2004). Grounding discourse in practice: exploring social capital debates at the World Bank. *Journal of Development Studies,* 40(5), 33-64.

[14] Brett, E.A. (2003). Participation and accountability in development management. *The Journal of Development Studies,* 40(2), pp. 1-29

[15] Brooke, C. (2002). What does it mean to be 'critical' in IS research? *Journal of Information Technology (17),* 49 - 57

[16] Brooke, C. (2002). Critical perspectives on information systems: An impression of the research landscape. *Journal of Information Technology (17),* 271 - 283

[17] Burrell, G. & Dale, K. (2003). Building better worlds?: Architecture and critical management studies, in *Studying Management Critically*, M. Alvesson, Mats & H. Willmott (Eds.), (pp. 177 - 196), London`: SAGE.

[18] Cecez-Kecmanovic, D. (2001). Doing critical IS research: The question of methodology, in *Qualitative Research in IS: Issues and Trends*, E. Trauth (ed.), (pp. 141 - 162) , Hershey: Idea Group Publishing.

[19] Cecez-Kecmanovic, D. (2001). Critical information systems research: A Habermasian approach. In: *Proceedings of the 9th European Conference on Information Systems,* Bled, Slovenia, June 27-29, 253-263

[20] Cecez-Kecmanovic, D.; Janson, M. & Brown, A. (2002). The rationality framework for a critical study of information systems. *Journal of Information Technology (17),* 215 - 227

[21] Chouliaraki, L. & Fairclough, N. (1999). *Discourse in late modernity - rethinking critical discourse analysis*. Edinburgh: Edinburgh University Press.

[22] Chua, W. F. (1986). Radical developments in accounting thought. *The Accounting Review* 61(4), 601-632.

[23] Ciborra, C. (2000). A critical review of the literature on the management of corporate information infrastructure., in C. Ciborra, Claudio and Associates, *From Control to*

Drift: The Dynamics of Corporate Information Infrastructures, (pp. 15 - 40), Oxford: University Press .

[24]   Cukier, W.; Middleton, C.,& Bauer, R. (2003). The discourse of learning technology in Canada: Understanding communication distortions and the implications for decision making, in E. Wynn; E. Whitley; M. Myers. & J. DeGross (Eds.), *Global and Organizational Discourse About Information Technology,* (pp. 197 – 221), Dordrecht: uwer Academic Publishers.

[25]   Cukier, W.; Bauer, R.,& Middleton, C. (2003). Applying Habermas' validity claims as a standard for critical discourse analysis, in B. Kaplan; D Truex; T. Wood-Harper & J. DeGross (Eds.), *Information Systems Research - Relevant Theory and Informed Practice,* (pp. 233-258), Dordrecht: Kluwer Academic Publishers.

[26]   Dawson, R. J. & Newman, I. A. (2002). Empowerment in IT education. *Journal of Information Technology Education* 1(2), 125–141.

[27]   El Sayed, H. & Westrup, C. (2003). Egypt and ICTs - how ICTs bring national initiatives, Global Organizations and local companies together. *Information Technology & People* 16(1), 76–92.

[28]   El Sherif, H. & El Sawy, O. A. (1988). Issue-based decision support systems for the Egyptian cabinet. *MIS Quarterly* 12(4), 551-569.

[29]   Elkjaer, B.; Flensburg, P.; Mouritsen, J. & Willmott, H (1991). The commodification of expertise: The case of systems development consulting. *Accounting, Management and Information Technologies* 1(2), 139 - 156

[30]   Escobar, A. (1995). *Development,* Princeton University Press, Princeton, NJ.

[31]   Ess, C. (1996) Introduction: Thoughts along the I-way: Philosophy and the emergence of computer-mediated communication, in *Philosophical Perspectives on Computer-Mediated Communication,* Ess, C. (Ed.), (pp. 1 – 12), Albany: State University of New York Press.

[32]   Fairclough, N. (2003) *Analysing discourse - textual analysis for social research,* London & New York: Routledge.

[33]   Fairclough, N. (1995) *Critical discourse analysis - the critical study of language.* London: Longman.

[34]   Fairclough, N. (1993) Critical discourse analysis and the marketization of public discourse: the universities. *Discourse & Society* (4:2), 133 - 168

[35]   Forester, J. (1992) Critical ethnography: on fieldwork in a Habermasian way. In M. Alvesson & H. Willmott (Eds.), *Critical Management Studies,* (pp. 4–65), London: SAGE.

[36]   Foucault, M. (1975) *Surveiller et punir: Naissance de la prison,* Paris : Gallimard.

[37]   Habermas, J. (1996) *Die Einbeziehung des Anderen - Studien zur politischen Theorie,* Suhrkamp, Frankfurt a. M.

[38]   Habermas, J. (1981) *Theorie des kommunikativen Handelns* - Band I, Suhrkamp Verlag, Frankfurt a. M.

[39]   Habermas, J. (1981) *Theorie des kommunikativen Handelns* - Band II, Suhrkamp Verlag, Frankfurt a. M.

[40]   Harvey, L. (1990) *Critical Social Research.* London: Unwin Hyman

[41]   Heng, M. S. H. & de Moor, A. (2003) From Habermas's communicative theory to practice on the Internet. *Information Systems Journal* (13), 331–352.

[42]   Hirschheim, R. & Klein, H. K. (2003) Crisis in the IS field? A critical reflection on the state of the discipline. *Journal of the Association for Information Systems* 4(5), 237 – 293.

[43]   Hirschheim, R. and Klein, H. K. (1989) Four paradigms of information systems development, *Communications of the ACM,* 32(10), 1199–1216.

[44] Howcroft, D. & Trauth, E. M. (Eds.) (2005) *Handbook of Critical Information Systems Research: Theory and Application*. Cheltenham: Edward Elgar.
[45] Howcroft, D. & Trauth, E. M. (2004) The choice of critical information systems research, in B. Kaplan, D. P. Truex, D. Wastell, A.T. Wood-Harper & J. DeGross, *Information Systems Research: Relevant Theory and Informed Practice* (IFIP 8.2 Proceedings) (pp. 196 – 211), Dordrecht: Kluwer.
[46] Howcroft, D. & Wilson, M. (2003) Paradoxes of participatory practices: the Janus role of the systems developer. *Information and Organization* 13(1), 1–24.
[47] ISDO, Information Society Development Office Mission Statement, available: http://www.isdo.gov.eg/mission.asp [accessed, 16.03.2005]
[48] Klein, H. K. & Myers, M. D. (1999) A set of principles for conducting and evaluating interpretive field studies in information systems. *MIS Quarterly* 23(1), 67–94
[49] Klein, H. K. & Huynh, M. Q, (2004) The critical social theory of Jürgen Habermas and its implications for IS research, in Mingers, J. & Willcocks, L. (Eds.), *Social Theory and Philosophy for Information Systems* (pp. 157 - 237), Chichester: Wiley
[50] Klenow, P.J. & RodrõÂguez-Clare, A. (1997) Economic growth: a review essay, *Journal of Monetary Economics* 40, 597-617.
[51] Kvasny, L.; Greenhill, A. & Trauth, E (2005) Giving voice to feminist projects in MIS research. *International Journal of Technology and Human Interaction* 1(1), 1-18
[52] Kvasny, L. & Trauth, E. (2003). The digital divide at work and home: The discourse about power and underrepresented groups in the information society, in E. Wynn, E. Whitley, M. Myers, & J. DeGross (Eds) *Global and Organizational Discourse About Information Technolog,* (pp. 273 – 291), Kluwer Academic Publishers, Dordrecht
[53] Kvasny, L. & Truex, D. (2000). Information technology and the cultural reproduction of social order: A research program, in: Baskerville, R.; Stage, J. & DeGross, J. (Eds.) *The Social and Organizational Perspective on Research and Practice in Information Technology.* (pp. 277 – 293) Boston: Kluwer.
[54] Levy, D. L.; Alvesson, M. & Willmitt, H. (2003). Critical approaches to strategic management, in in M. Alvesson, Mats & H. Willmott (Eds.), *Studying Management Critically* (pp. 92 – 110), London: SAGE.
[55] Lyytinen, K. (1992). Information systems and critical theory, in M. Alvesson & H. Willmott (Eds.), *Critical Management Studies* (pp. 159 – 180), London: SAGE.
[56] Lyytinen, K. & Hirschheim, R. (1988) Information systems as rational discourse: an application of Habermas theory of communicative action, *Scandinavian Journal of Management*, 4(1/2), 19–30.
[57] Marx, K. (1969). *Manifest der kommunistischen Partei*, Reclam, Stuttgart.
[58] Mason, R. O. (1986). Four ethical issues of the information age. *MIS Quarterly*, 10, 5-12.
[59] McAulay, L.; Doherty, N. & Keval, N. (2002). The stakeholder dimension in information systems evaluation. *Journal of Information Technology*, 17, 241 - 255
[60] McGrath, K. (2005) Doing critical research in information systems: A case of theory and practice not informing each other, *Information Systems Journal*, 15, 85 - 101
[61] Mejias, R.J., Palmer, J.W. & Harvey, M.G. (1999) Emerging technologies, IT infrastructure, and economic development in Mexico. *Journal of Global Information Technology Management* 2(1), 31-54.
[62] Mingers, J. (1992) Technical, practical and critical OR - past, present and future? in *Critical Management Studies*, M. Alvesson & H. Willmott (Eds.), (pp. 90–113) SAGE, London
[63] Montealegre, R. (1998) Waves of change in adopting the Internet: lessons from four Latin American countries. *Information Technology & People* 11(3), 235-260.

[64] Mubarak, H. (1999) Address by President Muhammad Hosni Mubarak to The National Conference on The Promotion of Technology and Information. Available: http://www.presidency.gov.eg/html/13_9.htm (accessed 16.11.2004), 13 Sep. 1999

[65] Mubarak, H (2000) President Mubarak's speech at the lunch hosted in his honor by Virginia's Governor. Available: http://www.presidency.gov.eg/html/27-Mar2000_speech.htm (accessed 21.12.2004), 27 March 2000

[66] Ngwenyama, O. K. & Lee, A. S. (1997) Communication richness in electronic mail: Critical social theory and the contextuality of meaning. *MIS Quarterly* 21(2), 145-167

[67] Nidumolu, S. R.; Goodman, S. E.; Vogel, D. R. & Danowitz, A. K. (1996) Information technology for local administration support: The governorates project in Egypt. *MIS Quarterly* 20(2), 197–224.

[68] Orlikowski, W. J. & Baroudi, J. J. (1991) Studying information technology in organizations: Research approaches and assumptions. *Information Systems Research* 2(1), 1-28.

[69] Probert, S. K. (2002) Ethics, authenticity and emancipation in information systems development, in A. Salehnia (Ed.), *Ethical Issues of Information Systems* (pp. 249–254), Hershey: IRM Press.

[70] Sahay, S. (2004) Beyond utopian and nostalgic views of information technology and education: Implications for research and practice. *Journal of the Association for Information Systems* 5(7), 282 - 313

[71] Saravanamuthu, K. (2002) Information technology and ideology. *Journal of Information Technology* 17, 79 - 87

[72] Schuurman, F.J. (2003) Social capital: the politico-emancipatory potential of a disputed concept. *Third World Quarterly*, 24(6), 991-1010

[73] Settle, A. & Berthiaume, A. (2002) Debating e-commerce: Engaging students in current events. *Journal of Information Systems Education,* 13(4). 279-285.

[74] Stahl, B. C. (2008) *Information Systems: Critical Perspectives.* Routledge, London

[75] Stahl, B. C(2008) The ethical nature of critical research in information systems. *Information Systems Journal*, Special Issue on Exploring the Critical Agenda in IS Research, edited by Carole Brooke, Dubravka Cecez-Kecmanovic, Heinz K. Klein, 137-163.

[76] Stahl, B. C. (2006) Emancipation in cross-cultural IS research: the fine line between relativism and dictatorship of the intellectual. *Ethics and Information Technology* 8(3), Special issue on Bridging Cultures: Computer Ethics, Culture, and Information and Communication Technologies, edited by Charles Ess, 97-108

[77] Stahl, B. C. (2005) The paradigm of e-commerce in e-government and e-democracy, in Huang, Wayne; Siau, Keng & Wei, Kwok Kee (Eds), *Electronic Government Strategies and Implementation* (pp. 1 – 19), Hershey: Idea Group Publishing.

[78] Stahl, B.C. & El Beltagi, I. (2004) Cultural universality versus particularity in CMC, *Journal of Global Information Technology Management* 7(4), 47-65

[79] Temple, J. (1998) *The New Growth Evidence*, Institute of Economics and Statistics, Oxford

[80] Thompson, M. (2003) ICT, power, and developmental discourse: A critical analysis, in: *Global and Organizational Discourse about Information Technology*, E. Wynn; E. Whitley; M. Myers. & J. DeGross, (pp. 347 – 373) Kluwer Academic Publishers, Dordrecht

[81] Ulrich, W. (2001) A philosophical staircase for information systems definition, design, and development. *Journal of Information Technology Theory and Application* (3:3), 55 - 84

[82] Varey, R. J.; Wood-Harper, T. & Wood, B. (2002) A theoretical review of management and information systems Using a Critical Communications Theory. *Journal of Information Technology* 17, 229 - 239

[83] Walsham, G. (2005) Learning about being critical. *Information Systems Journal* (15), 111 - 117

[84] Walsham, G. (2001) *Making a World of Difference - IT in a Global Context.* Wiley, Chichester

[85] Walsham, G. (1993) Decentralization of IS in developing countries: Power to the people? *Journal of Information Technology* 8, 74 - 81

[86] Warschauer, M. (2003) Dissecting the "digital divide": A case study in Egypt. *The Information Society* 19, 297 - 304

[87] White, G. (2006) Towards a democratic developmental state. *IDS Bulletin,* (37:4), 60-71.

[88] Wilson, M. & Howcraft, D. (2002) Re-conceptualising failure: social shaping meets IS research. *European Journal of Information Systems* 11, 236 – 250.

EGYPTIAN WOMEN ARTISANS: ICTs ARE NOT THE ENTRY TO MODERN MARKETS

Leila Hassanin
Information and Communication Technology for Development in the Arab World[1]

Abstract   Handicrafts are an income generating activity for many women in Egypt, though as producers these women are often receiving the lowest return in the trading chain. This research analyses the potential for Egyptian craftswomen to use information and communication technologies (ICTs) to improve their earnings. The research shows that while ICTs could be a useful tool for marketing and selling their products, there are various structural challenges to trading via micro-ICT outlets like websites to the international market. Though online sales of crafts are possible, the use of ICTs as a marketing outlet by the average craftswoman is not viable in today's Egypt. The findings show that in the case of handicraft trade the generic "export is best" attitude is not the solution. In fact, the global craft market is too competitive for the typical Egyptian craftswoman as they are generally not equipped to handle the global handicrafts business environment. If the purpose is to empower artisan women then it would be better to enhance the demands for Egyptian handicrafts among the average Egyptian and thus create a domestic market for these products.

Keywords: E-commerce, Egypt, artisans, ICTs

1.   Introduction

The idea for this research began as a project need. ArabDev had been promoting the use of the Internet among low income target groups throughout Egypt with a special focus on women. Several of the women in the training courses began asking if ArabDev can assist them in selling their goods online. The women and various supporting not-for-profits wanted to explore this option as a way to improve their earnings which are slim when they go through the traditional trading route.

The requests were in line with a strong focus in Egypt to promote micro-enterprises and to make handicrafts exportable. Donors and development practitioners working for income generating activities have been focusing on

---

[1] www.arabdev.org

Please use the following format when citing this chapter:

Hassanin, L., 2008, in IFIP International Federation for Information Processing, Volume 282; *Social Dimensions of Information and Communication Technology Policy*; Chrisanthi Avgerou, Matthew L. Smith, Peter van den Besselaar; (Boston: Springer), pp. 179–190.

micro- and small-enterprises (MSEs) as a tool for poverty alleviation. For example, the National Council for Women (NCW) in Egypt, presided over by the first lady, is spearheading income generation for rural women through handicrafts production. The council has trained 840 women in four governorates in craftmanshipand is tying this activity to traditional crafts. The products were showcased at the Global Summit of Women 2006 – the Davos for Women – in Cairo. The establishment of micro- and small-enterprises has been a poverty alleviation strategy for years in Egypt. Entrepreneurship is seen as a possibility for many people if they are given the adequate training. Through establishing their own businesses it is believed that females, even the ones who live in remote areas, can reach beyond their limitations and establish businesses.

According to this trend, development specialists believe that women will benefit by becoming entrepreneurs. But are the conditions for this entrepreneur-oriented model realistic? Is "entrepreneurship" a learnable skill for most of these women? Or are main components missing to make this entrepreneurship model a reality? Or does this notion of entrepreneurship, self-sufficiency, and "can make it" attitude need certain contextual circumstances taking into account the constraints that lower income and lower educated women face [4, 5]?

Egypt is planning to institutionalize e-commerce in coming years and therefore it was important to explore the potential of ICTs, the Internet especially, to market female crafts.

The study found that aside from the viability to use ICTs as marketing and selling tools, the underlying premise of micro entrepreneurship as a successful model for income generation is flawed. The findings question the assumption that women can be taught entrepreneurship, and that they can use ICTs successfully to improve their income. The research shows that ICTs were not widely used and, in fact, for many women constituted new sets of limitations, inequities, and barriers.

This concurs with Poojary's [2] findings that entrepreneurship is generally difficult to teach through training courses, but rather that entrepreneurial skills are learned from being in an entrepreneurial milieu. Therefore a person coming from an entrepreneurial family background is more likely to become an entrepreneur themselves [2].

The research concludes that an export oriented strategy for marketing crafts in Egypt is not a promising means to secure a better income for craftswomen. The Egyptian case study highlights the challenges faced by local craft producers who have a restricted domestic market for traditional, higher-end handicrafts. Increased local demand for their wares would make income generation easier for these craftswomen.

The findings show that ICTs are only a small part of the marketing cycle and that there are other fundamentals in the production and marketing process that are hindering exports of Egyptian handicrafts. The main barrier to micro-businesses by female artisans is the low of demand for Egyptian crafts in the domestic market. An Egyptian market for their crafts would make it more realistic for them to be able to establish independent businesses and local markets would make the use of ICTs as marketing tools feasible for some of the women artisans.

2.   Methodology

The analysis is based on case studies of women and organisations working in the crafts sector. To market crafts through ICTs extensive back office procedures involving quality control, transportation, and customs, among others, are needed. The study therefore reviewed the regulatory and transport issues involved in crafts export and made a quick market analysis of the national and international craft business as far as it relates to the female handicraft sector in Egypt.

The study is based on a series of qualitative interviews conducted during 2005-2006, field observations, and years of community development practice using ICTs to enhance livelihoods and education in Egypt. The research used open-ended, life-story interviews to encourage women to go beyond the specific focus of ICTs. This enabled the research to assess the use of ICTs in the women's lives and it brought issues that were important for the interviewees as females struggling with various life challenges that would not have been included in a more structured ICT focused interview.

It was not easy to locate and contact the craftswomen. There was reluctance, if not outright avoidance, especially on the part of traders to give information about their women producers, let alone allow direct contact with them. The unwillingness was mostly out of protectionism by the merchants who did not want to disclose their production sources. Even non-governmental organisations (NGOs) working in the field had to be approached through work relations and acquaintances. Due to these circumstances the research relied mostly on craftswomen working with NGOs.

Additionally, there were very few cases where artisan women had a combined experience with handicrafts and information technology. The ones who were found are more the exception than the rule; there is a weak relationship between crafts, women, and ICTs in Egypt.

Ten women from different regions of Egypt were interviewed. Varying geographical locations were chosen to account for some of the sub-cultures in the society. The research covers interviewees from Cairo, the community of Coptic solid waste collectors "Zabaleen" in Old Cairo, Siwa, Aswan, and Helwan an industrial district south of Cairo. In addition to the interview some of the NGOs' staff where interviewed.

The Egyptian society is predominantly Muslim, with a Coptic minority. Muslim and Coptic informants were included, the research did not find, in its scope, a difference between women from either religion. Both Coptic and Muslim women are subject to the same traditional, patriarchal norms. Additionally, Nubian and Siwan females were included as they have distinct traditional crafts and historical backgrounds.

Education ranged from university degrees to former illiterates, who through adult education attained diplomas. The interviewees' ages span from 18 to 53 years. Family conditions ranged from single, married, married with children, and separated. Financially, some of the women co-financed their households, some were saving the money in preparation for marriage, and one woman was the main provider for herself and her two children.

The study did not plan to extend beyond Egypt, but to comprehend the conditions for successful e-commerce for Egyptian craftswomen it was essential to understand the dynamics of the international crafts-market. I visited the New York Gift Fair, a major global crafts exhibit, to get a first hand experience of international competition.

3.   The female artisans

The interviews highlighted the fact that ICTs are, at present, only marginally used in the production, marketing and selling cycle for female handicrafts in Egypt. Randa, who was illiterate until her late teens is now a daily user of the Internet but not directly to market handicrafts.

> I used to be a weaver of rugs working with a local NGO. After I completed many years of literacy studies and I was able to earn my diploma I began working as a secretary for the NGO. That is when I stopped the weaving as I got a better income through my new job.

Asking Randa about how the NGO markets the rugs, she says that it is mostly done through traditional bazaars, a shop at the NGO, and contacts of the board members. She says that she sometimes takes questions for orders over email, but that the transactions are done via fax or in person.

Dalia has a B.A. in finance, she is a candle-maker, and wants to go into the wedding preparation business. Dalia is currently receiving training through a donor organisation (COSPE[2]) in enterprise design and management.

> The Internet is very useful for me. I own a computer and connect daily from home where I work. I browse online to get ideas for candle shapes. Lately I have been exploring to shift my business to wedding management as I am having a hard time finding the raw material for my candles. I sell the candles through fairs and at the Trade Egypt outlet. COSPE has a website but no orders ever came through the site. At present I do not see that there is enough demand to sell online.

Aida manages a recycled paper production line at an NGO. She sells paper products, cards, stationary, and artwork through an outlet located at the NGO and through fairs and direct contact with clients.

> We do not sell online. Some of our contacts use emails for orders though, but it is more a follow up on the orders than new business.

---

[2] See: http://www.utlcairo.org/ong/COSPE/our_projects.htm

We are browsing the net for ideas, but in general I would say that the Internet is not a major tool for us. I see the potential though and if you come back in some years we might be more active online. There are a lot of people now that browse the Net and use emails.

From the interviews it became clear that ICTs are used as a support for the design and production of crafts in Egypt, but until now are not a major marketing and sales tool. With the spread of ICTs, mobile phones, and the Internet in particular, this could change over time and should not be dismissed, but a realistic perspective should be maintained as to the context these women are working and marketing in.

4.   The challenge of limited demand for local crafts in the Egyptian market

In Egypt there is not much daily demand for locally made crafts, other than the simple, low-cost crafts used by lower income Egyptians, such as pottery to hold water, palm reed baskets, and iron works used in rural and semi-rural areas. These types of crafts are not covered in this research as they fall under the category of daily used objects which have a slim profit margin and are not marketable in their present crude form to other market niches. Most women in this study are involved in crafts that have lost their traditional use due to western styled modernization and have been relegated to the souvenir category.

The dress and interior design fashion in Egypt are geared towards Western models. Egypt has neither developed a modern design style using traditional motives like South Africa nor pioneered a contemporary design school like the Scandinavians. Nor did it maintain and cultivate its traditional crafts on a national scope like the textile industry in Senegal and Morocco, where the Caftan is still the national dress. There were short attempts by local designers to modernize the Islamic style in interior design, but these efforts remained at the level of well known designers and the elite, with most of the clientele in rich oil producing Arab countries. This style was not mainstreamed to the middle income brackets where the volume demand is. The leading Egyptian Décor magazine "Beity" ("My House") shows the design trends of the affluent who are beginning to incorporate Egyptian and Islamic elements into their homes. Yet, at present these trends are financially out of reach for most Egyptians.[3] Beity's showcase-houses though are a model for how traditional crafts could be used for a local design trend that could be adjusted to different income brackets.

A modern Egyptian design theme would allow for a more integrated craft production line where different crafts are combined to create design themes; this would include textiles, wood, metal, and glass, among other specialties. The

---

[3] A middle income Egyptian referred to the magazine to the researcher as offensive in its display of expensive, out of reach décor.

creation of such a design trend would create local markets for female artisans and would revitalize some of the traditional crafts in Egypt.

An adequate national market would be a starting point for handicrafts marketed through ICTs, in this case mobile phones could be even more viable than the Internet. Online marketing, though, would still have its clientele in the higher income brackets.

5.   Quality and design as marketing ingredients

The issue of quality as a prerequisite for successful sales came up with donors and with international NGOs that market crafts. At present, most products bought from the crafts women are not immediately sellable due to their poor finishing. The merchants are finishing many of the products and are reaping wide margins of profit by doing this. For example, they will take an exquisite, but frayed piece of stitching, line it, sew the edges and the piece will sell at a much higher price.

COSPE trained Siwan women artisans in quality improvement, such as finishing techniques. But COSPE experienced resistance by most women to clean up their embroideries because they had many household duties that needed their time and attention. So they set up a second production line with women sewers to finish the embroidery work. The multiple duties the craftswomen face in the domestic sphere prevents them from producing higher end finishes – despite the provided training and the promise of reaping better financial returns.

The use of professional designers has improved the marketability of some Egyptian crafts, putting a modern spin on them with stylish colours and by following fashion trends. El-Bashayer revived its crocheting by hiring a well known Egyptian designer with whose help the organisation improved its marketing quota through offering more attractive pieces. Their products range from floor length curtains, bedspreads, bath towels, to infant and adult clothes.

Negada, a weaving community in the Qena governorate at the Egyptian southern border, is another example of the importance of incorporating a designer in the production process. Negada shawls had been traditionally marketed to the Sudan, but with the civil war and the hardening of the Egyptian-Sudanese border the weavers lost their clientele and their main market. The craft was dying out. The Canadian International Development Agency (CIDA) funded a one-year project where a French designer was brought in to revive the fading weaving tradition. The designer worked directly with the weavers bringing in new colour combinations and weaving themes. Despite the project's short duration, the local weavers quickly absorbed the new designs and were able to expand their markets to Cairo and beyond.

Currently Negada fabrics are sold in an upscale outlet in Garden City, Cairo, with Japanese expatriates as its main clients. The prices of the Negada pieces are high, not affordable for most Egyptians. If the Negada experience could be adapted to the tastes of Egyptians and the prices adjusted to domestic consumers, even if at the higher income levels, there could be a wider domestic market for these textiles.

ICTs are an excellent tool to showcase product diversity, design ideas, and quality issues to local female producers. As the saying goes, a picture is worth a thousand words, and this technology enables to bring the message home in a visual manner.

6.   Challenges for Egyptian crafts in the global market

Internationally, Aid to Artisans (ATA)[4] is a leading US based fair trade organisation.[5] I met with the ATA board of directors, the marketing division, and visited their booth at the NY Gift Fair. ATA's products are attractively exhibited; a big difference from the quality and display of crafts in Egypt like the Fair Trade Egypt shop. In general the displays at the NYC Gift Fair were sophisticated in their designs, colour coordination, quality, and presentation. One has to take into consideration that the designs and colour schemes change from year to year. Seasonal items are marketed far in advance and a trend watch is critical at this level of marketing. In addition to be on the forefront of fashion trends, the crafts have to be financially competitive while maintaining the highest quality standards. This is a big ordeal, as - in their current state - most Egyptian crafts are not competitive internationally design and quality wise and their prices are mid-ranged at best.

In terms of the main competition to Egyptian goods, in fair trade terms and beyond, the Moroccan crafts are predominant and had an early entry into the global market, followed by Jordanian goods. Both the Moroccan and the Jordanian governments have been promoting handicraft exports for many years and have gained a foothold in the global market. The Egyptian government has only recently begun pushing crafts trade. It was obvious that this environment was not something a simple Egyptian craftswoman, or even a cooperative without external help, could handle. Even COSPE has been struggling to successfully export selected Egyptian crafts to Italy during their ten years of operation.

South Africa is a successful example of taking African crafts and designs to a broad based local and global clientele. This was possible by marketing the African "way of life" through interior design, literature, and a widening and increasingly sophisticated émigré base. One has only to step into Johannesburg airport's two dominant crafts shops: *Inside Africa* and the newly established *Into Africa*, to experience the designs, colours, and exquisite arrangements that have made this design style famous. There is no equivalent to this vibrant shopping experience in Egypt. South Africa was able to establish its design elements in the highest echelon of international interior design which has increased its marketability and

---

[4] ATA's website is a good starting point to explore the richness of global craft production and marketing, see: http://aidtoartisans.org/home.php
[5] ATA is also heavily supported by USAID funds.

appeal. The South African design is also popular within the country itself, this way it has a varied purchasing base.

7.   Selling crafts online

After having explored the macro-environment for the crafts trade in Egypt and globally, this chapter asks: what are the issues and challenges facing a woman who wants to establish an online crafts selling business? Are there other ICT tools beside the Internet that could help women market crafts? Are there examples from other fields that could guide economic development practitioners and decision-makers in invigorating trade in the crafts sector?

Davis [3] led a carpet selling project: *Women Weavers Online: rural Moroccan women on the Internet.* The project sold carpets traditionally made by Moroccan women through a website without the women leaving their respective villages. Some of these villages were in remote and isolated areas of Morocco. Davis shows that it was possible for her project to market and sell rugs through the Internet. Davis' article, however, also shows that establishing the website and marketing the rugs was based on the existence of the author who is a well-educated American and who used her social relations, her language, and technological skills to enable this commercial online outlet. Davis does not account for her expenses in the financial spreadsheet that shows a marginal profit for the women weavers through the international sale of their rugs. Not accounting for Davis' actual cost gives an unrealistic financial and technical viability to the initiative that could not have existed without her presence. This author is not optimistic about the possibility of training and recruiting a local person to substitute her to enable sustainability of the initiative.

8.   Suzanne the online crafts entrepreneur

Yet, given the right skills and circumstances it is possible to have a crafts selling business via the Internet as shown by the example of a young woman from Cairo, who is exporting handicrafts overseas through her website. Suzanne is a middle-class, single woman who, as is the custom in Egypt, lives with her parents. She attended a private, foreign language school and has a B.A. in Finance. After holding odd jobs for several years, she decided to establish her own business marketing Egyptian souvenirs at fairs and by establishing a website to sell internationally.

> *I am online daily for hours – my parents are constantly chiding me for running up the phone bill.*[6] *I search for wholesale traders online and have been using chat rooms and social networking sites like Facebook and others to find merchants. I have good and bad experiences, but selling needs a stick-to-it attitude and I have that in*

---

[6] In Egypt Internet use is paid through the phone bill.

*bundles. Overall I have been successful in the end. I am now dealing
with a trader in California whom I export bigger quantities to.*

Despite making business contracts, Suzanne has been discouraged by her sister
and her parents in her commercial enterprise. For them her work is very
consuming and requires a lot of upfront money, especially for the IT services, and
more than it has brought in until now, but Suzanne is persistent.

*Business is like that you have to give it time. I have made constant progress
since I began and I am optimistic about this enterprise.*

She has a website[7] that she constantly upgrades. Suzanne excelled in finding
back-office solutions to her e-business. One of the main challenges was the lack of
e-commerce in Egypt, which made it impossible to charge a customer's credit card
through an online transaction.

Egypt is planning to have e-commerce in the future, though an exact date has
not been set. Currently, the Information Technology Industry Development
Agency (ITIDA)[8], established by Law 15 in 2004, is responsible for e-signatures,
e-commerce, and e-business activities in Egypt. Paving the way for e-commerce,
e-signatures were established by the executive regulations, decree no. 109 of 2005.
E-signatures are a cornerstone for e-commerce because the electronic
authentication of signatures is essential for e-financial transactions.[9]

Under these circumstances Suzanne had to find a creative solution to be able to
offer credit card transactions on her site. Having a credit card payment option is a
necessity to be competitive in today's online craft business. Her site has a selling
link to a US company, 2Checkout.com, that "is the online distribution center for
over 300,000 tangible or digital products and services. 2CO provides turnkey e-
commerce solutions to thousands of business customers around the world."[10]

In addition to finding alternative solutions to be able to sell her wares, finding
reliable and cost effective transportation for her micro-business was a major
challenge for Suzanne. She researched all shipping and air companies and options
to find economic shipping rates from a dependable company she could trust in
handling the goods with care.

Suzanne had also dealt before with customs to be able to export her goods,
which proved to be quite complex, and she had to hire a person who knew how to

---

[7] See: http://www.charisma-arts.net/
[8] The Information Technology Industry Development Agency (ITIDa) online available at
http://www.itida.gov.eg/index.asp
[9] To pave the way for broader applications of online transactions the Egyptian government has
introduced some domestic e-financial transactions for citizens. For example, phone bills can be paid
through the e-government portal, a bi-lingual Arabic-English site, with a credit or debit card.
Credit/debit card use is limited in Egypt and are mostly restricted to higher income levels, but the
availability of such e-government service tools could open their use in future by the average citizen. At
present the economy is mostly cash based and computer diffusion is still low as is Internet use. All
these factors restrict the actual use of such e-financial services.
[10] See: https://shop.2checkout.com/2co/index

navigate the system. She now uses Aramex[11], as this company offered the most convenient solution for her micro-business.

Customs are handled by Aramex in Suzanne's case, but customs are a major issue with most import-exporters. At the NY Gift Fair an American merchant told the author that the US customs regulations change each year and that this is a problem for every exporter and importer as they never know what is permitted to be imported the following year. They make a deal to import a big lot of textiles, for example, only to find out that import regulations to bring them to the US has changed preventing them to import these textiles. Sometimes they circumvent this change by naming the import a different name and they get away with that. But it is not a guaranteed solution. Therefore, most merchants have contact points at the customs offices to know about new regulations as soon as possible, but problems regarding these changes still come up.

Suzanne is the epitome of persistence and the creator of inventive solutions that enabled her, through trial and error, to establish a successful online crafts selling business. However, the setting up of such a website requires a highly enterprising attitude, combined with education and technical skills or the money to afford outside technical assistance. Suzanne's command of English is excellent too – the absence of language skills with most of the artisan women interviewed is a major obstacle to use the Internet for international trading. In Suzanne's case she has been aided by her family's financial support; as a single, not yet married woman in Egypt she is expected to be, if not fully supported financially by her parents, then at least in great part so. This freed Suzanne from worrying about living expenses like shelter and food, which could have affected the input she has given and still is giving to her entrepreneurial project. Suzanne has a computer at home and has been an active Internet user for years before starting her enterprise. Her IT skills are quite sophisticated which made it possible for her to use the Internet as a marketing resource.

9.   Conclusion

The research began as a quest by ArabDev to fulfil the demands of some craftswomen and crafts related not-for-profits to use ICTs, especially the Internet to widen their markets. A pragmatic step-by-step approach to marketing and selling online and possibly through other ICTs, like mobile phones, was taken. The research showed the difficulties facing women artisans and women involved in the crafts trade to export Egyptian crafts competitively to global markets. The

---

[11] Among its services Aramex provides US and UK based mailboxes to its customers. With this system a customer has a US or UK based address to which they can send and receive mail through local transport charges. Then the contents of the mailboxes are shipped in bulk three times a week, reducing shipping costs for the mailbox owners. The Aramex mailbox option is the closest a micro business can come to wholesale shipping. Though the shipping destination is only Cairo in Egypt for example, anyone living in farther out governorates would need to arrange additional domestic transport. Due to the Aramex service offers, international trading for micro- and small enterprises has been made easier by allowing them to buy and sell as if they had a foreign domicile.

barriers involve literacy, language skills, technical know-how, knowledge of how to navigate the regulatory and legal aspects of the export trade, quality control, transport requirements, and the availability of e-commerce..

This study began with the premise that ICTs could offer access to wider markets and higher profit retention for Egyptian crafts women. The research findings, however, showed gaps with the design, production, and quality of the crafts that determine the competitiveness of Egyptian handicrafts and these issues have a greater impact on sales than the use of ICTs for marketing.   The Internet has been a resource for some of the interviewed women nonetheless. Among those women who use ICTs, several were formerly craftspeople and then increased their education, including computer, and Internet skills, and changed their earning venue to a clerical job.

Craft production is often abandoned once a woman has marketable ICT skills. More income can be earned through clerical work than through handicrafts. Some craftswomen who made it "up the ladder" through increased education became supervisors for other craftswomen but stopped their direct production of crafts. In Siwa, a computer trainer from a local development organisation who works at the local school continues to do the traditional Siwan stitching in the evenings for additional income. Yet she does not combine her artisan work with her IT skills. Overall, examples of craftswomen using ICTs were few and not the norm.

Suzanne's example shows that while some women, mostly the more educated and privileged, could indeed benefit from utilizing ICTs in their entrepreneurial quest, most Egyptian crafts-women face prohibitive barriers to use this technology.

There are few examples where craftswomen are directly involved in marketing their wares through the Internet in Egypt. Email is used by craft producing NGOs as part of the selling process, but not as a marketing tool. Even mobile phones were not a main vehicle used by women in the marketing cycle.

ICT enabled entrepreneurship for the female crafts sector is not yet realistic, especially if it is geared towards selling globally. There is a big difference between a woman selling her wares at a local market, while she sits on the sides of the street, and a woman marketing to outside venues, especially through the Internet. One cannot extrapolate the development of a street vendor to an online merchant. A business to consumer export model cannot compete with a wholesale website. The tactile nature of crafts lends them to more traditional marketing venues like craft exhibits.

The research shows that the global crafts market is a highly competitive sphere both in price and quality and that exporting is not the straightforward answer to craft marketing in the Egyptian case. Despite this fact, ICTs can be a vehicle for the marketing of crafts for entrepreneurially inclined women, as is shown in by an example in this chapter. Yet, the same is not true for the larger numbers of low income women. For these women to benefit from marketing through ICTs it would need to be institutionalized into a collective enterprise that handles the various stages of product design, quality control, and marketing.

ICTs though make a good venue for quality promoting education, for a more creative design process, and to give local craftswomen a taste of global wares so that they have more incentives to improve their crafts even for the local market.

The study found that the most promising market for local craftswomen would be a domestic outlet. If Egypt could establish a broad base of local demand for an Egyptian style in interior design, for example, lots of the traditional crafts, now at the brink of extinction, could be incorporated into products that are part of this revived design style. The establishment of such a market depends on creating demand and the making of crafts at various price ranges available to the Egyptian consumers. Decision makers and social leaders are the prime vehicles for creating more demand for Egyptian crafts in the interior design and fashion circles. This in turn would make it easier for craftswomen to market their crafts either individually, collectively, or through an intermediary and the use of ICTs would be a promising tool to help them in this endeavour.

Acknowledgements

This research was made possible by grants from the International Development Research Centre (IDRC) through the GRACE project and the Ford Foundation.

References

[1]   Alsever, J. (2006). Fair prices for farmers: Simple idea complex reality, *New York Times*, March 19, available online:
http://www.nytimes.com/2006/03/19/business/yourmoney/19fair.html.
[2]   Poojary, C.M. (1996). What creates an entrepreneur? Some observations from a micro study, *Journal of Entrepreneurship*, Sage Publications, 5 (2), 253-60.
[3]   Davis, S.S. (2004). Women weavers online: rural Moroccan women on the internet. *Gender, technology and development*, 8(1), 53-75.
[4]   Mueller, S.D. (2006). Rural development, environmental sustainability, and poverty alleviation: A critique of current paradigms, DESA Working Paper, No. 11, January 2006, available online: http://www.un.org/esa/desa/papers/2006/wp11_2006.pdf.
[5]   Ofreneo, R. P. (2006). Problematizing microfinance as an empowerment strategy for women living in poverty: Some policy directions, *Gender, Development and Technology Journal of the Asian Institute of Technology (AIT)*, Bangkok, available online:
http://www.upd.edu.ph/~cswcd/webpages/DOCUMENTS/facultypublications/PUBLI CATIONS_Ofreneo2.pdf.

INSTITUTIONAL STRATEGIES TOWARDS IMPROVING HEALTH INFORMATION SYSTEMS (HIS) IN SUB-SAHARAN AFRICA

Solomon Berhanu Bishaw
University of Oslo, Norway

Abstract   The development of "Health Information Systems" (HIS) in low-income countries have been on the agenda for the last three decades. Despite significant mobilization, however, little progress has been made in realizing improved systems. One among the popular reasons for such progress concerns the lack or unwillingness of some relevant groups of actors to participate in HIS initiatives. Such explanations often delimit participants to a project or organisation level, and scant attention has been paid to the institutional environment, web of values, norms, rules, beliefs, and taken-for-granted assumptions that has long been recognized to influence the day to day realities of organisational life. This chapter, drawing on an institutional theory of membership, and based on discursive data of more than a decade and half from a low-income county's HIS development endeavors, reveals institutional processes and pressures that constrain participation of relevant actors.

Keywords: Information systems, institutional perspective, participation, Africa

1.   Introduction

The importance of "health information" to support improvements in healthcare systems of developing countries has been emphasized for more than three decades. Policies on strengthening "Health Information Systems" (HIS) have, accordingly, been constituted globally [22, 25] and nationally [24]. Conceptualizations and advocacy as to what HIS constitutes, why it is so important, and how HIS development and implementation might be conducted have been delineated [23, 13, 10]. Technical and financial assistance have been mobilized to materialize the same [1, 6, 13]. However, three decades of policy and resource support appear to have done little to improve the situation [1, 25, 13].

One among the popular reasons for the limited progress made so far relates to the lack of, unwillingness, or superficial participation of relevant actors in HIS development endeavors. Too often constraints in human resource are to be blamed [24, 25]; either knowledgeable individuals or the financial and organisational resources required to hire such individuals are beyond reach. In this line of

Please use the following format when citing this chapter:

Bishaw, S.B., 2008, in IFIP International Federation for Information Processing, Volume 282; *Social Dimensions of Information and Communication Technology Policy*; Chrisanthi Avgerou, Matthew L. Smith, Peter van den Besselaar; (Boston: Springer), pp. 191–207.

argument, neither the types of expertise required nor the causes for such constraints are adequately explored; rather they are either overlooked or assumed and taken-for-granted. Then we have the politics of conflicting interests resulting in unwillingness, or superficial participation, of some relevant actors, for example, those "on the ground" in healthcare facilities, the policy makers "on the top" [7], and those among the different so called vertical health programs [6, 7]. Little effort was made, however, to account for the mechanisms or the ways such unwillingness was revealed. Furthermore, such explanations often delimit participants to a project or organisation level, which usually includes a subset of the potential stakeholders that might be affected by, and affect, the initiative.

There exists though, a wider recognition and frequent calls too, to broaden the sphere of research in the domain [18, 21]. Walsham and Sahay, for example, have called for critical studies as a way to open up "black boxes" surrounding IS initiatives, and called for the deployment of institutional theory as "topics and issues in developing countries are normally deeply intertwined with issues of power, politics, donor dependencies, institutional arrangements, and inequities of all sorts" [21, p. 19]. Smith and his colleagues also have suggested that "there is a need to first of all gain understanding of the existing social structures in place and then to carefully interpret to what extent and through which means participation of marginalized groups can be made possible" [18, p.16].

In this chapter, we aim to examine institutional processes and pressures that constrain, construct, and empower organisational or individual actor's participation in HIS development endeavors. We draw on "the institutional theory of membership", which emphasizes that participation in a specific domain by organisational or individual actors is seen not as a choice among unlimited options determined by purely internal arrangements, but rather as a choice among a narrowly defined set of legitimate actors determined by members composing a wider community [12]. By employing such a theoretical framework, I hope to deepen understanding, and stimulate appropriate action.

Section 2 provides the main constructs of the theoretical framework that guide the study. In section 3, we discuss the research context and the methodology employed. Section 4 presents construction of our analysis. Section 5 considers implication and limitations of the study.

2.   Theoretical framework

This study employs the *institutional theory of membership* [12] as an analytical lens to examine institutional processes and pressures that constrain, construct, and empower organisational or individual actors' involvement in HIS development endeavors. The notion of membership describes the basis of legitimate participation in a social arena [12]. *Legitimacy* here is "a generalized perception or assumption that the actions of an entity are desirable, proper, or appropriate within some socially constructed system of norms, values, beliefs, and definitions" [19, p. 574]. Central to the institutional theory of membership, accordingly, is its emphasis that organisational or individual actors are involved in a given social phenomenon is seen not as a choice among unlimited array of possibilities determined by purely internal arrangements, but rather as a choice among a narrowly defined set of legitimate actors determined by the members composing the organisational field. The form of this influence is manifested in *membership structures*: pragmatically oriented sets of rules that delineate membership, explaining who can participate and who can not in a given social arena, and if allowed to participate with what social position [12, 11].

Organisational field refers to the idea that a distinct "set of organizations" that comprises sets of "subject positions" (posts) bound together by institutionalized rules and standards [12, 8, 5]. This "set of organizations" represent "those organizations that, in the aggregate, constitute a recognized area of institutional life: key suppliers, resources and product consumers, regulatory agencies and other organizations that produce similar services or products" [8, p.148]. And for Bourdieu fields "present themselves synchronically as structured spaces of positions" [4, p. 72] cited in [12]. While the rules of membership that structure organizational fields reward particular strategic positions and practices, it also sanctions others, which makes the constitution of membership rules dynamic. Organizational and other actors continuously struggle to interpret or change membership rules so that their own identities are privileged [12].

2.1   Interaction rituals

Lawrence [12] argued that "membership in professional fields is produced through and enacted within sets of 'interaction rituals'" [12, p. 118]. *Interaction rituals* are "routinized interactions between two or more actors that are vested with some symbolic significance" [ibid]. For example, business lunches with colleagues, formal presentations at professional meetings, graduation ceremonies, or meetings of audit teams may represent interactive rituals.

Interaction rituals that govern membership can vary in terms of the degree to which they are formalized and taken-for-granted; or with respect to the actors involved. In this latter case, interaction rituals may involve relatively homogeneous sets of actors or in contrast, membership may be negotiated among a heterogeneous set of actors including multiple professional groups and clients. Membership is, therefore, conceptualized as a product of interaction ritual chains in which actors co-construct relationships with each other and membership boundaries. At the same time, membership boundaries produce the social space in which particular interaction rituals are understood as meaningful and valuable. Actors, therefore, through participation in these rituals, negotiate and signal their institutional membership [12].

As Lawrence [12] argued, neither the experience of membership nor its basis in interaction rituals is a simple, binary phenomenon. The social boundaries of some groups distinguish members sharply and powerfully from non-members, whereas for other groups the distinction is less clear and distinct. These differences reflect the way the interaction rituals vary in intensity and the extent to which they are self-reproducing. Fields with strong, enduring boundaries are built from powerful, self-reproducing rituals.

2.2   Membership strategies

Lawrence [12] argues that membership definitions of a field are of strategic interest to affected organisations and individuals. In a professional field, he argues that the interaction rituals define the boundaries of the profession by structuring the relationships among professionals, clients, regulators and other stakeholders, and also structure the distribution of the field's economic interests.

Membership in professional field is inherently dynamic, as membership boundaries can engender strategies of resistance in the part of those less privileged by the boundaries, who are often those excluded by the membership boundaries (See Figure 1). Social boundaries effectively associate various forms and amounts of "capital" with particular subject positions in the field [5]. Capital includes a diverse range of resources, including educational qualifications, social networks, and legitimate authority as well as economic capital. The differential allocation of capital based on the boundaries of institutional field sets up a situation in which conflict is embedded in their structures; actors will work to gain access to privileged positions or attempt to enact new rituals in order to change institutional rules and redistribute capital [5, 12].

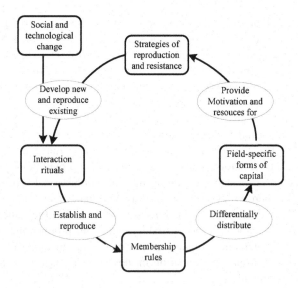

Figure 1: Membership dynamics in institutional fields (Source: [12, p. 122]).

Membership of professional fields may be transformed either through the impact of external disruption or through the strategies of interested actors.

Lawrence [12] argued that the starting point for understanding these dynamics is the set of interaction rituals that affect the membership rules for the field and in so doing differentially distribute the capital produced and motivate actors to reproduce or resist those rituals. A key issue then concerns the ways in which actors attempt to create new interaction rituals in order to reorient this process.

3.   Research approach

3.1   Research context and the HIS organisation field

This case study is based on Health Information System (HIS) development endeavours of a country located within the Sub-Saharan Africa. The modern healthcare system of the country has evolved over six decades as to its intra- and inter-organisational relationships, among other things. Internally, the organisational structure of the healthcare system has evolved with encounters between integration and separate health programs as well as centralization and decentralization. Externally, the system, being situated within a deprived economy, depends on others who are willing to augment the resources of the government to its operations. Since the outset, the system has been getting support from bilateral and multilateral agencies each of which have their own preferences as to the organisation and reporting mechanisms that has to be followed.

The introduction of what is known as the Sector Wide Approach to the health sector in the mid 1990s has bring such intra- and inter organisational relationships into the forefront through the structured consultations and documents produced through the process. One among the issues embedded in such encounters has been the development of HIS. While proprietary data collection and reporting systems persist all along for almost each separate health program, a department has been tasked\legislated to lead the development of an improved HIS system, at least since the end of the 1980s. The focus of this study to examine the institutional processes and pressures that constrain, construct and empower participation of various actors in HIS development endeavours this period.

Six relevant actors were identified in the HIS organisational field. Two groups are from within the Ministry of Health (MoH): the Planning Department and the "Other Departments". The Planning Department is the responsible division for the HIS function, initially informally and latter formally. Within this department there has been a unit, some times known as Health Statistics Unit and at times the HMIS unit, with a total of five posts two of which were professional at the end of 2006. The "Other Departments" within the MoH include Disease Prevention and Control (DPC), Environmental Health, and Mother and Child Health (MCH). Each of these departments has separate health programs such as Malaria and HIV\AIDS within the DPC; EPI and Family Planning within the MCH, and specialist experts. The third actor is the WHO, which is deeply embedded in the healthcare system. The WHO's staffs in the Country Office have increased from 3 to about 100 through a period of about half a century. The forth group represents Donors supporting the health sector broadly (more than two dozens) and the HIS component in particular. The other two groups are a public health group (which includes a private consultancy company and an academic department); and an Information Systems (IS) academic group.

3.2   Methodology and methods

This study employs Critical Discourse Analysis [15]. Discourse is defined as "an interrelated set of texts, and the practices of their production, dissemination and reception, that bring an object into being" [15, p. 3]. Texts are considered here to represent spoken, written, or any kind of artifacts that can be systematically investigated [15]. Discourse analysis as a methodology is used here to make sense of the processes whereby reality comes into being by examining and connecting individual texts to discourses, and locating both within a historical and social context. As our interest in this study rests on institutions, membership structures specifically, we rely on the discursive model of Phillips, Lawrence and Hardy in claiming that "institutions are constituted by the structured collections of texts that exist in a particular field and that produce the social categories and norms that shape the understandings and behaviours of actors" [16, p. 638]. We also base our data collection and analysis efforts in their suggestion that "particular discourses and institutions that affect an organization or sets of organizations could be studied historically, by tracing them back to key texts" [16, p. 647].

There were two distinct phases of data collection. The first of these was the gathering of "naturally occurring" key texts regarding the HIS under consideration. Two sets of texts were identified in this phase. The first set of texts relates to a long term (20 years) comprehensive Health Sector Wide Program, which covers all aspects of policy and planning, implementation, monitoring and management of all the areas that relate to the provision of healthcare to the whole country. Specific texts in this category include short-term (5-year) Sector Wide Programs (SWP), program action and implementation manuals, implementation performance reports, joint review meeting proceedings, and commissioned thematic consultancy reports. As HIS (also known as HMIS) together with Measurement & Evaluation being one among seven major components of the SWP, it has persistently been in the discourse in the iterative processes of planning, implementation, and evaluation. These texts collectively, and in a structured way, have left traces of more than a decade of experience in the sector. The second set includes HIS related texts produced before or during the SWP, but more or less independently from it. These include texts produced on pilot initiatives since 1990 and HIS related publications of the WHO and associates, particularly texts that were projected to the African Regional Office and Member States. The second phase of data collection involved web site visits and interviews with two senior staffs of the Ministry of Health (MoH). The focus of this phase was to gather background data on the different groups and individuals identified in the previous phase as to their place in the HIS field.

Data analysis was guided by the theoretical framework outlined in the previous section. Given the research focus on membership structures and strategies, we first examine each text in the discourse for traces of prescriptions for, or enactments of interaction rituals and their participants; strategies employed by the identified actors to introduce, reproduce or transform the rituals; the type of relationship among actors as to the coalition and competition as well as the resources available to each group. Backgrounds of individuals participating in the different rituals were explored as to their education, work experience, and organisational affiliation. Such background was sought besides the texts within the discourse, from websites associated to the different groups, and interviews with two senior employees at the MoH.

Finally, my extended involvement in the research domain needs to be mentioned here, which has enabled me to have a close look to the evolving interests and positions of the different actors in the field. I started involvement in the domain around mid 2003 with extensive visits to become acquainted with the government health care system broadly and HIS activities in particular. Over the subsequent one and half years, I was involved with a group of IS action researchers in initiating and enacting collaboration with authorities at autonomous "Provincial Health Departments" and undertaking pilot projects towards the development of an improved HIS in their constituencies. Over the latest three years, I have directed my attention and commitment to broader issues mainly following developments in the domain closely with a role of independent observer. In the entire five years, I was in the country for about twice a year and for an average of about six weeks each time. Prior to my entry into this research domain, I was mainly engaged in teaching and practicing Systems Analysis and Design as well as Database Design for about four years.

4.   Membership structures and strategies in the HIS field

4.1   Interaction rituals

The emergence of the HIS field in the country can be linked to the WHO and its recent development to the Sector Wide Program (SWP). This section presents the interaction rituals in more or less chronological order in three distinct periods: the early period before the introduction of the SWP; the formative years of the SWP; and the maturing SWP.

In the early period, two sets of interaction rituals dominate the HIS field under the sponsorship of the WHO. At the international/regional level major interaction rituals include *consultative workshops* such as study groups, technical discussion sessions, and workshops to develop, as well as disseminate, conceptualizations on HIS. One example of such early ritual is the technical discussion on "Strengthening Information Support for Management of District Health Systems" at the end of the 1980s. Participants in such rituals include the WHO and associates mostly public health academics and practitioners as well as authorities at the Ministries of Health of member countries.

At the country level, major interaction rituals include *consultations, committees, and workshops*. Consultations among officials of the WHO and the MoH were instrumental in the initiation of, and recruitment of a consultant for the pilot project, named "Strengthening District HMIS in [the country]", in 1990-91. Representatives of the WHO, as members of Policy Task Force or as "Resource Person" also did consult the MoH as in the inclusion of an HMIS provision in the Health Policy as well as in the SWP. Members of such consultation were mainly those responsible employees at the MoH and the responsible officers at specific departments within the WHO Country Office, but also consultants from the Regional Office and the Headquarters as well as funding agencies.

During implementation of the early mentioned pilot project, two *committees* and a series of *consultative workshops* were proposed and enacted. The two committees were a *Technical Working Group* (TWG) and a *National Advisory Committee* (NAC). The TWG was "established to prepare an implementation plan and to assume responsibilities for implementation". While it was lead by a "Statistician" responsible for the health statistics unit within the Planning Department\MoH, other named member also includes a "Statistician" from the Provincial Health Department' where the pilot districts were located. The NAC was proposed and constituted to support the TWG on "policy issues". This was said important because "on policy issues, the TWG had minimal leverage in negotiating with relatively well-financed vertical programmes". Accordingly, as reported by the WHO consultant, the committee was constituted with departmental and programme heads from the Ministry of Health and allied institutions, and were officially inaugurated with the presence of the Vice-Minster for Health. Besides these two committees, a series of workshops was proposed and at least a couple of them were enacted throughout the project period (in 1990-91). The objective of the workshops was to create a common understanding on issues surrounding district HMIS. Participants of such workshops were employees of the health care system, mainly from district health offices. For example, in the first consultative workshop there were 62 participants and 3 observers representing 18 districts, a Provincial Health Department, the MoH, the WHO and a donor agency, who had supported the project financially through the WHO.

Following the introduction of the SWP, two sets of interaction rituals, focusing on *governance* and *evaluation,* were introduced. The governance rituals comprise a set of structured "consultation forums" and "joint decision-making" framework which was developed and formalized over a decade. These structured rituals constitute, from top hierarchically, a Macro and Sector Level Joint Steering Committees, Intermediary Sectoral Consultative Forum, and Technical Coordinating Committee. The top level rituals often enacted once or twice a year and with a focus on policy issues; the intermediary level enacted once every two months and with a focus on operational and managerial issues; and the Technical Committee meets in almost a weekly basis focusing on implementation issues.

Membership in these rituals constitutes representatives of the Government and Donors fundamentally and often evolved to have more donor representatives than the government counterparts. The Technical Committee, for example, was set to include nine members four of which were set to the government. However, throughout the years there was only one member representing the government, head of the Planning Department, while at least five members represent donors. The chairmanship of this Committee has also been shared jointly by the head of the Planning Department and the WHO.

Each of these rituals has its own developmental history. If we take the Technical Committee, it was no where at the beginning of the SWP. At about midway in the implementation of the first five-year SWP, two individuals representing donors and the government coordinate a mid term review process together with "resource persons" from the WHO and another donor agency. This was to support the "inadequately staffed" and "highly overloaded" Secretariat of the SWP, the Planning Department. Subsequently, the Technical Committee was emerged informally to coordinate review missions, supporting recruitment of consultants, among other things, during the second SWP. In the third SWP, this Committee becomes formally embedded in the formal governance structure of the sector. As per a recent memorandum of understanding among some group of donors and the government on a certain Fund, "the [Planning Department] is responsible for receiving, processing and approving requests for funding, and ensure the appropriate and efficient use of the Fund in the spirit of its purpose. [Technical Committee's] endorsement is needed ... for activities which exceed the agreed budget".

The *evaluation rituals* are for "assessment of activities surrounding [SWP] implementation including monitoring of key performance indicators, periodic reviews, and joint donor supervision missions and thematic and evaluation studies". Four rituals can be identified in this category: frequent Joint Review Missions, Mid-Term and Final Evaluations, and ad hoc commissioned thematic studies. Evaluation rituals are said to be conducted "by specialists who have not been involved in the day-to-day management of a program" and with an "appropriate mix of national, international, Government and Donor personnel" and with a special preference to specialists already familiar with the domain.

If we consider, for example, one of two final program evaluations conducted so far, there were a total of 43 professionals participated from across various organisations (constituted into eight teams HMIS being one): 11 from the public sector; 23 from donor agencies; 1 local NGO representative; and about 8 individual consultants. Among a total of 12 expatriates participated in the evaluation was the team leader for the HMIS component hired for short term assignment from abroad. As per self-declared profile, the consultants' educational background, experience, as well as interest constitute a wide area of public health specialties: human nutrition, statistics, medical sociology; health systems research and development; health policy; monitoring and evaluation; health management information systems; and health financing. Other frequent participants in the

HMIS evaluation sub-team hold such positions as "health specialist" or "health sector development specialist" in multilateral and bilateral donor agencies. Such team members have been swapped to evaluate other components such as finance strategy or health services in different evaluation missions.

After about half a dozen of years since the implementation of the SWP was launched, and the governance and evaluation rituals maturing, calls were made to constitute, once again, the traditional rituals, namely the *Technical Working Group* (TWG) and the *National Advisory Committee* (NAC), which were enacted after a year and half latter. This time, the NAC was established "with a view to facilitate the development of a national policy and strategy on HMIS and M & E". Membership to the NAC was explicitly proposed to include representatives of the MoH, donor agencies, and an NGO initially; and "at a latter stage private sector and institute of higher learning"; and was enacted accordingly. The initial members of the NAC procured an international consultancy service for "Strengthening the National HMIS and Monitoring & Evaluation". Subsequently, the private consultancy company, who won the international bid, and an academic public health group who was tasked to handle the training component of the consultancy work have joined the ritual. Finally, an IS group from an informatics department of a university, who has competed and lost the consultancy bid, had joined the NAC.

The TWG was then proposed not only "to provide technical advice, and to monitor the implementation of the activities of the HMIS and M&E reform", but, since various stakeholders "have shown interest in supporting specific activities in different areas of the national HMIS and M & E reform (i.e. ICT, training etc)", it also has "to insure coordination between the institutions and synchronization in executing their respective, complementary activities". Membership into the TWG was, accordingly, been proposed to constitute the public health consultancy company, the public health academic group, the IS academic group, and a Foundation which has been involved in "Hospital Management Information Systems" in parallel but independently.

4.2   *Membership strategies*

Different strategies have been employed by the groups identified earlier in the construction, reproduction or transformation of the rituals in the field over the years. *The WHO* has been at the center of the field since the beginning and has influenced the rituals over the years as in many technical facets of the sector. The WHO, primarily had developed (through its own staff and collaborators) conceptualizations about HIS, embedded are - among other issues - the requisite expertise to participate in HIS related work and the location of professionals with such expertise both globally and within member states. While the expertise found within the WHO was emphasized, specific divisions within the WHO and collaborating centers were mentioned as sources of such consultants. At the country level, it was said that "emphasis should be placed on enhancing existing service staff and manager capacities in data generation, analysis and use, including the use of computers, rather than creating specialists in health data analysis and informatics". The WHO also employs its direct and well established relationship with the MoH to introduce, realize, and sustain its prescriptions. If we take the 1990\91 "District HMIS" pilot project, while the WHO had hired an expatriate consultant with the stated expertise to lead the project, "Epidemiology Coordinators (trained sanitarians)" were selected and trained from local staff for the "Information Coordinator" position. The latter were selected because of their "practical experience in relating numbers to decisions", "statutory responsibilities for management information systems", and for "being members of district health teams". Finally, the WHO advocates and facilitates adoption of resolutions on strengthening HIS by the World Health Assembly including its' own role in the field when and if needed. The latest resolution adopted in May 2007, besides once again reiterating the importance of HIS, notifies "the constitutional normative mandates of WHO in health information and epidemiological reporting" and requested the executive body "to increase WHO's activities in health statistics at global, regional and country levels and provide harmonized support to Member States to build capacities for development of health information systems and generation, analysis, dissemination and use of data".

Donors have employed *Colonization strategies,* which are "aimed at effecting a subject position within a field that gains its legitimacy and influence through its connection to positions outside the field". The SWP championed by the World Bank in mid 1990s was the basis for changes adopted by donors supporting the health sector. In subsequent years, three major processes were adopted by donors. First, the necessary conceptualizations for the health SWP including the major components of the program, governance structure and consultation forums, key documents and schedules were developed, and continuously refined. Secondly, Donors have managed to forge, formalize and institutionalize strong alliances among themselves. Also known as Donor's architecture, comprises a hierarchical, from a high level Donor Group (composed of head of missions for multilateral and bilateral donors), to Sector level Working Groups (Health Sector Donor Group is one among a dozen), to thematic Sub-Groups (HMIS being one among more than twenty), which was build over a decade. These were then have to join with government counterparts in creating the "joint consultation" and "decision-making" rituals, which were described in the previous section at least partly. Donors, as part of the alliance, are then expected to "speak with one voice" during consultations with their government counterparts as adopted by them as part of their "ways of working". Thirdly, donors embed and enact conditionality in their engagement with all concerned and the government in particular. For example, it was reported in one of the annual SWP performance reports that donors "were preparing to scale up their assistance… However, as a result of the [unacceptable] events in [year], donors have undertaken a joint-assessment of political and economic conditions for development. Also, they have suspended direct budget support".

The Public Health Group has employed *stratification strategies* that "involves the development or reformulation of interaction rituals into hierarchical chains such that professional groups in the field relate to each other through a series of order-giving and order-taking exchanges" [12, p. 136]. The public health consultancy group has created such a hierarchy when it hired local software developers in two occasions over the last five years. Earlier, two individual software developers were recruited for an autonomous provincial health department as part of a wider technical assistance, and very recently a software development company was subcontracted. In both cases, the developers were instructed to create "electronic version" of the data collection and reporting formats from page layout and formatting to positioning of selectable options. Similarly, at least initially, the public health academic department was tasked to participate in the training component of the HMIS consultancy work. In this regard, the public health academic group has mobilized and initiated a post graduate program in "Measurement and Evaluation", and "preparations are underway to begin diploma level training on HMIS... to support the new system with a sustainable human resource base".

The IS group employs *association strategies,* "which involve attempts to develop interaction rituals in which less established professional groups become engaged in common sets of activities and routines with more established groups" [12, p. 134]. This is to create and change "subject positions so that positions they are capable of occupying gain legitimacy from previously legitimated positions" [ibid]. The IS group has attempted a serious of activities in this regard. First, alliances were established with public health departments within universities, autonomous provincial health departments, and individual public health professionals. At the forefront of these activities was the collaboration with some autonomous provincial health departments to pilot test software for use in their constituencies. Such initiatives, however, had triggered such a comment during evaluation rituals "... uncoordinated provincial initiatives have been implemented to improve data collection and reporting; while well-intentioned, these initiatives threaten to further fragment an already fragile system". Secondly, efforts were made to introduce new rituals such as workshops, graduate level programs, and publications. Workshop tracks were organized on HIS in a mega continental ICT conference and another in a national ICT-for-health workshop. In these rituals invited participants, and panelists, include officials of the MoH/PD and Public Health Academics together with IS groups, the organizers. A call was made by this group in these workshops for a successive ritual for "sharing of best practices, know-how and software" among the different initiatives that were going on in parallel within the country. A graduate level program in HIS, another ritual, granting admissions to students from public health and informatics background, alike, was also introduced. Members of the IS group were also involved in proposal development and publishing articles together with public health professionals.

Last, but not least, we have the two groups within the Ministry of Health: the Planning Department and the "Other departments". *The planning department,* being in the center of the field, has all along been engaged with the WHO and donors intensively as well as with the new actors to a lesser degree despite its limited capacities. No traces of a unique kind were found in the discourse except the enactment and reproduction of existing prescriptions by this group. What was more is the participation of this group in other rituals (workshops and conferences), locally and abroad, with groups either at the periphery, or outside of the HIS field as has been constructed locally. In this rituals as well, this group reflects the prescriptions embedded in the HIS field. In a workshop organized by three ICT related departments of the national university and a government telecom company to deliberate on the challenges and prospects of appropriating ICT in the health sector, a senior staff from this department, who spoke on "Future Prospects on Telemedicine & HMIS", had emphasized that "support and technical assistance are expected from WHO in ICT area".

In the contrary, *the "other departments" within the MoH* has been taking the strategy of resistance by boycotting the rituals all along. Traces of such action are in abundant both in the rituals and in pilot implementation initiatives. As a recent SWP final evaluation emphasized "the participation of MoH in some of these joint arrangements ... seems to have been reduced to few staff from the Planning Department rather than the broad spectrum of MoH leadership. A broader and stronger representation of the MoH led by Planning Department would lead to a more effective Government-donor policy dialogue". It was also reported that among the factors to have constrained progress in HIS were "that several programs are coordinated by departments who all wish to monitor progress and performance in their own respective domains". Similarly "resistance" or "unwillingness" of members of this group in micro activities as in limiting "indicator" requirements, or using the new HMIS tools were many. In response to such resistance, the latest performance report of the SWP has revealed, that "preparation of legislation is underway in order to enforce the implementation of the new system."

5.   Discussion and implications

The empirical case presented in this study depicts the construction and transformation of membership structures in the HIS field and the varying strategies employed by the constitutive actors. We would argue that there has been membership structures in the HIS field that constrain some core groups of actors from participation. We also argue that the strategies employed by the various groups have failed to mobilize the necessary skills and support towards an improved HIS. In what follows a brief discussion on these issues is presented followed by highlights on the limitations and implications of the study.

Membership in the HIS field has been delineated almost exclusively to health related professionals as well as expatriate experts and with previous experience. In the early period, professionals within the WHO system and associates were the dominant sources of expertise. Through the SWP, new rituals have been introduced providing the basis for the ascendance of donors to the central position; existing rituals were then redefined to allow entry for new actors - private and academic public health groups and individuals. Furthermore, over the years, HIS related consultancy services have been exclusively directed to international consultants. Previous involvement in similar initiatives has also been preferential.

The strategies employed by the different groups have had mixed outcomes; but donors, and those backed by them, eventually shaped the membership structures significantly. The WHO, and the Planning Department of the MoH, both of which have been stayed central in the field reproduced the membership structures repositioning themselves as per the institutional dynamics. The "other departments" within the MoH have also persistently rejected to enact membership without any effect on the membership structures. Donor's colonization strategy, on other hand, has succeeded in transforming the membership structures facilitating entry for non-traditional actors such as for the private consultancy company. This could be attributed to their possession over scarce resources. Similarly, the stratification strategy of the public health consultancy group was also successful as they have managed to create hierarchical chains restricting - directly or indirectly - the IS professionals' access to field level rituals. Their success can be attributed primarily to their ability to influence donor(s) which could overcome any resistance from other groups, but also the enabling membership structures and their previous engagement in the broader health sector.

We also argue that the IS group's association strategy has had limited success so far. This group has been excluded from rituals in the field despite its visibility and interest. Its recent inclusion into a ritual is only at the periphery, after the issues surrounding HIS has been framed and almost all decisions have been made. Two explanations could be speculated as to the underlying reasons for the limited progress. First, since this group emerged after decades of institutionalization of membership structures, and after the governance and evaluation rituals of the SWP has more or less "stable and broadly acknowledged centers, peripheries, and status orders" [12, p. 135] the existing institutional structure is "less conducive to the construction of new positions or the transformation of existing ones" [ibid]. The second reason could be the inability of the IS group to offer a species of capital not readily available in the field as it is currently structured [12]. The latter reason could be attributed, at least partly, to the constraining institutional context.

To return to the issues raised at the beginning of this chapter, lack, unwillingness or superficial participation of relevant actors needs to be revisited and informed through the institutionally defined membership structures. In particular, I wanted to emphasis the *cognitive* and *normative* effects [19] of the membership structures. The *cognitive* aspect of membership structures makes actors unable to conceive different options as far as recruitment of professionals (organisational or individual) is concerned. Failing to recognize such options, they naturally also fail to act on them. One apparent example is the uncritical demand for support from the WHO in ICT matters in healthcare as presented by a senior representative of the Planning Department\MoH in a national workshop mentioned in the previous section. Such articulation considers neither the potential for collaboration with the ICT elites (academics and practitioners) who were present in the workshop with such a purpose nor the level of competence that can be found from the WHO in this domain. Prior research, however, identifies that the WHO has "a remarkably homogenous work force" with professional staffing "concentrated in medicine and public health" [14, p. 737] and has not made investments in ICT and related strategies [2] even for its own organisational use.

Membership structures also have *normative* aspect where actors conform to prevailing "appropriate" prescriptions. This is not only because the prescriptions might be proper or preferable, but also because of the awareness as to the incentives and\or disincentives that may follow for conformance or non-conformance. In the one hand, even when some of the actors participating in the field do perceive the need to include other professionals (with such backgrounds as IS or its reference disciplines) into the rituals, they may be reluctant to entertain such options because accepting existing membership structures that enjoys normative status may enhance their professional and\or organisational legitimacy, improving chances with interests that control important resources such as financing, professional labour, and managerial appointments and promotions [26]. On the other hand, even those disadvantaged groups such as the IS group or local professionals may prefer conformance to the prevailing membership structures against a sort of open dispute or demurring the existing membership structures. One possible explanation might be the costs that could be incurred with such act, in particular withdrawal of support for example in funding, or access to constituents. Individual and\or organisational interests may, then, best be served by following the crowd even if this is suboptimal (and even seems unacceptable at times) when considered merely on the basis of professionalism.

In another twist, the persistent boycotts of the "other departments" within the MoH to enact their membership in the HIS field could be interpreted as unwillingness to grant legitimacy either for the propriety of the HIS activity in general or for the validity of the constituting actors as practitioners [19]. This group may be unable to comprehend integrated HIS because of their entrenched cognitive frames through the separately managed health programs; or even if they do comprehend, they may not perceive the HIS field as it has been structured all along as valid and desirable (normative legitimacy); or as mentioned earlier, even when they do perceive the field's desirability, they may be reluctant to implement them because of their awareness of the risks of loosing\reducing their organisational power. The recent plan to impose this group to participate in the field through ratification of legal requirement is unlikely to succeed [20].

As a concluding remark, I suggest a collective effort to identify and transform such constraining structures in the field as a matter of priority. One way to do so is through *theorization*: the challenging of extant structures, the reasoned analysis of the limitations and latent possibilities of existing social patterns, the framing of alternatives, and mobilization of resources for the social construction of those alternatives [9, 17]. This may help actors, in this case, to perceive the requisite expertise to develop information systems, but could also be instrumental in defusing self-interested opposition. Finally, I would like to remind the suggestion made by Baskerville and Myers that the IS discipline has "a tremendous opportunity to take a prominent, leading role within the larger community of scholars interested in the development, use, and impact of information technology and systems in broadly defined social and organizational settings" [3, p. 8]. The health sector of low-income countries is one such arena.

The study has two limitations. First, the focus has been on the dominant voices in the field. Limited attempt was made to present dissenting voices within and across groups when traced. Neither the WHO nor the MoH are homogeneous; neither are donors and academics. Second, the discussion in this chapter is limited only to one "HIS" field, the one concerned with integration, implicitly or explicitly, and its discourse(s); other neighbouring and conflicting fields and their discourses were not examined.

Despite such limitations, however, this study has implications for research and practice. For practice, this chapter has shown not only the existence or effects of membership structures that needs to be considered in IS development endeavours, but the conception of such structures as socially constructed, and consequently manageable opens up strategic possibilities for IS practitioners and policy makers alike. For research, this chapter shows, focusing on a single institutional structure, that deepening understanding in such domains as IS in developing countries, necessitates the examination of the institutional context more than the actors in a single project or organisation.

References

[1]   AbouZahr, C. & Boerma, T. (2005). Health information systems: The foundation of public health. *Bulletin of the World Health Organization*, 83(8), 578-583.
[2]   Barrett, M, Fryatt, B., Walsham G., & Joshi, S. (2005). Building bridges between local and global knowledge: New ways of working the World Health Organization. *KM4D Journal*, 1(2), 31-46.
[3]   Baskerville, R. & Myers M. (2002). Information systems as a reference discipline. *MIS Quarterly*, 26(1), 1-14.
[4]   Bourdieu, P. (1993). *Sociology in question*. London: Sage.
[5]   Bourdieu, P. & Wacquant, J.D. (1992). *An invitation to reflexive sociology*. Chicago, IL: University of Chicago Press.
[6]   Braa, J. Eric, M., & Sahay, S. (2004). Networks of action: sustainable health Information Systems across Developing Countries. *MIS Quarterly*, 28(3), 1-26.
[7]   Chilundo, B. (2004). Integrating information systems of disease-specific health programmes in low income countries. Unpublished PhD Dissertation, Oslo: University of Oslo.
[8]   DiMaggio, P. J. & Powell, W. W. (1983). The iron cage revisited: institutional isomorphism and collective rationality in organizational fields. *American Sociological Review*, 48(2), 147-160.

[9]   Greenwood, R., Suddaby, R. & Hinings, C. R. (2002). Theorizing change: The role of professional associations in the transformation of institutionalized fields. *Academy of Management Journal*, 45(1), 58-80.

[10]   HMN/WHO (2008). Framework and standards for country health information systems.   http://www.who.int/healthmetrics/documents/hmn_framework200802.pdf. Accessed 20 April 2008.

[11]   Lawrence, T. (1999). Institutional strategy. *Journal of Management*, 25 (2), 161-188.

[12]   Lawrence, T. (2004). Rituals and resistance: membership dynamics in professional fields. *Human Relations*, 57 (2), 115-143.

[13]   Lippeveld, T., Sauerborn, R., & Bodart, T. (Eds.). (2000). Design and implementation of health information systems. Washington DC.: World Health Organization.

[14]   Peabody, J. W. (1995). An organizational analysis of the World Health Organization: narrowing the gap between promise and performance. *Social Science and Medicine*, 40(6), 731-742.

[15]   Phillips, N. & Hardy, C. (2002). *Discourse analysis: investigating processes of social construction*. Thousand Oaks, CA: Sage.

[16]   Phillips, N., Lawrence, T., & Hardy, C. (2004). Discourse and institutions. *Academy of Management Review*, 29(4), 635-652.

[17]   Seo, M., & Creed, W. E. D. 2002. Institutional contradictions, praxis, and institutional change: A dialectical perspective. *Academy of Management Review*, 27(2), 222-247.

[18]   Smith, M.L., Madon, S, Anifalaje, A., Lazarro-Malecela, & M., Michael, E. (2008). Integrated health information systems in Tanzania: experience and challenges. *EJISDC*, 33(1), 1-21.

[19]   Suchman, M. C. (1995). Managing legitimacy: Strategic and institutional approaches. *Academy of Management Review*, 20(3), 571-611.

[20]   Tolbert, P. S. & Zucker, L. G. (1983). Institutional sources of change in the formal structure of organizations: the diffusion of civil service reform, 1880-1935. *Administrative Science Quarterly*, 28(1), 22-39.

[21]   Walsham, G. & Sahay, S. (2006). Research on information systems in developing countries: current landscape and future prospects. *Information Technology for Development*, 12(1), 7-24.

[22]   WHO. (1978). Development of health information systems, Thirty-First World Health Assembly Resolution (WHA31.20).

[23]   WHO. (1993). Guidelines for the development of HMIS. WHO Regional Office for the Western Pacific, Manila.

[24]   WHO. (2006). Health of the people (The): The African regional health report.

[25]   WHO. (2007). Strengthening of health information systems, Sixtieth World Health Assembly Resolution (WHA60.27).

[26]   Zucker, L. G. (1987). Institutional theories of organization. *Annual Review of Sociology*, 13, 443-464.

A HUMAN ENVIRONMENTALIST APPROACH TO DIFFUSION IN ICT POLICIES

Elaine Byrne
University of Pretoria, South Africa
Royal College of Surgeons, Ireland

Lizette Weilbach
University of Pretoria, South Africa

Abstract   This chapter addresses the question: *Can a holistic model of ICT adoption and diffusion improve ICT policy formulation?* This question is answered by illustrating that in a globalised economy the existing models of ICT adoption are inadequate in explaining the process of adoption and diffusion, and that a human-environmental model can address this gap by explaining the duality of this process. The example of the South African draft White Paper on e-education is used to support this claim.

Keywords: ICT Policy; ICT for socio-economic development; ICT adoption and diffusion; ICT implementation context; human environmental model

1.   Introduction

Developing countries are well aware of the potential benefits of Information and Communication Technology for development: "There was at one time some debate as to whether information and communication technologies (ICTs) were relevant to developing countries, but this debate has been resolved with a clear yes answer. The question has become not whether, but how ICTs can be beneficial" [15]. Many policies promoting the use of ICT have resulted in large investments in ICT infrastructure and launching of e-governance initiatives. Many purport to support both economic and social development. However, when these policies are examined more closely the question of adoption and diffusion is often not, or at best simplistically, addressed. A rather linear trajectory from installation and training to adoption and diffusion is implicit. The basis for these assumptions regarding adoption is related to the rather flat view of the globalised world and resultant linear diffusion models that support this view.

This chapter explores the existing linear and universalistic models of ICT adoption and diffusion which are based on an underlying assumption of a globalised "flat" world (a term popularised by Friedman [6]). This simplistic view

Please use the following format when citing this chapter:

Byrne, E. and Weilbach, L., 2008, in IFIP International Federation for Information Processing, Volume 282; *Social Dimensions of Information and Communication Technology Policy*; Chrisanthi Avgerou, Matthew L. Smith, Peter van den Besselaar; (Boston: Springer), pp. 209–222.

of globalisation ignores the structural process of diffusion and adoption. In Section 2 of this chapter we discuss the classical diffusion theories and suggest an alternative model which addresses their shortcomings. The example of the South African ICT education policy [4] is used to illustrate that a more holistic multi-dimensional model of adoption of ICT – the human environmental model – needs to explore not just the various dimensions of the socio-economic context, but also the process by which these dimensions interact. Greater awareness of all dimensions of the context in which ICTs are proposed to be implemented are acknowledged in the policy, but the process of adoption and diffusion is largely ignored.

Thus, this chapter addresses the question: *Can a holistic model to ICT adoption and diffusion improve ICT policy formulation?* This question is answered by illustrating that in a globalised economy the existing models of ICT adoption are inadequate in explaining the process of adoption and diffusion, and that a human-environmental model can address this gap by explaining the duality of this process.

2.   Diffusion and innovation models

A one-dimensional view of ICT, inherent assumptions of the "goodness" of ICT, and an assumed linear trajectory from installation and training to adoption and diffusion, is apparent in many ICT policies. However, this assumes a "flat" world and ignores the structural conditions of diffusion and adoption. To take the latter into account implies having more holistic ICT policies based on contextual and socio-economic models of innovation diffusion. General trends, such as total quality management, business process reengineering, and the discourse on globalisation, support the rationale that there are standard ways in which ICTs should be used, and there are specific organisational features which ICTs should aim at supporting [1]. Avgerou [1] calls this approach to the exploitation of ICTs "a-contextual" and warns that it involves high risks of misleading and frustrating local efforts to make sense of and appropriate new technologies. Latter in this section we illustrate a model of ICT adoption and diffusion which can be used instead of these a-contextual models and assist in providing the context needed for a more human-environmental approach to ICT. However, before this discussion we describe some of the a-contextual and contemporary diffusion and adoption models.

In the late 1980's and early 1990's a lot of research in the field of information systems (IS) was done on IS implementation problems [9]. IS implementation research was mainly based on the theories of innovation diffusion, focusing on how the perceptions of the potential users of the information technology (IT) innovation influenced the adoption thereof. One of the most cited innovation-diffusion theories is that of Rogers [12]. Rogers' innovation-diffusion model shows that factors which influence the diffusion of an innovation are the characteristics of the innovation, communication channels, and the social system, all interacting over time. The five characteristics of an innovation which affect the rate of diffusion of that innovation, are: relevant advantage (the degree to which the potential adopter perceives the innovation to be better than its forerunner); compatibility (the degree to which the potential adopter perceives the innovation as being in line with his/her existing values, needs and past experiences); complexity (the degree to which the potential adopter experiences the innovation as being difficult to use); observability (the degree to which an innovation's results are evident to others); and "trialability" (the degree to which the potential adopter will try-out the innovation before adoption).

Moore & Benbasat [9] added two more innovation characteristics to the model of Rogers, namely: image (the degree to which a potential adopter's image or status is perceived to be enhanced in his/her social system because of him/her using the innovation) and voluntariness of use (the degree to which the potential adopter is perceived to willingly make use of the innovation). They furthermore split observability into result demonstrability (the degree to which the potential adopter's results of using the innovation are observable and communicable to others) and visibility (the degree to which information technology is apparent to the sense of sight). Moore and Benbasat [9] also pointed out that the key to whether or not an innovation diffuses is not really a result of the potential adopter's perceptions of the technology itself, but rather his/her perceptions of using the technology. They therefore rephrased Rogers' five innovation characteristics to reflect that it is the perceptions about using the innovation rather than the perceptions about the innovation itself which are of concern, and in addition labelled it "the Perceived Characteristics of Innovation (PCI)".

The social system's characteristics referred to in Rogers' model include those of the individuals, groups, the organisation, decision makers, and specific role players such as champions and senior managers, while the communication channels referred to could be internal or external to the organisation and could transfer either formal or informal communication [12].

According to Rogers [12, 13] the diffusion process consists of two stages: adoption and implementation. The adoption stage comprises of three sub-stages: knowledge acquisition, persuasion and learning, and the decision to adopt or reject the innovation. Implementation occurs when the individual starts to use the innovation. Kwon & Zmud [8] extended this model to also include post-implementation phases, such as confirmation, which occurs when the individual seeks the reinforcement of the innovation-decision already made.

Kwon & Zmud [8] combined the diffusion of innovation theory with application implementation research and as a result ended up with an enlarged model, which apart from Rogers' model, also includes task (uncertainty, autonomy, and variety) and environmental (heterogeneity, uncertainty, competition, concentration/dispersion, and inter-organisation interdependence) characteristics.

This model can be critiqued in a number of ways. For example, terminology in IT research seems to differ from that used in classic diffusion research, as for the former the adoption of technology is often a decision taken by a higher authority and the IS department then gets tasked to diffuse the technology through the rest of the organisation. The decision to adopt the technology is therefore made without consulting all the individuals in the organisation [2]. Adoption is therefore seen as the decision to use the technology, while diffusion is the process of implementing the decision.

Furthermore, in the IT field, voluntary decisions to adopt an innovation are not very common and Rogers' model does not address the resentment which is often caused by the enforcement of IT from a higher authority. Bayer & Melone [2] also argue that the characteristics of "non-diffusion" are of major importance to the IT field, due to the high incidence of IS failure, and that the classic diffusion theory does not explain why innovations are discarded in the same depth as why it is adopted.

The classic diffusion theory also fails to "consider interactions between various social systems" [2]. Information technologists tend to be more loyal to their discipline than to the organisations that employ them. It is therefore seldom the needs of their organisation that alerts them of a new technology, but rather their contact with other technologists. Aspects such as information politics and power bases seems to be important adoption factors and should therefore also be included in the innovation adoption theory.

According to Du Plooy [5] the classic diffusion theory disappoints as it makes no explicit mention of the social context or human environment of information systems adoption and use. Information technology is socially constructed and to cultivate and nurture a human environment in which the IS is to be implemented, one has to understand how people view technology and how they understand the meaning of technology. Innovation theory and the enhanced models of information technology diffusion/adoption not only fail in their lack of consideration of social interaction, but also because they are overly simplistic (even deterministic) in their view of the innovation process (or, in terms of information technology, of the process of implementation). According to Du Plooy [5]:

> "they fail to consider the type of social characteristics and dual interaction between information technology and the organisation, specifically with regard to factors and characteristics such as the different world views of the agent of change and the organisation within which the change is implemented; the duality of technology; the technological frames of reference of the agent of change and the organisation; organisational culture; organisational learning and emergence; the power bases of individuals and groups; empowerment/disempowerment of workers through information technology; resistance to change; the non-deterministic aspects of information technology; the determining capability of this technology; the influence of this technology on the values and judgement of an organisation; the influence of this technology on

business processes, organisational learning and internal communication; the application of technology in different work situations, e.g. managerial, individual office work, group work; the influence of organisations on information technology; the adaptation of the organisation to the technology; organisational norms and values; etc."

Du Plooy [5] therefore argues that the social context within which the adoption and diffusion of IT takes place is much 'deeper' than the pure demographic characteristics described by the characteristics of Rogers' model. Furthermore, Du Plooy argues that making sense of IT also means understanding the changes in structure, culture, work processes, and power bases that the adoption and use of IT bring to the organisation. Du Plooy extended the enhanced diffusion/ implementation model of Kwon & Zmud by adding a sixth dimension to the innovation-diffusion process, namely group characteristics. He also added "forces" and "elements" to the other five characteristics which he regarded as of importance to the human environment of IT adoption and use (see Figure 1).

Du Plooy's [5] enhancement of Kwon & Zmud's diffusion/implementation model is still a deterministic model as it seems to indicate that adoption and use will be successful if one takes the stipulated social factors into consideration when implementing an innovation. Du Plooy [5], however, believes the mechanistic causal interpretation suggested by the model to be incorrect and inappropriate since information technology is socially constructed and has non-deterministic characteristics. One cannot predict outcomes or determine cause and effect during information technology adoption and use that readily, because of these characteristics.

For more successful adoption and use, one needs to understand the social context of IT diffusion and implementation in its totality. This does however not mean that cultivating all six characteristics will guarantee success, while omitting one of these characteristics will also not necessarily lead to the adoption not being successful. According to Du Plooy [5] "such determinism cannot be superimposed on a process with so many non-deterministic characteristics." The six characteristics of Du Plooy's human environment of adoption and use framework (see Figure 2) should be viewed as an integrated totality which is not divisible into parts [5]:

"The six characteristics do not deterministically decide adoption and use. As a whole they are adoption and use in the sense that they constitute the full social context for adoption and use. Taken together they are the very substance of information technology adoption and use."

The "binding factor" between the various characteristics of the framework is their social contexts. Although each side of the cube points to a different dimension of the social context of information technology adoption and use, these dimensions cannot be isolated and considered on their own. The human environment only makes sense when considered in its totality, as a single environment which interacts recursively with information technology during its implementation and during its use [5].

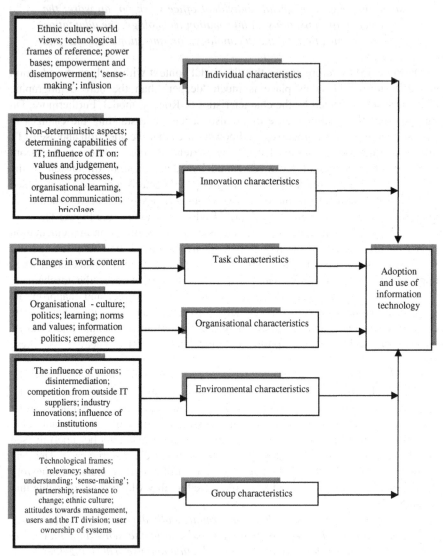

Figure 1: Du Plooy's enhancement of Kwon & Zmud's diffusion/ implementation model [5].

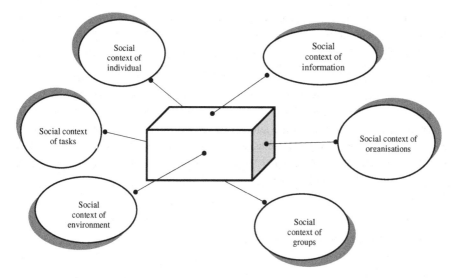

Figure 2: The human environment of IT adoption and use [5].

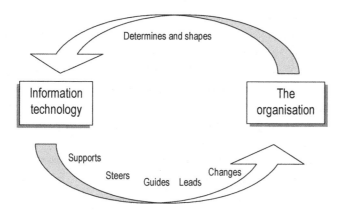

Figure 3: The recursive relationship between information technology and the organisation during the process of adoption and use [5].

Giddens' structuration theory [10] can be applied to describe the processes through which ICT's are themselves shaped, while they at the same time contribute to the shaping of the social relations of organisations within which they are implemented (the duality of technology) (Figure 3).

The use of Du Plooy's [5] framework to understand the full social context of information technology adoption and use is best understood when the recursive relationship between information technology and the organisation during the process of adoption and use (as illustrated in Figure 3) is integrated with the human environment framework (Figure 2) to show how the human environment actually encapsulates the process of information technology adoption and use (Figure 4).

If we therefore understand the interaction between the human environment and the process of IT adoption and use as shown in figure 4, we are able to make sense of this human environment. Only if we understand the human environment and its interaction with the adoption and use processes will we be able to cultivate and nurture such an environment to facilitate the adoption and use of this technology [5].

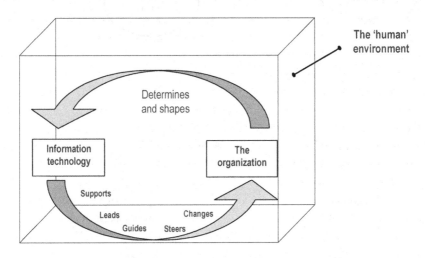

Figure 4: The human environment encapsulating information technology adoption and use [5].

According to Du Plooy [5], it is also important to note that the two dimensions of the adoption and use process shown here are "two sides of the same coin". They are not divisible into two distinct dimensions that can be considered separately because they are both contained and embedded in a human environment. The upper arrow of figure 4 shows that information technology is socially constructed, but this model even goes beyond that. Social construction is a term applied to the study of the meanings of technology and how those meanings affect the implementation (the adoption and use) of technology within the organisation [14]. This model includes that notion, but also shows that the human environment comprises of various integrated social contexts which transcend the study of meanings to include a large number of non-deterministic aspects that should be considered during information technology adoption and use. The lower arrow shows that information technology may also determine what an organisation is or may become. It does not do so deterministically, but it takes place within a particular human environment. It is the "other side" of the adoption and use "coin" [5].

This duality, however, is not a separation into two things that differ widely from or contradict each other, but it could rather be described as a concept expressed in a different way. Information technology, due to its close interaction with human actors in organisations, has in fact become the relic of modern society. We cannot perform our work in the modern organisation without this technology, but at the same time our organisations and we are changed when we adopt and use this technology [10, 11]. These two dimensions are impossible to disentangle or undo. We cannot understand the one dimension unless we also understand the other, and as Du Plooy explains "we can no longer even conceptualise information technology without thinking about its implementation", [5]. Thus, an ICT policy which aims to address socio-economic development should have this duality embedded in its policy if it is to address the process of innovation adoption and diffusion of ICTs in its country. The South African ICT policy for education is used as an example of a policy which aims to address socio-economic development, but in a rather linear manner, and inadequately deals with the process of innovation adoption and diffusion.

3.   The South African ICT policy in education

The draft White Paper on e-Education outlines the views of the South African Ministry of Education's position on the role of ICT in education in South Africa. The overall e-Education policy goal is:

> "Every South African learner in the general and further education and training bands will be ICT capable (that is, use ICT confidently and creatively to help develop the skills and knowledge they need to achieve personal goals and to be full participants in the global community) by 2013", [4, chapter 2, paragraph 2.23)].

The listed strategic objectives of the policy are [4, chapter 4]:

- ICT professional development for management, teaching and learning: Every teacher, manager and administrator in general and further education and training must have the knowledge, skills, and support they need to integrate ICT in teaching and learning.
- Electronic content resource development and distribution: The school curriculum in general and further education and training is supported through effective and engaging software, electronic content and online learning resources, and teachers, content developers, and administrators who contribute effectively to these resources.

- Access to information and communication technology infrastructure: Every teacher and learner in general and further education and training must have access to ICT infrastructure.
- Connectivity: Every teacher and learner in general and further education and training must have access to an educational network and the Internet.
- Community engagement: Schools must work in partnership with families and the wider community to ensure shared knowledge about ICT and extended opportunities for learning and development through ICT.

The key elements of the policy framework are equity, developing norms and standards, [4, chapter 4]. Content should be locally developed and technology should be viewed as a tool and not a solution.

The paper recognises that in order to achieve these objectives a socio-economic approach is needed:

> "for South Africans to cross over to the era of the knowledge economy, social exclusion should not be allowed. President Thabo Mbeki has underscored the importance of ICT for social and economic development at numerous South African and international fora. 'We must continue the fight for liberation against poverty, against underdevelopment, against marginalisation' and '... information and communication technology ... is a critically important tool in that struggle" [4, chapter 4, paragraph 1.11].

This encompasses a view of e-Education as going beyond computer literacy and the ability to operate various technologies. It means that learners (students) and educators (teachers):

- apply ICT skills to access, analyse, evaluate, integrate, present, and communicate information;
- create knowledge and new information by adapting, applying, designing, inventing, and authoring information;
- enhance teaching and learning through communication and collaboration by using ICT; and
- function in a knowledge society by using appropriate technology and mastering communication and collaboration skills.

e-Education views ICT as a resource for reorganising schooling and as a tool for whole-school development. It includes ICT as:

- a tool for management and administration;
- a resource for curriculum integration;
- a communication tool;
- a collaborative tool for teachers and learners; and
- a learning environment that advances creativity, communication [4, chapter 4, paragraphs 2.3 & 2.4]

Within the draft White Paper the Department of Education outlines some of the potential benefits of ICT, such as improving the quality of learning and teaching, providing students with life-long learning opportunities, and readdressing disparities within the educational system. Improved quality of teaching and learning are based on the premise that access to quality educational material is increased through access to technology and that diverse learning styles can be catered for. There is also recognition that simply placing computers in schools is not sufficient. The technology needs to be an integral part of the schools administration and teaching resources. Thus there is recognition that technology can decrease the time school staff spends on class administration, that school children need to be equipped in terms of technology to be fully functioning citizens when they leave school, and that technology should be used as an integral part of the curriculum. This requires capacity development and support mechanisms so that the technology can be sustained and efficiently utilised.

> *"There are three critical elements that will determine ICT's future as an effective tool for social and economic development. Firstly is cost. Any solution that South Africa adopts has to be cost-effective if we are to meet our developmental demands and to reach the most remote parts of our country. Secondly is sustainability. It is no use having state of the art technology unless it can be sustained. Thirdly is the efficient utilisation of ICT. Deployment of ICT does not guarantee its efficient utilisation. Capacity building and effective support mechanisms must accompany it", [4, chapter 4, paragraph 1.17].*

Thus a rather broad view of ICT is taken in the draft White Paper and there is recognition that it entails a social and economic approach. There is also some recognition, in terms of the stakeholders that need to be involved (school staff, students and parents), that the school is part of a broader context. We will now look at this policy in relation to our above discussion of diffusion and innovation models.

4. Discussion

It is interesting to note that in the e-Education policy there is recognition of many of the dimensions that are required for ICT to be adopted in schools, such as social context and capacity development. In Table 1, one can see that the e-Education policy addresses many of the elements of the human-environmental model. Furthermore, it is also interesting that in comparing the human environmental model (Section 2) and the South African ICT policy (Section 3) the diffusion and adoption of ICT is assumed. The elements are not viewed as a cohesive whole, but as separate sides to a box.

Social context element	Description	Current e-Education policy position
Individual	Ethnic culture; world views; technological frames of reference; power bases; empowerment and disempowerment; 'sense-making'; infusion	Recognition of the need for individual capacity development. Also recognised the role of mediators/champions. Aims for individual capacity development in terms of use, skills and knowledge gained.
Information Technology	Non-deterministic aspects; determining capabilities of IT; influence of IT on: values and judgment, business processes, organisational learning, internal communication; bricolage	Recognises that access to IT is necessary, but not sufficient and requires local support mechanisms.
Task	Changes in work content	Local content needs to be developed.
Organisation	Organisational culture; politics; learning; norms and values; information politics; emergence	Recognition of potential of ICT in decreasing time spent on administration and as a tool for more effective management.
Environment	The influence of unions; disintermediation; competition from outside IT suppliers; industry innovations; influence of institutions	Awareness of the influence of the environment on adoption (recognition of disparities caused by apartheid and that content should be locally developed). Thus, solutions must be cost-effective and reach the most remote parts of the country.
Group	Technological frames; relevancy; shared understanding; 'sense-making'; partnership; resistance to change; ethnic culture; attitudes towards management, users and the IT division; user ownership of systems	A team comprising teachers, content developers and administrators is required to implement the ICT policy. Also requires that a partnership should be formed with families and the wider community.

Table 1: The human-environmental dimensions and the South African e-Education policy.

There is mention of the need for a champion in the school to drive the process in the school, as well as a person in the community that can drive the external process. However, inherent in the policy is an assumption that by training and recognising that the technology at the school is a valuable resource, adoption will automatically follow. The draft White Paper implicitly adopts an overly simplistic (deterministic) way in which the adoption and use of IT will occur. The different world views of the agents of change and the organisation within which the change is implemented are not included [5]. Issues of power, politics, and culture are not mentioned and little is said about the impact of the innovation process on organisational culture, organisational learning, and change management. The dual interaction between IT and the school is not considered (the duality of technology). What is missing is an analysis of the process by which this will occur - the process by which local content is to be developed; how the different disparate technological frames of the individuals and groups who need to support this policy are aligned, and how support is to be given to teachers and students

5.   Conclusion

An organisation rarely chooses innovation freely, but it is rather determined by "events, trends, pressures, opportunities, or restrictions in the international or national arena" [1]. The situation with South African schools is not any different.

IS innovation should be studied as "a combination of technical/rational and institutional action" [1]. Not only is an IS implementation an intervention which is rationally planned, but several studies have shown that there are subjective, irrational elements of actions within organisations which tend to interfere with the "rational, planned and methodical actions". These social, cultural, or cognitive forces are located within and beyond an organisational setting and in many cases drive the overall organisational performance [1].

IS studies are in essence contextual, as they address a changing entity within its environment (the information system within the organisation). This is also the case when studying the diffusion and adoption of an IS in an organisation, such as a school. The "diffusion of an innovation" is spreading the word about a new idea or innovation. The adoption or rejection of the idea or innovation would, in time, follow diffusion. Adoption is in turn followed by some kind of change in the social system in which the adoption occurred.

When studying the social context of IS diffusion and adoption, one needs to study the technological change brought about (the "content" of change), and the socio-organisational conditions under which it happens (the "context" of change). An IT innovation and its context are so entangled that it would be an oversimplification to see the technology as the content and the society as the context [3]. Such a simplification makes it difficult to understand the multifaceted processes in which technology and humans take part to form socio-technical entities, or in terms of actor-network theory vocabulary, "heterogeneous networks". When studying change in the field of IS, one should therefore not only study the IS innovation as the content of change, but rather the change of heterogeneous networks of organisations and people within which these innovations will play a role.

A useful approach to the formation of ICT policy would be to develop the policy around the six dimensions of Du Plooy's human environmental model [5] and explain the multi-faceted approach of structuration using Giddens' structuration theory [7]. Thus, the authors are of the opinion that understanding, and as Du Plooy [5] puts it "cultivating", the human environment within which the IT is to be implemented, i.e., "the full social context of IT, the organizational, social, political and ethical concerns that govern and influence IT adoption and use", which in the case of ICT education policies relates to the social context of the individuals in the school, the school itself, the groups within the school and the community the school serves, the tasks performed and the IT used to perform them, and the broader environment within which the schools are positioned, would enable a more holistic and contextual ICT education policy to be adopted. This approach is currently being used by one of the authors in reviewing the adoption and use of a new open source content management solution in government in South Africa.

References

[1]   Avgerou, C. (2001) The significance of context in information systems and organisational change. *Information Systems Journal*, 11, 43-63.

[2]   Bayer, J. & Melone, N. (1989). A critique of diffusion theory as a managerial framework for understanding adoption of software engineering innovations. *The Journal of Systems and Software*, 9, 161-166.

[3]   Callon, M. & Law, J. (1989) On the construction of socio-technical networks: content and context revisited. *Knowledge Society*, 9, 57-83.

[4]   Department of Education. (2004) *Transforming learning and teaching through Information and Communication Technologies (ICTs)*. Draft White Paper on E-Education in Education, S. A. D. O. (Ed.), Pretoria: Formset Printers Office.

[5]   Du Plooy, N. F. (1998) *An analysis of the human environment for the adoption and use of information technology*. Unpublished DCom thesis, Department of Informatics. Pretoria, South Africa, University of Pretoria.

[6]   Friedman, T. L. (2006) *The world is flat. The globalised world in the twenty-first century*, London, Penguin Books.

[7]   Giddens, A. (1984) *The constitution of society. Outline of the theory of structuration*, Cambridge: Polity.

[8]   Kwon, T. H. & Zmud, R. W. (1987) Unifying the fragmented models of information systems implementation, in: *Critical Issues in Information Systems Research*, Boland, R. J. & Hirschheim, R. A., eds., John Wiley & Sons, New York.

[9]   Moore, G. C. & Benbasat, I. (1991) Development of an instrument to measure the perceptions of adopting an information technology innovation. *Information Systems Research*, 2(3), 192-222.

[10]   Orlikowski, W. J. (2000) Using technology and constituting structures: A practice lens for studying technology in organisations, *Organisation Science*, 11, (4 (July - Aug)), 404-428.

[11]   Postman, N. 1992. *Technopoly: the surrender of culture to technology*. Vintage Books: New York

[12]   Prescott, M. B. & Conger, S. A. (1995) Information technology innovations: A classification by IT locus of impact and research approach. *DATA BASE Advances*, 26(2 & 3), 20-41.

[13]   Rogers, E. M. (1995) *Diffusion of innovations*, Fourth edition, The Free Press, New York.

[14]   Sahay, S., Palit, M. & Robey, D. (1994). A relativist approach to studying the social construction of information technology. *European Journal of Information Systems*, 3(4), 248-258.

[15]   Walsham, G. & Sahay, S. (2006) Research on IS in developing countries: Current landscape and future prospects. *Information Technology for Development*, 12, 7-24.

ICT AND SOCIO-ECONOMIC DEVELOPMENT:
A UNIVERSITY'S ENGAGEMENT IN A RURAL COMMUNITY IN YOLA, NIGERIA

Jainaba M.L. Kah
American University of Nigeria, Nigeria

Muhammadou M.O. Kah
American University of Nigeria, Nigeria &
American University, U.S.A.

Abstract   This chapter explores ICT interventions, the role of universities in socio-economic development, knowledge creation and dissemination literature before taking a look at a university intervention in ICT for development in a small rural community in Yola, Northeastern Nigeria. The African Center for ICT Innovation and Training[1], an American University of Nigeria community engagement initiative is used as a case study to gauge its importance as an ICT resource center for the community and for small businesses and whether applied skills in information technology for university faculty and staff taught at the Center is leading to more productivity. The Yola and Jimeta Communities are also surveyed to find out whether the activities of the Centre and its interventions on developing ICT competencies and capacity building is helping to bridge the digital divide and empowering the community, especially women.

Keywords: ICT and Development, ICT social-economic development, ICT and women, Universities and Development

1.   Introduction

The potential of information and communication technologies (ICT) to transform communities and economies has been touted in the literature. The expectation of ICT playing a transformational role is more evident in Africa. Africa, being the last development frontier and known as the poorest continent has begun to look at ICT as the magic bullet to solve its developmental problems. A recent 2007 publication of the Africa Capacity Building foundation asserted that the level of interest in technology solutions to critical development challenges is

---

[1] Partly funded by a seed grant from the MacArthur Foundation.

Please use the following format when citing this chapter:

Kah, J.M.L. and Kah, M.M.O., 2008, in IFIP International Federation for Information Processing, Volume 282; *Social Dimensions of Information and Communication Technology Policy*; Chrisanthi Avgerou, Matthew L. Smith, Peter van den Besselaar; (Boston: Springer), pp. 223–239.

high in Africa, which raises a need to accelerate the penetration and application of technology on the continent, particularly in the public sector. Technology can assist in improving efficiency and effectiveness of public sector institutions by creating the enabling environment for the continent to increase her competitiveness.

Many declarations, such as the draft Ouagadougou Declaration, recognize the importance of good governance to promote sustainable development, poverty alleviation and the enhancement of the quality of life for Africans. These documents highlight and acknowledge the importance of access to information for healthy democracies, the challenge Africa faces in building the requisite ICT skills, and the fact that e-government wields great potential for making African governments more efficient, responsive, transparent and legitimate. The roadmap for the implementation of ICT best practices addresses issues of enabling environments, infrastructure development, security, harnessing citizen information for better government services, revenue, and online citizen services.

The challenge of how best to use ICT to empower communities and reduce poverty is still an area which needs further research; nevertheless, the debate on the utility of ICT in developing countries has largely been won [3, 38, 40]. In Africa, the public, governments and the donor community see ICT as a powerful tool in poverty reduction. Although the link between economic growth and ICT has been well established [24, 28], the exact processes of how ICT can be used for poverty reduction in developing countries need exploration and are open to challenge [26]. ICT as enablers in the development process and in poverty reduction can be envisaged using two approaches – ICT as a tool to promote economic growth (ICT-driven approach) or ICT used in support of development. In the ICT-driven approach, often underpinned by the assumption that better information improves how economic resources are allocated, one tries to empower the rural and urban poor by intervening to correct issues such as scarce, poor, inefficient, and untimely information by providing village knowledge centers. In this approach ICT can also be used to enhance health, education, social capital, etc. The other approach of using ICT in support of development first identifies the development goal (e.g., health care provision, increased agricultural yield, etc.), works out what the ICT needs of the target group are and then looks at how ICT and other media can play a role in providing and easing channels of communication. In using ICT to support development, the role of the poor in the identification of their information needs is greatly stressed [20].

Many international financial institutions (IFI) have issued reports on the economic arguments for ICT investments in developing countries and many recent reports discuss the distinct role ICT can play in bridging the information and knowledge gap for the poor [32].

This chapter explores the literature in areas such as ICT, socio-economic development, poverty reduction and the role of universities in knowledge creation and dissemination before taking a look at a university intervention in ICT for development in a small rural community in Yola, Adamawa State in Northeastern

Nigeria. This research aims to be a theoretical contribution and a description of the activities of the American University of Nigeria through its community engagement initiative, The African Center for ICT Innovation and Training, and a theoretical discussion of the approach used in this intervention.

2.   Methodology

A combination of surveys, interviews and an ethnographic study were chosen as the most appropriate methodologies to better understand the role of the Center since this will allow us to use an in-depth analysis of the social processes and economic histories of the community. Research included surveys which were handed out at the end of training modules and semi-structured interviews. The authors decided to use the Center as an area of focus since this is clearly an intervention whose role could possibly be ascertained from surveys of beneficiaries, the types of courses taught and the services offered by the Center and the perceived utility of the new skills learnt. By living within the community in the last three years and teaching at the Center, the authors were also able to use ethnographic methods such as unstructured interviews, and purposive trans-walks [7] by visiting the Center at least once a week unannounced to observe and interact with community members using the facilities and ask questions such as the utility of the courses offered, benefits accruing to them as a result of the new ICT skills being learnt, and how the Center has impacted their lives, etc. The survey was filled out by about 60 participants, about 40% of the total number of people trained at the Center during its first year of operations. Some of the findings are discussed in the case study.

3.   The role of universities in economic development

Universities have long been recognized as providers of basic scientific knowledge for industrial innovation through their research and related activities in the agricultural and manufacturing sectors [16, 17, 19, 37]. Neoclassical economic theory explained the productive performance and competitive advantages of firms largely in terms of relative resource endowments [18]. The role of knowledge and of institutions involved in the creation of knowledge was seen as exogenous, i.e. external to businesses, though not unimportant, to the production system [15]. Therefore, Gunasekara argues, knowledge creation, almost exclusively scientific in nature, and predominantly applying to agriculture, manufacturing and mining, was viewed similarly as an exogenous factor in a firm's production function. The development and diffusion of knowledge was viewed in linear terms, known as the science push model [37] in the sense that knowledge was created outside the production system, either in universities or the laboratories of large firms and then "pushed" out to industry for applied development and adoption [42]. The notion of university-industry linkage, whereby the two institutions jointly or cooperatively developed knowledge was weak, applying largely to the conduct of trials or other experiments by universities to prove concepts during research [37].

Many theories have been put forth regarding the role of universities in regional innovation systems. These theories have evolved in the last two decades from an approach which highlighted the importance of knowledge spillovers from the educational and research activities of universities in regional knowledge spaces, known as the innovation systems approach, to the development of a third role performed by universities in stimulating regional economic and social development [8, 11-14, 21].

The role of African universities in poverty alleviation and economic development has received additional attention in recent years as a result of success stories from India, Ireland and other economies that have managed to build human capital, especially in ICT areas, and have been able to attract companies and jobs thereby helping in the fight against poverty.

The first generation of post-independent African universities focused on nation building, with emphasis on providing functionaries for the civil service [2, 44]. African universities are now faced with new challenges and the need to be germane in dealing with issues such as globalization, meeting basic needs, and contributing to the transition towards sustainable development [35]. However, most universities have been saddled with dwindling budgets, massive increases in enrollment, lack of adequately trained professors, decaying infrastructure and have been unable to meet the new realities on the ground.

In the 1980's, African universities were criticized as being elitist centers of privilege, far removed from the development challenges facing the continent and not being actively involved in finding solutions [44]. Therefore, African universities have been trying to reinvent themselves by becoming more engaged with their host communities and countries. Many African governments faced with mounting debt repayment obligations, decaying infrastructure, stifling conditionalities under Structural Adjustment Programs, and meager resources to be distributed among mounting problems in agriculture, health, infrastructure, etc., agreed with donor advice to focus on universal primary education since investments in higher education without the corresponding improvements in African economies was leading to mass exodus of university graduates and academics (brain drain) to the developed world .

In response to these challenges, a number of African countries are exploring how universities could contribute directly to economic transformation through closer interactions with the private sector and government. Universities and other institutions of higher education, such as technical colleges, have been arguably the most under-utilized institutions in efforts to promote sustainable development [44]. Today, African universities are largely places to train people in areas that have little relevance to the acute developmental needs of the continent or to keep the youths from the streets and unemployment ranks for several years, instead of being the bastions for productive activities, scientific and technological innovation and in the forefront of the fight against poverty and underdevelopment. According to Zaglu, Sherrard & Juma (2006) [44] African universities can contribute to economic revival and growth in their surrounding regions, especially if they are located in rural areas where they can act as economic stimuli, facilitate the development of business and industrial firms, conduct Research and Development (R&D), create their own spin-off firms (bookstores, retail outlets, etc.), be involved in capital formation projects, such as technology parks and business incubator facilities, and introduce entrepreneurial and leadership training in their curricula. Universities can also ensure that students and faculty are involved in generating, adapting and diffusing available technical knowledge to meet local community and business needs.

4.   ICT for poverty alleviation and development

According to Urquhart, Liyanage, & Kah (2007) [38], ICT projects aimed at reducing poverty have often used models based on providing access to new technology, new skills and better ICT infrastructure with the expectation that ICT will primarily stimulate economic growth and production efficiency. Communities with low income and impoverished economies are expected to benefit from such ICT interventions because a direct correlation is assumed between ICT intervention and poverty reduction. Such a supply push approach has distinct limitations, because they do not take into account the endogenous capacity building and absorptive capacity of the community's knowledge, as well as the process of social capital formation.

Despite the complexity and cost of ICT, their uses in developing countries have ramifications for knowledge, information access and the economic and social welfare of communities. A strong correlation exists between the access to education and knowledge and poverty indicators such as infant mortality, family size, and women's health [32, 38]. Other studies have also established a close link between poverty and an information gap of the poor (see for example, [6, 22]). In this paper we look at an ICT intervention in Yola, Adamawa State, Nigeria.

5.   Why ICT interventions in Africa fail to have substantial developmental impact

Delivering and maintaining ICT projects in impoverished or remote areas is a major challenge due to technical and operational reasons [9]. Even though studies have shown that the commitment to access information and the realization that ICT is an important input has been high among poor people [25], getting the desired impact from ICT interventions is very difficult. From a supplier point of view, poverty alleviation can also be achieved by wealth distribution, and creation of infrastructure that can be activated only by direct intervention of governments and donors. Therefore, good governance is an important input for poverty alleviation and ICT has a role to play by disseminating information in impoverished areas.

ICT capacity building has been defined as the human capacity to utilize ICT. One problem for ICT interventions in developing countries is the lack of resident ICT skills and expertise, which may hinder sustained operation of implemented systems [1], and lack of information literacy hinders adoption [29]. As participants use ICT for development, they should become part of a process of building human and intellectual capital, which in turn should increase total social capital [3]. However, the lack of available avenues to stimulate and sustain social capital in networks and among people is one of the reasons why developing countries fail to fully exploit the existing global technologies [30, 4, 5, 29, 33]. According to Urquhart, Liyanage and Kah, it is therefore important to consider not only the lack of human capital, but also the fact that low absorptive capacity of individuals and organisations inhibits the use of ICT together with the weak social capital formation that acts as a barrier. Any definition of social capital will necessarily have limitations, as it encompasses complex social dynamics such as integration, sharing, relationship building, motivation, trust and commitment. Urquhart, Liyanage and Kah concluded that the weaker the social capital, the harder it is for knowledge and human capital to grow in a community, thereby perpetuating poverty.

In the next section we look at issues such as gender relations, access, prohibitive cost of ICT and how poverty impedes ICT adoption and diffusion.

5.1   Gender relations and ICT in Africa

The Centre in our case study is aware of the disadvantaged position and condition of women in much of Africa, which is why it has programs specifically targeting women. In recent years, people involved in development have argued that the education of girls is probably the most cost-effective development investment. Female education leads not just to better employment opportunities but to a better distribution of benefits within a family. It leads to improved child health, reduced fertility, and it improves agricultural productivity as women do most of the work in this sector. Even though the assertion that educating women is of the most cost-effective development investments and a key to poverty reduction is now widely accepted, some studies have found women still have little access to ICT. With the right enabling environment, ICT can provide a route for economic empowerment of women [23]. Khasiani [27] and Opoku-Mensah [34] both discuss women, ICT and governance issues and suggests that women lack the access to information compared to their male counterparts.

The Yola community, which is largely Muslim, practices purdah, a system of seclusion of women. In northern Nigeria, this practice is more prevalent. VerEecke in an ethnographic study of Muslim women traders looked at gender relations in Yola and argues that in Northern Nigeria, purdah (seclusion) exists as a viable institution in which married women, largely speaking, can only leave the house with due cause, such as to receive medical treatment, to attend marriages and funerals, to visit nearby relatives, or in recent years to go to one's place of work [36]. Women, in most instances, must seek their husbands' permission to leave the house. Violation of these regulations may result in such measures as the accusation of promiscuity by one's family or, in an extreme form, divorce. The women's modesty is further enhanced by the use of the veil, and in some instances by the use of escorts. In much of northern Nigeria, even at present, the purity of young Muslim girls is also preserved by early marriage which tends to preclude their continuation of school beyond the primary level. A few husbands may allow their wives to continue their education, at times to the university level. But they usually limit their wives' choices of work to those with minimal direct male-female interaction, especially as schoolteachers and nurses. However, increasingly there has been a gradual change in such rigidities. At AUN, the female students can be seen with their tight jeans, yet a headscarf to cover their heads. Even in recent times, many women, including some of our students believe that it is not their duty to work; for their husbands are obligated under Islam to provide for them and their children. This phenomenon was observed by the authors at the American University of Sharjah in the United Arab Emirates where women made up sixty-five percent of university students but were not joining the workforce in large numbers after graduation.

Despite Muslim men's control over their wives' extradomestic activities, women are in many respects politically and economically autonomous and develop activities that enhance their income or status, and provide them with an investment towards their future [39].

The Center has been very popular with women in Yola, with more women registering for courses compared to men. Being conveniently located within the community, the Center is accessible to young and married women making it possibly more likely that husband and parents will support their women to attend courses. Safety is also a major concern in Nigeria, therefore having the Center located in the community means students and people from the community do not have to travel to urban centers in other states to get advanced ICT training.

5.2   Lack of access, ownership and control as barriers to the adoption of ICT

Accessing ICT is a major impediment for many people in Nigeria and Africa. According to the Country Partnership Strategy for The Federal Republic of Nigeria (2005 - 2009) [43], teledensity though low has increased from .4 percent in December 1999 to over 6.5 percent in December 2004. The regulatory framework is state-of-the art. The response of the private investors has been remarkable. Private investments rose from $50 million at end-1999 to $5.4 billion at end-2004, so that the sector is second only to oil in Foreign Direct Investment (FDI). This shows unequivocally that the private sector can play a positive role in the economy. The IFC largest investment in Nigeria is in telecommunications. The National Monopoly (NITEL) is being prepared for privatization now. De-regulation of the telecommunications sector has been very effective.

According to the Economist Intelligence Unit (EIU) 2007 [10], Nigerians have been slow to embrace Internet technology, partly because of prohibitive local subscription charges and the poor state of the local fixed-line telephone system. However, despite the high costs the number of Internet users has risen rapidly in recent years; from under 300,000 in 2002 to around 2.5 million in 2005 and an estimated 3.5 billion by late 2006. This is reflected in the growth of Internet service providers. These have been licensed by the Nigerian Communications Commission (NCC) since January 1999; more than 100 have a basic license, although a large number of them are inactive. However, owing to the high costs and the problems associated with telephone lines, access to the Internet is mainly provided by Internet cafés (which tend to be expensive and offer slow connectivity in order to charge customers more), which are present in most urban centers. This situation of low access to ICT will hopefully improve with an Abu Dhabi's investment arm, Mubadala Development, recently completing a $400 million payment for a unified telecom license in Nigeria to offer services, such as fixed-line, voice, data services and establish an international gateway, areas previously restricted to the four existing GSM operators in the country. With the largest population in the region of about 140 million Nigeria has potential for significant growth.

Urquhart, Liyanage & Kah argue having access to computers alone does not guarantee transformation of communities and the positive impact of ICT being felt. Computers are not provided just for their sake. The aim of ICT interventions is to create desired transformation by giving people in rural areas access to a computer and the skills to use it. According to Urquhart, Liyanage & Kah, in some cases in Bangladesh, some villagers were quite fearful of trying out new technology and this was a barrier to use of the technology. For example, in one village where two computers were provided, the computers were kept at one of the villager's house for safe keeping instead of being used. Any attempt to move this computer to another location which is central for people to use or try out met with resistance from the person who took charge of the equipment. The fear was grounded on the belief that if people break it, who will repair it? Others are not ready to use it and if they do they have to pay a nominal amount to use it. As a result, inputs are rarely transformed into any usable outputs with tangible benefits. The presence of two computers in the village, however, is a symbolic social capital where villages felt that they were part of the rest of the world although there was no use out of the computers and information that it can deliver.

In their article, Urquhart, Liyanage & Kah argue that the transformation process envisaged in ICT interventions is also difficult due to the general level of education, where ICT education stands worlds apart from actual level of understanding. Villages require the information to be unpacked and presented to them. They were very interested in relevant information such as how to improve agricultural productivity. Indeed in the same village people were enthusiastic about a bee keeping project to be organized by Swedish Bee Keepers association – bringing wealth of knowledge and skills that can be put into practice immediately.

Villagers view ICT as intangible knowledge and an asset that can be of utility mostly for those who have knowledge to use it. As a result, two computers purchased for the village were left covered with a cloth over it, and served as a status symbol that indicates that the village now has educated people who can even use computers.

In our study area, Yola, Adamawa State, it was mostly the elites and some professionals who had access to computers and the internet at home. Given the poor state of electricity supply with rationing still prevalent, computer use at home is still low.

6.   Case study

6.1   The study area

Nigeria, Africa's most populous country, is composed of more than 250 ethnic groups. The following are the most populous and politically influential: Hausa and Fulani 29%, Yoruba 21%, Igbo (Ibo) 18%, Ijaw 10%, Kanuri 4%, Ibibio 3.5%, and Tiv 2.5%. Nigeria is large, diverse and complex. Nigeria's constitutionally powerful executive is constrained by the complexity of Nigeria's political system and the importance of ensuring national unity in a country with around 200 ethnic groups, 500 indigenous languages and two major religions (Islam and Christianity). Unfortunately, these potential cleavages in Nigerian society can be used for political ends. While there are indications that communal conflicts have subsided somewhat in the last two years, Nigeria remains vulnerable to resurgences of conflict. The Niger Delta despite its rich oil fields is very poor, with some community members feeling disenfranchised and excluded from the prosperity gained from oil revenues.

Nigeria's economic performance has improved in recent years partly due to improvements under a new reform-minded administration. Nigeria's former military rulers failed to diversify the economy away from its overdependence on the capital-intensive oil sector, which provides 20% of GDP, 95% of foreign exchange earnings, and about 65% of budgetary revenues. The largely subsistence agricultural sector has failed to keep up with rapid population growth - Nigeria is Africa's most populous country - and the country, once a large net exporter of food, now must import food [10].

6.2   Socio-economic activities in Yola, Adamawa State

Yola, the study area, is located in Adamawa state in Northeastern Nigeria. As with much of northern Nigeria, commerce and business (and of course government and military work), and not industry, have become the most popular and profitable enterprises. Following independence and the designation of Yola as the capital of Gongola State and the consequent new prospects of employment, migrations to Yola have accelerated greatly. Various peoples, especially the

Hausa, recently joined by Yoruba and Igbo from southern Nigeria, continue to dominate large- and small-scale trade industries in Yola as well as in many of its nearby towns, and finally, Hausa is beginning to replace Fulfulde as a lingua franca in many parts of the emirate [39].

As a result of the proselytizing mission of the Fulbe during the jihad, Adamawa and Yola have assumed a distinctively Muslim character. Christian missionaries were effective only in some rural areas, and only recently have some Christians migrated to the Fulbe towns. In the traditional part of Yola (Yola Town), one mainly finds Fulbe (those with pure Fulbe ancestry and those incorporated into the Fulbe identity), with non-Fulbe nowadays settling on the town's fringes. In the sabon gari (Jimeta), which was established early this century for "strangers," reside Fulbe, Hausa, and Kanuri Muslims, Igbo and Bachama Christians, and Batta, Kilba, Verre, and Yoruba, along with individuals from about twenty other minority ethnic groups whose members are either Christian or Muslim (VerEecke 1993).

Northern Nigeria, despite its political dominance of the country, currently lags behind the South in industrial development and Western education, so that this region's peoples, especially the poor, are among the most greatly affected. Northern peoples' sentiments of deprivation have been expressed, for instance, in local ethnic and religious antagonisms along with popular, at times destructive movements such as the Maitatsine riots in the early and mid-1980s [39, 41, 31].

6.3   The activities of the African Center for ICT Innovation & Training

In December 2005, American University of Nigeria (formerly Abti-American University of Nigeria) was notified of its successful grant application for $100,000 to build and run the African Center for ICT Innovation & Training to The John D. and Catherine T. MacArthur Foundation (henceforth MacArthur). The Founder of the university donated a building to which the chair of the Investment and Fund Raising Committee of the Board of Trustees donated N2,000,000 (Naira) (approximately $15,384) for renovations. The university, in turn, matched the renovation grant, and works on the Centre started in April 2006.

The Center's building is ideal in several respects. It is located adjacent to another university building near the campus and is situated close to the Yola business district. The proximity to the university building allows for the sharing of generators and diesel, water and sewage, and parking lots.

6.3.1   Incubator & techno-preneurship activities

The Center's goals include facilitating the development of ICT skills competencies of AUN staff, especially local staff, requisite for the operational needs of the university to coordinate library, admissions, registration and financial services to students and other related tasks. Further, the Centre recognized the value of training a small cadre of very bright, technologically advanced students excelling in ICT courses at AUN as well as recent top graduates from neighboring local universities and the local community of Yola and Jimeta by providing mentoring by ICT faculty and assigning supervised locally relevant software development activities with the expectation of developing product and services into marketable and usable software products. It is also the Center's aim that some of the ideas generated by students and faculty can result in next generation of software and ICT service providers responding to the needs of the local community and Sub-Saharan Africa.

An additional goal of the Center is to help provide advanced software technologies, internet connectivity/access to the community and ICT to some very bright students who graduated from the local Universities but were unable to have access to ICT during their undergraduate programs and/or at their institutions. The Center quickly recognized that very bright young men and women were graduating from these institutions with degrees in computer science, IT and other related fields but without the expected competencies. This is due mainly to the lack of access to ICT resources and capacity in most local and public universities. Access to modern software, Internet connectivity, ICT infrastructure and adequate faculty with the appropriate training/education in ICT is a rarity in most of institutions thus affecting the quality and competence of graduates. The center is also an ICT resource center for the community and for small businesses. The Centre continues to encourage particularly women in the communities of Yola and Jimeta to be trained in various aspects of ICT.

The group of students selected to be part of the Techno-Preneurship teams were mobilized to plan and create a registration application program that was used for the September 2006 intake of 300 students. This software was again adopted for the January 2007 intake. The students continue to enhance the functionality of the system that is evolving to be an adaptable and sustainable ERP system for higher education institutions in developing countries that will not be able to afford the Banner Solutions and/or DataTel Solutions. The applications being developed by the student Techno-Preneurship teams are designed to evolve as professional programs similar to the Banner system that will be adopted by the university. In the interim, AUN is using one of these Beta versions developed by one of the teams as its interim registration and admission systems. This system has great potential and we are working to enhance the modules to include a financial and advising module as well as convert it to Oracle. It is our hope that the students will be able to refine the application and introduce it to local universities for use.

The success of the Center's initial activity was spun off in October 2006 into another group of students which has begun to organize admissions data as well as another group adopting a local health care clinic (MATCO Clinic) based in the Yola/Jimeta community introducing the use and adoption of ICT as well as to design and develop a health care information systems. This has now evolved to a prototype knowledge support system for health informatics being developed.

A substantial percentage of students in the Center are female, amongst our most promising students, and are local to the community. These students are provided with a modest assistantship funded through the grant. It is also planned that these students will be the first to graduate and will thus lead AUN's employment profile in the business world.

6.3.2   Staff upgrading

The center is positioned to be a hub for ICT professional development and to improve the competencies of AUN staff as well as the larger communities of Yola and Jimeta. The Center is providing opportunity and access to ICT competency for the poor. The Center offers various levels of ICT training from basic to advanced to professional certifications. Another aim of the Center is to extend "self-paced, positive computer access and experience to local staff to create expectations of success and reliable performance," consistent with the work ethic of American universities. To date, this has happened in two ways. First, local staff members were given the opportunity to purchase AUN laptops and desktops in a heavily subsidized program. Second, recognizing occupational gaps in English competency, especially writing and e-mail messaging, the university offered free of charge a 4-week workshop in basic writing in spring 2006 and another in fall 2006. The class work and homework require the use of computers, and staff was released from duty in order to attend the courses.

All of the laptops and desktops in the distribution program were purchased by local staff, and the enrollment and attendance in the writing courses reached the maximum with classes remaining filled throughout the duration.

Further training leading to ICDL certification (International Computer Driver's License) progressed with 15 AUN local staff performing a diverse administrative function across the University with very minimum ICT skills. All these staffs were trained by highly qualified AUN faculty and learning is reinforced via self paced CBT's using SAM 2003 Training Assessment. These self paced CBT's are supported by the grant.

Furthermore, a group of 15 students from the Yola and Jimeta community were also trained along with the AUN University local staff. These are six week programs and all students that successfully completed the training will take the ICDL certification exams. The second batch of training for the local community commenced in May 2007. All the 30 participants currently undergoing training expressed interest to continue in the next level courses. The Center also fitted the infrastructure for the CISCO Academy and trained fifteen (15) community members for six weeks for the CCNA in May 2007. The center is also scheduled to offer short term training courses in Java and Web development.

6.3.3   Industry-university engagement

Selected students in the incubator worked on a prototype of "Knowledge Support Systems for Health Informatics" and this work continued through the summer of 2007 and is expected to be an application to be utilized by Health clinics in rural areas in Yola and Jimeta. Under the supervision of faculty, students were able to test these ideas developed in the Center and apply them to the needs of Yola and Jimeta rural communities.

The student activities also resulted in a Terms of Reference (TOR) and a Memorandum of Understanding (MOU) from The International Food Policy Research Institute (IFPRI) for collaboration and partnership with the Center to work with the Center's faculty associates and students to develop a Regional Strategic Analysis and Knowledge Support System (ReSAKSS) ICT Environment. A key element of the knowledge systems management component is the establishment of a ReSAKSS ICT and interactive website environment (RIE) to enable ready access to tools and information, promote mutual learning and peer-review, and facilitate dialogue on future priorities:

- Guiding the design and establishment of preliminary websites;
- Investigating and developing a comprehensive RIE;
- Coordination across nodes and select partners;
- Training and outreach for assessing and using the RIE resources.

Faculty Associates and students expect to commence work on these activities during summer 2008. Preliminary discussions and collaboration talks and project planning are taking place.

The Center also developed a program for "Women in ITC". This is an effort to increase the number of women at AUN studying and developing competences in computing as well as retention strategies for women enrolled in computing related programs. Several women from the community are undergoing training and mentorship at the Center. The center is contributing in the empowerment of women in the community via ICT competence and capacity development.

The center is also offering numerous IT industry certification programs such as Cisco, Microsoft, Oracle, IBM as well as programming (Java, C++, C##, Java script, PHP, ASP) Linux and Open Source Technologies and Unix. This is accomplished by housing a Cisco Regional Networking Academy; an Oracle Academic Alliance, a Microsoft Academic Alliance as well as an Open Source (Linux) and Unix Lab. This is progressing well with the establishment of the Cisco Academy and the CCNA certification.

6.3.4   The center's role in community engagement

The importance in developing a culture of "Techno-Preneurship" via the Center's Tech incubator as a mechanism to develop the next generation of business of IT companies as well as IT leaders in Nigeria and Sub-Saharan Africa is demonstrated via the current teams of students tasked with various real life applications development, including an health informatics system for the community and the partnership and collaboration to develop a Knowledge Support System for the IFPIRI, an international organisation based in Washington.

The Center, through applied research on ICT development and poverty reduction, tries to disseminate and/or share knowledge and results relevant to policy makers as it relates to their efforts in developing and adopting ICT to improve government and private sector processes. This is done via numerous publications on peer reviewed journals and presentations and/or publications to peer reviewed conference proceedings.

Through the Center the next generation of competent skilled IT labor force can be developed to avail themselves to compete for the million dollar software and IT outsourcing global market. This can have very positive economic effects. This is being demonstrated through the ongoing training activities of the Center for different levels of ICT training.

The first phase entailed the development of a lab at the Center to house the Cisco Networking Academy program at AUN-SITC providing students with a skills-based career path on the information technology industry. This has been completed. The second phase entailed development of the Labs for the other areas of Information Technology such as an Oracle Lab, Linux and Unix Lab and Microsoft Lab to facilitate the requirements for their certification programs.

6.4   Case study findings and discussion of the Center's impact

The impact of the Center on the communities of Yola and Jimeta is an ongoing study. On March 6, 2008, the Center held its first formal graduation ceremony in which 62 participants attended to receive their training certificates. In total more than 102 participants have gone through the Center for training. Some of the observable impacts are:

- Students hands-on learning experience equipping them with applied skill sets in different competencies in ICT;
- Faculty's ability to adopt and utilize ICT in their teaching in order to facilitate learning by enhancing the mode of delivery;
- In the case of staff of the university, the Center has greatly helped to enhance their skill sets and allow them to become more efficient and productive in the performance of their daily tasks;
- More than 20 participants from the State government of Adamawa have been trained at the Center. Many of these civil servants are at mid-career levels and have greatly appreciated the opportunity offered by the Center and have indicated that they are more productive at work due to the skills they have learnt. In addition, having these computer skills make them more marketable, and;
- An environment and training for internationally recognized industry certification in different areas in ICT, for example Cisco, MSCE, Oracle, DB2, Linux, Unix, Programming skills in Java, C++, C##, PHP, Java scripts etc, as well as web technologies and development skills.

7.   Conclusion

The Yola community is currently engaged in the activities of the Center mainly through the numerous trainings offered on ICT skills. Without the Center there was little hope of enhancing the community's skill sets and enabling the community to benefit from being part of the digital world. The women members of the community currently in various levels of ICT training had little hope of much ICT training being in a rural community like Yola. The Yola and Jimeta communities are very satisfied and encouraged by the activities of the Center and its interventions to help bridge the digital divide and empower women in the community with appropriate ICT skills.

An additional group that is benefiting from the Center is students who graduated from local universities such as the Federal University of Technology (FUTI) but were unable to have access to ICT during their undergraduate programs and/or at their institutions. The Center quickly recognized that very bright young men and women were graduating from public and substandard private universities, colleges and institutions with degrees and diplomas in computer science, IT and other related fields but without the expected ICT competencies. This is due mainly to the lack of access to ICT resources and capacity in most local and public universities.

References

[1] Adam, M.S. & Myers, M.D. (2003). Have you got anything to declare? Neo-colonialism, information systems, and the imposition of customs and duties in a third world country, in M. Korpela, R. Montealegre and A. Poulymenakou (Eds.) *Organisational information systems in the context of globalization.*   Dordrecht: Kluwer Academic Publishers.

[2] Amonoo-Neizer, E.H. (1998). Universities in Africa: The need for adaptation, transformation, reformation and revitalization. *Higher Education Policy*, 11, 301–309.

[3] Avgerou, C. (2001). The significance of context in information systems and organisational change. *Information Systems Journal*, 11(1), 43-63.

[4] Bhatnagar, S. (2000). Social implications of information and communication technology in developing countries: lessons from Asian success stories, *Electronic Journal on Information Systems in Developing Countries* 1(4): 1 9.

[5] Braa, J., Macome, E., Mavimbe, J.C., Nhampossa, J.L., Costa, J.L., Jose´, B., Manave, A. & Sito´i, A. (2001). A study of the actual and potential usage of information and communication technology at district and provincial levels in Mozambique with a focus on the health sector, *Electronic Journal on Information Systems in Developing Countries* 5(2): 1–29.

[6] Burch, J. & Grudnitski, G. (1986). *Information systems: Theory and practice*, (4th ed.). New York: Wiley.

[7] Chambers, R. (1997). *Whose reality counts: putting the first last.* London: Intermediate Technology.

[8] Chatterton, P. & Goddard, J. (2000). The response of higher education institutions to regional needs. *European Journal of Education*, 35(4), 475–496.

[9] Dymond, A. & Oestmann, S. (2002). ICTs, poverty alleviation and universal access: Review of status and issues, *ATPS Special Paper Series*, (9), Nairobi: Kenya African Technology Policy Studies Network, http://www.atpsnet.org/.

[10] The Economist Intelligence Unit Limited (2007), Country Profile 2007, 20-21 at www.eiu.com.

[11] Etzkowitz, H. & Leydesdorff, L. (2000). The dynamics of innovation: From national systems and "mode 2" to a triple helix of university-industry-government relations. *Research Policy*, 29(2–3), 109–123.

[12] Etzkowitz, H., Webster, A., Gebhardt, C. and Terra, B. R. C. (2000). The future of the university and the university of the future: Evolution of ivory tower to entrepreneurial paradigm. *Research Policy*, 29(2), 313–330.

[13] Etzkowitz, H. (2002). Incubation of incubators: Innovation as a triple helix of university-industry-government networks. *Science and Public Policy*, 29(2), February, 115–128.

[14] Etzkowitz, H. (2002). *MIT and the rise of entrepreneurial science*. London: Routledge.

[15] Freeman, C. (1995). The national system of innovation in historical perspective. *Cambridge Journal of Economics*, 19, 5–24.

[16] Gunasekara, C. (2006). The generative and developmental roles of universities in regional innovation systems. *Science and Public Policy*, 33(2), 137-150.

[17] Guston, D. H. (2000). Retiring the social contract for science. *Issues in Science and Technology*, 16(4), 32–36.

[18] Hall, P. (1994). *Innovation, economics and evolution*. New York: Harvester Sheaf.

[19] Hart, D. M. (1988). *Forged consensus: Science, technology and economic policy in the United States, 1921–1953*. Princeton: Princeton University Press.

[20] Heeks, R. (2002). I-development not e-development: Special issue on ICTS and development. *Journal of International Development*, 14(1), 1-12.

[21] Holland, B. A. (1999). From murky to meaningful: the role of mission in institutional change. In R.G. Bringle, R. Games, & E. A. Malloy (Eds.), *Colleges and universities as citizens* (pp. 48–73). Boston: Allyn & Bacon.

[22] Humphrey, J. (2006). Prospects and challenges for growth and poverty reduction in Asia, *Development Policy Review*, 24(s1), s29–s49.

[23] Huyer, S. & Mitter, S. (2003). ICTs, globalisation and poverty reduction: gender dimensions of the knowledge society part I, poverty reduction, gender equality and the knowledge society: digital exclusion or digital opportunity? Accessed on 9th August 2006 from http://gab.wigsat.org/partI.pdf.

[24] Jalava, I. & Pohjola, M. (2002). Economic growth in the new economy: Evidence from advanced economies. *Information Economics and Policy*, 14(2), 189–210.

[25] Kayani, R. & Dymond, A. (1997). Options for rural telecommunications development, *World Bank Technical Paper*, (359) http://www.inteleconresearch.com/pages/wbank.html.

[26] Kenny, C. (2002). Information and communication technologies for direct poverty alleviation: costs and benefits. *Development Policy Review*, 20, 141–157.

[27] Khasiani, S.A. (2000). Enhancing women's participation in governance: The case of Kakamega and Makueni districts, Kenya, in E.M. Rathgeber and E.O. Adera (Eds.) *Gender and the Information Revolution in Africa*, Ottawa: International Development Research Centre (IDRC), Chapter 8. http://www.idrc.ca/books/focus/903/11-chp08.html.

[28] Kraemer, K.L. & Dedrick, J. (2001). Information technology and productivity: results and policy implications of cross-country studies. In Pohjola, M. (Ed), *Information technology, productivity, and economic growth*, (pp. 257-279). Oxford: Oxford University Press.

[29] Lee, J. (2001). Education for technology readiness: prospects for developing countries, *Journal of Human Development*, 2(1): 115–151.

[30] Lim, E. (1999). Human resource development for the information society, *Asian Libraries* 8(5): 143–161.

[31] Lubeck. P. (1986). *Islam and urban labor in Northern Nigeria: the making of a Muslim working class*. Cambridge: Cambridge University Press.

[32] Marker, P., McNamara K., & Wallace L. (2002). The significance of information and communication technologies for reducing poverty. Report of the UK Department for International Development, 2002, retrieved from http://www.dfid.gov.uk/pubs/files/ictpoverty.pdf. Accessed 3 May 2006.

[33] Okunoye, A. (2003). Organisational information technology infrastructure in developing countries: A comparative analysis of national vs. international research organisations in two Sub-Saharan African countries, *Journal of Information Technology Cases and Applications*, 5(2):8–26.

[34] Opoku-Mensah, A. (2000). ICTs as tools of democratization: African women speak out, in E.M. Rathgeber and E.O. Adera (Eds.) *Gender and the Information Revolution in Africa*, Ottawa: International Development Research Centre (IDRC), Chapter 7, retrieved from http://www.idrc.ca/books/focus/903/10-chp07.html.

[35] Oyelaran-Oyeyinka, B. & Barclay, L. (2004). Human capital and systems of innovation in African development. *African Development Review*, 16(1), 115–138.

[36] Pitten, R. (1987). Documentation of women's work in Nigeria: problems and solutions in sex roles. In C. Oppong, (Ed.), *Population and development in West Africa*, (pp. 25-44). London: James Currey.

[37] Smith, B. L. R. (1990). *American science policy since World War II*. Washington, DC: The Brookings Institution.

[38] Urquhart, C., Liyanage, S., & Kah, M. (2007). ICTs and poverty reduction: a social capital and knowledge perspective. *Journal of Information Technology*.

[39] VerEecke, C. (1993). Muslim women traders of northern Nigeria: Perspectives from the City of Yola, *Ethnology*, 32(3), 217-236.

[40] Walsham, G., Sahay, S., & Robey, D. (2004). MIS Quarterly call for papers: Special issue on information systems and developing countries. www.misq.org.

[41] Watts, M. (1985). *Silent violence: food, famine, and peasantry in Northern Nigeria*. Berkeley: University of California Press.

[42] Webster, A. (1999). Technologies in transition, policies in transition: Foresight in the risk society. *Technovation*, 19, 413–421.

[43   The World Bank Group & Department for International Development (2005). Country partnership strategy for The Federal Republic of Nigeria (2005 - 2009).

[44] Zaglul, J., Sherrard, D., & Juma, C.   (2006). Higher education in economic transformation. *International Journal of Technology and Globalisation*, 2.3/4: 241-251.

LESSONS FROM A DROPPED ICT CURRICULUM DESIGN PROJECT: A RETROSPECTIVE VIEW

Roohollah Honarvar
AVEC Company

Abstract   Developing competent human resources is of crucial importance to policy makers aiming to move towards an information society. Universities are often designated the task of training Information Technology/Systems (IT/S) professionals for the economy of the future. This chapter critically reflects upon a dropped ICT curriculum design project which was to be used in ten Iranian universities. It aims to draw the attention of policy makers to the importance of practical considerations in issuing human resource development policies. The chapter focuses on the challenges of IT/S professionals' training to the centralised higher education system, as well as the challenge of providing social skills for IT/S professionals and the importance of national language. An analysis is given of the implicit assumptions behind Iran's national ICT policies and the deficiencies of those policies with regard to these challenges. Some practical recommendations and summary conclude the chapter.

Keywords: Developing countries, higher education, curriculum design, IT/S professionals' training, national ICT development policy

1.   Introduction

Developing competent human resources is of vital importance to policy makers aiming to move towards an information society. Four categories of people in need of ICT education or training are identified within the literature: the general public, the policy makers and managers at the governmental and organisational levels, technology users, and IT/S professionals [18]. This last group consists of professionals in different jobs with the primary role of creating information products/services in the society. Thus, they are the most important forces in the actual development of ICT within the country. Due to the high level of specialised education and training needed, universities are often designated the task of training these IT/S professionals (see for example [3, 5]).

As the first decade of the twenty first century comes to its end, ICT curriculum has been integrated into the educational programmes of the universities in most developed countries (see also [16]). The situation is much more heterogeneous in

Please use the following format when citing this chapter:

Honarvar, R., 2008, in IFIP International Federation for Information Processing, Volume 282; *Social Dimensions of Information and Communication Technology Policy*; Chrisanthi Avgerou, Matthew L. Smith, Peter van den Besselaar; (Boston: Springer), pp. 241–252.

the developing countries. In Asia, for instance, some pioneering countries (e.g. India, Malaysia, and Singapore) have become to some extent "powerful" players in the global information society by relying on their IT/S professionals, while some others (e.g. Nepal, Philippines, and central Asian countries) are just taking the first steps. More specifically, most countries do have a policy regarding the training of IT/S professionals[1], but the scope and depth of these policies vary considerably from one to another. Policy makers can share their experiences in the implementation of IT/S professionals' training policy to the advantage of their nations [6].[2] This is highlighted when one notes the relatively diminutive size of literature in this area of ICT policy.

Caryannis and Sipp [3] emphasise the need for renewing the educational system of most developing countries at the university level to become up-to-date and "more responsive to the ever-changing demands of the Knowledge Economy". This chapter discusses the practical challenges raised during the implementation of Iran's IT/S professionals' training policy (hereafter referred to as IT/SPTP), part of which was to design a standard ICT curriculum. The curriculum was to be implemented as a pilot project in ten Iranian state universities. The issues that emerged almost brought the project to a halt. Finally, the project, with a 350.000 dollars budget, was abandoned without any significant achievements. This was despite the great enthusiasm and ambition behind the project and the voluminous efforts and studies by the project team, to which the author was a modest contributor.

The rest of chapter is structured as follows. First, the reader is introduced to the context of Iran's national ICT policies within which IT/SPTP was formed and the idiosyncrasies of the country's university system. Then the case is described in terms of the steps taken by the project team pointing out the questions considered in each step and solutions offered. An analysis of the issues and obstacles which in one way or another insinuated the impossibility of reaching the final result is followed by a discussion of alternative possible solutions and an analysis of implicit assumptions behind the national IT/SPTP. This leads to some practical recommendations for policy makers. The conclusion highlights the main points addressed in the chapter.

2.   The context

Iran's National ICT agenda, usually known as TAKFA- Extension of Application of ICT in Iran- was established in 2002. The aim is to develop and maintain an advanced technological environment that will support and enhance education, learning and research as well as service and administrative functions all

---

[1] A recent study published by UNESCO [11] indicates that at least 15 of 28 countries included in the study have developed a specific policy for training IT/S professionals.

[2] One great step here has been the publication of *A curriculum for an information society: educating and training information professionals in the Asia-Pacific region* [17]. However, it is notable that the gap has not been narrowed since then.

over the country. Strategies and policies for using ICT are developed by the Supreme Council of ICT (chaired by the President) and the responsibility for carrying out strategies rests with The National ICT Agency.

The emphasis on human resource development as "the strategic priority" in TAKFA objective statement clearly shows that education and learning play a central role in country's ICT development policy [15]. There are specific policies written for developing information literacy, general information-handling skills (technology use) and training IT/S professionals.[3] These policies include, but are not limited to, providing basic ICT training for government employees, integrating ICDL training into school programmes and developing ICT-related degrees at university level.

In the same year, the Iranian Centre for Research in Telecommunications, under the then Ministry of Post, Telegraph and Telephone (PTT)[4], issued the National Strategy for ICT Development which was the result of an outsourced study on the prospect for developing ICT within the country [13]. This study highlighted the importance of human resource development and the need for developing new university programmes to educate adequately skilled IT/S professionals. The study also emphasised the need for a quantitative estimation of the number of IT/S professionals needed in near future.

The following year, a follow-up study was done on human resource development [14]. Looking at a five year horizon, the study assumed that the difference between vacant ICT-related careers evolving in this period and the number of graduates in ICT-related fields was to be filled by the professionals trained in the new ICT departments.[5]

Broadly speaking, the Iranian system of higher education consists of a relatively large number of state universities and a number of non-state universities (including a fee-charging university with many branches across the country, a distance learning university, a few recently established private universities and very few research institutions). These all are accredited by the Ministry of Higher Education.

The Ministry of Higher Education is also responsible for designing the standard curricula of degrees and syllabi of courses for all degrees. Since 1981, a prospectus for every programme must be proposed to the Supreme Council of

---

[3] The information regarding policies for training IT/S professionals is missing from Moore's report [11]. This may be the result of desk-based research approach of the study which has limited the sources of information to those available through the internet. But the study names Iran (along with some other countries like Japan) as "notable exceptions" which "take a broader view and aim to raise the level of information technology literacy throughout the population" in information literacy policy. The country is also recognised for requiring all government employees to have basic levels of ICT skills in order to develop ICT handling skills of the workforce.

[4] The ministry is now called the Ministry of Communication and Information Technology.

[5] It must be stressed here that neither TAKFA nor *The National Strategy for ICT Development* had not neglected the role of subsidiary educational institutions (such as technical and vocational training schools) in the training of ICT technicians as part of the IT/S professionals; but since we have focused our analysis on the role assumed for the universities in this process of development, we concentrate on sections in these policies that address this issue.

Higher Education Planning. This council will revise the programme and forward it to the Supreme Council of Cultural Revolution for final approval.[6] All accredited universities must follow the approved standard. Although no formal inspection has ever been made to check the conformity of the actual teaching process, the standard is followed with minor deviations in almost all universities' classes across the country. Most currently used curricula and syllabi were developed around 1982-1983, with only minor revisions since.

In this context, the Ministry of Higher Education was obliged to develop ICT departments covering both undergraduate and postgraduate levels in ten universities [15, Section 3.2.1]. As a prerequisite, the ministry assigned the BTF Institute to the task of designing a standard ICT department to be adopted in those universities. The project was initiated in late 2003.

3.   The case

A team of some 15 researchers was formed to execute the project. The first question to be addressed was "What is meant by an ICT department?" To answer the question, some 20 departments of IT were selected and studied along with other schools that provided some degrees in IT but did not have the title of "IT Department" or the like, notably business schools offering degrees in IT management. Other forms of ICT education at university level were also considered, such as the Multimedia University in Malaysia. The aim was to develop an understanding of alternative models of providing university-level ICT education and alternative forms of ICT departments and to find the most suitable model for Iranian universities. For reasons beyond the scope of this chapter, the choice was made to rename existing Computer Engineering departments to Computer Engineering and Information Technology departments and to extend their curriculum to offer technical degrees in ICT. Degrees in IT management were to be handled by business and management schools.

The next question was "what is taught in an ICT department?" There are differences between the standard curriculum in the sense described above and "model" curriculum discussed, for example, in [12]. However the methods for designing both are similar. Thus, this simple question led the team to study the curriculum of some selected departments. It is notable that Iranian universities do not award two-year associate degrees and therefore the search was limited to four-year undergraduate and postgraduate degrees.[7] To make a comprehensive review, the team explored in full detail the syllabus of every single course in relevant departments which in some cases included reading laboratory manuals. There was an incredible diversity of approaches to the subjects and the offered courses varied substantially from one department to another. Every department had its own selection of topics. Even for topics with the same title, two very different

---

[6] It was in 2005 that universities acquired the authority to revise course syllabuses or add new courses.
[7] The associate degrees are awarded by technical and vocational training schools.

approaches were pursued. This posed the third question "what should Iranian universities teach in ICT-related areas?" This included both designing new courses and redefining the existing ones which were taught at computer engineering departments.

Up to that time, no qualitative assessment of ICT education needs was made at national level. No information was present to make decision about which aspects of ICT to emphasise and which aspects to neglect or deemphasise. It was suggested by the author to map ICT-related careers against the national ICT plans to find out which careers are most required and which knowledge and skills must the future IT/S professional posses to perform his/her job competently.

This approach was criticised for undermining the role of private sector, but it was argued that the government will have the leading role in the diffusion of ICT in medium term and most private companies will be just contractors of governmental projects. This meant that they were to a large degree dependent on the government initiatives. Indeed, according to TAKFA, the government was obliged to provide support for the establishment of 500 ICT-related companies. Furthermore, the approach could help the planning of IT/S professionals' education by providing the time frame within which certain skills were needed. For example there was an immediate need for network-related professionals to support the development of national information network infrastructure. But postgraduate programmes in e-business and e-commerce were not needed until some 3 or 4 years later when e-business development plans would get underway.

The absence of a clear link between IT/S professionals' training programmes and their role in national ICT development has been a basic deficiency in most IT/SPTPs. Moore reports that most Asian countries follow what Walsham [18] calls the "standard route" in developing human resources, i.e. awarding ICT-related degrees [11] (for some exceptions, see Carayannis and Sipp [3]). Thus they usually have serious shortcomings regarding the inclusion of these trained specialties in the actual creation, manipulation, processing and use of information in society. By matching IT/SPTP to other national ICT development plans, the vision would become clear for future IT/S professionals.

Subsequently, the author was appointed as the manager of internal studies' group in mid 2004 and the team started to research about 1) knowledge and skills required for each career and 2) careers and job titles associated with implementation of ICT plans. The results were fascinating because they closely matched the previous quantitative studies and provided a plausible basis for designing the curriculum [9, 10]. But just then it seemed that further progress of the project was blocked by a number of overseen problems.

First, it was realised that the curriculum would have a short life, its material will soon be outdated and it will need to be revised. Given the resistance of the existing computer engineering departments to revise the obsolete course syllabi, this problem was not negligible. Moreover, revising the syllabus (of even one course) through the centralised mechanisms described above was not an easy task.

How should the process begin, who would decide about it and who would have the capabilities to revise the syllabus?

Second, such unified curriculum did not allow space for local peculiarities and regional differences. The spread of ICT was uneven and different provinces needed different combinations of skills and trainings [13]. Some flexibility had to be added into the system to allow some level of adaptation to local priorities.

Third, Walsham [18] points to the lack of broader social skills and capabilities in university graduates of computer sciences (in the most general sense of the word) due to the fact that their formal education focuses almost exclusively on technical training. This results in major difficulties when these graduates are introduced to the workplace, especially in developing countries.

Last but not least important, finding qualified lecturers seemed to be a very difficult task. Most of the current faculty members and people with formal educational backgrounds did not have the necessary background to teach new courses. Those who had technical qualifications to teach new courses did not have the educational background necessary to be faculty members. Very few individuals had both competencies and these could not be easily reached.

4.   Discussion

At this point, the reader may reasonably suggest: "Well, you did not have to abandon the project. A change of direction would have sufficed." But these obstacles jeopardised the vision of ICT department and blocked further investigation into the structure of department, its connections with other departments and etc. In fact, the practical obstacles were important but they were not the sole reasons for the early termination of project. The project was never formally dropped, but literally abandoned.

In this section a number of solutions for the above-mentioned obstacles are presented, followed by a discussion of their practical implications. The interrelationship of these problems and the paradoxical role of a centralized higher education system in regard to IT/S professionals' training are also highlighted.

4.1   The challenge to the centralized higher education system

It seems that little can be done in respect of the first issue, i.e. the short life of the curriculum. The fast changing nature of information technology and its unpredictability have proved to be an essential problem contributing to this issue. However, one strategy can be dividing the curriculum into core and non-core subjects, giving more persistence to courses with more fundamental importance [16, p. 29].

The slowness and complexities of bureaucratic mechanisms can be removed from the system by giving more authority to universities themselves. The situation here is very much like the classical distinction of centrally planned (bureaucratic) structure and market structure in organisation theory (see for example [4, 8]).

While the former is maintained through authority controls, the latter reacts to the dynamics of supply and demand, being coordinated by the communication of a "sufficient statistic" (e.g. price) which contains all the information one needs for decision making.

To draw more on organisation theory, one possible middle ground can be Sloan's Multidivisional form (or more shortly, the M-form). The M-form structure was essentially designed to simplify decision making structures within large firms [7]. By separation of strategic and operational issues, each division had more independency regarding its own operational and tactical decisions while committing to achieve some financial targets specified by central management team. The central management team, on the other hand, had more free time to investigate strategic issues and look at further horizons.

Such an approach can be very helpful in the context of national higher education system that faces the challenges discussed here. Universities can have some degree of freedom, given that they will not fall short of some educational standards. The policy makers can take a broader and strategic perspective on course selection as well as paying more attention to the issues concerning the whole higher education system. This is in line with our previous recommendation to divide curriculum into core and non-core courses and it perfectly matches the need for flexibility in adopting the curriculum for different provinces of the country.

If such implementation is not possible in the short run, it may be more appropriate to rely on more flexible options like non-degree programmes or vocational training certificates. This is particularly relevant if finding/training qualified lecturers are difficult or uneconomical (see below). For some specialties, it may be sufficient to invite professionals or, more appropriately, "professional services" from other countries. This is practical especially when some expert opinion is needed, as in the evaluation of the human-computer interface of a nation-wide system. Experts, by definition, will evolve through practice and expert-level practice cannot be included in formal education. But in sensitive areas such as system securities some cautionary measurements must be in place when relying on foreign professionals. However, it must be emphasised that in the long run, countries have to move to more flexible mechanisms in order to enjoy the full benefits of a dynamic and progressive national ICT development.

4.2   The challenge of IT/S professionals' social skills

To enhance the social and organisational capabilities of IT/S professionals, one simple option is to improve the curriculum by including some courses on social relationships. But a more challenging option is to re-skill the alumni of universities through continuing education courses held at universities. Alumni have the advantage of possessing practical experience and basic familiarity with the field. This can be effectively exploited to shorten the duration of specialised qualifications to less than one year. This re-skilled workforce who is equipped with both reliable theoretical knowledge and practical skills can be quickly absorbed for urgent needs of society while others are in preparation in formal undergraduate programmes.

Walsham [18] also mentions the shortage of senior IT/S professionals in developing countries who can help newer recruit to learn some of the organisational and behavioural skills and knowledge. These re-skilled professionals can also fill this shortage. Such continuing education programmes can also take the form of lifelong learning programmes which is of essential necessity for IT/S professionals but is often missing in the IT/S professionals' training policies.

4.3   The importance of national language

Finding qualified lecturers is a much more complex process than one might think. Here the language spoken in academic environments becomes of central importance. If it is English, French, Spanish or Portuguese (i.e. the languages which have many speakers around the world and particularly in the developed countries) it would be relatively easy to find foreign lecturers teaching in your language. But if the national language is relatively local with few or no speakers in the developed countries, it will be very difficult to find suitable lecturers. In fact, except for lecturers from your own country living abroad, there will be very little chance to find anyone and again it is very hard to attract these people.

One alternative strategy can be initiation of bilingual education, i.e. to lecture some courses in local language and some other in a foreign language; English for example. Thus you can invite and recruit foreign lecturers, bringing fresh air and dynamism to your academic environment. In Iran, the National Strategy for ICT Development had suggested moving towards the "bilingual-isation" of educational system, but broader policies regarding protection and propagation of the national language did not permit such ideas to be materialised.

Another alternative can be training of existing or potential faculty members by foreign lecturers (in a second language) and then assigning them to lecture on those topics in the local language. This approach seems to be the most practical solution because it makes existing faculty members more interested and poses the least threat to the national language. However, this option is usually expensive and time consuming.

Yet another option, more practical but more effectively limited, is to provide overseas education bursaries. The graduates of such programmes, usually with postgraduate degrees and up-to-date knowledge, are usually valuable potential candidates as faculty members and can be very helpful for the restructuring of ICT-related education in universities. However, their ultimate effectiveness is severely limited to the appropriate revision of curriculum to which they can be valuable contributors.

As it is clear from this discussion, these challenges are highly interrelated and policy makers must take a holistic view to understand the circumstances in full and plan accordingly. However, central to these challenges is the centralized planning system upon which higher education is heavily dependent in most developing countries. The centrally planned educational system is the primary institution by means of which governments are involved in implementing IT/S professionals' training policies. Hence, the governments have to "act upon" this system in apparently contradictory ways: on the one hand to supply the whole country with adequately skilled workforce in the long run and on the other to introduce more flexibility to the higher education system to cope with regional and temporal demands. While most countries pay considerable attention to the former issue, little attention is paid to the critical and vital role of the second in the long run. This is the subject we turn to in the next section.

5.   Retrospective view

Now, with the benefit of hindsight, a reconsideration of the general themes and implicit assumptions underlying TAKFA and other nation-level plans can be valuable. Surely, these plans were criticised on a number of grounds at that time but in most cases these criticisms were limited to sectoral boundaries such as e-government and e-health. In rare cases the whole policy was assessed. These evaluations usually attacked methodological aspects of national ICT policies (for example [2]), its technological implications or even the adopted privatisation policies. It is interesting, however regrettable, that both policy makers and critics were considering IT/S professionals' training as business-as-usual and, except for the "brain drain" problem, little attention was paid to the challenges of IT/S professionals' training in the higher educational system.

In TAKFA, the section on development of ICT in higher education consists of three elements: developing a network between universities, developing university-level ICT degrees and supporting ICT-related research in universities.[8] The policy also calls for a revision of university-level degrees based on the capabilities of ICT [15, section on *The Second Step Plan*]. No specific mechanism or advice is suggested for accomplishing any of these tasks. Expectedly, no potential practical obstacle has been addressed. Moreover, given the relatively successful centralised approach of the Ministry of Higher Education in planning and directing education in society, no adjustment of the usual approach was considered.

The National Strategy for ICT Development calls for a differentiation of ICT-related degrees in order to facilitate the planning of the IT/S professional workforce and puts more emphasis on vocational training of ICT technicians. However, it is interesting that it highlights "the existence of capable human resources and the growth ICT-related graduates" in the country as a point of strength [13, p.132]. This is despite the tiny size of ICT industry (less than 500

---

[8] Other sections on education consists of: developing the ICT infrastructure of schools and connecting them through a network, training the general public (most notably teachers and government employees), and developing e-learning and multimedia-enabled courses for the schools.

companies in 2001 and an estimated 210,000 employees overall, including the government employees in the ministry of PTT) and the inadequacies of appropriately trained IT/S in the workforce [2]. The report gives no guideline for training IT/S professionals except briefly mentioning the need to estimate the number of IT/S professionals needed and for continuous curriculum revision.

The subsequent report on human resource development has a more realistic picture of the workforce and explicitly concerns "the shortage of IT/S professionals" and "the lack of practical skills in existing professionals". The report also mentions the shortage of competent lecturers and the gap between the current curriculum and the actual needs of ICT sector [14]. However, it makes no reference to the need for regular curriculum revision and its challenge to the centralised approach of the ministry of Higher Education.

These reports give much less attention to the other challenges of IT/S professionals' training. As noted before, the National Strategy for ICT Development advocated the bilingual-isation of the educational system. It also briefly mentioned the need for more cooperation between industry and universities, but in both cases it did not provide any specific mechanism or guideline. This may be in part due to a lack of any institutionalised mechanism for cooperating with industry or to get any feedback from them which by no means is limited to only ICT-related degrees. This may be compared to the following recommendation made by the ACM Two-Year College Education Committee in its 'Guidelines for Associate-Degree Programs to Support Computing in a Networked Environment':

> Colleges should keep plans current through a comprehensive plan that includes ongoing professional growth and development for faculty and staff, continuous curriculum revision, periodic review, assessment and replacement of equipment and associated resources, and ongoing evaluation and updating of instructional methodologies and teaching materials.... An active industry advisory council, together with ongoing feedback from graduates and employers, provides an important mechanism to ensure that this occurs. These industry partnerships can provide many forms of support to the two-year college, including curriculum advice, industry training materials, in-service opportunities for faculty, a source of adjunct faculty, equipment donations, supplemental funding, student internships, placement opportunities, and recognition of program excellence [1].

Indeed, if such mechanisms had been in place, the curriculum would have been much more up-to-date and the centralised approach would have been enhanced by periodical quantitative and qualitative feedbacks from the industry. This would have also enabled the curriculum design project to be conducted in a much more flexible and demand-based manner. In the absence of such facilitating mechanisms, policy makers must clearly distinguish between what seems possible and what should actually be done.

6.   Conclusion

This chapter critically examined some conventional ideas about the training of IT/S professionals and the roles of universities in this regard. Drawing on a dropped ICT curriculum design project, the challenges of ICT education to the traditional higher education structure were explored. Several points can be drawn from the discussion presented.

One obvious message of this chapter is that developing university-level degrees for training IT/S professionals through standard rigid curriculum is not advisable. IT/S professionals' training is different from ICDL training. While central planning may be effective for developing information literacy and general information handling skills, it poses several challenges to the effective training of IT/S professionals. More often than not, central planning is conjoined with obstructive bureaucracies of higher education which dislike changes and cannot adapt to the rapid developments of the IT/S field. The M-form was suggested as a solution to some of these problems. However, it was suggested that four-year university degrees may not be the best options for educating IT/S professionals in some developing countries, at least for the short run. Policy makers must think out of the box and look for creative options. The opportunities provided by re-skilling the available workforce should not be overlooked.

Another message is that in line with Walsham and Moore, we suggest that policy makers must specify which ICT-related professions are needed and by how much. In other words, they must clarify how these trained specialists will be included in country's ICT development plans. This can lead to a categorization of the required IT/S professionals, their (possible/preferred) supply sources (including university education, vocational training, re-skilling programmes, and service importation contracts) and necessity time frames. This level of integration in the national IT/SPTP can give the graduates a clear vision of future and thus can contribute to maintaining graduates within the country, i.e. restricting the scale of brain drain phenomenon.

A third message is that policy makers must take into account the realities of available IT/S professionals especially in the academic environments before making any decision regarding further development of human resources. The role of language as a social phenomenon directly affecting the access to IT/S professionals and lecturers and the importance of public policies in this regard cannot be overstated.

Acknowledgements

The members of the research team, one and all, had valuable contributions to both the process and the goal of the research. The author appreciates their efforts without which this chapter would never be possible. The author also wishes to express his appreciation to the two anonymous reviewers for their constructive comments.

References

[1]   ACM Two-Year College Education Committee (2000). Guidelines for associate-degree programs to support computing in a networked environment. Rockford, Illinois.

[2]   BTF Institute (2002). A critique of national ICT policy and strategies. BTF Institute, Tehran, Iran.

[3]   Carayannis, E.G., & Sipp C.M. (2006). *E-development toward the knowledge economy*, New York: Palgrave Macmilan.

[4]   Coase R.H. (1937). The nature of the firm. *Eonomica*, Vol. 4, 386-405.

[5]   Fekri, M., & Jahangir M.R. (2004). The role of ICT department in planning and developing human resources. *Proceedings of the Second International Management Conference (IRIMC 2004)*, Tehran, Iran.

[6]   Grant G. (ed.) (2001). Regional initiative for informatics strategies. COMNET-*IT* and The Commonwealth Secretariat.

[7]   Gullien M.F. (1994). *Models of management*. Chicago: The University of Chicago Press.

[8]   Hayek, F.A. (1945). The use of knowledge in society. *American Economic Review*, 35(4), 519-30.

[9]   Honarvar, R., Jahangir M.R., & Rezaei A. (2003a). Report on shortages in current national ICT education, BTF Institute. Tehran, Iran.

[10] Honarvar, R., Jahangir M.R., & Rezaei A. (2003b). A comparative study of ICT human resources. BTF Institute, Tehran, Iran.

[11] Moore N. (2005). Information policies in Asia: A review of Information and Communication Policies in the Asia Region, Communication and Information in Asia. Bangkok: UNESCO.

[12] Noor, A. El Sayed (1984). Towards a model curriculum in computer-based information systems for developing countries: The case of Arab environments. *Computers and Education*, 8(2), 239-62.

[13] RADSAMANE (2002). National strategy for ICT development. Tehran, Iran.

[14] RADSAMANE (2003). Studies on human resource development. Tehran, Iran.

[15] Supreme Council of ICT (2002). TAKFA: extension of application of ICT in Iran. Tehran, Iran.

[16] The Joint Task Force for Computing Curricula 2005 (2005). Computing curricula 2005: the overview report. ACM and IEEE. United States of America.

[17] UNESCO (1998). A curriculum for an information society: Educating and training information professionals in the Asia-Pacific region. Bangkok: UNESCO.

[18] Walsham, G. (2000). IT/S in developing countries. In M. Zeleny (ed.) (2000) *The IEBM Handbook of Information Systems in Business* (pp. 105-109) London: Thomson-Learning.

Part 3:

The shaping of the institutions of the information society

15 YEARS OF WAYS OF INTERNET GOVERNANCE:
TOWARDS A NEW AGENDA FOR ACTION

Jacques Berleur
Facultés Universitaires Notre-Dame de la Paix, Belgium

Abstract: The "National Information Infrastructure: Agenda for Action" of the US Department of Commerce (National Telecommunications and Information Administration, NTIA) goes back to fifteen years (1993); the "3rd Internet Governance Forum" (IGF) will be held in Hyderabad (India) on December 3-6, 2008. Between those two dates, several events, documents, programmes, etc., may be regarded as signposts of Internet policy and governance: the European "Bangemann Report", followed quickly by similar proposals by different countries, the G7's "Global Information Infrastructure: Agenda for Cooperation", the two phases of the World Summit on the Information Society (Geneva, December 10-12, 2003 and Tunis November 16-18, 2005), and its subsequent Internet Governance Forums (Athens 2006, Rio de Janeiro 2007, and Hyderabad at the end of 2008), as well as the 2000 eEurope programme updated in eEurope 2002, and eEurope 2005 and the i2010 Initiative, "i2010 – A European Information Society for growth and employment." Although those documents are not always *per se* "policy documents" – they are called from time to time objectives, visions, framework, policy guidelines, programmes, etc. The goal of this paper is to derive some of the main social and political issues on Internet Governance that emerge from those programmes and documents. Our perspective and methodology are both historico-critical and thematic.

Keywords: Governance, World Summit on the Information Society (WSIS), Internet Governance Forum (IGF), NII, Bangemann, eEurope, i2010, deliberative and participative democracy

1. Governance

In its White paper on Governance, the European Commission states: "Governance addresses the question of how the European Union (EU) uses the powers given by its citizens. (...) The goal is to open up policy-making to make it more inclusive and accountable. (...) 'Governance' means rules, processes and behaviour that affect the way in which powers are exercised at European level,

---

Please use the following format when citing this chapter:

Berleur, J., 2008, in IFIP International Federation for Information Processing, Volume 282; *Social Dimensions of Information and Communication Technology Policy*; Chrisanthi Avgerou, Matthew L. Smith, Peter van den Besselaar; (Boston: Springer), pp. 255–274.

particularly as regards openness, participation, accountability, effectiveness and coherence." [53]

The Working Group on Internet Governance defines it: "Internet governance is the development and application by Governments, the private sector and civil society, in their respective roles, of shared principles, norms, rules, decision-making procedures, and programmes that shape the evolution and use of the Internet." [55] It is, as said today, a *multistakeholder* approach.

Finally, CPSR, makes explicit that "Internet governance encompasses a wide range of issues and organizations relating to the governing, financing and control of the Internet and its protocols", i.e., political, economic, social, and technical issues [11].

2.   The beginnings of Internet policies

2.1   The US NII Agenda for Action

The *National Information Infrastructure: Agenda for Action* (NII) is surely an event that "set fire to powders". The NII was conceived as "a seamless web of communications networks, computers, databases, and consumer electronics that will put vast amounts of information at users' fingertips" [42]. It was a priority *vision* of the US Administration, guided by nine principles and objectives. As stated in the section "Need for *Government Action* to Complement Private Sector Leadership" (emphasis added), the nine principles are: promote private sector investment; extend "universal service"; ensure that information resources are available to all at affordable prices; promote technological innovation and new applications, promote seamless, interactive, and user-driven operation; ensure information security and network reliability; improve management of the radio frequency spectrum; protect intellectual property rights; coordinate with other levels of governmental and with other bodies; and provide access to government information and improve government procurement. Each of these principles and goals were made explicit in terms of specific actions.

The NII Agenda for Action ended with the enumeration of benefits and applications that would assure its success: increased economic growth and productivity; job creation; technological leadership; regional, state, and local economic development; and electronic commerce. It was also said that NII could help solve America's health care crisis. Other domains of applications were highlighted: civic networking; technology in the public interest; research; life long learning; and creating a Government that works better and costs less.

The NII Agenda for Action was met with high hopes and expectations, but also raised warnings. Concerns were expressed regarding the reality of universal service, of a public space, the domination of a small number of big companies, the control by carriers, privacy, the restriction of global communication, the lack of consideration for socio-economic disadvantaged people, the haves and have-nots, and the promotion of only profitable applications [10, 15]. In brief, those warnings were about the NII lack of universality, i.e., the danger of an increasing digital divide. To avoid these dangers, it was considered essential to adopt policy and design guidelines that would serve the public interest.

To quote the conclusion of the NII Agenda for Action: "the principles and goals outlined in this document provided a blueprint for *government action* on the NII. Applying them will ensure that government provides constructive assistance to US industry, labour, academia and private citizens as they develop, deploy and use the infrastructure. (...) The NII will enable US firms to compete and win in the global economy..." It clearly stresses that it is a voluntary policy and in priority an economic policy.

2.2   The G7 GII

Let us mention briefly the US and European Commission initiative at the G7 level with the *Global Information Infrastructure: Agenda for Cooperation* (GII) [18]. The G7 Ministerial Conference on the Information Society (IS) launched the initiative at the occasion of a Round Table of Business Leaders on February 25-27, 2005, in Brussels. Eight core principles of the GII were listed as promoting fair competition, encouraging private investment, defining an adaptable regulatory framework, providing open access to networks, ensuring universal provision of and access to services, promoting equality of opportunity to the citizen, promoting diversity of content, including cultural and linguistic diversity, and recognizing the necessity of worldwide cooperation with particular attention to less developed countries. The differences with the NII are so narrow that it does not require more development here. The G7 initiated eleven specific projects, in order not to duplicate other projects: Global Inventory, Global Interoperability for Broadband Networks, Cross-Cultural Education and Training, Electronic Libraries, Electronic Museums and Galleries, Environment and Natural Resources Management, Global Emergency Management, Global Healthcare Applications, Government Online, Global Marketplace for SMEs, and Maritime Information Systems.

2.3   The European policies

Europe and the Global Information Society, Recommendations to the European Council, the so-called Bangemann Report, was surely a European response to the NII. It was published in preparation of the 1994 Corfu European Council, and at the occasion of a US-Europe industrial CEO meeting in Brussels, early 1995 [3].

The first European reflections however are not restricted to that core Report. Other reports were also very influential:

- Europe's Way to the Information Society. An Action Plan [1], and its Update [2],
- Building the European Information Society for Us All, First reflections of the High Level Group of Experts [21],

- The first annual report of the Information Society Forum, Networks for People and their Communities, Making the Most of the Information Society in the European Union [41].

The History 1993-2000 of the European Information Society is now archived and we do not reproduce it here [20].

No doubt that all this European brainstorming on the global information society was focusing on one of the main policies of that time: European economic competitiveness. The European Commission White Paper, *Growth, competitiveness, and employment* was published in 1993 [52]. The Bangemann Report was enlightening it. Chapter 1 envisaged "new ways of living" and its conclusion was about "new markets". Chapter 2 was clearly entitled "A market-driven revolution" and argued for the ending of, among others, the state-monopoly of the telecommunication operators. The worry is not about the "revolution" but about the driver! The slogan of the 1995 US-Europe industrial CEO meeting, "Let's put the private sector in the driver's seat" was winning out. But overall, the report appears as an attempt to create a policy to catch up with the US.

The Bangemann Report intended to promote the creation of a virtuous circle of supply and demand, and therefore launched a significant number of market testing applications across Europe to create critical mass. Priority applications were divided into two main blocks: the personal home market (interactive and transaction applications related to teleshopping, telebanking, entertainment, leisure) and business and social applications.

Priority applications had also to contribute to a number of macro-economic objectives: strengthening industrial competitiveness and promoting the creation of new jobs, promoting new forms of work organisation, improving quality of life and quality of the environment, responding to social needs, and raising the efficiency and cost-effectiveness of public services.

To blaze the trail, ten applications were proposed to launch the Information Society: teleworking, distance learning, universities and research centres, telematic services for SMEs, road traffic management, air traffic control, healthcare networks, electronic tendering, trans-European public administration network, and city information highways.

Were these applications coherent with the discourse or just following the "air of the time"? They were not far from the promise of the NII Agenda for Action.

We have also shown elsewhere that the real indicators of the Bangemann Report were most of them "economic and industrial" as seen in Table 1. Users, uses, and social and European values were not the top priorities [5].

Indicators	Ranking
Economic Values	21.7
Information and Communication Technologies	17.3
Information/Knowledge Society	14.2
Public Sphere	10.8
Actors	10.7
Uses	9.5
Methodology	7.1
User's representation	6.0
Social Values	5.3
European Values	2.5

Table 3: Indicators in the Bangemann Report

The Bangemann Report was accompanied by an "Action Plan" [1], and later by a "Rolling Action Plan" [2], whose 4 sections show the main preoccupations of the European Commission in agreement with the GII principles: regulatory and legal framework (towards a competitive environment; standardisation, interconnection and interoperability; tariffs, worldwide dimension; intellectual property rights; privacy; electronic protection, legal protection and security; media ownership; competition; audiovisual); networks, basic services, applications and content; social, societal and cultural aspects; and promotion activities. More than 40% of the actions were related to the regulatory framework whereas the social and cultural aspects represented the share of the poor!

As for the NII, the Bangemann Report raised many controversies, such as those already stressed by [15] for the NII, and others such as:

- The information society is presented as a means to reduce European unemployment, but the Bangemann report privileges an "infrastructure" and a pure "market driven approach", whereas what is to be solved first is a "social" problem.
- The Bangemann report presents the information highways as a tool for a better European cohesion, supporting the hypothesis that information diffusion is a medium of better participation by European regions. But, Europe is characterized by an enormous economic and social disparity between regions. The liberal approach of the Bangemann report could lead to a reinforcement of the dominant position of the ten leaders of the "Archipelago Europe" (the "ten best" regions).
- The Bangemann report is supposed to give a positive and democratic response to a wide range of social problems: education and training, marginalisation of unemployed youth, isolation and security of elderly and disabled population, better involvement in the public and cultural life. But, is it sure that open and equitable access for all citizens to the new services and applications will be provided? Would the "liberal" approach be

attracted to the non-profit sectors? Is the guarantee of "universal" access to the new services and applications sufficient?

2.4   First conclusions

15 years ago, the dreams of development through technology were in the minds, and not very different in US and in Europe! But, it cannot be denied that there were Internet policies. Moreover, they were policies from the highest level of policy makers. I am convinced that these policies were fundamentally economic policy, with a discursive accent on users regarded as consumers: "the best schools, teachers, and courses available to all students (...); the vast resources of art, literature, and science available everywhere; services that improve America's health care system and respond to other important social needs; (...) useful and fulfilling employment by 'telecommuting' to your office; small manufacturers get orders from all over the world electronically (...); see the latest movies, play the hottest video games, or bank and shop from the comfort of your home (...); obtain government information directly (...); government agencies, businesses and other entities all could exchange information electronically..." [42]. Many other Reports coming from Canada, Sweden, Denmark or organisations such as the OECD show how the Internet Governance was active.

It is important to note that the term governance was still in its infancy and covered mainly the way Governments used the powers given by their citizens.

Building the European Information Society for Us All [21], the report by the group of experts set up by Padraig Flynn, the Commissioner for Employment and Social Affairs, expresses rather well the mitigated acceptance of that kind of governance "Social policy merits equal if not more weight than economic policy in formulating our approach to the Information Society. We believe that the Commission has paid insufficient attention to these issues (...) So far, the Information Society policy debate has been dominated by technological issues and, more recently, the appropriate regulatory economic environment, neglecting by and large some of the broader issues implicit in the 'society' notion".

3.   15 Years later

Internet Governance has become an issue of the utmost importance in the World Summit on the Information Society [55, 56]. The question has surely been explored and scrutinized before, but we shall restrict our overview to its *status quaestionis* in the WSIS, and to the European policies during the last years.

This choice does not mean that there was no more policy at the federal level in the US. The Clinton–Gore Administration was very active after launching the NII, and the NII was well supported by the President's Information Technology Advisory Committee.[1] PITAC published different inspiring reports on specific IT

---

[1] See: http://www.nitrd.gov/pitac/

issues which are still worth reading: digital libraries, health care, learning, high-end computing, digital divide, cyber-security, etc. "Federal Policy Documents" in the form of laws, presidential decision directives and memorandums, and Office of Management and Budget (OMB) guidance have been enacted and partially cancelled [50]. President W. Bush transferred PITAC's role and responsibilities to the President's Council of Advisors on Science and Technology by 2005.[2] The PITAC's references are now archived.

On the European scene, the Commission remained very active trough its *eEurope* Plan of Action.

3.1   The World Summit on the Information Society (WSIS)

The WSIS has a very interesting history. It must be mentioned that the nature of the worldwide discourse has deeply changed. Many of the objections or warnings have vanished. The cost of infrastructure, for instance, is not mentioned anymore as an unbridgeable obstacle except in specific cases for rural areas of developing countries, although there are claims of *Taking ICT to every Indian village* [17]. The Digital Divide problematic has been deepened. The public service is more and more accepted as necessary. Unemployment is less emphasized. The elderly and disabled population have received specific applications and services. It is as if we had forgotten than 85% of the human beings are still excluded from the electronic communication networks. Whatever a critical view may object, the Internet is now considered as one of the biggest asset of our technologies and societies.

The WSIS has been really an exciting experience in terms of preparation and participation: 5 regional conferences (Africa, Asia-Pacific, Latin America and the Caribbean, Europe, and Western Asia) before the Geneva Summit, PrepCom (Preparatory Committees) PrepCom1, PrepCom2, and PrepCom3 before each of the Summit's phases, PrepCom3-II resuming just three days before the start of the Tunis Summit, etc.

Two documents are issued from the Geneva phase of the WSIS: the *Declaration of Principles, Building the Information Society: a global challenge in the new Millennium*, and a *Plan of Action* [53]. The first one explains the common vision, the key principles of an Information Society for All, and of an Information Society based on shared knowledge whilst the second states a Plan of Action to be achieved in 2015, in accordance with UN Millennium Development Goals [36]! This Plan of Action is setting up 11 action lines concerning the role of governments and all stakeholders in the promotion of ICTs for development: information and communication infrastructure, an essential foundation for the Information Society; access to information and knowledge; capacity building; building confidence and security in the use of ICTs; enabling environment; ICT applications that benefit all aspects of life: e-Government, e-Business, e-Learning,

---

[2] See: http://www.ostp.gov/cs/issues/information_technology.

e-Health, e-Employment, e-Environment, e-Agriculture, and e-Science; cultural diversity and identity, linguistic diversity and local content; media; ethical dimensions of the Information Society; and international and regional cooperation.

Those action lines will also be taken up in the Tunis Agenda, and specific UN Agencies will be in charge of implementing them (Table 2). Finally, the Plan of Action determines also a Digital Solidarity Agenda.

The Geneva Plan of Action was inspiring but failed on two of the crucial issues: Internet Governance, and the financial issues. Both questions were not solved and were then entrusted to the General Secretary. Let us quote the Geneva *Plan of Action*: "We ask the Secretary General of the United Nations to set up a working group on Internet governance, in an open and inclusive process that ensures a mechanism for the full and active participation of governments, the private sector and civil society from both developing and developed countries, involving relevant intergovernmental and international organisations and forums, to investigate and make proposals for action, as appropriate, on the governance of Internet by 2005.

The group should, *inter alia*: "develop a working definition of Internet governance; identify the public policy issues that are relevant to Internet governance; develop a common understanding of the respective roles and responsibilities of governments, existing intergovernmental and international organisations and other forums as well as the private sector and civil society from both developing and developed countries; prepare a report on the results of this activity to be presented for consideration and appropriate action for the second phase of WSIS in Tunis in 2005" [55, §13, b].

Regarding the financial mechanisms: "While all existing financial mechanisms should be fully exploited, a thorough review of their adequacy in meeting the challenges of ICT for development should be completed by the end of December 2004. This review shall be conducted by a Task Force under the auspices of the Secretary-General of the United Nations and submitted for consideration to the second phase of this summit. Based on the conclusion of the review, improvements and innovations of financing mechanisms will be considered including the effectiveness, the feasibility and the creation of a voluntary Digital Solidarity Fund, as mentioned in the Declaration of Principles." [55, §27, D2, f]

The *Tunis Agenda* did not make explicit any final recommendation, despite the efforts of the Task Force on Financial Mechanisms (TFFM) [56, §§3-28, and especially §27]. This is the most deceiving achievement.

Besides the Forum (see hereafter the section on IGF), the same *Tunis Agenda* decided a process of implementation and the UN organisations responsible for their follow-up (Table 2):

Action Line	UN organisations	
C1. The role of public governance authorities and all stakeholders in the promotion of ICTs for development	ECOSOC/UN Regional Commissions/ITU	
C2. Information and communication infrastructure	ITU	
C3. Access to information and knowledge	ITU/UNESCO	
C4. Capacity building	UNDP/UNESCO/ITU/UNCTAD	
C5. Building confidence & security in the use of ICTs	ITU	
C6. Enabling environment	ITU/UNDP/UN Regional Commissions/ UNCTAD	
C7. ICT Applications E-government E-employment E-business E-environment E-learning E-agriculture E-health E-science	UNDP/ITU WTO/UNCTAD/ITU/ UPU UNESCO/ITU/UNIDO WHO/ITU	ILO/ITU WHO/WMO/UNEP/ UN – Habitat/ITU/ ICAO FAO/ITU UNESCO/ITU/UNC TAD
C8. Cultural diversity and identity, linguistic diversity and local content	UNESCO	
C9. Media	UNESCO	
C10. Ethical dimensions of the IS	UNESCO/ECOSOC	
C11. International and regional cooperation	UN Regional Commissions/UNDP/ ITU/UNESCO/ECOSOC	

Table 4 Action Lines (Tunis Agenda – Annex)

3.2   The Working Group on Internet Governance (WGIG)

The WGIG has surely been a real battlefield, especially on our today focus, the Internet Governance. Between the two phases of WSIS, Geneva and Tunis, a Background Report reflecting the wide variety of opinions within the group as well as many comments made by stakeholders during the consultation process, 4 two-days meetings, the presentation of the "WGIG Final report" to PrepCom3 could not gain an agreement [54]. The Minutes of the PrepCom3 are laconic: "The Sub-Committee completed four readings of Chapter 3 (…); it proved possible to agree 23 paragraphs, and to consider a further 14 paragraphs that have some remaining square brackets or that remain open. However, due to lack of time, it did not prove possible to complete the work on sections 3a and 5 of the report dealing with follow-up and future arrangements" (Report of the Work of Sub-Committee A-WSIS-II/PC-3/DOC/11-rev.1).

The issues at stake were, to be brief, at least two-fold: the issue relating the creation of a space or forum for dialogue, and the issue relating the infrastructure and management of critical Internet resources. Objections came mainly from the US delegation, led by H.E. Mr David Gross (International communications and information policy, Department of State). PrepCom3 could not conclude, and was obliged to resume on 13-15 November, in Tunis, 3 days before the Summit, on the basis of documents among which an interesting input document, "Food for Thought", from the Chairman Designate of PrepCom-3 (WSIS-II/PC-3/DT/15) [46]. The idea of the Forum prevailed, but was adopted only as provisional.

Before coming to the Forum issue, and the creation of the Internet Governance Forum (IGF), we cannot avoid mentioning some words about the infrastructure and management of critical Internet resources. The WGIG Report stressed the three principles, which were already mentioned in the Geneva Declaration of Principles [55, §§48-49)]:

- No single Government should have a pre-eminent role in relation to international Internet governance.
- The organisational form for the governance function will be multilateral, transparent and democratic, with the full involvement of Governments, the private sector, civil society, and international organisations.
- The organisational form for the governance function will involve all stakeholders and relevant intergovernmental and international organisations within their respective roles.

Everybody was thinking of the US pre-eminent role and of the Internet Corporation for Assigned Names and Numbers (ICANN): this was explicitly said in the 4 models proposed by the WGIG. We shall come back on the question of ICANN, but the Resumed PrepCom3 did not adopt any change in the situation until the last minute.

The WSIS Plenary adopted the new texts on the basis of the Resumed PrepCom-3 Report (WSIS-II/PC-3/DOC/14). They were incorporated as chapter three in the Tunis Agenda for the Information Society [56, §§29-82].

Most of the objections to WSIS-inspired changes in Internet governance have been grounded in fears about top-heavy governmental meddling in Internet identifier policies, or concerns about the slow and restrictive nature of governmental processes [25].

In our opinion, although the focus has rarely been on the question, the clarification of the role of the civil society and its organisation should be developed. As spelled out in the Tunis Agenda, "Civil society has also played an important role on Internet matters, especially at community level, and should continue to play such a role" [56, §35]. This is still quite unclear. In the spirit of Habermas [19], L. Weerts wrote, "the civil society covers all the active networks in the political public space which do not depend upon either the administrative and governmental system, or the business system" [51]. The Civil Society Centre has more extensively defined it, in its Report on Activities 2005-6: "Civil society refers to the arena of uncœrced collective action around shared interests, purposes and values. In theory, its institutional forms are distinct from those of the state, family and market, though in practice, the boundaries between state, civil society, family and market are often complex, blurred and negotiated. Civil society commonly embraces a diversity of spaces, actors and institutional forms, varying in their degree of formality, autonomy and power. Civil societies are often populated by organizations such as registered charities, development non-governmental organizations, community groups, women's organizations, faith-based organizations, professional associations, trade unions, self-help groups, social movements, business associations, coalitions and advocacy groups." [8]

Taking into account those definitions, the role of the civil society, and above all its organisation, should be scrutinized in depth more carefully.

3.3   The Internet Governance Forum (IGF)

"The Internet (…) governance should constitute a core issue of the Information Society agenda." [56, §29]

"We ask the UN Secretary-General, in an open and inclusive process, to convene, by the second quarter of 2006, a meeting of the new forum for multistakeholder policy dialogue – called the *Internet Governance Forum* (IGF). The mandate of the Forum includes the discussion of public policies, advise all stakeholders in proposing ways and means to accelerate the availability and affordability of the Internet in the developing world, identify emerging issues, (…) and, where appropriate, make recommendations, publish its proceedings…" [56]. This mandate is fully described in [56, §72]. Regarding the review of progress made in the implementation of and follow-up of the IGF, as well as of the WSIS, a proposal is submitted to the next Commission on Science and Technology for Development (CSTD) Meeting to be finally submitted to the Economic and Social Council of the United Nations ECOSOC).[3] It was not obvious, due to the UN system, that CSTD participants would include representatives of governments, civil society, the private sector, and international organisations.

The first two meetings of the IGF were held in Athens (30 October to 2 November 2006), and Rio de Janeiro (12-15 November 2007). The next meetings will take place in Hyderabad (December 2008) and Egypt (2009).

The main issues under discussion were nearly the same in Athens and Rio: openness, setting the scene, security, diversity, access, the way forward, and emerging issues. Rio IGF added one theme: critical Internet resources. A good overview of those themes may be found in [28]. "Internet for All" was chosen as the overall theme for the Hyderabad meeting, and the suggested agenda is as follows: reaching the next billion (access, multilingualism); promoting cyber-

---

[3] See:
htttp://www.unctad.org/Templates/meeting.asp?intItemID=1942&lang=1&m=15018&info=highlights

security and trust (the battle against cyber-crime, fostering security, privacy, and openness); managing critical Internet resources (transition from IPv4 to IPv6, arrangements for Internet governance – global and national/regional); and emerging issues: the Internet of tomorrow.

The governance of the Internet encompasses, as stressed in the CPSR definition [11], both technical and public policy issues. But the Tunis Agenda [56, §35] trying to distribute to the different multistakeholders their different tasks, and *inter alia* the policy authority for Internet-related public policy issues to the sovereign right of States, and "especially the community level" to the civil society, looks like a division of labour between the stakeholders.

The Internet Governance Project (IGP) has established the issue areas and the issues that are under the responsibility of specific organisations and must be approached in a multistakeholder manner (Table 3).

Issues areas	Issue
Human rights	Privacy
	Content Regulation and Freedom of Expression
Intellectual Property Rights	Copyright
	Trademark
	Other IPR Issues
International Economic Relations	Trade and eCommerce
	Consumer Protection
	Competition Policy
	Taxation
Enforcement of Order	Network and Information Society Security
	Crime
	Authentication and Identity
	Cyberterrorism
	Spam
Operational Policies for the Internet	Global Resource Management
	Interconnection

Table 3. Issue areas and issues in the Internet Governance Process

Among the main critical issues related to the technical governance, it is clear that many authors focus on the fact that technical regulators encroach beyond their limits. The IGP has shown that, among the issues that can be linked to Internet Governance, ICANN covers all the issues in terms of policy development, rules, and recommendations, whilst the other organisations including UN ones are most often strictly limited to their domain of competence [34]. ICANN is covering, in one way or another, all the issues areas of Table 3, whereas most of the other organisations, including UN ones, are covering 2 and at a maximum 3 of them. Is it normal that a private not-profit organisation under the Californian law, whose first task should be technical, takes decision in domains that are outside its field of competence, or out of "the rule of law" [27]?

Recently (May 2008), "A subcommittee of the US Congress on Telecommunications and the Internet has expressed its opposition to any move by the Commerce Department to alter its unilateral oversight of ICANN". (...) "Legally and operationally, the root server operators have no contractual obligations to ICANN or, for that matter, to anyone else; they are the last remnants of the informal yet effective stewardship model of the early Internet pioneers, in which a self-selected group of trusted technical experts assumed operational and policy responsibility for key internet coordination functions" [38]. "ICANN has quasi-governmental powers over Internet identifiers, yet lacks both of these mechanisms of *external accountability* (voting for Board members, and independent judicial review)" [40]. Any change in ICANN should also have to face the strong US position in the so-called "331 words note", *US Principles on the Internet's Domain Name and Addressing System* [43]. NTIA in its mid-term review of the "Joint Project Agreement" stated: "ICANN has made significant progress in several key areas, but most participants agree that important work remains to increase institutional confidence through implementing effective processes that will enable: long term stability; accountability; responsiveness; continued private sector leadership, stakeholder participation; increased contract compliance; and enhanced competition" [44].

Finally, it has never been said that IGF was promised a perennial existence; the WSIS 2005 explicitly notes: "We ask the UN Secretary-General to examine the desirability of the continuation of the Forum, in formal consultation with Forum participants, within five years of its creation, and to make recommendations to the UN Membership in this regard" [56, §76].

4.   From *e*Europe to i2010 Initiative

Let us come to the last step of our panorama of policies by looking again at the European scene.

In the late '90s, the former "Information Society Project/Promotion Office" (ISPO) has become a Directorate General, the DG of "Information Society". That reveals the driving force that European Commission was intending to assign to ICT. It invented a new Europe, the "*e*Europe" (that *Le Monde Diplomatique* labelled "Europe, Inc."), and its application all in "e" (eBusiness, eGovernment, eWork, eHealth, eLearning, etc.). We shall not repeat here all the history of "*e*Europe," "*e*Europe 2002," "*e*Europe 2005": we developed it in our *ICT policies of the European Union: From an Information Society to eEurope* [5]. But we must add the latest, the "i2010 Initiative": *i2010 – A European Information Society for growth and employment* [22].

The Lisbon strategy of the Commission is explicit: the strategic goal for 2010 set for Europe is "to become the most competitive and dynamic knowledge-based economy in the world, capable of sustainable economic growth with more and better jobs and greater social cohesion." [30] The "knowledge-based economy" became a "knowledge-based Europe" in the final version [31]!

To reach that goal, the *eEurope* 2005 Action Plan has been replaced by the *i2010 initiative*, "a comprehensive strategy for modernising and deploying all EU policy instruments to encourage the development of the digital economy: regulatory instruments, research and partnerships with industry" (IP/05/643, 1 June 2005) [22]. It is an umbrella policy "to foster growth and jobs in the Information Society and media industries."

The supporting policies can be presented in 3 main policy priorities: increasing EU investment in ICT research to promote innovation and technical leadership, mainly within the 7th Framework Programme [23]; building a regulatory environment for an open competitive single market for the digital economy; ensure sustainability by promoting an inclusive European Information Society. Astonishing surprise: not one word in this three-fold policy about the World Summit! The European Parliament has a more active position [45].

The differentiated weight of those policies could be measured by their respective budget. This operation is not an easy one. The easiest part to detect is the ICT 7th FP: the European Parliament and the Council (18 December 2006) have earmarked a total of 9050 million for funding ICT over the duration of the 7th FP (2007-2013), making it the largest research theme in the programme (nearly 18%), the total budget of the 7th FP Budget being 50521 million [7]. The objective of the ICT 7th FP is spelled out without ambiguity: improving the competitiveness of European industry and enabling Europe to master and shape future developments in ICT so that the demands of its society and economy are met. Specifying the policy and the social context, "the Commission underlines that our innovation performance is crucially dependent on strengthening investment in and the use of new technologies, particularly ICTs, by both the private and public sectors. ICTs provide *the backbone for the knowledge economy*. They account for around half of the productivity growth in modern economies." [23, *emphasis ours*]

Second policy priority: building a regulatory environment. To take account of the changed sectoral landscape, since the last regulatory package was in 2002, the Commission launched a review of the current regulatory rules in November 2007. Viviane Reding, the EU's Telecoms Commissioner sets the tune: "The European regulatory model is designed to increase competition in the telecoms market and this certainly is starting to pay off." (May 2008) The 2002 framework was made up of 6 Directives: common regulatory framework, access and interconnection, authorisation, universal service, privacy, and markets competition [47]. The logic of those policies was rather clear: protection of the investments (through IPR and Neighbouring Rights, parallel to the US 1998 Digital Millennium Copyright Act), protection of the business transactions (identification, authentication, confidentiality, eCommerce, etc.), and fight against cyber-criminality. The revised regulatory framework should include: more competition by ensuring that competing operators have access to infrastructure without discrimination; radio spectrum management more flexible and market oriented; reducing the costs of roaming to mobile phone users; facilitate transfer of customers from one service provider to another; and develop suing criminal misuse of financial information [48].

The third policy priority intends to ensure sustainability by promoting an inclusive European Information Society. According to unofficial sources, the budget should not be more than   1600 million for the same period 2007-2013, excluding the 7th FP [22].

Examining the proposal as well as the annual reviews, it appears that the argumentative discourse has not changed: it refers to the Lisbon strategy in terms of competitiveness, economic growth, and uses' development. Unfortunately, i2010 lacks an integrated vision and is bursting in tight budgets. A fragmented approach still prevails. A pessimistic prospective is that the end of i2010 will probably result in the end of a real European ICT policy, or at least the end of the current "cycle". However, the Commission has already announced that between 2008 and 2010 it will develop a long-term agenda, examining *inter alia* the challenge of future networks, the policy for users in the digital environment, and the contribution of ICT to a "true Single Market" and to the Lisbon strategy. Let us wait and see, and hope that the "pro-users policy" will gain more consideration than in the past!

5.   Towards a new agenda for action

None of the early documents, the NII [42], the Bangemann Report [3], and the GII [18] use the word "governance". Even the famous Lisbon strategy ignores it [30, 31]. "Government" and "govern" are the words to speak of the traditional ways in which the authority is exercised. The word eGovernment appears 8 times in the 2003-revised document of the Lisbon strategy [31]. But in the i2010 document, "governance" is used 10 times,   "eGovernment" 3 times, and "Government" 0 times, in a document that is 25% shorter [22]. Does this mean anything? One could be tempted to believe that the first years of our 15 years period start with a strong policy investment on the side of the governments. That it is true, but at the same time governments call on the private sector for investing in infrastructure that they cannot afford. The price to be paid was then the content of their discourse, which became, as it appeared in our analysis, more and more liberal in the European sense, i.e., market oriented – which is not a sin – mentioning the social needs only when they are at risk to be profitable! Let us repeat the warning of the European Group of Experts: "the Information Society policy has been (…) neglecting by and large some of the broader issues implicit in the 'society' notion." [21] Since the 1993 Delors White Paper on *Growth, competitiveness, and employment*, liberalisation has become the major keyword [52]. Social policies of the Information Society will no longer be at the forefront, if they have ever been. "People first", or "people centred" information society have been misleading metaphors. There was a policy, no doubt, but out of the hands of those who are commonly called "policy-makers".

The Internet governance concept – as defined by the WGIG –, the WSIS, and its follow-up through the IGFs are signs of a new approach of policies, and even of democracy, in the line of today search for a participative and even deliberative governance. The emphasis, since the beginning of the WSIS PrepComs has been on the "multistakeholder" approach. This word has yet to be realised to its full meaning, but new issues and challenges of a *new agenda of action* are emerging from the hesitating paces of different events in an ICT governance environment that shows more and more that it lacks a strategy. Let us mention some of them [13], being conscious that the question of Internet governance, in today's process of globalisation, is part of a more philosophical and political reflection on the contemporary forms of "living together" and societal organisation [32, 29].

- How to reach the 5 billion people who are not "connected"? The question of access is crucial – the core issue of Internet Governance – but not only in terms of access to infrastructure, but at the same time, access to knowledge, which means the capacity of structuring information, i.e., education, etc. What does mean a socio-economically inclusive Information Society with access "on an equal footing"? What do mean policies including enabling environment?
- The lack of public strategy is becoming more and more obvious. This kind of laisser-faire policy, covered over by a sometimes empty discourse, is surely not favourable for developing that the "market" is not willing to pay!
- A social and cultural divide is doubling the digital divide in a more and more digital-driven society. The current legislations on Internet Property Right (IPR) that is very often considered as obvious is by and large protecting the vested interests and surely not inspired by a multistakeholder approach.
- The diversity of issues and local situations is such that the Internet Governance must be thought through "national and/or regional IGFs". This should ensure a wider participation, and open the path to a deliberative democracy. The idea is pending. The process of "Dynamic Coalitions", multistakeholder working groups, must be encouraged at all levels.4 There is also a need of increasing the regional cooperation, mainly between the small countries that do not have the capacity of their own autonomy.
- The diversity has multiple dimensions: linguistic, cultural, and social. Real attention is needed to overcome all the obstacles such as IPR and linguistic predominance. Developing multilingualism on the Internet is a must and is already on the agenda of UNESCO.
- A focus on "Internet rights" is claimed to cover issues such as increasing surveillance, traceability, privacy, intimacy, and right to diversity. A "bill of rights" would be a first step [6]. The human rights are too often

---

4 See: http://www.intgovforum.org/Dynamic%20Coalitions.php

constrained to discussions about specific countries (China, Vietnam, Iran, etc.), but should also include big businesses (CISCO, Yahoo!, Google, etc.).

- The ethical dimension of the Internet and of its governance, even if already advocated in documents, is too often hidden behind legal consideration. It has to be scrutinized as such, in its multi-polarity.
- The Digital Solidarity Fund and its "1% digital solidarity principle" must have more consideration, in the spirit of the Millennium [36], as well as the financial mechanisms that are insufficiently innovative in the Tunis Plan of Action [14].
- Many controversies about the role of ICANN in Internet Governance are raised: its unilateral control must be replaced by a multistakeholder approach. "Foreign governments want control of the Internet transferred from an American NGO to an international institution. Washington has responded "with a Monroe Doctrine – as re-interpreted in the Roosevelt corollary5 – for our times, setting the stage for further controversy, a Monroe doctrine conceived as a license for the US to practice its own form of colonialism"? [12] The Rio IGF assembly has recommended the gradual transfer of ICANN to the authority of the international community.
- "Multistakeholder" is today a password in many policy circle, mainly in international circles. The word is accepted. But isn't it sometimes an empty shell? As we already said for the civil society, the concept should be clarified, and explored in depth. Moreover, a multistakehloder organisation and governance especially in the perspective of "global governance" has still to be invented. We are perhaps in a period of testing new ways of governance and democracy, and surely of living and deciding together. Our new challenge is, as said earlier, to invent a participative and deliberative democracy at a worldwide level.

A final remark: Where is IFIP in this debate? Unfortunately, we should say that its visibility is not substantial, or at least that its name does not appear pre-eminently!

References

[1] Action Plan 1994, Commission of the European Community, Europe's way to the information society. An action plan, Communication from the Commission to the Council and the European Parliament, and the Economic and Social Committee and the Committee of Regions, Brussels, COM(94) 347 final, July 19, 1994.
[2] Action Plan 1996, Europe's way to the information society. Updated version of the Action Plan, Status of April 1st, 1996. ISPO Office, (COM(96) 0607 - C4-0648/96).

---

[5] "Chronic wrongdoing, or an impotence which results in a general loosening of the ties of civilized society, may in America, as elsewhere, ultimately require intervention by some civilized nation, and in the Western Hemisphere the adherence of the United States to the Monroe Doctrine may force the United States, however reluctantly, in flagrant cases of such wrongdoing or impotence, to the exercise of an international police power"? [49]

[3]   Bangemann M., Europe and the global information society, recommendations to the European Council, The Bangemann Report, Brussels, May, 1994 http://europa.eu.int/ISPO/infosoc/backg/bangeman.html.[6]

[4]   Berleur, J., Avgerou, C (Eds.) (2005), *Perspectives and policies on ICT in society*, An IFIP TC9 (Computers and Society) Handbook, Springer Science and Business Media, Series: IFIP International Federation for Information Processing, Vol. 179, viii + 290

[5]   Berleur, J., Galand, J.-M. (2005), ICT policies of the European Union: From an information society to *e*Europe. Trends and visions, in Berleur J., Avgerou C., (Eds.), *Perspectives and policies on ICT in society* (pp. 37-66)

[6]   Bill of rights (2008), The Internet Bill of Rights, A Dynamic Coalition of the Internet Governance Forum, http://www.internet-bill-of-rights.org/en/ and http://www.intgovforum.org/dynamic_coalitions.php?listy=4

[7]   Budget breakdown of the Seventh Framework Programme (7th FP) of the European Community (EC) (2007-2013) and Euratom (2007-2011), http://cordis.europa.eu/fp7/budget_en.html

[8]   Centre for Civil Society (2007), London School of Economics, Report on Activities, July 2005 – August 2006, http://www.lse.ac.uk/collections/CCS/publications/

[9]   Clements B., Comyn G., Rouhana K., & Burgelman J.-Cl., (2004), Building the Information Society in Europe: The contribution of socio-economic research, *IPTS Report* n°85, http://www.jrc.es/home/report/english/articles/vol85/EDI1E856.htm

[10]   *CPSR Newsletter* (1994), Vol. 11, No. 4 & Vol. 12, No. 1, Winter 1994

[11]   CPSR (2008), Internet Governance, http://cpsr.org/issues/ig/index.html.

[12]   Cukier, K.N. (2005), Who will control the Internet? *Foreign Affairs*, November/December, http://www.foreignaffairs.org/2005/6.html.

[13]   Desai, N (2007), Chairman's Summary, IGF, Rio de Janeiro, November 2007, http://www.intgovforum.org/

[14]   DSF-FSN (2003), Global digital solidarity fund, Reducing the Digital Divide, Geneva, http://www.dsf-fsn.org.

[15]   Dutton, W., J. Blumler, N. Garnham, R. Mansell, J. Cornford, and M. Peltu, The information superhighway: Britain's response, A Forum Discussion, Paper Nr. 29, Programme on ICT, Economic and Social Research Council, Brunel University, UK, December 1994.

[16]   G7 Pilot Projects (1995), http://www.ispo.cec.be/g7/projidx.html

[17]   Garai, A., Shadrach, B. (2006), *Taking ICT to every Indian village: Opportunities and challenges.* New Delhi, India: One World South Asia.

[18]   Global Information Infrastructure-GII (1995), Ronald H. Brown, Secretary of Commerce, Chair Information Infrastructure Task Force, *Global Information Infrastructure: Agenda for Cooperation.* Washington, D.C: US Gov. Publ. Off., 1995. http://www.ntia.doc.gov/reports/giiagend.html.

[19]   Habermas, J. (1989), *The Structural Transformation of the Public Sphere: An Inquiry Into a Category of Bourgeois Society.* Trans. Thomas Burger. The MIT Press.

[20]   History, Towards an Information Society 1993-2000, 2001 http://web.archive.org/web/20030210221623/europa.eu.int/ISPO/basics/i_history.html.

[21]   HLGE (1996), *Building the European Information Society for us all*, First reflections of the High Level Group of Experts, Interim Report, January 1996.

[22]   i2010 (2004), i2010 – A European Information Society for growth and employment (COM (2005) 229 final), 2005 http://ec.europa.eu/information_society/eeurope/i2010/index_en.htm

---

[6] Many of the former European Commission links do not exist anymore. Most of them can be found back through Wayback Internet Archive, http://www.archive.org

[23] ICT (2007-2013), Information and Communication Technologies, European Commission, 7th Framework Programme,
http://cordis.europa.eu/fp7/ict/programme/home_en.html.

[24] Internet Governance Forum – IGF (2005) United Nations WSIS,
http://www.intgovforum.org

[25] Internet Governance Project, Political Oversight of ICANN: A Briefing for the WSIS Summit, Concept Paper by the IGP, 1 November, 2005
http://www.internetgovernance.org/pdf/political-oversight.pdf.

[26] Internet Bill of Rights, A Dynamic Coalition of the Internet Governance Forum,
http://www.internet-bill-of-rights.org/en/.

[27] Klein H., ICANN Reform: Establishing the rule of Law. A policy analysis prepared for WSIS 2005, http://www.IP3.gatech.edu

[28] Kleinwächter W. (Ed.) (2007). *The Power of Ideas: Internet Governance in a Global Multistakeholder Environment,* Germany Land of Ideas.

[29] Lenoble J. & Maesschalck M. (2006), Beyond neo-institutionalist and pragmatist approaches to governance., Working paper series : REFGOV-SGI/TNU-1,
http://refgov.cpdr.ucl.ac.be/.

[30] Lisbon European Council (2000), Presidency Conclusions, European Council 23-24 March 2000, http://www.europarl.europa.eu/summits/lis1_en.htm.

[31] Lisbon (2003), European Commission, *Towards a knowledge-based Europe. The European Union and the information society,* Office for Official Publications of the European Communities,
http://www.europa.eu.int/comm/publications/booklets/move/36/index_en.htm.

[32] Maesschalck, M. (2001), *Normes et contextes. Les fondements d'une pragmatique contextuelle,* New, York; Olms Verlag : Hildesheim-New York

[33] Markey E.J. et al., (May 2008), Committee Members Comment on Possible Changes to Internet Watchdog Agency,
http://markey.house.gov/index.php?option=content&task=view&id=3342&Itemid=125

[34] Mathiason J., Mueller M., Klein H., Holitscher M., & McKnight L. (2004), Internet Governance: the State of Play, Internet Governance Project,
http://internetgovernance.org/pdf/ig-sop-final.pdf.

[35] Mathiason J., Hofmann J., Mueller M., McKnight L., & Cogburn D. (2006), The Distributed Secretariat. Making the Internet Governance Forum Work, Internet Governance Project, http://internetgovernance.org/pdf/distrib-sec.pdf.

[36] Millennium (2000), UN Millennium Development Goals, Keep the Promise 2015,
http://www.un.org/millenniumgoals/.

[37] Monroe, J. (1823), US Department of State, Monroe Doctrine,
http://www.state.gov/r/pa/ho/time/jd/16321.htm.

[38] Mueller, M. (2008a), The US Congress and 'free speech principles on the Internet', May 11, 2008, Internet Governance Project,
http://blog.internetgovernance.org/blog/_archives/2008/5/11/3685901.html.

[39] Mueller, M. (2008b), F Root Server Makes its Peace with ICANN, 2008, Internet Governance Project, http://blog.internetgovernance.org/blog/offset=20.

[40] Mueller, M. (2008c), Comments of the IGP on Midterm Review of the Joint Project Agreement submitted to the NTIA, US DoC, February 15, 2008,
http://www.ntia.doc.gov/ntiahome/domainname/jpacomments2007/jpacomment_026.pdf.

[41] *Networks for People and their Communities* (1996). Making the Most of the Information Society in the European Union, First annual report to the European Commission of the Information Society Forum, Brussels, June 1996.

[42]   National Information Infrastructure-NII (1993). National Telecommunications and Information Administration (NTIA), *National Information Infrastructure: Agenda for Action*, Washington, DC, Department of Commerce, September 1993, http://www.ibiblio.org/nii/.

[43]   National Telecommunications and Information Administration-NTIA (2005), US Department of Commerce, *US Principles on the Internet's Domain Name and Addressing System*,
http://www.ntia.doc.gov/ntiahome/domainname/usdnsprinciples_06302005.htm.

[44]   National Telecommunications and Information Administration-NTIA (2008). Statement on the Mid-Term Review of the Joint Project Agreement (JPA) between NTIA and ICANN, Released April 2, 2008
http://www.ntia.doc.gov/ntiahome/domainname/ICANN_JPA_080402.html.

[45]   Parliament (2008) European Parliament resolution on the second IGF, held in Rio de Janeiro from 12 to 15 November 2007, B6-0041/2008,
http://www.europarl.europa.eu/sides/getDoc.do?type=MOTION&reference=B6-2008-0041&language=EN

[46]   PrepCom3 and PrepCom3-Resumed (2005), The third meeting of the Preparatory Committee (PrepCom-3) of the WSIS Tunis phase:
http://www.itu.int/wsis/preparatory2/pc3/index.html.

[47]   Regulation (2002), European Commission, Regulatory framework for telecoms in the EU today,
http://ec.europa.eu/information_society/policy/ecomm/current/index_en.htm.

[48]   Regulation (2008), European Commission, Reforming the current telecom rules,
http://ec.europa.eu/information_society/policy/ecomm/tomorrow/index_en.htm.

[49]   Roosevelt Th. (1904), Theodore Roosevelt's Corollary to the Monroe Doctrine [37], http://www.state.gov/r/pa/ho/time/ip/17660.htm.

[50]   US IT Policy (2000), Information Technology Policy Document – Official Federal government-wide policy or guidance
http://policyworks.gov/policydocs/policy_list.htm. (covers the period 1986-2000), whilst the Office of Management and Budget gives reference from 1997 to today. http://www.whitehouse.gov/omb/inforeg/infopoltech.html.

[51]   Weerts, L. (2004), Quatre modèles théoriques pour penser la société civile dans l'ordre juridique international, Séminaire Société civile et démocratisation des organisations internationales, 28-29 mai 2004, à l'Université libre de Bruxelles, http://www.ulb.ac.be/droit/cdi/fichiers/modeles_theoriques.pdf.

[52]   White Paper of the Commission (1993), Growth, competitiveness, and employment, (COM(93)0700 – *Official Journal of the European Union* C3-0509/93)

[53]   White Paper of the Commission (2001), European Governance, COM(2001) 428, July 2001, http://europa.eu/documents/comm/white_papers/index_en.htm#2001.

[54]   Working Group on Internet Governance-WGIG (2005), WGIG Final Report, Château de Bossey, June 2005, http://www.wgig.org/.

[55]   WSIS (2003), Documents issued from the World Summit on the Information Society, WSIS, phase 1: *Declaration of Principles, Building the Information Society: a Global Challenge in the New Millennium*; and *Plan of Action*, 12 December 2003; http://www.itu.int/wsis/index.html.

[56]   WSIS (2005), Documents issued from the World Summit on the Information Society, WSIS, phase 2, Tunis (2005): *Tunis Agenda for the Information Society*, 18 November 2005; and *Tunis Commitment*, 18 November 2005, http://www.itu.int/wsis.

GOVERNMENTAL POLICIES FOR ICT DIFFUSION AND LEADERSHIP LEGITIMACY IN GRASSROOTS MOVEMENTS

Magda Hercheui
London School of Economics and Political Science, UK

Abstract   This empirical investigation focuses on environmental-education virtual communities and points out how the Brazilian government, through specific legislation, has increased the legitimacy of some of their members in relation to others in decision-making processes in the studied collectives. In demanding that some anchor organisations assume the formal responsibility for funded projects that aimed to diffuse Internet communication channels among environmental educators, the Brazilian government affected how community members perceived the power distribution in online collectives. Although other forces were behind the construction of legitimacy of community leaders, members broadly recognized that the law was an important factor in the construction of a common understanding on who had power in decision making. Drawing upon institutional theory, this chapter analyses how the specific legislation influenced the way community members perceived the legitimacy of their leaders. The chapter claims that policies for spreading the use of ICTs among grassroots movements and civil society organisations have direct effects in relation to their governance structures, and thus these policies should be under broader scrutiny.

Keywords: Information society, policy, ICT, social movements, institutions

1.   Introduction

The objective of this chapter is to argue that governmental policies for the diffusion of information and communication technologies (ICTs) affect how social movements and civil society organisations perceive the legitimacy of their leaders, with consequences for their governance structure. In other words, in reinforcing the leadership legitimacy of some members in relation to others, governmental policies may favour the centralization of decision making, working against more participatory and democratic governance structures. In a broad sense, this chapter thus aims to highlight the need of reflecting on the consequences of such policies

Please use the following format when citing this chapter:

Hercheui, M., 2008, in IFIP International Federation for Information Processing, Volume 282; *Social Dimensions of Information and Communication Technology Policy*; Chrisanthi Avgerou, Matthew L. Smith, Peter van den Besselaer; (Boston: Springer), pp. 275–286.

for movements whose objectives include the creation of democratic social structures.

In order to construct this argument, this chapter draws upon an empirical investigation of a group of three Brazilian environmental-education virtual communities. These three communities are informal collectives that emerged from the voluntary interaction of individuals who are concerned with the theme of environmental education. Members of the studied communities interact mainly through Internet channels, although they also cultivate face-to-face interactions.

As informal collectives, these communities cannot assume legal responsibilities, such as directly contracting governmental funding. In the beginning of the 2000s, nonetheless, these three communities received funding from the Brazilian federal government (FNMA – Fundo Nacional do Meio Ambiente). The money was given to support specific projects, mainly to allow these collectives to buy servers and computers, to organize their websites and information services, and to promote the Internet-mediated interaction among environmental educators. In exchange for the money, the communities compromised to feed a centralized federal databank with information on environmental education.

The legislation related to this funding imposed rules which were not coherent with the official governance structure of the benefited communities. In a nutshell, the legislation demanded that formal organisations (legally responsible) assume the representation of these communities in the specific projects. In order to receive the money, each community was formally represented by an anchor organisation, which was endowed with differentiated rights and obligations in relation to other members. Although the process of choosing the anchor organisations cannot be explored in this essay, it is worthy to highlight that some leaders chose them, without consulting all members.

This differentiation between *formal representatives* and *other members* clearly opposed the way these communities established their governance structures, at least rhetorically. Recalling their inherent condition as grassroots movements, these communities defended what they call the network way of organizing: when collective decisions are necessary, such as organizing a public demonstration against the government or a corporation, the final decisions should be grounded in the consensus among all members.

Community members revealed that this alleged network model is inspired by ideals of *participatory democracy*, in which all members would have the same rights in decision-making processes [13, 22, 30]. In practice, however, the studied communities did not adopt such a network way of organizing. The empirical investigation revealed that the communities had a centralized decision-making process, even before the introduction of the specific legislation (in the beginning of the 2000s). In other words, the studied communities cultivated, in parallel, two paradoxical governance structures: one idealized model of network, horizontal decision making, and another model of centralized decision making, in which few members (called here "leaders") make decisions in name of the community, excluding "ordinary" members.

This paper takes for granted this situation of contradictory and parallel models of decision making, and examines how the specific legislation has interfered in the way members perceived the legitimacy of leaders in these communities, supporting the centralization of governance structures. Other forces and mechanisms have also influenced the legitimacy of community leaders, but for lack of space this paper focuses only on the role of the specific legislation in this process.

The concept of legitimacy in this paper draws upon institutional theory. As summarized by Suchman [31], legitimacy is the perception (or assumption) that specific actions are appropriate within a social system of norms, values, and beliefs, which implies that legitimate actions are understood as natural and meaningful. In a more systematic fashion, Scott [26] argues that legitimacy depends on conformity to formal rules, to moral bases, and to taken-for-granted frames of reference. The author adds that in modern societies authorities such as the government have the role of conferring legitimacy [26]. This chapter focuses on discussing how the governmental action and the conformity to rules reinforce the legitimacy of community leaders as community representatives, thus undermining the relevance of other members as leaders.

The next sessions develop this argument. Session 1 presents the empirical objects and methodology of this research. Session 2 summarizes the main findings of the empirical study. Session 3 discusses the findings through the lens of institutional theory, arguing that the government, through creating legislation, has influenced the way community members perceive the legitimacy of their leaders. Finally, session 4 concludes, reflecting on the need of having awareness of the impact of governmental projects to diffuse ICTs among civil society and grassroots movements.

2.   Empirical object and methodology

In the academic literature, the term virtual community (and similar ones such as online communities and virtual or online social networks) is used generically to describe collectives which emerge from voluntary computer-mediated interaction [2, 3, 23, 30]. More restrictedly, Graham [10] defends the use of the term only for those Internet-mediated collectivities that have (i) *voluntary membership* of people who have (ii) *common interests* and (iii) adhere to *a set of rules* (such as procedures for admission and exclusion). This investigation adopts this more restricted meaning of virtual community, as the studied communities have these three characteristics.

This research investigates three Brazilian environmental-education virtual communities:

Rebea (Rede Brasileira de Educação Ambiental) (Brazilian Environmental-Education Network): created in 1992 and active at a national level. The community had around 380 members (membership numbers in the three communities are related to 2006) on the general discussion list and around 600 members on Orkut – the Google's online social network (some members are in both lists). Website: http://www.rebea.org.br .

Repea (Rede Paulista de Educação Ambiental) (São Paulo Environmental-Education Network): created in 1992, but active more regularly since 1999, in the State of São Paulo. The community had around 560 members on the general discussion list. Website: http://www.repea.org.br/.

Reasul (Rede Sul Brasileira de Educação Ambiental) (Brazilian South-Region Environmental-Education Network): created in 2002 and active in three states of the Brazilian south (Rio Grande do Sul, Santa Catarina and Paraná). The community had around 2,000 members on the general list. Website: http://www.reasul.org.br/mambo/.

Although the communities have received financial and material support from formal organisations (governmental offices, universities, and non-governmental organisations), their members understood that these communities are independent social movements (called *networks*), because their links with organisations are informal and membership is voluntary.

The main stated goal of these communities is to organize the diffusion of information and knowledge, to debate technical and political issues related to the field of environmental education, and to mobilize their members to collective action in order to influence the government, other institutions, and private organisations. Their main communication channels are the discussion lists (such as Yahoo! and Google), through which members receive and send messages daily.

In order to investigate *how the specific legislation affected the legitimacy of community leaders* (research question), this research adopted a qualitative methodology (in-depth, semi-structured interviews), grounded in an interpretive approach. The interpretive perspective understands that social research may investigate phenomena through uncovering the inter-subjective meanings social actors attribute to them [9, 11]. Community members are thus the primary source of data [12, 18]. A total of 43 in-depth interviews were conducted, between April and June 2006. The selection of interviewees was done by a snowball process [7]: key informants (listed in the communities' websites) were first contacted and they indicated other members.

In spite of the inherent ambiguities of qualitative research [1, 11, 14], this study adopted a rigourous set of criteria to elaborate a coding process which permitted the construction of an understanding which is convincing and logically consistent [1, 9]. The research obtained a great level of agreement among respondents, which is an indicator of reliability in qualitative research [18, 21, 32]. The findings are combined here into a singular case, as this paper does not have space for conducting a multiple-case study in details.

Furthermore, the findings are consistent with institutional theory (see session 3), which is also an indicator of rigour in qualitative research [6, 21]. Indeed, institutional theory has been chosen as an adequate lens for understanding the studied phenomenon because it provides a consistent framework on how institutions influence legitimacy and how legitimacy support institutions [26, 27, 31]. The coding process started from the institutional framework, in a deductive fashion. The interaction with data, however, has improved the original coding, in an inductive fashion. Thus, the final result presented in this article is the consolidation of a coding process which has elements of deduction (theory structuring coding) and induction (codes emerging from the data).

The original interviews were in Portuguese and were translated into English by the researcher. The presented transcriptions respect the original meaning, but some editing has been done, avoiding expressions and digressions which do not help the understanding of the discourse [8, 16, 24]. The interviewees are identified by the name of their communities (Rebea, Repea, and Reasul) and a number created at random to preserve the anonymity of respondents.

3.   Main findings

Members of the three studied communities highlighted the relevance of the governmental funding (FNMA) for their collectives in terms of empowering the communities. With this funding, these communities bought servers, produced their websites (improving their visibility to the general public), and contracted professionals to organize and feed information into their communication channels (mainly the discussion lists and websites). As summarized by a Rebea 1:

> The FNMA funding mobilized the communities and permitted things to work better. Because of this money, the communities achieved a higher level in their activities. It was a partnership between communities and the government, with common objectives.

Also Rebea 2 agreed:

> The governmental funding permitted the community to organize itself, to construct a website and to contract a professional in communication [to support community activities]. These improvements were not coming through voluntary work.

Members of the three communities emphasized, nonetheless, that the funding was grounded in a specific legislation, which forced the communities to be represented in the contracts by formal organisations. Recall that these communities do not have a formal, legal existence, thus they could not be accountable for public contracts.

In order to overcome this obstacle, the government created an intermediary solution: the communities could keep their informality, as far as one formal organisation (called an "anchor") could assume the responsibility in name of the community. In other words, these formal organisations would sign up contracts, receive the money, and be accountable for both the use of the funding and the contractual commitments (mainly the feeding of the federal databank). These formal organisations could be prosecuted by the government if the contracts were not respected. As explained by Repea 1:

> *The legislation imposed the conditions to provide funding. The community [through the anchor organisation] accepted the governmental demands: one formal organisation should represent the community.*

Also Rebea 5 argued in the same direction:

> *It is a legal impasse: the government cannot give money to informal communities. Someone should be accountable for the money. If individuals had received money directly in their personal bank accounts, which would be the priorities?*

The governmental concern about accountability appeared to be broader than the distinction between informal communities versus formal anchor organisations. As explained by Rebea 14, the government would not have accepted a non-relevant organisation as a representative of the communities:

> *The government wanted a "good" formal organisation [to represent the community in the project]. One small non-governmental organisation would not be acceptable as a representative [although this is not a formal rule, the member argued it was a known norm].*

This is also the opinion of Repea 4:

> *The anchor organisation should have the structure to face the legal demands. The received money would not be enough if the organisation did not have its own structure working.*

Consequently, these formal organisations that were responsible for the contracts either obtained a leadership role in these communities or reinforced their previous leadership. Indeed, although these communities emphasized that all members have equal rights and power in their collectives, members recognized that the legislation favoured a more centralized perception of their governance structure. Rebea 2 summarizes:

> *This is the drama with civil society organisations: the work is directed by the ones who fund the collectives. The problem is not to receive money from the government, but to balance whether community members have capacity to negotiate with the government about how the money would be expended.*

The common understanding of members was that the only way of obtaining the governmental funding was to accept this rule of being represented formally by an anchor organisation. In other words, members legitimated the acceptance of an organisational structure mediated by formal organisations because they believed the funding would benefit the whole community. As defended by Repea 2:

> *Without the governmental money, the things happen in a slow way in the communities. When we had the FNMA project, we had goals. Without the funding, the process was free, without planning.*

Members linked with the anchor organisations were endowed with differentiated rights (they received the money and had legal power to decide about the projects) and obligations (they needed to guarantee that resources have been used correctly) in relation to other members. The contracts were enforced by the specific and general legislations: the government could use coercive mechanisms to force the anchor organisations to fulfil the contract. Consequently, the legislation favoured the centralization of decision making because only the anchor organisation would face coercive sanctions if the contract was not fulfilled, argued Repea 9. The same reasoning is formulated by Repea 5:

> *Some discussions should be restricted to a group of people in order to not damage the project. The organisation which received the money for the project was selected to make decisions in the way it wanted. It would not be possible to discuss the project with the whole community. Those organisations which asked the money should manage the project.*

Other community members argued in the same direction:

> *We cannot put 600 people discussing a project. We discuss among few leaders, because one organisation is accountable for the money* [Repea 8].

> *In the FNMA, people were accountable for the money. If the person is not legally responsible, she will not commit. People may contribute, but not in the way it is demanded formally [considering the contract]* [Reasul 10].

Interestingly, this legislation could only affect the governance structures of the projects ruled by the specific contracts. In other words, the government demanded an anchor organisation to respond for specific funding, not for the community as a whole. As stated by Reasul 9:

> *The FNMA demanded a coordinator for the funded projects, not for the communities [as a whole], but the group which managed the projects extended their attributions to manage other community issues.*

Thus, the community could keep parallel structures of governance, as far as the one responsible for the funding followed the legal imposition of having a formal representative. Furthermore, the legislation did not impose any rule in relation to how decisions should be made even in the funded projects. In other words, the legislation imposed accountability for anchor organisations, but it did not imply necessarily that these organisations should make decisions in a more centralized or decentralized way. Although respondents identified that the legislation had limited scope in terms of interfering in the way communities make decisions, the leadership of the anchor organisation in decision making related to other issues was accepted as legitimate.

In practice, using the argument that the legislation imposed a more centralized governance structure, interviewees legitimated the leadership of members who were linked to the anchor organisation. Members of the anchor organisations, for instance, argued that they would not be able to fulfil the contracts, considering the complexity of tasks and bureaucratic procedures, if they had not centralized the decision making. As explained by Repea 1, representative of the anchor organisation:

> *The accountability was very detailed, demanding receipts and public scrutiny in the contracting of people. It was a lot of work, which really overwhelmed the anchor organisation. This legislation forced the community to differentiate between the anchor organisation's members and the other members.*

Also Reasul 1, representative of the anchor organisation, confirmed:

> *The money was managed by the anchor organisation, which reduced the autonomy of other members. The boundaries of the FNMA project and the community as a whole become blurred, because we [the anchor organisation] had deadlines and formal goals [which was not the case for the members who were not affiliated to the anchor organisation].*

Furthermore, the interviewees also called attention to the fact that even after the end of the funding projects, the anchor organisations in the three communities kept their relative leadership, at least for a while. As the representative of an anchor organisation (Repea 1) explained:

> *The money had finished, but not the work. We continued to work, and people understood that our organisation [anchor] kept the leadership of the community. Although we formally are not anymore the executive secretary, I do not know if people acknowledge this change, as we keep answering the telephone and the emails [as community representatives].*

This impression is confirmed by Repea 3:

> *In my opinion, after the project, the very same people [representatives of the anchor organisation] kept going as executive secretaries, although now they call themselves management group.*

4.   Discussion

In this part, this chapter discusses the findings considering the insights provided by institutional theory [5, 26, 27]. In sum, the findings point to the conclusions that the discussed legislation (FNMA funding) has reinforced the legitimacy of specific leaders, related to the anchor organisations, through two sanction mechanisms: the recognition of legitimate authority (rewarded by the funding) and the possibility of imposing punishment (in the case of contractual breaking). These claims are developed below.

As defined by Scott [26, p. 48]: "Institutions are social structures that have attained a high degree of resilience [...] [which] are composed of culture-cognitive, normative, and regulative elements, that, together with associate activities and resources, provide stability and meaning to social life."

Considering the scope of this paper, there are two aspects of this definition that should be explored. First, Scott claims that *institutions are resilient social structures*. In this specific study, the legislation favours the reproduction of a very traditional social structure – the centralization of decision making. Indeed, this is a governance social structure which is pervasive in hierarchical organisations [29]. In other words, the studied legislation formalised instruments which could influence the communities in adopting a centralized decision-making model, in spite of their intentions (at least in the rhetorical level) of cultivating network governance structures.

Second, Scott [26] proposes the idea that institutions are composed of different sort of elements. In the studied case, the *regulative* element is the main focus of interest, as the legislation fostered centralized decision making through *coercive mechanisms*: if something went wrong, the anchor organisation would be legally accountable. Although the legislation imposed only an accountability structure rather than a decision-making one, members in general legitimated the empowerment of the anchor organisations as they were the ones which risked suffering punishment. In this example, the coercive mechanisms favoured the diffusion of centralized decision-making structures [5, 26].

Clearly, members recognized the logic of instrumentality, brought by the legislation, as proposed by Scott [28]. In other words, the legislation is interpreted as having legitimate means (enforcement mechanisms and centralization of decision making) and ends (beneficiating the communities with funding). In regulative systems, the basis for legitimacy is legally sanctioned [28].

In legitimating centralized decision-making models, which are mainly managed by the anchor organisations, the legislation has facilitated the institutionalization – the diffusion of social structures through settings in time and space [25, 26] – of hierarchical governance models in informal communities. In addition, these centralized models have affected the perception of community members of the legitimacy of the leadership of individuals who were associated with the anchor organisations.

As explained by DiMaggio and Powell [5], coercive mechanisms are supported by formal and informal pressures, from the legal environment to the political influence, including persuasion and even cultural expectations. The authors argue, for instance, that the objective of obtaining funding from hierarchical institutions is an obstacle to any organisation creating a more egalitarian governance form [5]. Indeed, the findings support this idea: many members have accepted the reproduction of hierarchical structures as a mean of obtaining funding in spite of their rhetoric of nurturing horizontal, network forms of organizing.

The findings also support the idea that the communities adopted hierarchical structures in order to improve their legitimacy in society, as proposed by Meyer and Rowan [20] and Meyer [19]. More specifically, they adopted centralized decision making in order to legitimate themselves and their leaders as accountable actors. At a more normative level, the centralization of decision making in the hands of legitimate leaders is considered appropriate within the specific set of values and beliefs [17, 26, 31], i.e., the perception that it would be acceptable to recognize the legitimate authority of the anchor organisations in order to receive governmental funding, as expressed by respondents.

Furthermore, the process of institutionalization is not static. As soon as some members are legitimate as leaders, they have further possibilities of controlling the methods of enforcement to foster the reproduction of centralized decision-making model [15, 25]. Indeed, the findings echo this institutional perspective: some leaders were benefiting from the described perception of legitimacy even after the end of the funded projects, as they kept themselves in strategic positions in the communities' governance structures.

5.   Conclusion

Interpreting the empirical findings, this paper concludes that the Brazilian government, through specific policy, has affected the way members of the studied environmental-education virtual communities perceived the legitimacy of their leaders. Although the legislation itself has not impose rules of governance for the community as a whole, the fact that the government established a contractual relationship with some community representatives (anchor organisations) rather than with others (or the community as a whole) has affected the perception of legitimacy of these representatives. The very simple fact that the government cultivates interactions with some members instead of others affects the perception of who is a legitimate leader.

The findings show that the funding legislation affected the legitimate authority of some community leaders through sanctions mechanisms. On the one hand, the communities accepted the legal impositions in order to qualify for receiving governmental money (reward mechanism). On the other hand, the communities altered their perception of legitimate governance structures through recognizing the fact that the anchor organisations were the ones taking the risk (punishment mechanism). Furthermore, the communities kept legitimating the leadership of the anchor organisations even after the end of contracts, which calls attention to the inertial forces present in process of institutionalisation.

Considering the concern related to policies, the findings contribute to the discussion on the diffusion of ICTs and democracy. Many have claimed that the organisation of grassroots movements and civil society organisations through computer-mediated channels would empower these collectives [2, 3, 4, 10, 23], permitting more participatory, democratic decision-making processes [13, 22, 23, 30].

The findings, however, to some extent challenge these arguments. First, the interviewees revealed that the communities committed rhetorically with a network, participatory decision-making model meanwhile in practice they cultivated other governance structures. Second, the findings showed that in some circumstances grassroots movements may be inclined to accept new rules in order to receive direct and indirect incentives, such as funding. Third, the data indicated how a specific legislation which aimed to diffuse the appropriation of ICTs through communities of environmental educators has affected the way these collectives perceive the legitimacy of their leaders, reinforcing centralized governance structures.

To be clear, these communities did not already have an effective network organisation and for this reason it is not possible to say that the legislation has changed the governance structures of these communities. Members did express, however, that the legislation has reinforced the legitimacy of some community leaders. Although other factors have also influenced the distribution of power among members, the fact that the government legitimated some leaders rather than others has been recognized as an important fact in the definition of who is more central in the process of making decisions.

In conclusion, this chapter claims that although ICTs may be related to processes of cultivating more democratic and participatory decision-making in society, it is important to be attentive to the way traditional social structures influence the new forms of interacting through computer-mediated channels. Naturally, this paper does not deny the relevance of ICTs to the empowerment of grassroots movements and civil society organisations; rather, it calls attention to the need to be aware of how institutional forces in society may influence the kind of interactions in virtual collectives. In observing how policies related to ICTs affect in practice the governance structures of grassroots movements, citizens may organize themselves to favour regulations which do not go against the interests of the democratic aspirations of these collectives.

References

[1]   Bauman, Z. (1978). *Hermeneutics and social science – approaches to understanding.* London: Hutchinson of London.
[2]   Castells, M. (1996). *The rise of the network society.* Massachusetts; Oxford: Blackwell Publishers.
[3]   Castells, M. (2001). *The internet galaxy: Reflections on the internet, business and society.* Oxford; New York: Oxford University Press.
[4]   Delanty, G. (2003). *Community.* London; New York: Routledge.
[5]   DiMaggio, P.J. &Powell, W.W. (1991 [1983]). The iron cage revisited: Institutional isomorphism and collective rationality in organizational fields. In W.W. Powell and P.J. DiMaggio (Eds.), *The new institutionalism in organizational analysis.* Chicago; London: The University of Chicago Press.
[6]   Eisenhardt, K.M. (1989). Building theories from case study research. *The Academic of Management Review,* 14(4), 532-550.
[7]   Esterberg, K.G. (2002). *Qualitative methods in social research.* Boston: McGraw-Hill.
[8]   Flick, U. (2002). *An introduction to qualitative research* (2nd edition). Thousand Oaks; London; New Delhi: Sage Publications.
[9]   Gadamer, H. (1989 [1975]). *Truth and method.* (2nd revised edition). London: Sheed & Ward.
[10]   Graham, G. (1999). *The internet: A philosophical inquiry.* London: Routledge.
[11]   Habermas, J. (1981 [1968]). *Knowledge and human interests.* London: Heinemann.

[12] Hakim, C. (2000). *Research design – successful designs for social and economic research* (2nd edition). London; New York: Routledge.

[13] Juris, J.S. (2005). The new digital media and activist networking within anti-corporate globalization movements. *Annals*, AAPSS, 597, 189-208.

[14] Klein, H.K. & Myers, M.D. (1999). A set of principles for conducting and evaluating interpretive field studies in information systems. *MIS Quarterly*, 23(1), 67-94.

[15] Knight, J., and Ensminger, J. (1998). Conflict over changing social norms: Bargaining, ideology and enforcement. In M.C. Brinton and V. Nee (Eds.), *The new institutionalism in sociology*. Stanford, CA: Stanford University Press.

[16] Kvale, S. (1996). *InterViews: An introduction to qualitative research interviewing*. Thousand Oaks; London; New Delhi: Sage Publications.

[17] March, J.G. (1994). *A primer on decision making: How decisions happen*. New York: The Free Press; London: Maxwell Macmillan International.

[18] Mason, J. (2002). *Qualitative researching* (2nd edition). London; Thousands Oaks; New Delhi: Sage Publications.

[19] Meyer, J.W. (1994). Rationalized environments. In W.R. Scott and J.W. Meyer (Eds.), *Institutional environments and organizations*. Thousands Oaks; London; New Delhi: Sage Publications.

[20] Meyer, J.W., and Rowan, B. (1977). Institutionalised organizations: Formal structures and myth and ceremony. *The American Journal of Sociology*, 83(2), 340-363.

[21] Patton, M.Q. (2002). *Qualitative research & evaluation methods* (3rd edition). Thousand Oaks; London; New Delhi: Sage Publications.

[22] Pickard, V.W. (2006). United yet autonomous: Indymedia and the struggle to sustain a radical democratic network. *Media, Culture & Society*, 28(3), 315-336.

[23] Rheingold, H. (2000 [1993]). *The virtual community: Homesteading on the electronic frontier* (revised edition). Cambridge, MA: MIT Press.

[24] Rubin, H.J., and Rubin, I.S. (2005). *Qualitative interviewing – the art of hearing data* (2nd edition). Thousand Oaks; London; New Delhi: Sage Publications.

[25] Scott, W.R. (1998). *Organizations: rational, natural and open systems* (4th edition). Upper Saddle River, NJ: Prentice Hall International.

[26] Scott, W.R. (2001). *Institutions and organizations* (2nd edition). Thousand Oaks; London; New Delhi: Sage Publications.

[27] Scott, W.R. (2003). Institutional carriers: Reviewing modes of transporting ideas over time and space and considering their consequences. *Industrial and Corporate Change*, 12(4), 879-894.

[28] Scott, W.R. (2005). Institutional theory: Contributing to a theoretical research program. In K.G. Smith and M.A. Hitt (Eds.), *Great minds in management: the process of theory development*. Oxford: Oxford University Press.

[29] Simon, H. (1997 [1945]). *Administrative behaviour: A study of decision-making processes in administrative organization* (4th edition). New York: Free Press.

[30] Steinmueller, W.E. (2002). Virtual communities and the new economy. In R. Mansell (ed.), *Inside the communication revolution – evolving patterns of social and technical interaction*. Oxford: Oxford University Press.

[31] Suchman, M.C. (1995). Managing legitimacy: Strategic and institutional approaches. *Academy of Management Review*, 20(3), 571-610.

[32] Yin, R.K. (2003). *Case study research: design and methods* (3rd edition). Thousand Oaks; London; New Delhi: Sage Publications.

EXAMINING TRUST IN MOBILE BANKING TRANSACTIONS:
THE CASE OF M-PESA IN KENYA

Olga Morawczynski
University of Edinburgh, Scotland

Gianluca Miscione
University of Oslo, Norway

Abstract: This chapter examines how trust can emerge and be sustained in the context of mobile transactions. It focuses on M-PESA, a mobile banking system in Kenya, using data from an ethnographic study that was deployed in Kibera—one of Africa's largest slums. We present research in progress and discuss two main findings. Firstly, interpersonal trust relations between the customers and agents are weak. Customers do not trust the agents with their money. Secondly, the institutional trust relations between the customer and Safaricom, the mobile service provider offering M-PESA, are strong. This means that customers use the M-PESA service because they believe that their money will be kept safe by Safaricom. After providing empirical evidence to substantiate these claims, this study concludes by suggesting questions for future research.

Keywords: Mobile banking, M-PESA, trust, Kibera.

1. Introduction

This chapter examines how trust can emerge and be sustained in the context of mobile transactions, through an ethnographic study of M-PESA, a mobile banking system deployed in Kibera—one of Africa's largest slums.

The topic of trust was chosen for analysis because we are dealing with economic transactions and the exchange of e-money via the M-PESA application. Such exchange, as pointed out by several authors, is contingent upon trust [13, 15]. We can thus make the argument that the trajectory of M-PESA is dependent upon the trust relations that are established between the actors involved in these exchanges. Using this argument as a starting point, we will examine the nature of these relations and identify the actors involved in establishing and maintaining them in the context of Kibera.

This work intends to be situated between what Avgerou [4] termed social embeddedness and transformative discourses in IS in development contexts. The

Please use the following format when citing this chapter:

Morawczynski, O. and Miscione, G., 2008, in IFIP International Federation for Information Processing, Volume 282; *Social Dimensions of Information and Communication Technology Policy*; Chrisanthi Avgerou, Matthew L. Smith, Peter van den Besselaar; (Boston: Springer), pp. 287–298.

former type of discourse views ICT innovation as "a locally socially constructed course of action" [4 pp.7] and focuses on locally embedded meanings of a technology. The latter also pays attention to the social context and local embeddedness of a technology. However, "while socially embedded analyses tend to take social, economical and political relations in a developing country community or the world as large as a given, the transformative is explicitly concerned with the way ICT are implicated in the dynamic of their change" [4, p. 8]. Through ethnographic research, we aim at understanding how local meanings are ascribed to the technology. We also want to examine how the M-PESA application is implicated in the dynamics of social, economic, and political arrangements. Such understandings must take into consideration trust relations. These relations, as mentioned above, affect the trajectory of innovation.

2.   Introducing mobile banking

The pervasiveness of the mobile phone in developing countries has recently instigated the development of applications designed to alleviate poverty. One of the most recent is m-banking—a platform for the delivery of financial services via the mobile phone. According to the international development community, the aim of these initiatives is to empower poor constituents by providing them access to formal financial services. The main concern within the m-banking literature is related to adoption. Many studies pose the question of whether or not these applications have the potential to be *transformational*[1], or appropriated by a large segment of the unbanked population [11, 18]. To date, there is very little empirical work examining the adoption of m-banking applications and discussing the numerous barriers to this process.

3.   Presentation of the case

M-PESA is an m-banking application that facilitates branchless banking via the mobile phone. It targets the unbanked, prepaid segment of the population and was officially introduced onto the Kenyan market in March of 2007 by Safaricom, the Kenyan mobile service provider. It was funded by Department for International Development (DFID), the part of the UK government that provides aid to developing countries in conjunction with Vodafone, the UK telecommunications company [20].

This m-banking application facilitates numerous financial services such as checking account balances, making deposits and withdrawals, transferring money and phone credit to other users. To access these services, individuals must register at one of the retail agent outlets, and deposit cash. This cash is thereafter reflected

---

[1] Please note that the definition of "transformational" in the literature cited is still vague. It is not made explicit when a technology becomes transformational or what constitutes "a large segment of the unbanked population". We have used this definition in the context of this research to emphasize the interest placed in adoption and usage by the international development community.

as e-money in a virtual account that is managed by Safaricom. This is called the non-bank led model of m-banking because the customer has no direct relationship with a bank. After this account is created, and an e-money balance established, all of the aforementioned transactions can be conducted via the mobile phone. To access e-money transferred via M-PESA, the recipient must also visit a retail agent. They provide the agent with identification, verify the transaction number, and convert the e-money balance on their phone into cash.

The transferring money option is particularly interesting in this context because it facilitates the transfer of remittances—both domestic and international. In regards to the latter, Safaricom is currently testing the transfer of e-money between Kenya and the UK. If successful, there are plans to extend this service to other countries that are major sources of remittances because they have a large segment of Kenyan emigrants. This includes the US, France, and Germany [3].

Safaricom reports that within one year of its launch it had close to two million M-PESA customers register with the service and over 2000 active M-PESA agents [24]. Over 9 billion Ksh^2 had been transferred through the system during the first year [1]. Reports emerging from the international development community are quite optimistic that such growth rates will continue and argue that these applications have the potential to be "transformational" [18, 19]. They further assert that such appropriation will instigate economic development as poor constituents will be provided the opportunity to participate in the formal economy—some for the first time. However, before M-PESA has this so-called "transformational" effect, it must first be adopted and appropriated by a large segment of the unbanked population. As will be discussed in more detail later, the establishment and maintenance of trust is vitally important in this process.

4.   The empirical setting

Kibera is one of the most impoverished areas in Kenya. The slum is located 7kms southwest of Nairobi and it is estimated that one million people, or 60% of the population in Nairobi, call Kibera their home [10]. The unemployment is some of the highest in the country and only 17% of the adult population is reported to be permanently employed [10]. The rest are casual labourers or employed in the informal sector. The health indicators in the slum are also extremely poor. It is estimated that 20% of the community is infected with the HIV virus [10]. This is almost four times the national average. Although Kibera is situated on property that is government owned, the social amenities are extremely poor. There are no government clinics or hospitals and the police are reported to visit the slum only to collect bribes. The majority of dwellers do not have electricity. During the evenings the slum becomes engulfed in darkness and, because of the security risks, few residents leave their homes. Water is also a problem, as the supply is not

---

^{2} Approximately £73 million.

reliable. The residents must either depend on private vendors selling the water by cart or the nearby river, into which Kibera's sewage drains.

There are no formal financial institutions in Kibera. The majority of the population cannot afford the monthly fees required by the larger banks. They also do not have a steady income which they can put away in an account. Money transfer services such as Western Union and Postapay are also not available and residents must travel into town to access such services. It must be noted that in Kibera there is a demand for both banking and money transfer services. In regards to the former, many of those interviewed asserted that they did want to put away their limited savings in a safe place. Many of those interviewed who were unbanked would store their money under their mattresses in "home banks". These were small tin boxes with a slit on the top that was used to insert the money. There was also a great demand for money transfer services. Most of the residents in Kibera are migrants from rural areas who have come to the city to work. They thereafter send remittances to relatives and friends in the rural area. This under-representation of these institutions can be explained by the lack of security within the slums. As mentioned previously, there is very little police presence. This means that the organisations dealing with money may not receive adequate protection should there be trouble. It also means that close to one million people in Kibera have limited access to formal financial services.

Although there are no financial organisations within the boundaries of Kibera, there were, at the time of the study, five M-PESA agents. It must be noted, however, that after the disputed Presidential elections that took place in late December 2007 riots broke out in Kibera. Only one of these agents was operational during these riots. The rest closed due to security concerns. Two of the shops were vandalized and remained closed as at May 2008. Despite these security issues, it has been reported by Safaricom that the number of agents and the customer base is expected to increase rapidly in Kibera. As will be discussed below, the telecommunications company has been aggressively marketing the m-banking application focusing on capturing the unbanked segment of the population.

5.   Discussing trust

There exists a wide body of literature on the topic of trust. However, a concise definition of the term remains elusive as it holds a variety of meanings across disciplines. Because we are examining trust in the context of exchange around m-banking, we will appropriate a definition that is inherently *relational* [12, 14, 15, 16, 20]. The starting point to our definition of trust is that it possibly emerges as a property of relations between two or more social actors. These actors can be individuals. They can also be institutions such as corporations or political parties [22]. These actors are interacting in some way and have *expectations* regarding each other's future behaviour [5, 8]. They expect that the other actor will fulfil their obligations, behave in a predictable manner, and will act fairly in situations of opportunism. In this regard, trust is the expectations that people have of each other, and of the institutions with which they deal. According to Barber [5], these expectations are socially learned and socially confirmed. They change over time, as the actors involved in the trust relations interact and gain more information about each other.

There are several levels at which trust can be examined because, as mentioned above, different types of actors are involved in trust relations. Some scholars pay attention to the trust relations that emerge between individuals, which is known as interpersonal trust [6, 7, 16]. This type of trust is established between two or more interacting individuals who through time learn about each other. As they learn, they make judgements regarding each other's disposition, intentions, and motives. Several authors have also pointed to something called extended trust to explain trust relations that extend beyond those that we know personally [21]. They argue that this type of trust is essential for an efficient market economy because it fosters co-operation between individuals who may not have prior information about each other. Several explanations have been given as to why individuals choose to co-operate, even without this information. Some argue that an individual's role in society can form a basis of presumptive trust. It is not the actual person that is trusted but the system of expertise that produces and sustains role-appropriate behaviour [12]. For example, Dawes [9] asserts that "we trust engineers because we trust engineering and believe that engineers are trained to apply valid principles of engineering, moreover, we have evidence everyday that these principles are valid when we observe planes flying" [12, p. 9].

Whilst some pay attention to relations that emerge between individuals, others examine those that exist between individuals and institutions such as corporations or political parties. This is commonly referred to as institutional trust [17, 25]. It is different from interpersonal trust because it is based on trust in institutional arrangements rather than in people. Institutional trust, however, also includes an element of interpersonal trust [22]. This is because the beliefs held about a particular institution can be contingent upon the personnel which they staff. For example, Zimmer [26] argued that institutional leaders can greatly affect the way in which the entire institution is perceived. To make this point, Zimmer examined the impacts of the Watergate scandal on perceptions of trust by the public of the government. He concluded that the violated trust of Nixon led to a generalized distrust for the American government.

In this research, we will use the aforementioned discussion on trust to delineate how it emerges and is sustained in mobile transactions in Kibera. Using M-PESA as an example, we will examine inter-personal trust relations between the customer and agent. We will further explore the institutional trust relations between the customer and Safaricom—the mobile service provider offering the M-PESA service.

6.   Questions for discussion and data gathering techniques

At this early stage of research, the focus will be on answering the following:

- What type of trust is needed in the context of mobile transactions?
- How does it emerge?
- How is it negotiated?
- Who is involved in these negotiations (directly and indirectly)?

To help answer the aforementioned questions and instigate discussion on the concept of trust in mobile transactions, we will use data gathered in an ethnographic study in Kibera from September 2007-December 2007. During this period, we used participant observation and semi-structured interviews in Eva's Impressions, a mobile phone shop that provides M-PESA services. The shop is situated along Kibera Drive, which is the main passageway to town. It has been opened since 2006 and sells a variety of Safaricom products including scratch cards, SIM cards and mobile phones. The shop started offering M-PESA services in June of 2007. Based on our visits to other M-PESA agents in Kibera, we found Eva's to be the busiest. We visited the shop from one to two times per week and spent time speaking to three classes of individuals—the users, the non-users, and the agents.[3]

We hired two research assistants to help with the interviews. They both spoke Swahili and were familiar with Kibera. One of the assistants lived in the slum and thus knew many of the people that came into the shop. This facilitated the interview process.

7.   The preliminary findings

7.1   Findings related to usage

Before we discuss the findings in regards to trust and mobile transaction, let us first examine how the application was used. There are two ways in which we monitored usage. Firstly, we counted the number of transactions that were recorded in the agent's logbook, and noted the transaction type. In Eva's we found that there were between 50-65 transactions per day. There are usually more deposits than withdrawals, but at times the amount of deposits and withdrawals were equal. However, according to the agents, customers would often make large deposits and several small withdrawals. This led us to suspect that the service was being used not just to send, but also to store money. We further learned that the frequency of transactions increased at particular points of the year. September was reported to be the busiest month because it is the beginning of the school term.

---

[3] It must be noted that these particular groups are not stable. For example users may become non-users should they find that the application is too difficult to use, or does not adequately fit in with their financial habits. It is also important to recognize that actors may fit into more than one of these groups. For example, the users may also be agents.

During this period, many Kenyans send their relatives in rural areas money for school fees. The last week of each month was also reported to be busy. This is when Kenyans receive their paychecks.

We also monitored usage by speaking with the customers in the shop. Our preliminary findings show that most individuals were using M-PESA to send money to their relatives, or to top-up their mobile phone credit. We also found that some were using the application to exchange money with business partners. For example, a female resident of Kibera, who had her own spinning business, used M-PESA to send money to her suppliers in Mombasa and collect debts from her customers. She claimed that M-PESA "makes business easier" because it saves her both time and money. There were also occasions when M-PESA was being used to "help a friend in need". An interview with a young woman revealed that she was using M-PESA to send money to a friend who was "stranded" and needed "fare for the bus" because she had been robbed. The woman sending the money said that she'd never had a bank account, and did not know of any other way that the money could be sent.

Some customers also claimed that they were using M-PESA to store their money. We were surprised to find, however, that the majority of these individuals had one or more bank accounts in town. They claimed that they were using M-PESA because they could access their money without having to travel outside of Kibera. According to our interviewees, such travel was both costly and time consuming. We also found that many of the customers who were using M-PESA to send money were unaware that it could be used for other purposes. In fact, several individuals that we interviewed asked us whether the application had "other uses". This lack of information on the various functionalities of M-PESA can be attributed to the way in which the application is being marketed. M-PESA is being presented mainly as an application that facilitates money transfers from urban to rural areas. Radio adverts and billboards advertising M-PESA throughout Nairobi also fail to mention the other uses. The slogan used for such advertisements is *"Tuma pesa kwa simu"*, meaning *"Send money by mobile phone"* in Swahili.

7.2   Findings related to trust

We also have several results that can be used in our discussion of trust. One of our first findings is that many of the M-PESA customers do not trust the agents with their money.

The agents often complained that they would receive the blame for all the problems with the M-PESA system. Because M-PESA utilizes the same data channel as text messages, it often becomes congested at "peak texting times". The result is that many M-PESA transactions fail. They are either not processed in the system, or are processed but the SMS that confirms the M-PESA transaction to the agent and customer is not sent. The agents asserted that in both of these cases, they were accused of stealing the customer's money after a deposit was made and no confirmation SMS received. A conversation with an M-PESA agent in Eva's revealed the following:

I asked the agent whether she, or her customers, had lost money when the system became congested. She said no. She then added that on several occasions her customers "thought that they had lost money". Last week, she explained, she had a customer come in to make a deposit. He wanted to send the money to his relatives. This customer gave her the money and he was told to wait for the confirmation SMS. However, after waiting around for nearly an hour, he told the agent that he had to leave for work and would be back if he did not receive the confirmation. He came back the next day to "hassle" her, she explained. She tried to make it clear to him that the money was "in the system", but the customer demanded his "stolen" money back. He then became "angry" and began to "quarrel". She had to call the Safaricom people to reverse the transaction so that she could give the man his deposit.

Most of the agents interviewed had similar stories and told us that they were often accused of stealing money from the customers.

Our data further revealed that some customers did not expect others to trust the agents. In fact, the agents told us that some customers would come into the shop with their debtors and attempt to withdraw money. This was even when the customers did not have enough money in their accounts to make the requested withdrawal. We saw one incidence of this with a man who had a debt with a peanut seller:

We heard some yelling outside of the shop before we saw a man stumble in with a cigarette in one hand and a pack of peanuts in the other. He smelled of alcohol and his white shirt had large brown stains, and what appeared to be cigarette burns. He was followed by another man who was holding a large basket of peanuts. They were exchanging words in Swahili, and the man in the white shirt was yelling in English "get the money from the agent" as he entered the shop while pointing at Cheryl [the agent]. Before the peanut seller could make his way into the shop, the man in the white shirt pushed passed him and they ran out into the street. They continued to yell at each other, and a crowd was beginning to gather.

Once they left, we all started to laugh. Christine [my research assistant] turned to me and explained that the man told the peanut seller to collect the "5 bob"[4] for peanuts from Cheryl. The peanut seller demanded his money in cash, and refused to believe that the man in the white shirt had "5 bob" in an M-PESA account. Cheryl explained that this sort of thing happens very often. Customers who are in debt will come in with their debtors and try to withdraw money from their M-PESA account. The agent will check the account and realize that the customer does not have enough money for the requested withdrawal and inform the customer. The customer will then become angry and inform the debtor that the

---

[4] "Bob" is the slang name used for Kenyan shilling.

agent is lying and that the agent does not want to give the customer their money. Cheryl emphasized that "it is always our fault".

Our interviews with the customers confirmed that many do not trust the M-PESA agents. One on occasion, an angry customer complained to us that the agent at Eva's had stolen money from him. He asserted that he had made a deposit of "400 bob" the week before and when he checked his balance that morning he only had "399 bob". He demanded that the agent return the "1 bob" that was stolen. The M-PESA agent had to spend several minutes explaining that there was "1 bob" deducted from his account every time that he checked his balance. The man was not convinced and asked for some evidence. The agent showed him a leaflet with the different transaction costs. The customer then stamped out the door with leaflet in hand.

From these findings we can make the argument that interpersonal trust relations between the customers and agents are still weak. This could be because the application has only recently been introduced into Kibera. Many of the customers interviewed had signed up within the last few months and used the application monthly or bi-monthly. This means that they have had limited interaction with the agents. It can thus be argued that at this stage M-PESA customers are gaining information and making judgments regarding the disposition, intentions, and motives of the agents. Such information will help them to form expectations regarding the future behaviour of the agents. As we have seen from the field notes above, one such expectation is how money deposited will be handled by the agent. Customers want to make sure that their money is fully reflected in their M-PESA account and that it can be accessed when needed. We can further make the argument that trust relations are weak because all of the agents in the shop live outside of Kibera. They are thus not known personally by the customers. In this case, what we earlier called extended trust relations need to be established between the customer and the agent.

If many customers do not trust the agents with their money, then we must ask ourselves why they use M-PESA. The data gathered suggests that they use the service because they trust Safaricom. This means that the trust relations between the customers and Safaricom are much stronger than those between the customers and agents. This could be because the company has a history in Kenya. It has provided mobile services since 1997. As at May 2008, the company was reported to have 70% of the Kenyan market, which amounts to 9.5 million subscribers (in a country of 36 million) [2]. As such, many of the M-PESA customers have been using Safaricom as their mobile service provider before the M-PESA service was introduced. They have thus had more exposure to the mobile service operator and more time to assess the quality of the institutional arrangements. These assessments, as mentioned above, are vital for the emergence of institutional trust. In the context of m-banking transactions, such trust is important because customers are handing over their money to be held in a virtual account managed by Safaricom. As such, they must have faith that the institution will protect such deposits and make them available to the customer when needed.

It was also previously discussed that institutional leaders may affect the way in which the institution is assessed, and whether it is trusted. From the fieldwork data, we found this to be correct. An interview with an M-PESA customer revealed the following:

Andrew made clear that there were several problems with Equity [the name of his bank]. I leaned forward and asked him what they were. "I don't mean to be tribal" he replied, "but the president of Equity is too close to Kibaki [the CEO of Kenya]". I asked him to explain and he told me that the president of Equity Bank, who was Kikuyu like Kibaki, was giving "too much" of the "common man's" money to support Kibaki's electoral campaign. If this went on, he emphasized, the bank would crash and the money of the "common man" would be lost. He then said that this is why spreading out your money in several accounts was a "good idea"...I asked him whether he was afraid that Safaricom would crash and that he would lose the money in his M-PESA account. He shook his head. He said that everyone knew that Safaricom would not involve themselves in "tribal politics" because Micheal Joseph (the president of Safaricom) did not belong to any of Kenya's tribes.

In the case of Andrew, he trusted Safaricom with his money because Micheal Joseph, its President, did not have tribal affiliations. Our interviews with other customers also revealed that Joseph was well respected in the community. Because of his South African background, he seemed to be excluded from accusations of tribal favouritism. We can thus make the argument that many of those interviewed trust Safaricom because they trust Joseph. We can further argue that they trust Joseph because they believe that he is politically neutral. Such a finding confirms the aforementioned research suggesting that the organisational leader affects the way in which an institution is perceived. In this case, Joseph's good standing in the community has positively impacted public opinion of Safaricom.

8.   Conclusions

From these few early examples, we can see that trust is a vital element of social relations, and is shaping the trajectory of the M-PESA application. Our preliminary findings suggest that many of the customers trust the M-PESA system because it is affiliated with Safaricom. This means that institutional trust relations between the customers and the mobile service provider are strong. Our findings further suggest that interpersonal trust relations are weak as customers do not trust the agents within the M-PESA network. We have shown that on numerous occasions the agents were accused of stealing the customer's money when there was a problem with the application. As the study progresses, other examples will be gathered and used to discuss the issue of trust.

Finally, based on the results collected thus far, further research will focus on the following questions:

- Do people establish trustworthy relations beyond their immediate circles? If so, why do they extend their trust beyond these boundaries?
- What about brand trust? How did Safaricom gain trust? How does it sustain it?
- What about distrust and power? How can these concepts be incorporated into the analysis?

References

[1]   (2008, March 28). Kenya: Clear M-Pesa's legal hurdles. Business Daily. Nairobi.
[2]   (2008, March 14). Kenya sets $3bn Safaricom IPO price. Reuters. Retrieved April 20, 2008, from http://www.engineeringnews.co.za/article.php?a_id=129263.
[3]   Aron, M. (2007). Kenya: trend-setting M-Pesa goes international. Business Daily. Nairobi.
[4]   Avgerou C. (2007) Information systems in developing countries: a critical research review, London School of Economics and Political Sciences, Innovation Group, Working Papers Series, October 2007.
[5]   Barber, B. (1983). *The logic and limits of trust*. New Brunswick: Rutgers University Press.
[6]   Boon S.D. & Holmes J.G. (1991). The dynamics of interpersonal trust: Resolving uncertainty in the face of risk. In Cooperation and Prosocial Behavior, ed. RA Hinde, J Groebel (pp. 167-82). New York: Cambridge University Press.
[7]   Brann, P. & Foddy, M. (1988). Trust and the consumption of a deteriorating resource. *Journal of Conflict Resolution*, 31, 615-30.
[8]   Dasgupta, P. (1988). Trust as a commodity in D. Gambetta (ed.) *Trust: Making and breaking cooperative relations,* (pp. 49-72). New York: Basil Blackwell.
[9]   Dawes, R.M. (1994). *House of cards: Psychology and psychotherapy built on myth*. New York: Free Press.
[10] Ilako, F. & Kimura, M. (2004). Provision of ARVs in a resource-poor setting: Kibera Slum. International Conference on AIDS. Nairobi, Kenya, African Medical and Research Foundation (AMREF).
[11] Ivatury, G. & Pickens, M. (2006). Mobile phone banking and low-income customers: Evidence from South Africa, Consultative Group to Assist the Poor/The World Bank.
[12] Kramer, R. (1999). Trust and distrust in organizations: Emerging perspectives, enduring questions. *Annual Review of Psychology*, 50, 569-598.
[13] Luhmann, N. (1979). *Trust and power*. New York: Wiley.
[14] Mayer, R., Davis, J., & Schoorman, FD. (1995).An integrative model of organizational trust. *The Academy of Management Review*, 20,709–34.
[15] Malinowski, B. (1922). Argonauts of the Western Pacific: Account of native enterprise and adventure. London, Routledge and Kegan Paul Ltd.
[16] McAlister, D.J. (1995). Affect- and cognition based trust as foundations for interpersonal cooperation in organizations. *The Academy of Management Review,* 38, 24–59.
[17] Mishler, W. & Rose, R. (2001) What are the origins of political trust? Testing institutional and cultural theories in post-communist societies, *Comparative Political Studies,* 34 (1), 30-62.
[18] Porteous, D. (2006). The enabling environment for mobile banking in Africa. Boston, DFID.
[19] Porteous, D. (2007). Just how transformational is m-banking?, Finmark Trust.
[20] Putnam, R. (1993). Social capital and public life. *The American prospect*, 13.

[21] Raiser, M., Haerpfer, C., Nowotny, T., & Wallace, C. (2001). Social capital in transition: a first look at the evidence. Working Paper No 61. European Bank.

[22] Smith, M.L. (2007). Confianza a la Chilena: A comparative study of how e-services influence public sector institutional trustworthiness and trust. PhD Thesis. London School of Economics and Political Science.

[23] Vaughan, P. (2007). Early lessons from the deployment of M-Pesa, Vodafone's own mobile transactions services. The transformational potential of m-transactions, Vodafone Group PLC: 6-10.

[24] P. Vaughan, personal interview, March 27, 2008.

[25] Williamson, O.E. (1985). The economic institutions of capitalism. New York: Free Press.

[26] Zimmer, T. (1972). The impact of Watergate on the public's trust in people and confidence in the mass media. *Social Science Quarterly*. 59,743-751.

SOCIAL NETWORKS WITHIN FILTERED ICT NETWORKS:
A CASE STUDY OF THE GROWTH OF INTERNET USAGE WITHIN IRAN

Farid Shirazi
Ryerson University, Canada

Abstract   This chapter investigates the growth of the Internet in Iran, the effect of Internet filtering, and the impact on marginalized groups including NGOs, female activists, religious minorities, the younger generation and the increase of the digital divide. Using secondary data from multiple sources, the chapter presents the current use of the Internet in Iran and makes comparisons with other countries in the Persian Gulf region. The chapter argues that Internet filtering and severe restrictions on SMS messaging negatively affect not only ICT expansion, but also civil liberties— thus increasing the digital divide regionally, as well as on a global scale.

Keywords: ICT, digital divide, filtering, weblogging, gender digital divide, NGO, civil liberties, democracy

1.   Introduction

In a report published by the United Nations Conference on Trade and Development, former UN Secretary General Kofi Annan observed, "Information and Communications Technology (ICT) have considerable potential to promote development and economic growth. It can foster innovation and improve productivity. It can reduce transaction costs and make available, in mere seconds, the rich store of global knowledge. In the hands of developing countries, and especially small and medium sized enterprises, the use of ICTs can bring impressive gains in employment, gender equality, and standards of living"" [63].

Kofi Annan's articulation of the influence and impact of ICT on socio-economic development is supported by many researchers in the field of ICT development. Some researchers argue that ICT provides an environment for political freedom [49, 46], freedom of information [41], virtual rights [22] and digital rights [34]. It involves people in a new form of governance, that is, e-government [9, 15, 36], public participation in the form of e-democracy [12] and fosters engagement of associations and communities [13, 40, 48, 65] by utilizing civil societies, NGOs, human rights activists groups and marginalized groups [14,

Please use the following format when citing this chapter:

Shirazi, F., 2008, in IFIP International Federation for Information Processing, Volume 282; *Social Dimensions of Information and Communication Technology Policy*; Chrisanthi Avgerou, Matthew L. Smith, Peter van den Besselaar; (Boston: Springer), pp. 299–317.

18, 21, 33, 42, 47, 51, 53], providing them with the opportunity to access information and knowledge and disseminate it within the public sphere [46].

Scholarly research on ICT development in developing countries has identified that ICT and the Internet in particular, positively correlate with the proliferation of democracy [10, 51]. Other scholars consider ICT and globalization as a means of imposing Western culture onto other cultures through hegemonic power and dominance [45].

Some researchers believe the Internet is undermining the foundation of authoritarian regimes in the Middle East and Arab world [35, 8]. Wheeler [66] emphasizes that the use of the Internet to openly oppose the states' political agendas is often punished by imprisonment. Ghashghai and Lewis [23] state that many Middle Eastern governments fear the Internet will facilitate communication among "subversive" individuals and other organisations such as special interest groups that have political agendas that challenge the legitimacy of their governments. These governments justify Internet content filtering by appealing to a constructed Islamic "moral majority" and claiming to uphold the moral values of their society [66]. In particular, filtering is justified as sustaining Islamic values by protecting citizens from sites that contain pornography and other "depravities."

This chapter raises two questions: 1) To what extent do ICTs and in particular, the Internet, promote freedom of speech and gender equality in Iran? and 2) What is the impact of ICT filtering on these activities in Iran? I use narratives of the Internet's usage along with a comparison study with other Middle Eastern countries to analyze the impact of ICT tools such as the Internet and SMS on Iranian citizens' freedom of expression especially the pursuit of gender equality.

2.   Background

Iran is a Theocratic Republic consisting of several interconnected governing bodies, with an Islamic Shi'a Law constitution. The chief of state is the Supreme Leader, a lifelong position appointed by the Assembly of Experts, who maintains the decisive edict in major political, cultural, religious, judiciary, foreign policy, and economic issues. The Expediency Council is a policy advisory body, which represents all major government factions, as well as clerics from the Council of Guardians. The Supreme Leader chooses the members of the Council of Guardians of the Constitution. Parliament (*Majles*) selects six jurists from a list of candidates recommended by the judiciary (controlled by the Supreme Leader). The Council of Guardians and the Supreme Leader have the power and authority to veto any proposed bills if deemed inconsistent with the constitution or Islamic Law. The President is head of government and is elected for a four-year term from a list of candidates adjudicated by the Council of Guardians. In the 2005 election, over 1000 individuals sought candidacy for election to the presidency. The Council of Guardians banned all but six [20].

Since 1987, Iran has seen the emergence of many political parties and activist groups. The government has a stronghold on freedom of expression by repressing organized and individual freedom of speech. It regulates the press through censorship and restraints, supported by extensive laws. The government issues controls on publication, television and radio broadcasting, issuing gag orders on media coverage of specified events/topics, and has successfully jammed broadcasts. Website censorship is justified by authorities to prevent social immorality, preserve the religious or political authority, or to preserve national security. According to Reporters Without Borders [55], Iran has one of the worst press freedom records in Middle East.

Country	Land area (mil Sq. km)	Pop. (mil)	LE 2006	Adult Literacy 2006	GDPP (US$) 2006	HDI index 2006	HDI rank 2006	EFR rank 2006	Democ rank 2005	PF rank 2005	Constit
Iran	1.648	68	70.7	77	7,525	0.746	96	156	132	164	Islamic Shi'a

Table 1: Demographic Data, LE= Life Expectancy, EFR= Economic Freedom Rank, HDI=Human Development Index, PF= Press Freedom. Sources: UN, ITU, Freedom House, World Audit, The Heritage Foundation, Reporters Without Borders

2.1   ICT development in Iran

ICT development in Iran could have revolutionized communication capabilities among its people by facilitating news reporting, supporting cultural events, broadening the expression of political views and the dissemination of research articles, and engaging thousands of bloggers. Iran's initial ICT development dramatically increased the capacity and speed of its telecommunication networks but the government's control over and monopoly on ICT infrastructure impeded future development of the ICT industry. Many Middle Eastern countries took a liberal approach towards ICT development. Bahrain, Jordan, Kuwait, Qatar and United Arab Emirates (UAE) privatized their government-owned telecom sector, reduced Internet censorship, and successfully increased the volume of operations and services to meet the demand of their markets. In contrast, Iran implemented strict controls on ICT development, particularly by deterring expansion of high-speed internet connections. The government banned high-speed Internet accessibility [60] thus slowing the country's development and modernization. Most developed nations either have established, or are moving toward high-speed access to enable Internet-based applications such as e-commerce, e-banking, e-government and other information-based services that require a higher speed and more reliable Internet connections.

Rahimi [54] states that the Internet in Iran was first promoted by the government to provide an alternative option to scientific and technological innovation during the troubled economic period followed the Iran-Iraq war (1980-1988).

The growth of ICT from 1995 to 2005 was 4.9 fold due to the government's investment in an ICT infrastructure. According to the World Bank [69], Middle Eastern countries had the highest Internet growth in the world (370%) during the period of 2000 to 2005. The Iranian Internet usage had a growth of more than 2900% for the same period. Iran has not only seen an increase in the number of Internet users, but also a significant increase in the number of Persian "weblogs", especially among the younger generation. Alterman [8] argues that while the Internet is not yet a mass medium in most countries, in the Middle East and North Africa (MENA) region, it is growing in popularity among young elites. The use of the Internet to mobilize citizens for democratic changes in Iran challenged the conservative rulers in Iran. The massive usage of the Internet, e-mails, chat rooms and online meetings during the student uprising in 1999 followed by the shut down of reformist newspapers in 2000 [54] made the powerful conservative Supreme Council for Cultural Revolution declare a vague order to all ISPs in Iran to remove anti-government and "anti-Islamic" sites from their servers [54]. The order also mandated all ISPs to operate under government approved monitoring system to filter the Net content [54]. Despite these restrictions millions of Internet users found the Net to be a forum to express their opinions, thoughts and ideas on personal and social levels; expressions that could not otherwise be published through conventional media due to the degree of control by the Iranian government. Many NGOs, minority groups, religious groups, political groups/organisations, and silent voices have used this venue to attract more people to their agenda and programs.

3.   The Iranian Digital Society

Thousands of educated young men and women use one of the core components of ICT, the Internet, for promoting democracy, human rights, freedom of speech and gender equality in Iran. The increase in the weblogs and the proliferation of text messaging have enabled the formation of organized socio-political groups in Iran, reflecting the fact that young Iranians strive for changes in traditional Iran to allow for a space for the creation of ideas, promoting gender equality and respect for human rights.

The Iranian digital society seeks and finds freedom of expression on the Internet. Opinions, concepts, ideas normally filtered or suppressed, due to the monitored and controlled media, are expressed freely on the Internet. In this way, the Internet is becoming an increasingly popular tool among the young generation and those who want access to an unrestrained/uncontrolled source of information. Thousands of Iranian youths, men and women, are active in today's blogging and are among the world's leading Bloggers.

This activity has changed the social boundary that is drawn between men and women in their society; crossing the "red line" over which one cannot step and being a faceless opinion maker is a new experience that internet users in Iran are practicing. Bloggers have also changed the conventional way of publishing ideas, namely the official means of publication.

A review over two Iranian web hosting servers, namely PersianBlog and Mihanblog, during the period of June 6th 2004 to August 5th 2005 (Table 2) shows that 78% of web postings receive responses of one or more comments. These response comments and their subsequent conversion into a multilateral discussion about social, political or cultural issues is a phenomenon that will slowly but undoubtedly help the emergence of a multi-voice society rather than the current single voice. As one Iranian blogger explains, "In my previous weblog there was no 'comments' section. I mean, I didn't allow others to voice their opinions.... When I enabled the comment section in my new weblog, I began to find it very interesting. As others commented and I responded, I noticed a gradual change in my real life as well" [9].

3.1   Weblogging in Iran

A more popular method of Internet usage in Iran includes both active and passive capacities that have enabled people to disseminate articles regarding social/political issues, art and humanities and personal expression (Table 2).

Some bloggers have and are using pseudonyms to avoid prosecution or other social problems whereas others do not go incognito. Various issues are discussed openly and brought forward to share and challenge the judicial system. This culls sympathy and empathy in order to place social and political pressure on government to overturn or rescind legal decisions. In a country controlled by Shi'ite Sharia law, there is little tolerance towards other religions. The Internet provides a secular environment. Weblog postings have challenged the theocratic system in Iran. Table 2 shows no more than 3% of all web postings relate to supporters of the theocratic Shi'ite system. It is of no little consequence that many of the government sectors including the judiciary have implemented harsh law enforcement against bloggers. The practice of Bahaism, one of the minority religions not recognized as legitimate in Iran, is forbidden. This and other religious minorities such as Sunnit Muslims, Christians, Zoroastrians, Sufis, and Jews have established their own web sites outside Iran [71] with the hope that their readers will forward their articles to users in Iran. Most Iranian bloggers are more interested in social and political issues rather than the religious Islamic practices that are discussed on official Islamic Shi'ite institutions' and schools' websites.

Weblogs contain art in the form of music and poetry. Many active music weblogs promote Western music. For example, the punk metal [17] groups and Rap lovers (such as Eminem supporters) that are officially forbidden in Iran are accessible on the Internet. Along with many Farsi-based music weblogs there are also weblogs belonging to the growing underground music scene. One of the most famous Iranian rap groups widely introduced on the Internet is "Emziper " [17].

Although access and exposure to the underground music scene is denied in the official Iranian media or public, it is widely accepted on the Internet.

Weblogs	Persianblog	Mihanblog
News	666	89
Journalism/ Literacy composition	2557	26
Trade and commerce/ e-commerce	2312	344
History	302	13
NGOs	176	-
Philosophy & Mysticism	1572	34
Islamic religion	2564	77
Computer Games	272	69
Humorous and Satiric webs	2559	227
Literature	5406	241
Cinema	991	51
Music	1015	530
Arts	2314	78
Sport	395	121
Technology	7202	31
Information and Communication Tech	4047	299
Health and Medicine	281	9
Nature and Environment	302	4
Research and Education	6694	142
Diary	14115	314
Public issues	29600	433
Neighboring countries	563	-
Total	85905	3132

Table 2: Number of blogs and topics hosted by two Farsi Weblog servers

Personal weblogs bring private domain issues into the public domain. A private domain is defined by the restricted and traditional society (as opposed to open society). Weblogs provide a platform for the expression of personal thoughts, sometimes using stream of consciousness, discovering intrapersonal and interpersonal areas such as self-regard, emotional self-awareness, assertiveness, independence, self-actualization, empathy, social responsibility, and interpersonal relationships. Iranian bloggers use this medium to express their inclusion within a group that has a common goal: to have their opinions/views heard and validated. As one blogger states, "I am alive because I am writing a weblog. Weblog is my identity exact like my fingerprint that uniquely identifies me...I found freedom in cyberspace, I got self confidence by writing a weblog...I am not only a citizen of my country but also a citizen of cyberspace... "

Iranian women write some of the most popular blogs. A female Iranian pioneer blogger [32] stated: "I could talk very freely about things I could never talk about in any other place, about subjects that are banned...Women in Iran cannot speak out frankly because of our Eastern culture and there are some taboos just for women, such as talking about sex or the right to choose your partner...I have the opportunity to talk about these things and share my experiences with others". ICT has enabled communication to transgress gender boundaries in a gender-segregated society. While female bloggers enjoy the freedom of speech outside of Iran through the exchange of information such as the criticism of political situations in Iran with their homeland bloggers, their postings receive responses from within Iran, a phenomenon not experienced before. Some female bloggers within Iran have posted their weblogs to those hosted outside of Iran, freely criticizing political issues in Iran.

3.2   The Iranian women active on the Internet

Although Iran is a male dominated society, there are a growing number of intellectual and educated women making demands for a constitutional change in law to support gender equality. This has been a major impetus for many female weblogs to grow rapidly. The recent demonstrations by Iranian women [43], organized by Iranian Women NGOs and female bloggers, are examples of their struggle for raising their social status through gender equality.

Although primary schools and high schools are all same-gender schools, universities in Iran do not have this limitation. The assimilation of young boys and girls in universities in smaller cities has created cultural changes in these cities.

More than 58% of the country's students are women [58]. Iranian women enrolled in universities and other educational institutions are becoming highly qualified specialists in the field of medicine and ICT. This has resulted in promoting women's freedom and equality rights. Women are becoming more socio-politically active and taking their first steps in campaigning for equal rights, a campaign that is one of the strongest social movements in the Middle East, especially in the Persian Gulf. Li [39] points out that the female population is involved in social activities despite the social limitations placed on their liberty by the constitution and other laws of this Islamic republic.

The literacy rate for Iranian female adults increased from 68% in 1999 to 82.6% in 2004, an increase of 14.6%. The rate for Iranian male adults in the same period increased by 5.7% from 82% to 87.7%.

Although the number of educated women in Iran increased dramatically, the employment rate decreased during this period. The statistics published by the

Statistical Center of Iran shows an interesting picture for changes in higher education in Iran [58]. According to UNICEF [62] women's employment, which had reached a high of 13.8% of total persons employed just before the Revolution (1979), has actually declined since (12% in 1996). The desire for equality in employment opportunities is frequently expressed in hundreds of Iranian women's weblogs.

3.3   Civil society and NGOs online

Mostashari [44] argues that NGOs are an important part of social movements within a civil society. In Iran, NGOs are playing an important role in strengthening the foundation of an emergent civil society. In the Middle East, Iran is considered as having a highly developed civil society. It has many different active NGOs ranging from women's issues, development (school construction, cultural centers), community health promotion and education, emerging health crises (HIV/AIDS education and support [52]), community social problems (runaway girls, street children), environmental, to economic (career services, skill training, micro-loans). For example, the NGO "The Society for the Protection of the Socially Disadvantaged Individuals" is actively present on the Internet which aims to increase awareness and enhance discussion on social issues [57].

Other civil society groups in Iran presently active in cultural activities with enormous presence on the Internet include "The Iranian Writers Association" (http://www.Kanoon-nevisandegan-iran.org). Defending freedom of speech is the most important goal of the Iranian writers association. Their members are very active both online and printed publications in Iran through their personal weblogs.

At the same time, the presence of Iranian women in different NGOs (the number of Iranian Women NGOs increased from 67 in 1997 to 480 in 2005), and on the Internet has provided them with important tools to battle the social injustices dictated by Islamic laws. Publishing Internet weblogs has been a release valve to express and communicate their current situation to their audience, and is a means by which to increase pressure on Iranian policy makers.

Shirin Ebadi, one of the most appreciated Iranian female NGO activists, a recipient of the Nobel Peace Prize in 2003, played a vigorous role in Iranian NGO activities by taking part in the formation of the two most important NGOs in Iran. One is the "The Children Rights Society" in 1994 and the other is the "Human Rights Society of Iran" in 2001. Activities of the Children's Rights Society include sending informative news through the Internet to schools and giving access to students in order to identify problems and society's responsibility toward the matter. These activities will have a long term effect on the culture of Iran.

Iranian women are active in guiding NGOs. They not only attend NGO meetings, but also promote a movement in support of women's rights. Many of these NGOs question their "male dominated" society and have requested equal rights for men and women. Many websites and weblogs support this demand. Articles posted which pertain to social injustices advocate for changes in the

Iranian constitution. Many female-oriented NGOs instigated demonstrations in support of women's rights in Iran such as the one in Tehran on June 12, 2006 which protested the violation of women's rights in the constitution and the general humiliation of women in Iranian society. Unfortunately, if not unexpectedly, many of the female activists were arrested [43].

The "Stop the violence against women" movement is gaining substantial momentum particularly with the engagement of bloggers who campaign for cultural change and equal rights for Iranian men and women. These are examples of successful female-oriented sites. Several Iranian women's rights activists recently initiated a wide campaign demanding an end to discriminatory laws against women in Iranian law. Their Campaign "One Million Signatures Demanding Changes to Discriminatory Laws" went online to attract more people to their agenda [5].

3.4   Online news

Weblogs related to news and political topics were among the first weblogs censored by the Iranian government. The judiciary decision to shut down many reformist papers [54, 61] was one of the main reasons for going online to publish what authorities censored. There were firm restrictions on the allowable content for media publication. The atmosphere of censorship and self-censoring on publications caused rapid development of weblogs to compensate for the current lack of sources of information. Many Iranian university students converted weblogs into an important source of political and human rights debates. Thousands of weblogs became a fast and reliable source for collecting and distributing news and political discussions in response to the lack of reliable sources of information since the government controls all of the major broadcasting institutions including national radio and TV. The judiciary helps to maintain state control of the media. The government's reaction to the proliferation of weblogs was to filter popular sites, weblogs, and arrest many blogging activists, especially those who posted articles challenging the political hardliners [1]. "We have suffered under unjust press laws," said one of the members of the Iranian branch of the Committee to Protect Journalists. "We are afraid of more to come with this new parliament" [1],

3.5   Mobile SMS

Another ICT tool widely used for communication and exchange of text, image, and video messages is the mobile cell phone. The Short Message Service (SMS), commonly known as "text messaging", is particularly popular among young people. It has transformed the means of communication within that generation for personal, social, business, and political purposes. A popular feature of mobile cell phones is their video transmission capability, the Multimedia Messaging Service (MMS), which makes it possible to capture visually events as they occur. The increased number of posted cell phone captured video clips on YouTube that originate from Iran attests to the importance of this type of ICT to support freedom of expression. Since most clips are politically motivated criticizing the current socio-political situation, they are not available through official media. In a recent video clip posted on YouTube called "No More Lies" [19] the video editor chides authorities for their persecution of Iranian young people who flout the dress code. The video is based on an Iranian underground rap song directed towards the political leadership and describes the official repression of young people. The 29-year-old editor of the video says that he simply pieced together snippets of videos and other images that were already on the Internet. The posting has received messages of support from Iranians around the world – including people inside Iran. "I've received many e-mails," he says. "I see there is a lot of discussion about [the video], it has already [more than] 95,000 hits. The message is the same – all Iranians are upset, there is lots of anger in their messages, they're really concerned" [19].

Surarez [59] argues that mobile cell phones have the potential to mobilize people and impose changes in certain aspects of political activities, including public participation in the political process. Regarding the use of SMS mobile messages in the Philippines Lallana [37] explains that text messaging is used as the medium for organizing rallies, spreading information, and stating political positions. SMS helped to develop the political account or interpretation of current events in the Philippines.

During the June 2005 Iranian presidential election, millions of young Iranians sent SMS messages to boycott the election or to support the other candidates. The massive use of SMS messages angered hardliners who appealed to the Ministry of Justice to ban SMS messaging [3].

4.   Iran state censorship on ICT

According to Reporters Without Borders' annual press freedom index [55], the Middle East region has one of the worst press freedom records in the world. In its press freedom ranking report, RWB announced that Denmark had the best press freedom record in 2005, while North Korea was placed at the bottom of the list (167th place). Some Middle Eastern countries ranked near the bottom including Iran (164th), Iraq (157th), Saudi Arabia (154th), and Syria (145th), while Lebanon (108th), United Arab Emirates (100th) and Qatar (90th) ranked somewhat higher. Kuwait had the best press freedom record in Arab world (85th).

Studies on Internet content filtering show systematic Internet filtering typically targets political and religious sites as well as those that promote gender equality and women's rights [50]. The Iranian government actively tracks and filters six major types of Internet sites. The sites under surveillance are primarily related to political and religious issues, ethnic minority groups, women's rights, or contain sexual content, or links to various international organisations. With the assistance of some well known international Internet companies [37], the government has implemented an effective Internet filtering mechanism to track millions of Internet users searching the Internet for the latest news and information that is otherwise censored by the traditional local media.

OpenNet Initiative[1] (ONI) [50] reports that Iran's Internet filtering system is one of the world's most substantial censorship regimes. It was adopted at a time of extraordinary growth both in general Internet usage and in the number of its citizens who write online in Farsi. ONI explains that blogs have become an important forum for personal, social and political expression in Iran, and the move to control this content is consistent with the regime's overall Internet censorship strategy. The filtering Internet content has a negative impact on accessibility and increases the digital divide between developed and developing countries. It has a direct and profound impact on NGOs, minority groups, religious groups and other marginalized voices in the country. It further increases the gap between genders and their ability to access information technology. A "gender digital divide" is the ultimate result of Iran's Internet filtering especially when the number of special interest group web sites is on the rise. These groups and other individuals use the Internet to express their concerns about the current situation and are using it as a venue by which to increase pressure on Iranian policy makers [26].

Historically, women in the Middle East and North Africa region have had low levels of formal political participation, and little access to the political process or to state power as well [56]. However, a growing number of studies about the region clearly demonstrate that women are extensively involved socially and politically in local and international NGOs, local and transnational social movements and networks, including feminist ones, and the media [, 43, 44, 28] where they are actively working towards women's empowerment. A review of ONI's documents shows that the filtering applied on sites related to women's rights is placed among the highest on the filtering list (fourth place).

Filtering and censorship are also applied to other ICTs such as satellite TVs. According to Guardian news agency report [60], millions of Iranians use satellite dishes to watch Western television. In a recent crack down, Iranian police seized thousands of dishes in an attempt to end access to uncensored programming. The government further restricted ICT access by declaring it illegal for internet service providers to offer broadband internet connections. The government justified this action as an effort to protect the country's Islamic beliefs from Western influence.

5.   ICT development in Iran vs. other Persian Gulf states

Over the last decade, governments in the Persian Gulf region invested heavily in ICT, enabling them to not only renew but expand their ICT infrastructures via the implementation of new technologies. During the period of 1995 to 2002, expenditure on equipment, software and telecom services in these countries was an estimated 5.2% of the combined GDP of these countries. Overall ICT

---

[1] The OpenNet Initiative is a collaborative partnership of four academic institutions: University of Toronto, Harvard Law School, University of Cambridge, and Oxford University.

investment during the period of 2000 to 2003 increased from 2.8% of the combined GDP to 3.02% [67].

ICT development in the Middle East was accomplished by the use of two different approaches. One approach was oppressive control of ICT development imposed by governments such as Iran in the area of Internet development, radio, and television broadcasting. In Iran, the telecommunication sector has been viewed as a key element of national military and economic security, too important to be left in private hands, whether domestic or foreign [24]. The second, more liberal approach, has been deployed by countries such as Bahrain, Kuwait, Oman, Qatar, and UAE. Their approach emphasized partial privatization of the state owned telecommunication sector. For example, Bahrain, one of the leading countries in ICT development, introduced telecommunication privatization in 2001 and opened its telecommunication sector to the private sector and foreign investors. The Kuwaiti Mobile Telecom company (Zain) became the largest private operator in the region providing wireless services to seven Middle Eastern and 15 sub-Saharan African countries [70].

The government of Qatar owns the telecommunications system Qatar Telecom (Q-Tel), which was partially privatized at the end of 1998. In 2004, the Supreme Council for Communication and Information Technology was created to enable and regulate the country's ICT sector [16, 4]. Similarly, the UAE's telecommunications entity "Etisalat" was 40% privatized [2]. Finally, in 2004, the Omani telecommunication sector opened its doors to the private sector as part of an agreement with the World Trade Organization (WTO). The government of Oman recently completed the privatization of Omantel [4], the country's primary provider of Internet services in October 2005 when its shares became available to foreign investors.

As Table 3 indicates, Bahrain, Kuwait, Qatar and United Arab Emirates not only had the most successful ICT implementation and digital access in the region, but also gained a ranking well above the world average. Iran on the other hand had the least ICT development in the region. According to ITU's 2007 dataset [29] Iran ranked in 105th place in ICT expansion among 183 economies. Countries such as United Arab Emirates, Qatar, Bahrain and Kuwait were ranked in 45th, 46th, 47th and 57th place respectively. This shows that the digital divide exists at both the regional and global levels.

Period	1996		2005	
Country	Internet	Mobile	Internet	Mobile
Bahrain	0.83	6.65	21.33	103.04
Iran	0.02	0.10	10.07	10.39
Kuwait	0.79	7.97	26.05	88.57
Oman	0.00	0.67	11.10	51.94
Qatar	0.99	5.69	28.16	92.15
Saudi Arabia	0.03	0.99	6.62	54.12
United Arab Emirates	0.39	7.78	31.08	100.86
World Average	1.27	2.5	15.25	34.02

Table 3: Mobile and Internet growth per 100 inhabitants, Source: ITU.

ICT development in Iran and Saudi Arabia warrants further comparison. As Table 3 indicates, Saudi Arabia saw enormous expansion in mobile development due to the establishment of a regulatory telecommunications authority in 2001 to implement ICT privatization [6]. However, Saudi Arabia's Internet growth is not particularly encouraging due to restrictive government policy in this area. According to ONI [50] and Reporters Without Borders [55], Iran and Saudi Arabia not only have ultimate control of Internet expansion but they also impose the most active filtering of Internet content [55, 50]. Iran, in contrast to Saudi Arabia, also imposes heavy governmental control on mobile expansion. Both Iran's Internet and Mobile growth show very limited growth despite the citizens' demands for services in these areas [31].

The Middle East's digital gap is best illustrated by comparing ICT expansion in Iran and Bahrain. As the Figures 1 (ICT index[2]) and 2 (Internet growth) indicate the digital gap between Iran and Bahrain increased by 1.2 fold during the period of 1995 to 2005. Two main reasons for this digital gap are: 1) Bahrain implemented partial privatization of its government owned telecom sector in 2001 and 2) Bahrain implemented a liberal policy towards Internet usage. According to the ONI report [50], Bahrain has the least amount and level of Internet filtering in the Persian Gulf region.

---

[2] ICT index is a measure of four main ICT infrastructure indicators: fixed telephone lines per 100 inhabitants, mobile cellular subscribers per 100 inhabitants, computers per 100 inhabitants and Internet users per 100 inhabitants.

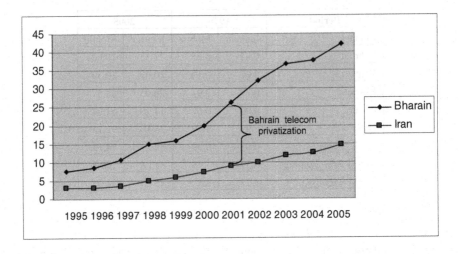

Figure 1: ICT index, the growth of digital divide between Iran and Bahrain. Source: ITU.

Many scholars view ICT privatization in developing countries as the key catalyst for modernization and expansion of public telecommunications networks [30, 27, 64, 11]. Specifically, the World Bank [67] emphasizes that governments can create competitive markets that grow faster, cost less, facilitate innovation, and respond better to user needs if they open their telecommunications markets through well-designed reforms resulting in increased private investment and ICT development.

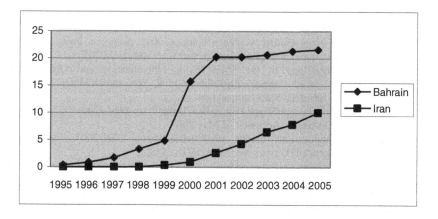

Figure 2: Internet users per 100 inhabitants. Source: ITU.

6.   Conclusion

During the last decade the digital divide increased between Iran and the rest of the world [29]. The digital gap is particularly pronounced when comparing Iran's position in ICT development with other Persian Gulf states. Even though Iran was one of the first countries in the region to go online [25] its Internet infrastructure development has lagged drastically from other countries in the region. State control of ICT development and Internet filtering by the Iranian government remain the two main impediments to Iran's ICT expansion. These barriers undermine future development of this industry. Perhaps more importantly, they negatively impact on Iranian citizens' freedom of expression and civil liberties.

The social need for individuals and groups to continue to interact and participate in social dialogue is growing with intensity in Iran despite governmental control and constraints on Internet content and activity. Government censorship drives a wedge in the ability of Iranians to communicate and share information thus inhibiting the development of social knowledge within their society. Because the mass of Iranian citizenry seeks secularization and liberalization of social and moral values [7] and mistrusts governmental information and intentions, they forge through and around political and physical obstacles by connecting with and creating cyber communities. These masses sift through opinions and facts to piece together a semblance of life outside their own world, seeking to learn about what they do not know. It is through this process that active and passive Internet users have developed a self and social awareness, a comprehension that they do not have what they need. They know that they do not know, and are willing to risk state sanctions to gain knowledge and inclusion in the global social network. Their journey of personal and cultural change continues in the face of official ignominy.

References

[1]   Blogging boom gives Iranian women a voice. (2004). American Press. Retrieved from: http://www.iranian.ws/cgi-bin/iran_news/exec/view.cgi/2/2705.

[2]   Information Technology in the UAE (n.d.). Liberalization and Deregulation. http://www.american.edu/carmel/lr2962a/liberal.html. Accessed 18 March 2008.

[3]   Iranian judiciary threatens SMS campaigners. (n.d.). http://www.iranmania.com/News/ArticleView/Default.asp?NewsCode=32749&NewsKind=Current%20Affairs. Accessed 12 May 2007.

[4]   Oman telecommunications market intelligence report 2006/2007. International Telecoms Intelligence ITU news magazine. ICT in Qatar, http://www.itu.int/itunews/manager/display.asp?lang=en&year=2006&issue=02&ipage=ICTinQatar&ext=html. Accessed 5 May 2008.

[5]   One million signatures demanding changes to discriminatory laws. (n.d.). http://www.we-change.org/spip.php?article19. Accessed 20 Januray 2008.

[6]   Telecom privatization and learnings in the kingdom of Saudi Arabia (2002). OECD Global Conference on Telecommunications Policy for the Digital Economy, Dubai, United Arab Emirates, January 2002 htttp://www.oecd.org/dataoecd/52/17/1810617.pdf. Accessed 25 April 2007. See also: Telecommunications in the Middle East, http://www.mideastlaw.com/article_telecommunications_in_the_middle_east.html. Accessed 25 April 2007.

[7]   Abootalebi, A. (2004). Iran's Struggle for democracy continues: An evaluation of twenty-five years after the revolution. *Middle East review of International Affairs Journal*, 8(2).

[8]   Alterman, J. B. (2005). IT comes of age in the Middle East: Focus on IT and diplomacy. *Foreign Service Journal*, December.

[9]   Amir-Ebrahimi, M. (2004). Bad Jens, Iranian Feminist Newsletter. http://www.badjens.com/rediscovery.html. Accessed 26 April 2008.

[10]   Baliamoune-Lutz, M. (2003). An analysis of the determinants and effects of ICT diffusion in developing countries. *Information Technology for Development*, 10, 151-169.

[11]   Bortolotti, B., D'Souza, J., Fantini, M., & Megginson, W.L. (2002). Privatization and the sources of performance improvement in the global telecommunications industry, *Telecommunications Policy*, 26, 243-268.

[12]   Brücher, H. & Baumberger, P. (2003). Using mobile technology to support eDemocracy. *Proceedings of the 36th Annual Hawaii International Conference on System Sciences*, Hawaii.

[13]   Burrows, R., Nettleton, S., & Pleace, N. (2000). Can public policy widen participation in cyberspace? Networks, interests and initiatives in North-West England, *Proceedings of DIAC 2000 Conference Shaping the Network Society*, Seattle.

[14]   Castells, M. (1996). *The rise of the network society*. Oxford: Blackwell.

[15]   Clift, S. (2004). *E-Government and democracy: Representation and citizen engagement in the Information Age*. United Nations. http://www.publicus.net/articles/cliftegovdemocracy.pdf. Accessed May 2007.

[16]   Dahel, R. (2001). Telecommunications privatization in Arab countries: An overview, Arab Planning Institute, http://www.arab-api.org/wps/wps0107.htm. 5 Accessed May 2008.

[17]   Emziper. (n.d.). The Persian RAP group. http://www.emziper.com. Accessed 10 June 2007.

[18] Escobar, A. (1999). Gender, place and networks: a political ecology of cyberculture. In W. Harcourt (Ed.), *Women@internet: creating new cultures in cyberculture* (pp. 31-54). London: Zed.

[19] Esfandiari, G. (2007). Internet video tells leaders to 'Leave The Youth Alone', http://www.rferl.org/featuresarticle/2007/08/29da6771-bb8b-4896-a8c4-738cf37c1679.html. Accessed 8 April 2007.

[20] Esfandiari, G. (2005). Reformists outraged over exclusion of candidates from presidential race. http://www.rferl.org/featuresarticle/2005/05/cbc7caf0-4671-4284-b587-fe6b7cba9318.html. Accessed 30 May 2006.

[21] Ferdinand, P. (Ed). *The Internet, Democracy and Democratization.* Frank Cass & Co: London.

[22] Fitzpartick, T. (2000). *Building the virtual state: information technology and institutional change.* Washington D.C.: Brooking Institute.

[23] Ghashghai, E. and Lewis, R. (2002). *Issues affecting Internet use in Afghanistan and developing counties in the Middle East.* Santa Monica, CA: RAND Corp.

[24] Gholami, R., Moshiri, S. and Lee, S. (2004). ICT and productivity of the manufacturing industries in Iran. *The Electronic Journal of Information Systems in Developing Countries*, 19(4), 14.

[25] Goodman, S., Burkhart, G., Foster, W., Press, L., Tan, Z., & Woodard, J. (1998). *The global diffusion of the Internet project: an initial inductive study.* Center for Information Strategy and Policy. http://mosaic.unomaha.edu/GDI1998/0CONTENT.PDF. Accessed January 2007.

[26] Guardian Unlimited (2005, September 14). Publish and be banned. http://blogs.guardian.co.uk/news/archives/2005/09/14/publish_and_be_banned.html. Accessed 8 November 2007.

[27] Gutiérrez, L.H. (2003). Regulatory governance in the Latin American telecommunications sector, *ScienceDirect*, 11(4), 225-240.

[28] International Freedom of Expression Exchange (n.d.). Government moving to silence Internet and web-log communications. http://www.ifex.org/frleftz/content/view/full/62403. Accessed 3 May 2008.

[29] International Telecommunications Union.(2007). Measuring the information society - ICT opportunity index and world telecommunication/ICT indicators.

[30] International Telecommunications Union. (1997). World telecommunication development report 1996/97: Trade in telecommunications. Geneva: ITU.

[31] Iran Daily (n.d.). Telecommunication round-up, April 5, 2007. http://www.iran-daily.com/1386/2809/html/focus.htm. Accessed 2 August 2007.

[32] Hermida, H. (2002). Web gives a voice to Iranian women. http://news.bbc.co.uk/2/hi/science/nature/2044802.stm See also: http://www.iranian.ws/cgi-bin/iran_news/exec/view.cgi/2/2705, Aessed July 2006.

[33] Jones, A. (2001). Wired world: Communications technology, governance and the democratic uprising. In F. Webster (Ed), *Culture and politics of the information age* (pp. 145-163). London: Routledge.

[34] Jupp, B. with Perri 6 (2001). Divided by Information? The 'digital divide' and the implication of the new meritocracy. London: Demos.

[35] Kalathil & Boas, T.C. (2003). *Open Networks, Closed Regimes: The impact of the Internet on Authoritarian Rule.* Washington, DC: Carnegie Endowment for Peace.

[36] King, J. (2006). Democracy in the information age. *Australian Journal of Public Administration* 65(2), 16–32.

[37] Lallana, C. (2004). SMS in Business and Government in the Philippines. ICT4D Monograph Series 1.

http://www.apdip.net/projects/e-government/capblg/casestudies/Philippines-Lallana.pdf. Accessed 20 April 2007.

[38] Lenihan, D. (2002). Realigning Governance: From E-Government To E-Democracy. *OECD E-government project Seminar: Vision, Responsiveness and Measurement*, Paris.

[39] Li, X. (2006). Iranian women's rights severely restricted, The WashingtonTimes, March 8.http://www.learningpartnership.org/en/news/press/030806iran. Accessed 2 May 2008.

[40] Lin, N. (2001). *Social capital: A theory of social structure and action.* Cambridge, UK: Cambridge University Press.

[41] Loader, B. (Ed). (1998). Cyberspace Divide. London: Routledge.

[42] Meier, R. (2000). Late blooming societies can be stimulated by IT. *Futures*, 32, 163-181.

[43] Mir-Hossein, Z. (2006). Is time on Iranian women protesters' side? Middle East Report Online, http://www.merip.org/mero/mero061606.html. See also: http://www.hrw.org/english/docs/2007/02/27/iran15416.htm. Accessed 18 August 2007.

[44] Mostashari, A. (2005). An introduction to non-governmental organizations (NGO). Management. Iranian Studies Group, MIT. web.mit.edu/isg/NGOManagement.pdf. Accessed 10 April 2007.

[45] Neyestani, M. R., (2006). Cultural and religious identities in era of information and communications globalization. *Turkish Journal of International Relations*, 4(4), 33-39.

[46] Norris, P. (2006). Democratic divide? The impact of the Internet on parliaments worldwide, *Journal of Communication*, 56(1), 218-219.

[47] Noveck, B.S. (2000). Paradoxical partners: electronic communication and electronic democracy. *Democratization*, 7(1), 18-35.

[48] Nwagwu, E. W. (2006). Integrating ICTs into the globalization of the poor developing countries. *Information Development*, 22(3), 167-179.

[49] Nye, J. S. and Kamarack, E. (1998). Preface. In J.S. Nye and E. Kamarack (Eds.), *The information revolution: Impacts of governance* (pp. 161-178). Princeton: John F Kennedy School of Government, Harvard University.

[50] OpenNet Initiative. (n.d.). Internet filtering in Iran in 2004-2005: A country study. http://www.opennetinitiative.net/studies/iran/
see also: http://opennetinitiative.net/bulletins/004/
http://opennet.net/research/regions/mena http://opennet.net/research/profiles/bahrain
http://opennet.net/studies/saudi/ Accessed 28 September 2007.

[51] Ott, D. & Rosser, M. (2000). The electronic republic? The role of the Internet in promoting democracy in Africa. *Democratization*,7(1), 137- 155.

[52] Persiaplus. (n.d.). Persians living positive. http://persiaplus.org/about_us.php. Accessed 18 January 2007.

[53] Quan-Haase, A., Wellman, B., with, Witte, J., and Hampton, K. (2002). Capitalizing on the Internet: Social contact, civic engagement, and sense of community. In B. Wellman & C. Haythornthwaite (Eds.), *Internet and everyday life* (pp. 291-324). Oxford: Blackwell.

[54] Rahi, I. B.(2003). Cyberdissent: The Internet in revolutionary Iran, *Middle East review of International Affairs (MERIA) Journal*, 7(3). http://meria.idc.ac.il/journal/2003/issue3/jv7n3a7.html. Accessed 5 April 2007.

[55] Reporters Without Borders (2005). Press freedom report. http://www.rsf.org/rubrique.php3?id_rubrique=554

See also: http://www.rsf.org/article.php3?id_article=15201. Accessed 18 October 2007.

[56] Rizzo, H. and K. Meyer. (2006). Women's dissent in the Middle East: Political and civic engagement and gender and religious norms. *Paper presented at the Annual Meeting of the American Sociological Association*, Montreal.

[57] Spasdi (n.d.). The organization for the protection and assistance of socially disadvantaged individuals. http://www.spasdi.org/eng-pagas/report80.htm. Accessed 5 January 2007.

[58] Statistical Center of Iran. http://www.parstimes.com/statistics/. Accessed 29 September 2007.

[59] Suarez, S. (2005). Mobile democracy: Text messages, voter turnout, and the 2004 Spanish general election. *Prepared for Annual Meeting of the American Political Science Association,* September 1-4.

[60] Tait, R. (2007, November 23). Iran bans fast internet to cut west's influence. *The Guardian.*http://www.guardian.co.uk/technology/2006/oct/18/news.iran. Accessed 8 November 2007.

[61] Tarock, A. (2001). The muzzling of the liberal press in Iran, *Third World Quarterly*, 22(4), 585-602.

[62] UNICEF. (2007). Islamic Republic of Iran - The big picture. http://www.unicef.org/infobycountry/iran.html. Accessed 8 January 2008.

[63] United Nations Conference on Trade and Development (UNCTAD). (2004). E-Commerce and Development Report 2004. http://r0.unctad.org/ecommerce/ecommerce_en/edr04_en.htm. Accessed 22 April 2007.

[64] Wellenius, B. (1999). Mitigating regulatory risk in telecommunications In Public Policy for the Private Sector. Washington, D.C.: The World Bank Group.

[65] Wellman, B. (1999). The network community. In B. Wellman (Ed.), *Networks in the global village* (pp. 1- 48). Boulder, CO: Westview.

[66] Wheeler, D. (2006). Empowering publics: Information technology and democrat ization in the Arab World—lessons from Internet cafés and beyond.Oxford Internet Institute, Research Report, 11.

[67] World Bank. (2006). Information and communications for development, global trends and policies.

[68] World Bank. (2005). Financing information and communication infrastructure needs in the developing world: Public and private roles.

[69] World Bank. (2005). World development report. http://econ.worldbank.org/WBSITE/EXTERNAL/EXTDEC/EXTRESEARCH/EXTWDRS/EXTWDR2005/0,,menuPK:477681~pagePK:64167702~piPK:64167676~theSitePK:477665,00.html. Accessed 18 April 2007.

[70] Zain (n.d.). CEO message, http://www.zain.com/muse/obj/lang.default/portal.view/content/About%20us. Accessed 20 April 2008.

[71] Zoroastrian Organizations. (n.d.). http://www.avesta.org/zgroups.html See also: http://www.farsinet.com/ici/ and http://www.isl.org.uk/farsi/index.php Accessed 18 July 2007.

A NO-IPR MODEL AS SOLUTION TO REUSE AND UNDERSTANDING OF INFORMATION SYSTEMS

Kai K. Kimppa
University of Turku, Finland

Abstract   This work in progress paper argues that a reason why reuse of software components in information systems development is not more common and why users do not and cannot understand the systems they use partly depends on the implementation of the current IPR[1] system and the repercussions it has for the proprietary software model. A full blown anti-IPR system, modified from the GNU GPL and CC Attribution-ShareAlike licenses, is offered in its place. Furthermore, reasons why both reuse of software components and understanding of software would be enhanced are given. Also, some business models viable in that environment are tentatively suggested. Finally, how to—at least partially—implement this in the current IPR environment is explored.

Keywords: Information systems, information systems development, social informatics, work informatics, IPRs, free source software, GNU GPL, object-oriented development

1.   Introduction

The potential of the object-oriented development approach has largely not come to fruition. The idea of reusing objects easily as modules for further development has only been realised within organisations, if even there. This results in reinventing the wheel again and again, even for very similar purposes. The reason for this is obvious: it is not a fault of the object-oriented programming paradigm, on the contrary, object-oriented development strongly supports the idea, but rather it is due to the Intellectual Property Rights (IPRs) system in use in previously Western societies but now globally due to World Intellectual Property Organization (WIPO) negotiations and World Trade Organization (WTO)/ TRIPS (trade-related aspects of intellectual property rights) treaties.

On top of this, as many (e.g., [1-3]) have proposed, the users of information systems typically do not understand how the information system works. The user interface does not use the language of the users, nor does it inform the users of the

---

[1] IPR is a loaded term which presupposes that immaterial things can be owned. In this paper immaterial is often used in place of IPR.

Please use the following format when citing this chapter:

Kimppa, K.K., 2008, in IFIP International Federation for Information Processing, Volume 282; *Social Dimensions of Information and Communication Technology Policy*; Chrisanthi Avgerou, Matthew L. Smith, Peter van den Besselaar; (Boston: Springer), pp. 319–325.

system logic which is used to give the users an understanding of the way the system works.

This further complicates the situation by transferring control of the information system from the user to an unidentifiable party, often the information system itself which then seemingly is in control [4-5]. This is visible through expressions such as "the system told me to do this", which of course is true in a sense, but the users often actually do not know who or what is behind the requirements of the system.

At the organisational level this is visible through lack of user confidence, unnecessary work being done, and work being done wrong. Even though participatory design and other more user-centred design methodologies (such as SSM, socio-technical method(s), trade unionist approaches, etc., for a comparison of some of these see [6]) suggest heavy user participation in the design of the systems, the participation has not actualised except in isolated cases and where it has, the lower level understanding of the now typically wide variety of information systems in use remains impossible. There are various reasons for this, of course, one of which being the inability to actually view and modify the specifications and the code itself..It is clear, however, that if problems remain, a knowledgeable worker in an organisation could understand both the working system as well as the information system better than an external developer – and in the current situation this kind of modification remains extremely rare and hard to accomplish.

In work informatics research, an operationalisation of the social informatics research methodology (or methodologies) [7] made famous by Rob Kling[2], the main idea has been to use what works to solve the issues raised. One potential direction to take to solve some of the problems presented is adaptation of the no-IPRs model proposed by Kimppa [8], which would change the current information systems development situation dramatically.

The current proprietary model, based on the IPR structure in place can be seen as a cause of why the potential of reuse of software components is not happening. The current IPR model encourages closing source code and its parts from both the public and competition. This, naturally, leads to "inventing the wheel" again in a situation where someone other than the original creator of the system needs a similar part.

The current proprietary model does not encourage user participation. Users are not privy to the internal functioning of the information systems they use as the proprietary model keeps the source code a trade secret and thus deprive the users from both understanding of the system and the possibility to adapt it better to their and their colleagues use.

There are, of course, current alternatives, such as Free Libre Open Source Software (FLOSS) and Creative Commons (CC) Attribution ShareAlike models. Unfortunately they have not spread widely, and the current IPR systems do not

---

[2] See e.g., "Social Informatics: An Information Society for All? In Remembrance of Rob Kling" for the various ways in which social informatics has been developed [20].

encourage their use and at times even actively prohibit it. The situation is contradictory to their use, as copyright for any "literary" work such as software is the default position and the creator of software needs to actively seek to bypass this to enable free (or open) use of the software they create. Thus, the playing field is by default heavily tilted towards the proprietary model.

There are also plenty of examples of clearly using IPRs to prefent FLOSS or CC usage even in situations which previously would have been possible, typically due to the strengthening of copyright via methods such as DMCA (Digital Millennium Copyright Act), its European counterpart, DRM (Digital Rights Management) systems, etc. Some illustrative cases include Vivendi vs. BnetD (see e.g. [9]) where DCMA was used to stop reverse-engineering. Another example provided by Lessig [10] was the creation of the the Grey album by mixing the White and the Black albums.

2.   A suggested solution

Kimppa [8] has proposed a no-IPRs model that would closely resemble the Free Software Foundation's GNU GPL model (e.g., [11]) to completely replace the current IPR legislation. The idea is not to offer a new model, but to replace the current model with the default being no IPRs instead of strong protection. In the model any published material would be free to be used and further developed by any other, be it an organisation or an individual user. This does not mean that information systems would magically become available at no cost. Development of systems would still be necessary for various reasons. Of course, it would mean rethinking of current models of software business. The benefits and draw backs of the system would undoubtedly be various; some are presented in this work in progress paper.

2.1   Benefits and draw backs from organisational perspective

First, any modules written for any published information system would be reusable for any other system needing them. That would significantly cut back in the need to recode same or similar parts (e.g., [12]). The main benefit of the object-oriented thinking in software development could be fully utilised by extensive object libraries as well as larger parts of systems available for the basis of new or further developed systems. As good systems are designed to strengthen the business strategy of an organisation and is thus dependant on the aims and working practices of that particular organisation; almost no information system is directly applicable to another organisation. This helps in keeping the benefit from internal/out sourced development alive even in an environment where parts of systems could easily be copied or adapted to another organisation.

Management of information system projects would fall more squarely within the companies needing the software. This would mean inside development for integration combined with selecting from the existing what can be integrated to the needed product. This would, however, mean more selection possibilities since there would be no need to take fully outside developed systems, which would translate to more choice than currently exist. This would also offer a possibility to integrate other modules than the ones offered by the proprietary company (i.e., any existing or any that are wanted and can be created either through buying from an outside supplier or through inside development). A possibility to tie information system development more firmly to the strategic goals of the company would also emerge.

CIOs (Central Information Officers) and IT Managers would be more capable of supporting the business strategy if they were able to make more concrete choices between modules they choose for the organisations information systems (for a call for CIOs to understand business strategy and be able to better support it see [13]). With the possibility to use previous modules and the need to understand them creating information systems which would support the general strategy of the organisation would be more important than the capability "to make the best deal" for the software obtained. New skills in the managerial portfolio of an information system development manager would become valuable and this would likely also change the education required for the position.

Cooperation instead of competition would become a more viable option if others could access the software in any case. Thus, the costs of implementing a system could be shared with others operating in the same field. This would be especially beneficial for SMEs (Small and Medium Sized Enterprises) which now are largely dependent on certain distributors for their internal software and cannot afford internal development.

Of course, for off-the shelf software making end user products this would mean hard times—at least with the current business models. Luckily other models exist already. Models such as offering "handholding" services [14] such as help desk services from the producer of the software (as is done by Red Hat or other major GNU/Linux distributors), or further development of the software package, where the customer should expect to be able to get better service than from an external competitor.

Trying to hold the current model of many copies at low price would likely not be a profitable model, however. The model presented by Kimppa [8] would likely be closer to the mark (figure 1).

As noted in the figure 1, the first sale of a new system would be the main profit maker. This would entail finding new ways for producing systems, such as finding partners willing of cooperation to finance a new system instead of attempting to compete with each other.

2.2   Benefits for user understanding of systems

As previously used modules could be reused widely, some functions of the information systems would already be widely tested with other users, thus making it simpler for the next users to take the system in use. Also, similar functions would be more likely to function in a same manner in other systems if the same generic pattern of design would be reused instead of reinvented—a feature commonly found in various usability heuristics (e.g., [15]).

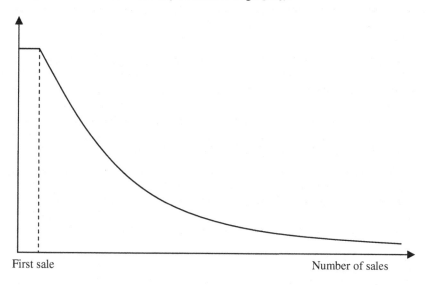

First sale   Number of sales

Figure 1: The new profit model for regular sales. Note: other functions that would add profit such as modifications and support are excluded [8].

For the more ambitious user even the internal functioning of the system would be—at least theoretically—available. As "[u]sers [would] no longer be at the mercy of one programmer or company which owns the sources and is in sole position to make changes" [15] they could actually make relevant changes to the information systems they need or want to use. This would give them a wholly new understanding of the systems they use.

With the return of more internal development and organisation directed development the needs of the users could be taken into account more in the development process. As the directors of information system development processes would be internal to the organisations, their understanding of the needs of the organisation and its employees would be greater than in the current out sourced system development model.

3.   Current possibilities to adapt the model

Entirely internal development is typically not an option in the current systems development climate. Most organisations are not mainly systems development organisations and thus do not have the competence needed for extensive system development from within the organisation nor is it plausible to expect this to change.

Entirely external development would likely encounter problems as well. It would essentially be the same situation as exists with the current proprietary system development models: understanding of the system would remain mainly in the hands of the external organisation while the understanding of the work processes would remain internal to the organisation needing the information system.

Free Libre Open Source Software development offers possibilities even in the current IPR environment. For this to work, however, cooperation between organisations would seem to be the key factor. This would provide both the internal understanding of work processes, external help for the coding available from 1) external companies integrating existing FLOSS and coding the necessary parts for the system, 2) enthusiasts in the field, and 3) even "competition" in the field who need the same or similar information system.

This would be especially beneficial for SMEs, however public sector organisations such as hospitals could also benefit by cooperation instead of competition. Unfortunately, the current proprietary system and its unfortunate side-effects, such as requirements for competition from both EU and national decision makers, do not encourage this.

4.   Discussion

In this work in progress paper an alternative to the current IPR regime was briefly introduced (for more details, see [8, 16-19]). It was argued that the alternative could bring benefits through enabling the reuse of software components and systems as well as increasing the understanding of information systems by the users and organisations. Some reasons, such as the openness of the source code as well as the encouragement to cooperation, were discussed. Unfortunately, in the current environment, this model is unlikely to be largely adapted, although some signs of its usability for SMEs are evident. Actual examples in the field of the current situation are clearly needed for verification/falsification of the proposals made.

The logical next step for this research would be to look into these issues to see whether the model is actually used (the author has seen some minor examples), and especially whether the proposed benefits present themselves in such cases.

References

[1]   Norman, D. A. (1988-1989). *The design of everyday things*, New York: Doubleday.
[2]   Eriksson, I. & Nurminen, M. I. (1991). Doing by learning: Embedded application systems. *Journal of Organizational Computing*, 1, 4, 323-339.
[3]   Faulkner, C. (1998). *The essence of human-computer interaction*, Essex: Prentice Hall.
[4]   Langefors, B. (1970). *Theoretical analysis of information systems*. Lund: Student Litteratur.

[5]   Kimppa K. K., Lahtiranta J., & Nurminen, M. I. (2007). Agentization in computing: How to ameliorate history today? *History of Nordic computing* - HiNC2.

[6]   Iivari J., Hirschheim R., & Klein K (1998). A paradigmatic analysis contrasting information systems development approaches and methodologies, *Information Systems Research*, 9(2), pp. 164-193.

[7]   Nurminen, M. I. (2006). Work Informatics – An operationalisation of social informatics. In Berleur, J., Nurminen, M. I., and Impagliazzo, J. (Eds.), *Social informatics: An information society for all? In Remembrance of Rob Kling* (pp. 407—416). Boston: Springer.

[8]   Kimppa, K. K. (2007). Problems with the justification of intellectual property rights in relation to software and otherdigitally distributable media. PhD thesis. University of Turku, Finland

[9]   Corante (2004). Major DMCA/EULA Loss - District Court Clueless in BNETD Case, Corante, *Tech News*. October 01, 2004, Available at http://www.corante.com/importance/archives/026273.php. Accessed 28 April, 2005.

[10] Lessig, L. (2004). The black and white about grey Tuesday. http://www.lessig.org/blog/archives/001754.shtml. Accessed 25 August, 2006.

[11] Free Software Foundation (1996-2007). The free software definition, http://www.gnu.org/philosophy/free-sw.html. Accessed 30 November, 2007.

[12] Stallman, R. M. (1992). Why software should be free, http://www.gnu.org/philosophy/shouldbefree.html. Accessed 30 November, 2007.

[13] Sambamurthy, V., Straub, D. W., and Watson, R. T. (2001). Managing IT in the digital era. In Dickson, G. W. and DeSanctis, G. (Eds.), *Information Technology and the Future Enterprise: New Models for Managers* (pp. 282—305). New Jersey: Prentice Hall.

[14] Stallman, R. M. (1985-2007). The GNU manifesto, http://www.gnu.org/gnu/manifesto.html. Accessed 30 November, 2007.

[15] Nielsen, J. (1993). *Usability engineering*, Boston: Academic Press.

[16] Kimppa, K. K. (2004). Consequentialist considerations of intellectual property rights in software and other digitally distributable media. Ethicomp 2004, *Challenges for the Citizen of the Information Society*, Apr 2004.

[17] Kimppa, K. K. (2004). Intellectual property rights – or rights to the immaterial – in digitally distributable media gone all wrong?. In Lee Freeman & A. Graham Peace (Eds.) *Information Ethics: Privacy and Intellectual Property* (pp 53—67). Hershey: Idea Group.

[18] Kimppa, K. K. (2004). Intellectual property rights in software—Justifiable from a liberalist position? The free software foundations position in comparison to John Locke's concept of property. In Richard A. Spinello, Herman T. Tavani (Eds.), *Intellectual Property Rights in a Networked World: Theory and Practice*. (pp 67—82). Hershey: Idea Group.

[19] Kimppa, K. K. (2005). Kantian duty ethics compared with current intellectual property rights laws. Ethics of New Information Technology: Proceedings of the Sixth International Conference of Computer Ethics: Philosophical Enquiry (CEPE2005).

[20] Berleur, J., Nurminen, M. I., & Impagliazzo, J. (Eds.) (2006). *Social informatics: An information society for all? In remembrance of Rob Kling*, Boston: Springer.

MEASURING INFORMATION SOCIETIES: A CRITICAL STUDY OF THE INFOSTATE FRAMEWORK

Anouk Mukherjee
London School of Economics and Political Science, UK

Abstract   In this chapter, I use critical theory to explore the underlying philosophy of the infostate framework for measuring information societies in developing countries. I find the hallmarks of instrumental reason when examining the framework and argue that this risks giving policymakers a false sense of clarity when shaping poverty reduction policies in developing countries. Given the influence of the infostate framework on the shaping of policy, this could have serious negative consequences for international efforts. I suggest a thorough critical study of a wider set of frameworks used for policymaking. The study could form the basis for the development of alternative frameworks for the measurement of information societies in developing countries.

Keywords: Information society indicators, measuring ICT for development, infostate framework, critical theory, instrumental reason

1.   Introduction

Information and communications technologies (ICT) have come to assume an important role in international efforts to reduce poverty at the beginning of the 21st century. In 2003 and 2005, the United Nations held two world summits on the information society (WSIS) to support the Millennium Development Goals (MDG). These conferences produced a plan of action upon which efforts to close the global "digital divide" could be based. One of the key objectives of the plan is to develop benchmarking and indicators to measure information societies and hence assess progress towards internationally agreed goals. This undertaking is no doubt a major challenge and has revealed deep divisions in the global discourse on ICT and development.

Countless frameworks to measure the global information society have been constructed. Kim and Nolan [9] present them in three broad categories: the economic, the technological, and the information stock approach. A survey of literature suggests that frameworks used in practice are generally based on an economic approach that is focused on the growing information vector in economic activity. In essence, the economic approach sees ICT as powerful tools for productivity growth which drive overall economic growth which in turn contribute

Please use the following format when citing this chapter:

Mukherjee, A., 2008, in IFIP International Federation for Information Processing, Volume 282; *Social Dimensions of Information and Communication Technology Policy*; Chrisanthi Avgerou, Matthew L. Smith, Peter van den Besselaar; (Boston: Springer), pp. 327–334.

to the overall well being of society. Advocates of this approach frequently point to the economic success of ICT-rich societies such as the US as evidence for support [17]. This concentration on economic approaches has become an increasing preoccupation for those promoting a broader theoretical treatment of the problem.

Concern over the lack of a unified meta-theory in the measurement of the information society has been voiced for some time [6, 9, 10, 11, 24, 25]. Grigorovici et al. [6] are particularly critical of the self-referential nature of many frameworks used by international organisations. Other critics argue that past approaches have been too fractured and specialised to provide a comprehensive framework for the measurement of the information society [3, 11]. However, the call for broader theories is being heeded and some very diverse and original frameworks for improved measurement of the global information society have been developed [3, 14, 25]. For instance, Petrič [14] has elaborated a framework based on Habermas' theory of communicative action to measure the use of personal Web sites in Slovenia.

In this chapter I explore the basis for the criticism of the current dominant economic approaches. I critically examine one of the leading economic frameworks and discuss its limitations. By gaining a better understanding of the challenges faced by those developing frameworks, I hope to inform further research into better ways of measuring information societies.

I am guided in my reflection by critical theory, and more specifically the ideas or "fragments" exposed by Theodor Adorno and Max Horkheimer [1]. I specifically chose to explore the thinking behind the infostate framework, which is used to study the link between ICT and development [18, 20] and used by the International Telecommunication Union (ITU) for its ICT Opportunity Index.[1] The application by the ITU gives the infostate framework wider recognition and therefore could have significant influence on policymaking and the development of other frameworks.

I draw from semi-structured guided interviews with experts who construct and use frameworks for the measurement of information societies: the Chief of the ICT Policy and Analysis Section, United Nations Conference on Trade and Development (UNCTAD); Associate Economic Affairs Officer, UNCTAD; Visiting Fellow and creator of the infostate framework, International Development Research Centre (IDRC); and independent telecoms policy consultant, Antelope Consulting.

The rest of the chapter is structured as follows: Section 2 provides a description of the infostate framework and traces its origin and use. Section 3 discusses the biases and limitations of the framework, drawing from a critical theoretical perspective; in particular, my critique highlights the instrumental reasoning underlying the framework and its use and comments on the risks such an approach implies for the cause of development. Finally, in the conclusions I suggest how this research could be taken further.

---

[1] See: http://www.itu.int/ITU-D/ict/publications/ict-oi/2007/index.html.

2.   The infostate framework and model

Orbicom (Network of UNESCO Chairs in Communications) developed the infostate framework in response to the G8 Digital Opportunities Task (DOT) Force Genoa Plan of Action of 2001. The project was sponsored in large part by the Canadian government through the Canadian International Development Agency (CIDA) but also had the backing of the InfoDev Programme of the World Bank [18]. The framework was developed to satisfy the need for "adequate approaches to quantify and monitor ICT-related gaps between info-poor and info-rich countries" [17]. The perception was that there were no satisfactory frameworks available for policymakers and a new one needed to be constructed urgently. The infostate framework is aimed at policymakers at all levels of governance - donors, investors, and NGOs - and seeks to guide policymaking or investment choices and also to evaluate the results of these choices over time [18, 20].

The infostate framework is based on the assumption of a very strong link between ICT and development. Evidence for this link is drawn from research on ICT and productivity in developed countries. In the first publication exposing the framework, Sciadas, cites research from 2000 on the US economy by Jorgensen and Stiroh [17] for support. The experts I interviewed confirmed their belief in this strong link as does the latest publication updating the framework: "Concerted efforts have been devoted to the specific issue of untangling the linkages between the diffusion and the use of ICTs and economic development. Almost instinctive early beliefs that ICTs represent a powerful new addition to the development arsenal are increasingly coupled with hard evidence that this is so" [20].

The fundamental belief that ICT can drive growth makes it the focus of the infostate framework. The framework follows a very clear and linear logic based on neo-classical economic theory where the distinction between the consumptive and productive capacity of an economy is crucial. The standard of living - and by extension well-being - of a society depends largely on its current consumption of goods and services. Its well being in the future, however, is ensured by the productive capacity of the economy. Increased well-being therefore can be reached by growth of the productive capacity which also translates to economic development. ICT participates in this development both as a consumptive and productive asset. For example, home broadband would be considered a consumable service and the word processing skills of an office worker a productive asset. An infostate is defined as the level at which ICT is integrated in economic activity as both consumptive and productive assets in a given economy [17].

In order to make this framework operational in practice, an infostate needs to be broken down into measurable entities. Consumptive and productive ICT assets are subdivided into categories that are in turn subdivided repeatedly until an elementary measure is reached. For example, productive ICT assets can be subdivided into two categories – capital and labour. Capital can then further be subdivided into networks and machinery. This exercise can be repeated until one arrives to measurable items such as cables, keyboards, and routers. The resulting tree structure represents the model applied for determining the infostate of an economy. The aggregation of indicators makes the infostate a composite index. In this manner, the infostate indicator is similar to the consumer price index (CPI). An infostate can be measureable over time and could allow comparison between countries at a given point in time [17].

In 2001, the model was used to measure the infostate of countries representing 99% of the world's population. Countries in Western Europe, North America, Australia, New Zealand, Japan, and Singapore had the highest infostate, while Myanmar, Bangladesh, and the poorest nations in Africa scored the lowest. Not surprisingly, the results also showed a strong correlation between infostate and per capita GDP [18].

3.   Critique of the infostate framework

To begin, the development of such a framework would have to overcome one fundamental problem of measuring information societies. Without rich and appropriate data, understanding the phenomenon is almost like guesswork, while without an appropriate framework, the collection and representation of data is difficult. Menou in 1985 likened this to a "chicken and egg" problem [10] and Grigorovici et al. echoed the analogy in 2002 [6]. In order to overcome this challenge, the infostate framework was designed to be "conducive to empirical application" and to make "maximum sense out of existing data sources" [19].

In practice, such an approach carries the risk of becoming self-referential. The result of the 2001 study ranking countries by infostate finds a strong link between ICT and economic growth. Therefore, according to the publication, the link is confirmed and the framework validated for application. The empirical application of the framework reveals that the underlying assumption is true and the framework is valid.

The assumption of a universal link between ICT and development is questionable. The link in the infostate framework is a static set of relationships between ICT, productivity growth, and human development. Sciadas frequently points to the success of developed nations that have ICT virtually penetrating all economic activity as evidence of this link [17]. In this perspective, the success of nations is judged on the basis of various economic indicators such as GDP, technological infrastructure, and innovation. The nations are then classified accordingly as developed, developing, or least developed. The logic follows a top-down approach where economies at the bottom should emulate those at the top in order to progress and attain the same levels of success. Critics see this as a narrow economic view of development because it disregards evidence that one cannot predict the impact of introducing ICT into a certain social context based on the results in a different social context [2, 4, 21]. Being based on the experience of ICT and economic growth in the West, the infostate framework could be overlooking key differentiating factors in developing countries. One of these factors is what Kim and Nolan call the "technoeconomic heritage" of different countries and regions [9]. No consideration for such factors is provided in the elaboration of the infostate framework [17, 19]. In fact, it is founded upon the basic assumption that the laws of society are universal and constant over time. This is despite the fact that Sciadas acknowledges the use of the framework may only be useful when comparing similar economies [17].

Heeks and Kenny state that the assumption of a universal link between ICT and development ignores the failures of information systems in developed nations [7]. There is a significant lack of evidence that ICTs are radically improving the efficiency and effectiveness of organisations. Heeks and Kenny further argue that developed countries would benefit most from the global diffusion of ICT since it embodies Western institutions - or "scripts" [22] - and the production of the technology is dominated by developed nations.

Sciadas believes that ICT presents an "historic" opportunity for the evolution of our societies [17, 20]. This perception is consistent with the idea that ICT has changed the rules of history and its arrival represents a break from the past. The belief that the classic stages of economic development - the historical path of the West - are no longer valid is widely held by the interviewed experts. They believe developing nations can "leapfrog" the classic stages of development by exploiting the benefits of ICT. They further argue that ICT is changing the rules of international development economics and acknowledge it is an emerging phenomenon. But how can one rely on a framework to measure an emerging phenomenon over time when the foundations of the framework itself are expected to shift?

The context surrounding development of the infostate framework can be a cause of bias. Specifically, the urgency given by politicians to measuring the global information society has favoured those approaches that can deliver results in a speedy and short-term, cost effective manner. This situation can make extensive and thoughtful research into the issue difficult [3]. Furthermore, frameworks based on broader social theory face the danger of not being taken seriously because they are not universally recognised. They therefore risk being rejected by international organisations for practical use in measuring the global information society [11]. In this environment, economic frameworks such as infostate are perceived as having a solid empirical track record in the West and will likely carry favour by policymakers.

This critical reflection on the infostate framework suggests that its development may have been grounded in instrumental reason. Under instrumental reason, moral reason is disconnected from the subjects' aspirations and desires. Each person or living being is considered to be an object of science. These objects are catalogued, standardised, and quantified into an abstract form of reality which can be manipulated for the purposes of science, industry, and utility in general. In order to have the power of prediction over space and time, instrumental reason consists of universal laws that are presumed to be all encompassing. It ignores the specificities of context whether geographical or temporal and considers anything that eludes it to be of mythological or superstitious origin. Instrumental reason has come to replace the emancipatory reason of the Enlightenment and has dictated the subservience of human consciousness to economic and political interest. Instrumental reason provides society with a sense of false clarity and always uses "the devices of familiarity and straightforward dismissal to avoid the labour of conceptualization" [1].

The notions of universality, detachment from context, tacit and unfounded assumptions, and praxis – hallmarks of instrumental reason - appear through the lens of critical theory when examining the infostate framework. Universality, detachment from context, and tacit and unfounded assumptions take root in the link between ICT and development used by the framework. Praxis is present in the concurrent development and validation of the framework in a pressurised political environment. These predispositions may be inappropriate grounding for a framework that measures a complex and evolving phenomenon that is intricately linked to the historical path of nations. Consequently, the embedded instrumental reason risks giving policymakers a false sense of clarity when shaping poverty reduction policies in developing countries. This would imply that the infostate framework could misguide international efforts and perhaps even work against the goals of the Millennium Declaration. Such a failure would not only be a major setback for international organisations fighting for global equity, but also a tragedy for those suffering the blight of poverty.

4.   Conclusions

Although the efforts to measure the information society take root in the highly desirable goal of poverty reduction, as embodied by the MDGs, the philosophical underpinnings of these efforts should be critically examined. This is vital especially given the failures of the past in reducing poverty on the planet.

In this chapter, I have explored the infostate framework that is currently used by the ITU for its influential ICT opportunity index. This preliminary examination suggests that its roots in instrumental reason limit its ability to help in unpacking the complex relationship between ICT, poverty, and development. It is principally handicapped by its unawareness of the wider social, political, cultural, and historical contexts in the measurement of the information society. The solidity of the framework is further undermined by its use to validate the questionable assumption of the strong link between ICT and development – an assumption upon which the framework itself is based.

If these patterns of thinking are confirmed and are shared with other dominant frameworks used to measure the global information society, then questions should be raised about their potential effectiveness. Can such frameworks provide an accurate and meaningful picture to help guide poverty reduction in developing countries? Could they in fact work against the achievement of MDG objectives and reinforce existing disparities?

These questions could form the basis of a more thorough critical study supported by empirical evidence. It should cover a wide spectrum of frameworks that are in use today to measure the information society in developing countries. From this study, alternative multidisciplinary approaches could be developed in order to provide a broader perspective on the problem at hand.

References

[1]   Adorno, T. W., M. Horkheimer, & J. Cumming (1997). *Dialectic of enlightenment*, London: Verso Editions.

[2]   Avgerou, C. (2002). *Information systems and global diversity*, Oxford: Oxford University Press.

[3]   Barzilai-Nahon, K. (2006). Gaps and bits: Conceptualizing measurements for digital divides", Information Society, 22(5), 269-278.

[4]   Ciborra, C. & Lanzara, G. F. (1994). Formative contexts and information technology: Understanding the dynamics of innovation in organizations", *Accounting, Management and Information Technology*, 4(2), 61-86.

[5]   Freeman, C. (1997). The "national system of innovation" in historical perspective. In D. Archibugi and J. Michie.(Eds.) (pp. 24-49) *Technology, Globalisation and Economic Performance*, Cambridge: CUP.

[6]   Grigorovici, D. M., Schement, J.R., & Taylor, R.D. (2002) .Weighing the intangible: Towards a framework for information society indices, E-Business Research Center Working Paper.

[7]   Heeks, R. & Kenny, C. (2002). ICTs and development: Convergence or divergence for developing countries? Proceedings of the 7th International Working Conference of IFIP WG9.4, 29-31 May 2002, Bangalore, India.

[8]   Held, D. (1980). Introduction to critical theory: Horkheimer to Habermas, London: Hutchinson.

[9]   Kim, S. & P. D. Nolan (2006). Measuring social "Informatization": A factor analytic approach, *Sociological Inquiry*, 76 (2), 188-209.

[10]   Menou, M. J. (1985). An overview of social measures of information, *Journal of the American Society for Information Science*, 36 (3), 169-177.

[11]   Menou, M. J. & R. D. Taylor (2006). A "Grand Challenge": Measuring information societies, *Information Society*, 22(5), 261-267.

[12]   Mowshowitz, A. (1980). Ethics and cultural integration in a computerized world, *Human Choice and Computers*, 2, 251-269.

[13]   Mowshowitz, A. (1981). On approaches to the study of social issues in computing, *Communications of the ACM*, 24 (3), 146-155.

[14]   Petrič, G. (2006). Conceptualizing and measuring the social uses of the internet: The case of personal web sites, *The Information Society*, 22 (5), pp. 291 - 301.

[15]   Porter, M.E., Sachs, J.D., Cornelius, P.K., McArthur, J.W., Schwab, K. (2002) The global competitiveness report 2001-2002, New York, Oxford University Press.

[16]   Pruulmann-Vengerfeldt, P. (2006) Exploring social theory as a framework for social and cultural measurements of the information society, *The Information Society*, 22 (5), pp. 303 - 310.

[17]   Sciadas, G. (2002) Monitoring the digital divide, Orbicom.

[18]   Sciadas, G. (2003). Monitoring the digital divide... and beyond, Orbicom.

[19] Sciadas, G. (2005). Infostates across countries and over time: Conceptualization, modelling, and measurements of the digital divide, *Information Technology for Development*, 11 (3), pp. 299-304.

[20] Sciadas, G. (2005). From the digital divide to digital opportunities: Measuring infostates for development, Orbicom.

[21] Suchman, L. (1987). *Plans and situated action*, Cambridge: Cambridge University Press.

[22] Suchman, M. (1995). Managing legitimacy: Strategic and institutional approaches, *The Academy of Management Review*, 20 (3), pp. 571-610.

[23] UNCTAD (2006). Information economy report 2006, the development perspective.

[24] van Dijk, J. A. G. M. (2006). Digital divide research, achievements and shortcomings, *Poetics*, 34 (4-5), pp. 221-235.

[25] Vehovar, V., et al. (2006). Methodological challenges of digital divide measurements, *The Information Society*, 22 (5), pp. 279 - 290.

[26] WSIS (2003). Building the information society: A global challenge in the new millennium, Geneva Declaration of Principles.

OPEN ACCESS BARRIERS:
AN ACTION RESEARCH

Mathias Klang
University of Lund, Sweden

Abstract   ICT has provided the infrastructure to enable easy access to scientific information. Despite this, libraries are suffering from the rising of journal subscriptions. Additionally, the structure of scholarly publications is creating a wasteful situation where publicly funded research is being paid for several times over. University libraries are struggling to deal with these new realities at the same time as they provide a level of service with acceptable access to publications. The work of librarians is being heavily affected by the influence of copyright and licensing which together are creating barriers to open access. The work in this chapter draws from an action research in progress undertaken by Lund's University in order to explore the barriers to open access to scientific research output in Sweden.

Keywords: Open access, action research, scholarly publication

1.   Introduction

In the early stages of the development and dissemination of ICT as a communications infrastructure a great deal of optimism about its potential to provide an equal open democratic access to the public sphere was expressed. The technology in focus in this chapter is Internet based communications technology. Much of the discussion in the early stages of the development of the Internet dealt with its uncontrollable nature. For those outside traditional power structures it was hailed as an important alternative to achieve wide spread communication while many of those inside the power structures were concerned with the negative effects of this new found freedom [14].

Both the cyberlibertarians and the cyberpaternalists agreed that the Internet provided a global information and communications infrastructure and that it could be used to create a public sphere [14]. In addition to this, a fundamental basis for such a development was the access to information and, in particular, access to scientific information.

Yet while the developments in communications technology provides an infrastructure it is not without limitations. Developments in technology make access to information possible and yet there still remain great barriers to access to scientific information. These barriers have moved from the technical to the legal

Please use the following format when citing this chapter:

Klang, M., 2008, in IFIP International Federation for Information Processing, Volume 282; *Social Dimensions of Information and Communication Technology Policy*; Chrisanthi Avgerou, Matthew L. Smith, Peter van den Besselaar; (Boston: Springer), pp. 335–348.

and administrative and in the field of free access to scientific journals this is expressed in the form of copyright law and licenses.

The use of this barrier to open access (OA) has created a wasteful situation where important scientific data is locked away and were universal access to vital information remains unfulfilled. The purpose of this chapter is to explore the effects of copyright law and licenses on the ability to provide open access to scientific information. This chapter will use semi-structured interviews which are used to illustrate the way in which different actors are attempting to adapt to the new realities of the technical, legal, and academic structure in order to achieve a greater efficiency in the access to scientific knowledge.

The following section will describe the fundamentals of open access and scientific publications. This will be followed by an explanation of the methodology used in this chapter and the results of the method. This will be followed by an analysis of the results and the chapter will close by drawing some conclusions on the results.

2.   Theory

The Internet was developed as an open (end-to-end) system with a focus on the non-discriminatory transportation of content. In other words the Internet is not concerned about the content but focuses on delivering from sender to receiver. Compared with print, such a system radically alters the ability of users to access information in addition to this the creation of digital copies is associated with low costs. Lastly, providing a digital copy online ensures that multiple users can access the same information without prejudicing each other's ability to do so, and without incurring additional costs for the sender. In this way, Internet technology has radically disrupted [11, 14] the non-digital models for the publishing scientific journals. This is recognized in the 2003 Berlin Declaration, which states in its preface:

"The Internet has fundamentally changed the practical and economic realities of distributing scientific knowledge and cultural heritage. For the first time ever, the Internet now offers the chance to constitute a global and interactive representation of human knowledge, including cultural heritage and the guarantee of worldwide access."

The barriers to knowledge therefore shift from being a barrier of being able to physically access and interpret the scientific knowledge to being one of legal access to the knowledge. This does not mean that other barriers have completely disappeared. Ability to use the new technology and to interpret scientific data is by no means universal. However the main focus has *shifted from transportation to law*. The basis of this new barrier to access lies in the use of copyright law and licensing.

The technology of the printed word has long held a unique position in the dissemination of scientific knowledge; its most specialized form, the scientific journal, was established 300 years ago [23]. Since the establishment of the scientific journal as a publishing model the popularity and growth has been steady. Even so, in the last half century the growth in the number of journals has been unprecedented [23]. According to Tenopir [20] there were almost 50,000 academic journals in 2003.

In addition to the growth in the number of journals there has also been a concentration of media, which has entailed a decrease in the number of independent publishers. In other words, fewer publishers are producing a larger number of journals. The situation is made more precarious by the evolution of the so-called serials crisis [21]; this is the rapidly rising cost of academic journals. It is generally recognized that the cost of scientific journals has risen at a rate that exceeds that which can be motivated by inflation [5, 6, 13, 17]. As a result university libraries are struggling to provide researchers with access to the necessary journals.

The recent development of the open access ideology comes from two primary driving forces: the desire for openness and the need to resolve the so-called serials crisis.

This has led to multiple responses in order to achieve greater levels of open access [11, 23]:

(1)   Open access Journals;
(2)   Institutional repositories;
(3)   Policy statements (declarations); and
(4)   Changes in research funding policy.

The launch of open access journals has come from a few different directions. Some have been developed as new journals, some are established journals that have changed their policy to become open access, and finally there are the declarations of independence where journal editors or whole editorial boards have resigned in protest and launched open access alternatives.

An important aspect to remember about the open access journal is that there are several alternative forms. For example the journal content is made freely available to readers. In the so-called green route the material is made freely available to readers because the journal itself has an alternative method of financing its existence (for example advertising, grants, unpaid labour). While in the "gold" route the author pays the publisher a fee prior to publication and the material is then free to all readers.

A practice closely connected to the open access journal is self-archiving. This system has been developed to enable the archiving of content on an institutional level. Self-archiving can entail practices such as the author maintaining his/her own publications via a personal web page and the use of institutional repositories. From the point of view of an organisation, longevity and searchability of the institutional repositories, for example in libraries, have been recognized as far superior.

From these developments a level of institutional policy support has materialized in the form of different declarations in favour of open access systems.

Some of the more important such declarations are the Declaration on Science and the Use of Scientific Knowledge (UNESCO-ICSU World Conference on Science, 1999), a United Nations Economic and Social Council ministerial declaration (2000), the Declaration of Havana (2001), the Budapest Open Access Initiative (2001), the Third World Academy of Sciences (TWAS) issued the Beijing Declaration on scientific advancement, openness, and cooperation (2003), the Berlin Declaration on Open Access to Knowledge in the Sciences and Humanities (2003), the UN World Summit on the Information Society approved a Declaration of Principles and Plan of Action (2003), the Valparaiso Declaration for Improved Scientific Communication in the Electronic Medium (2004), and Ministerial representatives from 34 nations to the Organisation for Economic Co-operation and Development (OECD) issued the Declaration on Access to Research Data From Public Funding (2004).

While these declarations vary in exact content they all intend to provide greater levels of access to scientific publications. If we take the wording of the Berlin Declaration as an example we see that open access contributions must satisfy two conditions:

1.   The author(s) and right holder(s) of such contributions grant(s) to all users a free, irrevocable, worldwide, right of access to, and a license to copy, use, distribute, transmit, and display the work publicly and to make and distribute derivative works, in any digital medium for any responsible purpose, subject to proper attribution of authorship (community standards, will continue to provide the mechanism for enforcement of proper attribution and responsible use of the published work, as they do now), as well as the right to make small numbers of printed copies for their personal use.

2.   A complete version of the work and all supplemental materials, including a copy of the permission as stated above, in an appropriate standard electronic format is deposited (and thus published) in at least one online repository using suitable technical standards (such as the open archive definitions) that is supported and maintained by an academic institution, scholarly society, government agency, or other well-established organization that seeks to enable open access, unrestricted distribution, inter operability, and long-term archiving.

Declarations such as these have been echoed in many other professional organisations and university bodies. Additionally they have collected signatories and supporters around the globe. The effect has been to prove that there is a wide support for the principles of open access.

These practical and political developments are also being reflected in the ways in which scientific research is being funded. The best example of such action is the policy changes carried out in 2005 by the Wellcome Trust when it began to implement its new open-access mandate for Wellcome-funded research.

As this all too brief overview of open access developments shows, many of the actors involved in the production and dissemination of scientific knowledge are working towards creating an environment where open access becomes a norm.

3.   Librarians & action research

As we have seen above there is a need to ensure that the access to scientific publications is enhanced through open access since the alternative is proving to be too costly and too wasteful a system. In attempting to operationalise the goals and visions expounded in the different declarations it has fallen upon the university libraries to ensure that open access visions are made practicable. Without the ability of these information systems specialists to provide solutions the individual authors can only make piecemeal attempts in securing access to scientific information.

The initial steps that have been taken have focused upon creating institutional repositories [1, 3, 10] and ensuring that the material being made available by individual publishers and journals was being made available to a wider audience. The next step in the process was to convince authors of the viability, sustainability and value of the open access alternatives. Much of the latter work has been to show the resulting impact of publishing in open access environments [7, 9].

A recent project launched at the University of Lund in Sweden has taken the action research approach in order to actively explore and impact on the use of open access. Action research builds upon a close collaboration between the researcher and the reality that is being studied. There are several different forms of action research recognised within IS research [4]. However, as Holwell [12] points out, these forms all share certain characteristics to enable them to fall into the action research field. These common characteristics are (1) that the researcher is immersed within the research object, (2) the work is not driven by the needs of the researcher, (3) problems arise from the local context, (4) descriptions and theories are built and tested empirically and iteratively within the local context [2, 4, 16, 22].

The process of action research consists of re-iterating a research cycle consisting of (1) identifying the problem (diagnosis), (2) creating goals/planning, (3) implementation, and (4) evaluation [19]. The method is not uncontroversial. Baskerville and Wood-Harper [4] identify three important pitfalls (issues of impartiality, discipline, and context-dependency), which the researcher using this method must be aware of, and address. Action research was chosen as the method for this research since the method supports both positivist and interpretavist approaches [15] irrespective of this the results arising from this method can be used "across varying epistemologies, ontologies, and methodologies" [8]. In addition to this, the method is openly an approach that attempts to develop important contributions to practice while carrying out research within that practice, and at the same time providing valuable insights to the research community [18].

In the aforementioned project, the university library of Lunds University began by conducting a survey among all the university libraries in Sweden in order to find out more about their procedures in dealing with copyright law and licensing in relation to achieving a greater level of open access. The initial survey phase will then be followed up by the creation of best practice models for the university libraries. These models are intended to create a consensus among the university libraries and also to provide a better basis of understanding of the varying problems when dealing with copyright and licensing. In addition to this it is hoped that the development of consensus among university libraries will provide researchers and authors of scientific articles with a clearer image of the way in which open access solutions can enable them to reach a wider audience for their work.

The purpose of the project is to develop competencies and provide legal support in relation to copyright issues brought about by open access publishing. The primary focus group is researchers, administrators, research funding offices, and universities in general.

The two-year project began in September 2007 with preliminary planning and research for the project and the data collection phase of the project. The resulting plan was a long-term research project with several concrete short-term goals. The project also has a goal to provide legal support throughout the project.

In the aforementioned project the university library of Lunds University has begun by conducting a survey among all the university libraries in Sweden in order to find out more about their procedures in dealing with copyright law and licensing in relation to achieving a greater level of open access. The initial survey phase will then be followed up by the creation of best practice models for the university libraries. These models are intended to create a consensus among the university libraries and also to provide a better basis of understanding of the varying problems when dealing with copyright and licensing. In addition to this it is hoped that the development of consensus among university libraries will provide researchers and authors of scientific articles with a clearer image of the way in which open access solutions can enable them to reach a wider audience for their work.

Action research is a reflective process of progressive problem solving led by individuals working with others in teams or as part of a "community of practice" to improve the way they address issues and solve problems. Action research can also be undertaken by larger organisations or institutions, assisted or guided by professional researchers, with the aim of improving their strategies, practices, and knowledge of the environments within which they practice.

The *action* component of this research stems from the need not only to conduct empirical research and report findings but also to actively present changes locally and lobby for policy changes nationwide. The process will be carried out iteratively by conducting interviews with different groups affected by the open access problem complex and successively attempting to overcome each groups problems by suggesting best practice models and then returning to evaluate the results of these changes within the organisation.

3.1 The interviewees

University College of Borås: The University College of Borås, UCB, consists of six academic Schools. In total, UCB has now 11,000 registered students, where approximately 6.300 are (registered) Degree programme students. The university has 536 employees.[1] The interview at the University College of Borås was conducted on the 20 February and lasted a little over an hour.

Linköping University: The university is organized in four faculties and 14 departments. It has a student population of 25,000 and 3,500 employees.[2] The interview at the university was conducted on the 21 February and lasted an hour and a half.

Jönköping University: Jönköping University Foundation is one of three independent institutions of higher education (not state-owned) in Sweden that are entitled to offer postgraduate programmes. Research and education is carried out in four schools: Jönköping International Business School, School of Education and Communication, School of Engineering and School of Health Sciences.[3] The interview was carried out on the 22 February and lasted one hour.

Chalmers Technical University: Number of students 6,343 and number of teachers and researchers 1,433.[4] The interview was conducted on the 26 February and lasted 75 minutes.

Stockholm University: Stockholm University has over 50,000 undergraduate and master's students, 1,800 doctoral students and 5,200 employees.[5] The interview was conducted on the 27 February and lasted 50 minutes.

The *University of Gävle* is comprised of six departments that offer approximately 50 degree programmes and 800 elective courses. There are approximately 13,000 registered students and approximately 800 employees.[6] The interview was conducted on 8 April and lasted almost one hour.

The *University of Halmstad* has around 50 programmes, 10,000 students and around 550 employees.[7] The interview was carried out on 10 April and lasted 50 minutes.

The *Göteborgs University* has about 50,000 students and more than 5,000 employees.[8] The interview was conducted on 11 April and lasted 75 minutes.

---

[1] http://www.hb.se/english/ucb/
[2] http://www.liu.se/en/presentation/
[3] http://www.hj.se/doc/4417
[4] http://www.chalmers.se/en/sections/about_chalmers/facts_and_figures_1
[5] http://www.su.se/pub/jsp/polopoly.jsp?d=3807&a=26335
[6] http://www.hig.se//ufk/is/introduction.html
[7] http://www.hh.se/omhogskolan.10.html
[8] http://www.gu.se/omuniversitetet/

Umeå University has 29,000 students and close to 4,000 employees. The university offers 1,900 courses and 240 programmes. The interview was conducted on 12 April and lasted one hour.

4.   Results

The resulting nine hours of interviews reflect different areas of concerns presented by the interviewees. The main thrust of these concerns can be divided into the following groups:

1.   Copyright Concerns;
2.   Research Culture;
3.   Administrative Concerns;
4.   University Context;
5.   Legal Culture; and
6.   Information Needs.

In order to preserve the anonymity of the interviewees the material presented in the analysis will not be identifiable with any particular university.

5.   Analysis

All the universities involved identified copyright as a major source of concern in their everyday work. The main source of trouble was the lack of information about the way in which copyright and copyright licenses could and should be interpreted in the workday experience of the library.

The concern with copyright was more serious among the libraries that had a larger amount of researchers and a well functioning self-archiving system. However, even the smaller universities expressed concern with the complexities of copyright in relation to their everyday work.

The lack of information was made more acute since the libraries experienced that they are receiving more copyright and licensing questions from researchers that they were expected to answer with a fair level of certainty.

Some of the universities also expressed concerns that they did not have access to sources of legal advice. Libraries without access to university legal departments felt that the lack of such a function was an important flaw in the organisation in relation to copyright. Libraries with access to university legal departments felt that these departments tended not to resolve the issues at hand and felt a need for a more specialized legal position dedicated towards copyright.

During some of the interviews the interviewees demonstrated an erroneous understanding of copyright. The result creates additional barriers to open access. Despite the fact that the interviewees were misinformed the result is equally problematic.

These copyright concerns reflected in the interviews show that copyright is perceived as a problem for libraries and that the libraries do not have access to adequate training, readily available information, or dedicated legal counsel. The larger universities' concerns become more acute since the larger universities are also those with more researchers and research publications and therefore more likely to come into contact with copyright and licensing questions. In addition to this the larger universities also are more active in open access questions and self-archiving practices and therefore more likely to come into contact with copyright concerns.

5.1   Research culture

The librarians all spoke of the difficulties in changing the culture of the researchers who ignore open access and publish in the traditional journals. Additionally there was little interest among the researchers to attempt to re-negotiate with journal publishers in order to preserve their rights or to maintain rights for the university library to self-archive. One interviewee quoted a researcher as saying that open access was unnecessary as all his peers had access to the journals that counted. However, the interviewees also maintained that the researchers are open and sympathetic to the open access idea once it was explained to them.

Therefore the problem with the research culture was therefore not that the researcher could not be convinced but rather the problem was reaching the researchers. It was widely admitted that information via email or paper was not effective since it could be readily ignored. Information meetings were seen as having the best effect but there is also a risk of preaching to the converted and not being able to reach those who are disinterested.

The smaller universities whose researchers either belong to larger research groups or whose researchers are PhD students with supervisors at other universities are difficult to convince as they tend to follow the norms and recommendations of the external groups or supervisors.

The interviewees all leaned towards a carrot and stick system – the carrot for the researcher being the advantage of additional readers in an open access system. This is the part where the librarians work hard to convince the researchers to adopt open access practices. The stick, almost all libraries think was required, was the need for a strong university leadership to be able to place demands on the researchers to adopt open access practices. An additional stick was seen in the potential of funding bodies to demand that money be connected to open access. Those interviewees who did not feel the need for coercing researchers into open access belonged to the smaller universities with few researchers.

5.2   Administrative concerns

The administrative concerns consist partly of the need to convince those involved in adding material to the database or reporting publications that such practices are both relatively easy and well worth carrying out. These tasks are organized and carried out differently at the many departments and faculties at the interviewed universities; however, the task falls either on the author, the local administrator, or a librarian. This administrative concern is not considered to be of great importance but it is recognized as being necessary to do something in order to overcome it to ensure widespread self-archiving and reporting of publications.

A more difficult concern related to the administration of self-archiving among librarians is the wrongful use of metadata. In all cases where those entering data were not librarians the high levels of errors among the metadata raised concerns for librarians since this entails additional work for them. However, only in universities with low levels of research publications was it seen as an option to allow librarians to add material. All other universities represented by the interviewees pointed out that this was an impossible task for the librarians to carry out.

A further administrative issue, which occurred in cases where pre-prints were used, was the issue of versions. This problem is one of being able to identify a "correct" version, i.e., ensuring that the archived version is the same as the published version. In most cases the interviewees expressed concerns that researchers did not have an adequate control over different versions of their publications and that self-archiving erroneous or flawed versions would inevitably decrease the value of the archiving system.

The final administrative concern was with dealing with copyright itself. This concern was in two parts: the issue of license changes and the issue of copyrightable content included in the archived publications. The problem with changes to established licenses, either between library and publisher or between author and publisher, was a source of major concern as it was recognized that these changes occurred with little or no warning and the consequences could be great.

The second copyright related concern was that of publications which include copyrightable content. Most interviewees were relatively relaxed in that the archiving required that the author sign a license granting the university use and ensuring that the author had full right to use the publication in this manner. However, certain interviewees expressed concern that they had no way of knowing what the author understood or which content was included in the publication with correctly acquired permission. All universities adopted a "don't ask don't tell" approach in that they adopted a license upon which they relied totally and did not exercise any copyright control.

5.3   University context

The differences in size, age, organisation, and culture of the universities all affected the way in which the adoption of open access was proceeding at the different universities. All these factors affect the way in which the university can demand action from its researchers and the way in which the researchers will react towards the demands.

Generally speaking the newer, smaller universities were better controlled in that the faculties and departments had not developed independently. Older and larger universities tend to be better at resisting centralized control and therefore do not quickly follow the demands of the university to adopt open access.

5.4   Legal culture

The legal culture at the university was felt by the interviewees to present a particular set of problems in relation to open access issues. Generally speaking, the universities without access to legal departments to consult felt that this was a major problem, while universities with such departments did not feel that the legal departments understood what the libraries needed.

The latter group realized that the university legal department had many varying administrative tasks and therefore could not be dedicated enough to the questions of open access and copyright to fill the needs of the library.

In addition to this, the role of the legal department is to ensure that any potential liability the university may risk is limited. This position causes the legal department to be negative towards interpreting legal documentation in favour of the libraries needs to adopt open access. This has the effect that the legal departments do not recommend open access and in some cases actively work against such adoption.

In most cases, as described earlier, the universities have a reliance on the copyright licenses entered into between the university and the researcher guaranteeing that the researcher has the right to archive and that all copyrightable material in the publication is there with permission. However in some cases the legal administration of these licenses is carried to such extremes that open access is possible in theory but in practice it is difficult to implement. One such example is the university that demands that such a license be signed by the authors in duplicate and stored physically at the library.

5.5   Information needs

Many of the interviewees felt that the resources allocated towards open access were adequate. What was missing was reaching researchers and administrators with more information. It was felt that this information in itself would convince the readers that open access was a worthwhile activity.

These informational needs could be broken down into different types of information. Many interviewees felt that a copyright helpdesk was necessary; others felt that additional documentation was required to educate both librarians and researchers. Many pointed to the lack of courses and seminars that needed to be held in this area.

6.   Conclusions

The project is going strong with initial results showing that there is indeed a need for more work in order to help libraries in their transition to adopting effective open access solutions.

The lack of universal access to scientific publications only serves to strengthen the knowledge divides within the knowledge society. In part the lack of access to scientific data has created a wide-ranging growth in the amateur dissemination of data. Projects such as Wikipedia have shown that there is a great universal interest in the dissemination of scientific knowledge. Projects such as Wikipedia also show that if the professional dissemination of scientific data will not adequately provide what people need then alternatives will arise. However, projects based upon amateurs lack the necessary scientific rigor in ensuring the validity of scientific results.

Looking beyond such amateurish attempts we have seen that the economics of scholarly publishing is moving us deeper into the serials crisis and has already forced universities to discontinue subscriptions to necessary scientific publications. Thus, we are building a greater rift between those that can afford scientific data and those who cannot.

Beyond the economics of publishing there also lays an important philosophical approach to open access and this is the fact that the current incumbent system of economic publishing is highly wasteful and drains research resources from the production of research to the dissemination of results. Therefore it is hoped that open access solutions, through methods such as the one based in Lund, will act towards rebalancing the system of scientific research and the dissemination of results.

1.   Aside from conducting additional interviews to ensure the validity of the results there are several areas that require work for the future. Some of the areas requiring additional work are: Licensing: All universities use licenses in order to ensure that the researchers' results are archived and can be accessed. These licenses appear in different forms at the different universities. The licenses appear in everything from notices that appear to those entering full texts into the database to the opposite extreme of requiring all authors to physically sign paper documents. No matter what form they appear in the protection afforded by these licenses is questionable and therefore a great deal of work should be carried out in order to streamline and standardize the licensing system in order to strengthen the transition to open access.

2.   Documentation: The university libraries require documentation in the form of information brochures and educational documents. These documents are needed to inform librarians, researchers, and administrators.

3. Licenses: One way to help open access would be to strengthen the position of the author. This can be done by creating licenses and author addendums which the universities can adopt and recommend to their researchers.
4. Education: Among the recurring requests that came up in the interview was the need for further education for librarians. Therefore seminars and lectures should be held to ensure that the level of copyright knowledge among librarians is increased.
5. Policy study: The importance of administrative policies cannot be underestimated and there is a need for a study of the policies and policy documentation available at universities.
6. Helpdesk: Another issue that was raised in the interviews was the need for a copyright and licensing helpdesk. Among the future uses for the project would be to provide this service.

References

[1] Anderson, B (2004). Open access and institutional repositories. *Behavioral & Social Sciences Librarian* 23(1), 97–101.
[2] Argyris, C. Putman, R. & Smith, D. (1985). *Action science: Concepts, methods and skills for research and intervention.* Jossey-Bass, San Francisco.
[3] Bailey, C. W. (2005). The role of reference librarians in institutional repositories. *Reference Services Review*, 33, 259-267.
[4] Baskerville, R. & Wood-Harper, T. (1996). A critical perspective on action research as a method for information systems research. Journal of Information Technology, 3 (11), 235-246.
[5] Björk, B-C. (2004). Open access to scientific publications - an analysis of the barriers to change? *Information Research*, 9(2). January.
[6] Dingley, B. (2006). U.S. periodical prices – 2005, U.S. Periodical Price Index 2005, American Library Association.
[7] Eysenbach, G. (2006). Citation advantage of open access articles. PLoS Biology 4(5).
[8] Germonprez, M. & Mathiassen, L. (2004). *The role of conventional research methods in information systems research.* In Proceedings of IFIP 8.2 (Kaplan, B. et al Eds.) Kluwer Academic Publishers, Boston.
[9] Harnad, S. et al. (2004). The access/impact problem and the green and gold roads to open access. *Serials Review* 30(4), 310-314.
[10] Harris, M. (2005). Institutional repositories: is the open access door half open or half shut? *Learned Publishing* 18(2), 85-90.
[11] Hedlund, T., Gustafsson, T. & Björk, B-C. (2004). The open access scientific journal: an empirical study. *Learned Publishing* 17(3), 199-209.
[12] Holwell, S. (2004). Themes, iteration, and recoverability in action research. In *Proceedings of IFIP 8.2* (Kaplan, B. et al Ed.) Kluwer Academic Publishers, Boston.
[13] Kaufman P. (1995). Why we must subscribe to fewer journals. Information Issues. University of Tennessee, Knoxville Libraries.
[14] Klang, M. (2006). Disruptive technology: Effects of technology regulation on democracy, Doctoral Dissertation, University of Göteborg. Defended publicly 2nd October 2006.
[15] Kock N. (1997). Myths in organizational action research: Reflections on a study of computer-supported process redesign groups. *Organizations and Society* 4 (9) 65-91.
[16] Lincoln, Y. & Guba E. (1985). *Naturalistic enquiry.* Sage Publications, London.

[17] Peters, J. (1995). Hard choices for the libraries' collections. Information Issues. University of Tennessee, Knoxville Libraries.

[18] Rapoport, R. (1970). Three dimensions in action research. *Human Relations* 23 (4), 499-513.

[19] Susman, G. & Evered, R. (1978). An assessment if the scientific merits of action Research. *Administrative Science Quarterly* (23), 582-603.

[20] Tenopir, C. (2004). Online scholarly journals: How many? *Library Journal* 129 (2), 32.

[21] Van Orsdel, L. C. & Born, K. (2005). Choosing sides: Periodical price survey 2005. *Library Journal*, April.

[22] Whyte, W. (1991). *Participatory action research.* Sage Publications, Newbury Park, CA.

[23] Willinsky, J. (2006). *The access principle: The case for open access to research and scholarship.* MIT Press, Cambridge Mass.

Section 4:

Panel

FREE AND OPEN SOURCE SOFTWARE IN LOW-INCOME COUNTRIES: EMERGENT PROPERTIES?

Panel

Gianluca Miscione
University of Oslo, Norway

Dorothy Gordon
Advanced Information Technology Institute, Ghana

Kevin Johnston
University of Cape Town, South Africa

Free and Open Source Software (FOSS) is becoming an increasingly important element in strategies for development and implementation of information and communication technologies (ICT) in low-income countries (LICs). Such initiatives often have strong public sector orientation, as government ICT policies are expected to shape and support further socio-economical development. The usual mismatch between bureaucracies and trajectories of development initiatives (mostly run by international agencies) provides a promising field for empirical research.

This panel intends to discuss the connection between FOSS and organisational learning in contexts where usual assumptions about them cannot be taken-for-granted. It will be argued that the relevance of open technologies as public goods rests in allowing increased organisational learning in public administrations. Such a focus on the organisational aspects would complement existing studies on economical relevance of FOSS.

Common assumptions about FOSS dynamics emphasize the spontaneity of open and distributed development, as the FOSS-related organisations emerged on themselves. This panel proposal invites to explore what are the hidden regulations which constrain or en-act development, use, further development, and further use of FOSS-based ICT in LICs. These processes need to be understood to be explicitly considered in ICT for development policies. With this aim, three cases are presented and discussed, two from Africa and one from Kerala, a Southern state of India.

Please use the following format when citing this chapter:

Miscione, G., Gordon, D. and Johnston, K., 2008, in IFIP International Federation for Information Processing, Volume 282; *Social Dimensions of Information and Communication Technology Policy*; Chrisanthi Avgerou, Matthew L. Smith, Peter van den Besselaar; (Boston: Springer), pp. 351–355.

Challenges of IT decision-making for government in Africa and the implications for e-government solutions

Dorothy K. Gordon

Governments all over Africa are engaged in the rapid deployment of new ICT systems intended to improve efficiency and improve G2C services. There is increasing interest in Africa from globally recognized companies that are in the business of marketing solutions. Also some donor agencies aggressively link funding with procurement of solutions designed by their nationals.

Companies in the local IT ecosystem benefit from a subsidiary market in the area of customization of proprietary solutions in order to adapt them to local needs. The high cost of these solutions and the relative paucity in government experience in large-scale IT procurement raises issues relating to fiscal management.

On the other hand the capacity for FOSS deployment and maintenance is weak in Africa. Local FOSS businesses find the environment difficult for a variety of reasons. What real options exist for transferring knowledge and building capacities in these areas? Is there a viable strategy for informing Governments of their options in the face of aggressive marketing of proprietary solutions? What is the role of local FOSS businesses? What policy elements could ensure a level playing field?

Free/Libre & Open Source Software (FLOSS/OSS) in low income countries

Kevin Johnston

In the paper "Why South Africans don't FLOSS?" (with Dr Seymour, published in IBIMA, 2005 International Conference proceedings) we attempted to identify the factors that influence and limit the usage and intended usage of Free/Libre Open Source Software (FLOSS) within South Africa. Private and public sectors were examined.

We found that South African (SA) Small Medium Enterprises (SMEs) are often in favour of purchasing proprietary software rather than using OSS, as seek immediate resolution of technological issues, brand equity is important (tried & tested), and risk of unknown.

Strategically, SA government has expressed strong intentions to use OSS since 2001, given its focus on local skill development, foreign exchange exposure and national security. On a practical level, we found limited OSS usage within the SA government. Political influences and risks associated with the scale and complexity of large government organisations nullify their OSS strategic usage intent. Through the need to leverage off their existing skill base and infrastructure, and the political pressure to eliminate additional risk by not going through unchartered territory, government remains tied to proprietary software.

If software procurement was predominantly cost driven, OSS would be considered and used by more organisations. Too few people are aware of what OSS can achieve and of the multiple success stories. Unless OSS distributors aggressively reorient themselves towards marketing, it will be impossible for them to effectively compete with proprietary organisations such as Microsoft.

In surveys of key issues for Chief Information Officers in South Africa, OSS did not feature at all. It should be noted that the list represented issues that CIOs regard as important, and not necessarily as problematic.

Organisations need to be aware that OSS can alter and shape strategy without senior management being aware of it. Staff can and do download OSS onto corporate platforms without permission (as it's free) or authority. This software may then start to be used and integrated into the business and business processes, and so changes the strategy.

Organisations need to be aware that although OSS is free, using it is not free, there are costs to run it on hardware, people costs, data conversion costs, etc.

Situating FOSS for organisational learning

Gianluca Miscione

The Kerala case moves from the development and implementation of a project by an international action-research network, locally supported by the government. The case involves the implementation of reporting software for aggregated health data from the public health system in primary health care facilities in the region of the capital. The argument addresses FOSS-related emphatic expectations for emancipation in the "knowledge society" on one side [4], and implementation and use, on the other. Then, a meso-level between global trends and local specificities is identified as crucial in situating FOSS for development potentialities. FOSS technologies are locally desirable both for practical and ideological reasons: practically, the software is expected to be more under control of the local authorities and developers' team. Ideologically, the Kerala government sustains that FOSS can be used to enact and guarantee cooperation and communal property, which is more consistent to its own ideological dispositions and long term development strategies.

A crucial challenge for FOSS in LICs concerns the establishment of functioning and sustainable implementations. Given the novelty of organisational forms required and implied by FOSS, the local elaboration and eventual consolidation of FOSS-based systems cannot take place without going through trial and error heuristic. Because of this, it is relevant to relate the discourse surrounding and legitimizing FOSS, with the politics and practice of implementation.

This case shows that the (formal and informal) institutional constraints which FOSS implies and relies on are fragmented or absent, whereas others can be relevant. Nevertheless, FOSS narrative proves to be present and effective both in negotiations between stakeholders, and in facilitating local participation to information system development.[69]

FOSS fluidity allows inscribing a variety of context-bound socio-technical arrangements [3], and can also avoid path-dependencies and vendors' lock-ins [6]. But this is not spontaneous: software development process needs to be designed and carried on in a way that allows local organisations to "indigenize" FOSS.[70]

The interactions around local technical skills improvement, and the increased ability for organisations to formulate, express, negotiate, and inscribe their needs in technology is proposed as a chance for organisational learning. This is proposed as a case for discussion about co-evolution between remote organisations, and the (mutually) transformative character of FOSS and ICT.

Panelists

Dorothy K. Gordon is the Director-General of Ghana's Advanced Information Technology Institute (the Ghana-India Kofi Annan Centre of Excellence in ICT), which provides IT training and consulting and promotes context-appropriate R&D in information and communication technology. As a specialist in international development with more than 20 years experience, she has consulted to businesses and governments and has worked globally in the public sector and with civil society organisations, with increasing management and leadership responsibilities. She is currently Chair of the E-Government Commission of WITFOR 2009 (the World IT Forum) and President of the IPv6 Forum-Ghana. She is also the Africa spokesperson and Eminent Expert for World Summit Awards-Ghana, and a member of the Champions Network of UNGAID (the UN Global Alliance for ICT for Development).

Kevin Johnston is currently senior lecturer and Head of Department of the Department of information Systems at the University of Cape Town (UCT), South Africa. Kevin taught Mathematics & Science at High Schools, before working for 24 years in industry for companies such as Wilson-Rowntree, De Beers, Liberty Life, Lifegro (Legal & General Volkskas) and BoE. He joined UCT in 2001 as Senior Lecturer in the Department of Information Systems. His main areas of interest are ICT Management and Project Management. He has presented papers at conferences in Africa, Americas, Asia, Australia, and Europe.

Gianluca Miscione received his Ph.D. in Information Systems and Organization from the Sociology Department of the University of Trento (Italy) with a dissertation focused on the interplay between information and

---

[69] Myths and narratives are discussed by Czarniawska [2] in Neoinstitutional terms. The legitimizing role of myth is clearly presented by Noir and Walsham [5] through a case from Kerala, as well.

[70] Camara and Fonseca [1] relates modalities of participation to code writing, and software modularity.

communication technologies and health care change in "developing" contexts. At the University of Oslo, his research activity line is situated between information infrastructures and organisational studies. Gianluca can be reached at gianluca.miscione@gmail.com.

References

[1] Camara G. & Fonseca F. (2007). Information policies and open source software in developing countries, Journal Of The American Society For Information Science And Technology, 58(1), 121–132.

[2] Czarniawska B. (1997). Narrating the organization: Dramas of institutional identity, University of Chicago Press, Chicago, 1997

[3] De Laet, M. & Mol A. (2000). The Zimbabwe bush pump: Mechanics of a fluid technology, Social Studies of Science, 30, 225-263.

[4] Government of Kerala - Department of Information Technology (2007). Information technology policy - Towards an inclusive knowledge society, Thiruvananthapuram

[5] Noir C. & Walsham G. (2007), The great legitimizer: ICT as myth and ceremony in the Indian Healthcare Sector, Information Technology & People, 20(4), 313-333(21).

[6] Weerawarana S. & Weeratunge J. (2004), Open source in developing countries, SIDA.

EVALUATING "CONNECTING FOR HEALTH": POLICY IMPLICATIONS OF A UK MEGA-PROGRAMME

Panel

Kathy McGrath
Brunel University, UK

Jane Hendy
Imperial College, UK

Ela Klecun
London School of Economics and Political Science, UK

Leslie Willcocks
London School of Economics and Political Science, UK

Terry Young
Brunel University, UK

Around the world the implementation of information and communication technology (ICT) is proposed as a way of transforming healthcare, making it "better" (e.g., safer, more accessible, and patient-centred) and more efficient by facilitating the management of healthcare organisations and processes. The implementation of ICT has been a vital component of UK government strategy for the National Health Service (NHS) for at least a decade, most recently expressed in the National Programme for IT (NPfIT) for England, considered to be the biggest non-military initiative of IT implementation in the world and now subsumed in the wider institutional structure of "Connecting for Health" [2].

The National Programme is a 10-year change initiative dating from 2002, which was originally estimated at a procurement cost of £6.2 billion, although recent projections suggest it may cost £20 billion in the end [4]. The aim of the programme is to deliver a "system of systems" supported by a nationwide IT infrastructure and network covering all of the strategic health authorities in England. The critical applications will provide electronic facilities for sharing patient records, booking appointments, transmitting prescriptions, and transferring digital images (e.g., X-rays and scans) and will be supported by ancillary services such as email, online directories, and websites.

Please use the following format when citing this chapter:

McGrath, K., Hendy, J., Klecun, E., Willcocks, L. and Young, T., 2008, in IFIP International Federation for Information Processing, Volume 282; *Social Dimensions of Information and Communication Technology Policy*; Chrisanthi Avgerou, Matthew L. Smith, Peter van den Besselaar; (Boston: Springer), pp. 357–362.

The vision of fully informatized health is clinically, economically, socially, and politically attractive, yet no country has found it easy to realize. Many reasons have been put forward for a slow pace of ICT adoption in the UK NHS, including the gap between the government's vision and the realities "on the ground" manifested, for example, by the lack of adequate resources (e.g,. skills and technologies), attitudes to ICTs and reforms in general, as well as the complexity of the systems needed.

The panellists will examine the implementation issues surrounding various aspects of the Connecting for Health programme and present policy implications from their research. Each panellist will offer a different perspective on the programme, acknowledging both the diversity of agencies shaping the proposed systems and the multiple loci for decision making and interpretation of the government's vision. To that end, they will address different application areas (e.g., electronic patient records and electronic prescribing), a range of implementation issues (experienced by suppliers, trust managers, and staff) and the diverse expectations of various interested parties (e.g., politicians, government agencies, patient groups, academics, and the press). The presenters will illustrate the issues raised through the use of practical examples drawn from their own research and secondary data available from government publications, academic journals, and other documentary sources. Assuming a 90-minute session, the presentations of the five panellists are planned to take 60 minutes, allowing 30 minutes discussion time at the end.

Panel Presentations

Kathy McGrath

Kathy McGrath will open the panel session. She will provide an introduction to the context and purpose of the Connecting for Health programme as outlined above. She will then draw on her research on the use of an electronic patient record system in a London teaching hospital to suggest why the promising vision associated with this innovation is proving difficult to realize. She will argue that calls for better training and increased efforts to engage the support of staff address no more than symptoms of the issues surrounding the new electronic application. More broadly, NHS trusts are facing a number of operational challenges, including staff shortages, very busy wards, and the need to contain spending, alongside spiralling implementation costs for the information systems mandated by the National Programme. In these circumstances, cutbacks on training and support activities associated with the new applications are a short-term, pragmatic response by trust managers striving to balance their budgets while improving their performance ratings.

Following a brief summary of the policy implications from her work, Kathy will ask each of the other panellists to present their findings on particular aspects of the National Programme.

Jane Hendy

More than 5 years from inception of the NHS National Programme for IT, it is clear that many of original goals have not been realized. Having studied the implementation of the programme from its inception, in four NHS acute hospitals, Jane Hendy will outline the problems encountered and discuss lessons that can be learned from England's experiences.

From interviews with hospital managers over a two year period, Jane will describe organisational factors that have resulted in sub-optimal implementation. In particular, the impact of financial deficits, poor communication between central and local managers, and staff disengagement will be discussed. Staff concerns about the potential outcomes of delayed implementation, such as risks to patient safety and the loss of the programme's original vision, will also be addressed. Lastly, Jane will explore the gap between national policy making and local decision-making, and the difficulty in achieving an appropriate balance of responsibility between government and local healthcare organisations.

Ela Klecun

The prescribing and administration of medicines is one of a number of critical applications within the National Programme which is seen by the UK government as having the potential to transform healthcare through technology. Originally, government strategy was committed to electronic prescribing (EP) in all acute hospitals by 2005 [5], but at present Connecting for Health is asking local service providers to provide a solution to e-prescribing in hospitals by 2008 to 2010. However, EP is at an early stage of development in UK hospitals. Such systems only exist across a whole hospital at a handful of sites, despite the UK being among the world leaders in the introduction of e-prescribing into primary care.

Ela Klecun will describe a study of the deployment of EP systems in two UK hospitals, contrasting their models of implementation and focusing on challenges faced during the introduction and subsequent use of the systems. She will then present some lessons from the studies and suggestions for future implementations. She will argue that acquiring a technology is the start of the process: time and effort are required for it to become embedded into any particular clinical context. Furthermore, as resulting systems span professional boundaries, departments, and (potentially) organisations within and beyond the NHS, their implementation and use require negotiating diverse professional and organisational cultures and different needs and goals.

Leslie Willcocks

Mega-programmes such as Connecting for Health pose management dilemmas since their sheer scale implies that they will not meet initial expectations. Thus, a more realistic approach is required to the assessment of performance than measuring progress against plans and outcomes against targets. Furthermore, action is required by institutions to engage in more honest public debate about the prospects for such programmes, which will better serve the public interest.

Leslie Willcocks will highlight the characteristics of mega-programmes that make them easy targets for criticism. He will then argue that the supporters and advocates of the UK's National Programme should not be surprised at the criticism currently being levelled since it is a logical consequence of the way they have chosen to play. In offering a pragmatic assessment of what should have been expected, Leslie will draw out the policy implications of his approach to evaluating mega-programmes like Connecting for Health.

Terry Young

Human interaction with various information sources, required during the processes of delivering healthcare, may be viewed in terms of three critical tensions [1, 3]: the local-national tension, the management-clinical tension, and the tension between the interactive (i.e., sharing of data or information) and the interpersonal (i.e., face to face, either physically, or mediated through the IS). Terry Young will explore the impact of these tensions on the UK's Connecting for Health programme and argue that each dimension suggests policy implications.

Terry will examine the national-local tension as a series of debates around where records should be kept, and indeed how the specification, procurement, and installation of IS should be managed. He will address the clinical-managerial tension in the way that many clinical applications simply cannot be installed until the management-based foundational systems are in place, impacting heavily on the drive to provide a range of clinical services uniformly across the country. Finally, he will argue for greater attention to the interpersonal element of healthcare IS provision, opening the way to highly beneficial options in terms of patient-centred and lifelong delivery of care. Terry will present the implications of his work for policy development.

Panellists

Jane Hendy is a Research Fellow at Tanaka Business School, Imperial College, London. Her main interests are the adoption and implementation of complex health service innovations, particularly ICT innovations. Jane worked for 3 years in the Public Health and Policy department of the London School of Hygiene and Tropical Medicine, researching the implementation of the NHS National Programme for IT in acute hospitals. Jane is currently researching the outcome of £100m of government funding aimed at developing telecare (health and social care delivered remotely to the user in their home). The work aims to understand processes and outcomes of developing a mainstream telecare service, with the goal of identifying local and national facilitators and barriers to progress.

Ela Klecun is a lecturer in information systems at the London School of Economics and Political Science (LSE). She holds a Ph.D. in information systems from the LSE. Her research interests include the implementation and use of health information systems, evaluation of information systems, digital exclusion, and the application of critical theory and actor-network theory in the field of information systems. Ela studied the local implementation of ICT policies and strategies in South London, and reviewed a number of telehealth initiatives around London. More recently she has been involved in an EPSRC/ESRC/MRC sponsored project evaluating electronic prescribing systems at two UK hospitals, and developing evaluation activities, frameworks and methods needed to assess such systems. Ela can be reached by e-mail at e.klecun@lse.ac.uk or through her home page at http://personal.lse.ac.uk/klecun/.

Kathy McGrath is a Senior Lecturer in Information Systems at Brunel University in West London. She has extensive experience as an IT practitioner, including 8 years as an IS and management consultant working in the public and private sectors. More recently, she gained an MSc and PhD in Information Systems from the London School of Economics and Political Science. Her teaching and research interests focus on IS innovation and management, and the relationship between information technology and organisational change. Kathy studied the implementation of ICT-based modernization initiatives in the ambulance service, including the changes arising from a government review of ambulance performance standards. She has also been involved in a project evaluating the use of an electronic patient record system at a London teaching hospital. Kathy can be reached by e-mail at kathy.mcgrath@brunel.ac.uk or through her home page at http://www.brunel.ac.uk/about/acad/siscm/disc/people/all/kathymcgrath.

Leslie Willcocks is Professor of Technology, Work and Globalization in the Information Systems and Innovation Group, Department of Management at the London School of Economics and Political Science. He has studied major project implementations and IT outsourcing since 1986 including major public sector programmes. In September 2007 he co-edited a special issue for the *Journal of Information Technology* devoted to the NHS National Programme for IT. He has an international reputation for his work on large-scale outsourcing in the private and public sectors and is author of 28 books and over 180 refereed papers on this subject and on IT issues, organisational change and IT management.

Terry Young is Professor of Healthcare Systems at Brunel University in West London. He joined Brunel in 2001 after a career in industry which spanned research to strategy in broadband communications. He is currently the Principal Investigator of two multi-university research projects into healthcare technology and delivery: MATCH and RIGHT. His research interests centre around the processes of care delivery and the technology needed to support it.

References

[1]   Avison, D. & Young, T. (2007). Time to rethink health care and ICT? *Communications of the ACM*, 50(6), 69-74.

[2]   Brennan, S. (2005). *The NHS IT project: The biggest computer programme in the world ...ever.* Oxford: Radcliffe Publishing.
[3]   Connell, N. & Young, T. (2007). Evaluating healthcare information systems through an 'enterprise' perspective. *Information and Management*, 44(4), 433-440.
[4]   National Audit Office. (2006). The national programme for IT in the NHS. London: The Stationery Office, 16 June.
[5]   NHS Executive. (1998). Information for health: An information strategy for the modern NHS 1998-2005. London: NHS Executive, September.

GENDER RESEARCH IN AFRICA INTO ICTS FOR EMPOWERMENT (GRACE)

Panel

Ineke Buskens
GRACE, South Africa

Gertrudes Macueve
Eduardo Mondlane University, Mozambique

Ibou Sane
Dakar Sheikh Anta Diop University, Senegal &
Gaston Berger de Saint Louis University, Senegal

Anne Webb
GRACE, Canada

This panel arises from a three-year research project (2005-2008) entitled Gender Research in Africa into ICTs for Empowerment[71]. The project, which is ongoing into a second phase, was undertaken to find out how and why women use ICTs and how the use (or non-use) affects their lives. This study engages with issues sometimes referred to as the gendered digital divide [6, 7, 5], the recognition that men are participating and benefiting to a greater degree than women in the Information Society [9]. It is recognized that the gender divide is more than a matter of access and use of tools, or designing content. While there is "global agreement that gender equality is essential for building a 'sustainable, just and developed society' [WSIS *Declaration of Principles* 2003]" [9, p. 135], there seems to be a gap in terms of understanding the implications of gender discrimination in relation to the potential benefits to society of the new technologies. This is a problem if societies as a whole are to benefit from ICTs and use them to further their development, if the vision of development pursued is to equitably reflect and fulfill the interests and needs of the population, not only those in positions of power.

The use of ICTs has the potential to enhance our lives and contribute to our wellbeing, effective use of time, economic development and so forth. Because they are merely tools whose meaning is defined by the use and the users, they can

---

[71] This project was funded by the International Development Research Centre of Canada. The views expressed in the paper are those of the authors, and do not necessarily represent the opinions of the funder. For more information on the GRACE project, please see our web site www.GRACE-Network.net.

Please use the following format when citing this chapter:

Buskens, I., Macueve, G., Sane, I. and Webb, A., 2008, in IFIP International Federation for Information Processing, Volume 282; *Social Dimensions of Information and Communication Technology Policy*; Chrisanthi Avgerou, Matthew L. Smith, Peter van den Besselaar; (Boston: Springer), pp. 363–367.

also enhance gendered life situations, relationships and images and play thus a conservative, reactionary role. The GRACE project was undertaken to try to understand how women in Africa are engaging ICTs to improve their lives, and to try to understand when and how ICTs are beneficial to them and their pursuits, and when and why they are not.

The GRACE project

The GRACE project is unique on two levels: the subject matter of the research and the research coordination approach. The project explores the ways in which women in Africa use information and communication technologies (ICTs) to empower themselves. It focuses on the external, structural barriers women experience, as well as on the internal/conceptual factors which prevent or enable them to use ICTs to their advantage, and the strategies they use to overcome impediments [4].

The project comprises 14 sub-projects, reflecting 14 research sites in 12 countries in Africa. Approximately 30 researchers have been involved (women and men), with academic and NGO affiliations, supported by a coordination team.

The sub-projects differ from each other greatly in terms of target group and research focus, although they are all coherent with the general aim of the overall research initiative. Furthermore, the concepts of gender and empowerment which frame the project's general direction and commitment to women's equality do not have unequivocal meaning within the sub-projects. These concepts were understood and interpreted in various ways at the start of the project, and became increasingly multifaceted and contextualized through the duration of our work.

In terms of the research coordination approach, and the approaches taken by the researchers, emphasis was placed on the use of qualitative research techniques as these techniques yield in-depth data and are able to highlight the various dimensions and aspects of phenomena. The research questions and methodologies, the research trainings, as well as the ongoing mentoring and support program accompanying the research were grounded in the principles of critical emancipatory research [1, 3].

The methods used in each case were identified by the researchers as the best suited to learning about the lives and the thinking of their respondents. The respondents were approached as active agents in determining their own reality, rather than as victims of their situation. This may seem to contradict the point that women's lives are not well understood and are not setting development directions; however, we wanted to find out how women understood their current situations, we wanted them to think beyond their current realities, and to consider what needed to be in place for them to pursue their visions. To do this sort of reflection and thinking women had to see themselves as having the capacity for action on their own behalves [1, 2, 3, 8, 11]. It is this sort of thinking that produces practical, functional knowledge that can lead to change.

Another significant aspect of the research approach taken in GRACE is that the research teams conducted their research in their own contexts. They conducted their study either in their own region, their community, in their own workplace, or in some cases including themselves as respondents. While working in a familiar environment facilitates building rapport with research participants, and one's recognition of local specificities, researchers are faced with the task of also recognizing local norms for what they are – normalized social, cultural, gender, economic (and so forth) relations, not inevitables. Thus, as with an "outsider," a researcher working as a "native anthropologist" is also confronted with the task of revealing and questioning her own assumptions and biases, becoming aware of her own lenses [1], and managing to "'make strange that which appears familiar, and make familiar that which appears strange'" [2, 13a]. This condition of self-awareness or reflexivity is a key quality of the qualitative research approach engaged in the project.

Panel presentations

Anne Webb/Ineke Buskens

The panel moderators will open the session providing an introduction to the GRACE project as outlined above. They will introduce the research coordination approach and process engaged in the GRACE project and the significance of this approach. They will then introduce each of the panelists who will speak to their specific GRACE research project and the methods used, research context and analysis.

Gertrudes Macueve

"A number of studies suggest that information and communication technologies (ICTs) can contribute to empowering women. We selected two rural districts, Manhiça in the south and Sussundenga in central Mozambique, to investigate whether women in Mozambique's rural areas with access to ICTs through existing telecentres and the expanding mobile phone networks are becoming more empowered. Through qualitative research, we reached the conclusion that the main tools being used by women in these areas and playing an empowerment role are the community radio and the mobile phone, rather than ICTs such as computers, e-mail and Internet. The women are either unaware of the possibilities of the latter tools or do not find what is available sufficiently relevant to their immediate survival needs" [5].

Ibou Sane

"The massive movement of women into the popular and solidarity economy in Senegal reflects the state of the economic crisis that exerts great pressure on the fate of a large number of people affected by this situation aggravated by structural adjustment programmes implemented by the Bretton Woods international institutions. It is within this context that women's associations and women's promotion groups play key roles in mobilizing women to relax the economic and social constraints which weigh heavily on families. In this respect, women fishmongers and fish processors in Dakar intend, through entrepreneurship, to strengthen their creative capabilities in income-generating activities, and affirm their financial autonomy as a process of gradual questioning of the distribution system of the gendered social relationships. In this endeavour to conquer space for freedom and achievement, the mobile telephony as a working tool plays an important role in business transactions" [10].

Panelists

Ineke Buskens is a Cultural Anthropologist with a passion for research methodology and women's empowerment and a deep appreciation for cultural diversity and individual human uniqueness. Graduated in Leiden, the Netherlands, she has lived in Ghana, India, and Brazil and since 1990 she has lived in South Africa. After having been Head of the Centre for Research Methodology at South Africa's Human Science Research Council for 5 years, she founded Research for the Future in 1996. She works since as an independent international research and process facilitation consultant. In her research she focuses on emancipatory approaches that envision a sustainable, just and loving world, in her research training on bringing out the genius in every participant, in her facilitation work, on gender awareness and authentic collaboration. Ineke is a student of Ramtha's School of Enlightenment in Yelm, Washington, USA and this learning journey inspires her to become all she can be.

Gertrudes Macueve is a lecturer in computer sciences at Eduardo Mondlane University in Mozambique. She is currently doing her doctoral studies in the field of Information Systems. Her research interests include ICTs for development in general, and e-government and gender in particular. She has been involved in telecentre research activities since 2000, and was lead author for the Mozambique study.

Ibou Sane is a researcher and lecturer at the departments of sociology at Dakar Sheikh Anta Diop University and Gaston Berger de Saint Louis University (Senegal). He teaches urban sociology, political sociology, development sociology, informal sector sociology, sociology of associations' movement, methods of research on social science, assessment projects methods and sociological theories. His works focuses on the Senegalese commercial informal sector, on development, historical demography, and presently he is looking into gender, ICT and development.

Anne Webb's commitment to feminist qualitative research is rooted in participatory action research approaches. She has worked with communities and research teams for the past fifteen years pursuing the reduction of inequalities. Trained in sociology, adult education and gender studies in Toronto (Ontario Institute for Studies in Education) and Den Hague (Institute for Social Studies), her education has involved people from all walks of life and locations, formally and informally, in Canada, Europe, and Southern Africa, and is a continually enriching process. Anne currently resides in Hull, Quebec, Canada.

References

[1]   Buskens, I. (2002). Fine lines or strong cords? Who do we think we are and how can we become what we want to be in the quest for quality in qualitative research?, *Education as Change*, 6 (1), 1-31.
[2]   Buskens, I. (2006). Gender research in Africa into ICTs for empowerment, *IICBA Newsletter UNESCO* 8(2).
[3]   Buskens, I & Earl, S. (2008), Research for change – Outcome Mapping's contribution to emancipatory research in Africa, *Action Research* 6(2), 173-194.
[4]   Buskens, I., Esterhuysen, A., & Radloff, J. (2004). GRACE: Gender Research in Africa into ICTs for Empowerment, project proposal
       www.grace-network.net/publications/GRACE%20proposal.pdf
[5]   Gertrudes Macueve, G., Mandlate, J., Ginger, L., Gaster, P., & Macome E. (2009, forthcoming). Women's use of ICTs in Manhiça and Sussundenga: A tool for empowerment? In Buskens, I. and A. Webb (Eds), *Creating New Realities?*, London: Zed Books.
[6]   Hafkin J.N. (2000). Convergence of concepts: Gender and ICTs in Africa, in *Gender and the Information Revolution in Africa*, Ottawa: IDRC.
[7]   Hafkin, J.N. & S. Huyer. (2006). *Cinderella or Cyberella? Empowering women in the knowledge society*. Bloomfield: Kumarian.
[8]   Hannan, C. (2004). Women's rights and empowerment: Gender equality in the new millennium, Presentation to the United Nations Day Banquet, Dallas Chapter of the United Nations, October 24.
[9]   Huyer, S., Hafkin, J.N., Ertl, H., & Dryburgh, H. (2005) Women in the information society in Sciadas, G. (ed.) *From the Digital Divide to Digital Opportunities: Measuring Infostates for Development.* Orbicom/ITU, Ottawa. http://www.orbicom.ca/media/projets/ddi2005/index_ict_opp.pdf, 134-194.
[10] Ibou Sane, I. & M. Balla Traore. (2009, forthcoming). The mobile telephone as a tool for promotion of emancipation and strengthening of the entrepreneurial initiatives of women fish processors and wholesalers in Dakar. In Buskens, I. and A. Webb (Eds.), *Creating New Realities?*, London: Zed Books.
[11] Kabeer, N. (2003). Gender mainstreaming in poverty eradication and the Millennium Development Goals. Commonwealth Secretariat/IDRC/CIDA, Ottawa, p. 171.
[12] Rathgeber, E.M. (2000). Women, men, and ICTs in Africa: Why gender Is an issue in E.M. Rathgeber and E.O. Edera (Eds.) *Gender and the Information Revolution in Africa*, Ottawa: IDRC.
[13] Strega, Susan (2005). The view from the poststructural margins: Epistemology and methodology reconsidered. In L. Brown and S. Strega (Eds.) *Research as resistance: critical, indigenous and anti-oppressive approaches.* Toronto: Canadian Scholars Press.
       a. Hekman 1999, p. 138 cited p. 231.